Principles of Computer Organization and Assembly Language

Using the Java™ Virtual Machine

PATRICK JUOLA

Duquesne University

PEARSON
Prentice
Hall

Upper Saddle River, New Jersey 07458

Library of Congress Cataloging-in-Publication Data

Juola, Patrick

Principles of computer organization and Assembly language : using the Java virtual machine / Patrick Juola.
   p. cm.
   Includes bibliographical references and index.
   ISBN 0-13-148683-7
   1. Computer organization. 2. Assembler language (Computer program language) 3. Java virtual machine. I. Title.
   QA76.9.C643J96 2006
   004.2′2–dc22

2006034154

Vice President and Editorial Director, ECS: *Marcia J. Horton*
Executive Editor: *Tracy Dunkelberger*
Associate Editor: *Carole Snyder*
Editorial Assistant: *Christianna Lee*
Executive Managing Editor: *Vince O'Brien*
Managing Editor: *Camille Trentacoste*
Production Editor: *Karen Ettinger*
Director of Creative Services: *Paul Belfanti*
Creative Director: *Juan Lopez*
Cover Art Director: *Jayne Conte*
Cover Designer: *Kiwi Design*
Cover Photo: *Getty Images, Inc.*
Managing Editor, AV Management and Production: *Patricia Burns*
Art Editor: *Gregory Dulles*
Manufacturing Manager, ESM: *Alexis Heydt-Long*
Manufacturing Buyer: *Lisa McDowell*
Executive Marketing Manager: *Robin O'Brien*
Marketing Assistant: *Mack Patterson*

© 2007 Pearson Education, Inc.
Pearson Prentice Hall
Pearson Education, Inc.
Upper Saddle River, New Jersey 07458

TRADEMARK INFORMATION
Java is a registered trademark of Sun Microsystems, Inc.
Pentium is a trademark of Intel Corporation.
Visual C++ is a registered trademark of Microsoft Corporation.
PowerPC is a registered trademark of IBM Corporation.

10 9 8 7 6 5 4 3 2 1

ISBN 0-13-148683-7

Pearson Education Ltd., *London*
Pearson Education Australia Pty. Ltd., *Sydney*
Pearson Education Singapore, Pte. Ltd.
Pearson Education North Asia Ltd., *Hong Kong*
Pearson Education Canada, Inc., *Toronto*
Pearson Educación de Mexico, S.A. de C.V.
Pearson Education—Japan, *Tokyo*
Pearson Education Malaysia, Pte. Ltd.
Pearson Education, Inc., *Upper Saddle River, New Jersey*

To My Nieces
Lyric Elizabeth, Jayce Rebekah, and Trinity Elizabeth

Contents

Preface

Statement of Aims

What

This is a book on the organization and architecture of the `Java Virtual Machine` (JVM), the software at the heart of the `Java language` and is found inside most computers, Web browsers, PDAs, and networked accessories. It also covers general principles of machine organization and architecture, with llustrations from other popular (and not-so-popular) computers.

It is *not* a book on Java, the programming language, although some knowledge of Java or a Java-like language (C, C++, Pascal, Algol, etc.) may be helpful. Instead, it is a book about how the Java language actually causes things to happen and computations to occur.

This book got its start as an experiment in modern technology. When I started teaching at my present university (1998), the organization and architecture course focused on the 8088 running MS-DOS—essentially a programming environment as old as the sophomores taking the class. (This temporal freezing is unfortunately fairly common; when I took the same class during my undergraduate days, the computer whose architecture I studied was only two years younger than I was.) The fundamental problem is that the modern Pentium 4 chip isn't a particularly good teaching architecture; it incorporates all the functionality of the twenty-year-old 8088, including its limitations, and then provides complex workarounds. Because of this complexity issue, it is difficult to explain the workings of the Pentium 4 without detailed reference to long outdated chip sets. Textbooks have instead focused on the simpler 8088 and then have described the computers students actually use later, as an extension and an afterthought. This is analogous to learning automotive mechanics on a Ford Model A and only later discussing such important concepts as catalytic converters, automatic transmissions, and key-based ignition systems. A course in architecture should not automatically be forced to be a course in the history of computing.

Instead, I wanted to teach a course using an easy-to-understand architecture that incorporated modern principles and could itself be useful for students. Since every computer that runs a Web browser incorporates a copy of the JVM as software, almost every machine today already has a compatible JVM available to it.

This book, then, covers the central aspects of computer organization and architecture: digital logic and systems, data representation, and machine organization/architecture. It also describes the assembly-level language of one particular architecture, the JVM, with other common architectures such as the Intel Pentium 4 and the PowerPC given as supporting examples but not as the object of focus. The book is designed specifically for a standard second-year course on the architecture and organization of computers, as recommended by the IEEE Computer Society and the Association for Computing Machinery.[1]

---

[1] "Computing Curricula 2001," December 15, 2001, Final Draft; see specifically their recommendation for course CS220.

How

The book consists of two parts. The first half (chapters 1–5) covers general principles of computer organization and architecture and the art/science of programming in assembly language, using the JVM as an illustrative example of those principles in action (How are numbers represented in a digital computer? What does the loader do? What is involved in format conversion?), as well as the necessary specifics of JVM assembly language programming, including a detailed discussion of opcodes (What exactly does the i2c opcode do, and how does it change the stack? What's the command to run the assembler?). The second half of the book (chapters 6–10) focuses on specific architectural details for a variety of different CPUs, including the Pentium, its archaic and historic cousin the 8088, the Power architecture, and the Atmel AVR as an example of a typical embedded systems controller chip.

For Whom

It is my hope and belief that this framework will permit this textbook to be used by a wide range of people and for a variety of courses. The book should successfully serve most of the software-centric community. For those primarily interested in assembly language as the basis for abstract study of computer science, the JVM provides a simple, easy-to-understand introduction to the fundamental operations of computing. As the basis for a compiler theory, programming languages, or operating systems class, the JVM is a convenient and portable platform and target architecture, more widely available than any single chip or operating system. And as the basis for further (platform-specific) study of individual machines, the JVM provides a useful explanatory teaching architecture that allows for a smooth, principled transition not only to today's Pentium, but also to other architectures that may replace, supplant, or support the Pentium in the future. For students, interested in learning how machines work, this textbook will provide information on a wide variety of platforms, enhancing their ability to use whatever machines and architectures they find in the work environment.

As noted above, the book is mainly intended for a single-semester course for second-year undergraduates. The first four chapters present core material central to the understanding of the principles of computer organization, architecture, and assembly language programming. They assume some knowledge of a high-level imperative language and familiarity with high school algebra (but not calculus). After that, professors (and students) have a certain amount of flexibility in choosing the topics, depending upon the environment and the issues. For Intel/Windows shops, the chapters on the 8088 and the Pentium are useful and relevant, while for schools with older Apples or a Motorola-based microprocessor lab, the chapter on the Power architecture is more relevant. The Atmel AVR chapter can lay the groundwork for laboratory work in an embedded systems or microcomputer laboratory, while the advanced JVM topics will be of interest to students planning on implementing JVM-based systems or on writing system software (compilers, interpreters, and so forth) based on the JVM architecture. A fast-paced class might even be able to cover all topics. The appendices are provided primarily for reference, since I believe that a good textbook should be useful even after the class is over.

Acknowledgments

Without the students at Duquesne University, and particularly my guinea pigs from the Computer Organization and Assembly Language classes, this textbook couldn't have happened. I am also grateful for the support provided by my department, college, and university, and particularly for the support funding from the Philip H. and Betty L. Wimmer Family Foundation. I would also like to thank my readers, especially Erik Lindsley of the University of Pittsburgh, for their helpful comments on early drafts.

Without a publisher, this book would never have seen daylight; I would therefore like to acknowledge my editors, Tracey Dunkelberger and Kate Hargett, and through them the Prentice Hall publishing group. I would like to express my appreciation to all of the reviewers: Mike Litman, Western Illinois University; Noe Lopez Benitez, Texas Tech University; Larry Morell, Arkansas Tech University; Peter Smith, California State University–Channel Islands; John Sigle, Louisiana State University–Shreveport; and Harry Tyrer, University of Missouri–Columbia. Similarly, without the software, this book wouldn't exist. Aside from the obvious debt of gratitude to the people at Sun who invented Java, I specifically would like to thank and acknowledge Jon Meyer, the author of `jasmin`, both for his software and for his helpful support.

Finally, I would like to thank my wife, Jodi, who drew preliminary sketches for most of the illustrations and, more importantly, has managed to put up with me throughout the book's long gestation and is still willing to live in the same house.

I

Part the First: Imaginary Computers

Computation and Representation

1.1 Computation

A computer

Also a computer

1.1.1 Electronic Devices

How many people really know what a computer is? If you asked, most people would point to a set of boxes on someone's desk (or perhaps in someone's briefcase)—probably a set of dull-looking rectangular boxes encased in gray or beige plastic, and surrounded by a tangle of wires and perhaps something resembling a TV. If pressed for detail, they would point at one particular box as "the computer." But, of course, there are also computers hidden in all sorts of everyday electronic gadgets to make sure that your car's fuel efficiency stays high enough, to interpret the signals from a DVD player, and possibly even to make sure your morning toast is the right shade of brown. To most people, though, a computer is still the box you buy at an electronics shop, with bits and bytes and gigahertz that are often compared, but rarely understood.

In functional terms, a computer is simply a high-speed calculator capable of performing thousands, millions, or even billions of simple arithmetic operations per second from a stored program. Every thousandth of a second or so, the computer in your car reads a few key performance indicators from various sensors in the engine and adjusts the machine slightly to ensure proper functioning. The key to being of any use is at least partially in the sensors. The computer itself processes only electronic signals. The sensors are responsible for determining what's really going on under the hood and converting that into a set of electronic signals that describe, or represent, the current state of the engine. Similarly, the adjustments that the computer makes are stored as electronic signals and converted back into physical changes in the engine's working.

How can electronic signals "represent" information? And how exactly does a computer process these signals to achieve fine control without any physical moving parts or representation? Questions of representation such as these are, ultimately, the key to understanding both how computers work and how they can be deployed in the physical world.

1.1.2   Algorithmic Machines

The single most important concept in the operation of a computer is the idea of an **algorithm**: an unambiguous, step-by-step process for solving a problem or achieving a desired end. The ultimate definition of a computer does not rely on its physical properties, or even on its electrical properties (such as its transistors), but on its ability to represent and carry out algorithms from a stored program. Within the computer are millions of tiny circuits, each of which performs a specific well-defined task (such as adding two integers together or causing an individual wire or set of wires to become energized) when called upon. Most people who use or program computers are not aware of the detailed workings of these circuits.

In particular, there are several basic types of operations that a typical computer can perform. As computers are, fundamentally, merely calculating machines, almost all of the functions they can perform are related to numbers (and concepts representable by numbers). A computer can usually perform basic mathematical operations such as addition and division. It can also perform basic comparisons—is one number equal to another number? Is the first number less than the second? It can store millions or billions of pieces of information and retrieve them individually. Finally, it can adjust its actions based on the information retrieved and the comparisons performed. If the retrieved value is greater than the previous value, then (for example) the engine is running too hot, and a signal should be sent to adjust its performance.

1.1.3   Functional Components

System-Level Description

Almost any college bulletin board has a few ads that read something like "GREAT MACHINE! 3.0-GHz Intel Celeron D, 512 mg, 80-GB hard drive, 15-inch monitor, must sell to make car payment!" Like most ads, there's a fair bit of information in there that requires extensive unpacking to understand fully. For example, what part of a 15-inch monitor is actually 15 inches? (The length of the diagonal of the visible screen, oddly enough.) In order to understand the detailed workings of a computer, we must first understand the major components and their relations to each other (figure 1.1).

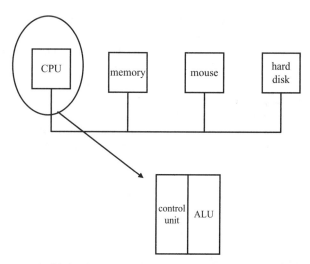

Figure 1.1 Major hardware components of a computer

Central Processing Unit

The heart of any computer is the **Central Processing Unit**, or CPU. This is usually a single piece of high-density circuitry built on single **integrated circuit** (IC) silicon chip (figure 1.2). Physically, it usually looks like a small piece of silicon, mounted on a plastic slab a few centimeters square, surrounded by metal pins. The plastic slab itself is mounted on the **motherboard**, an electronic circuit board consisting of a piece of plastic and metal tens of centimeters

Figure 1.2 Photograph of a CPU chip

on a side, containing the CPU and a few other components that need to be placed near the CPU for speed and convenience. Electronically, the CPU is the ultimate controller of the computer, as well as the place where all calculations are performed. And, of course, it's the part of the computer that everyone talks and writes about—a 3.60-GHz Pentium 4 computer, like the Hewlett-Packard HP xw4200, is simply a computer whose CPU is a Pentium 4 chip and that runs at a speed of 3.60 gigahertz (GHz), or 3,600,000,000 **machine cycles** per second. Most of the basic operations a computer can perform take one machine cycle each, so another way of describing this is to say that a 3.60-GHz computer can perform just over 3.5 billion basic operations per second. At the time of writing, 3.60 GHz is a fast machine, but this changes very quickly with technological developments. For example, in 2000, a 1.0-GHz Pentium was the state of the art, and, in keeping with a long-standing rule of thumb (Moore's law) that computing power doubles every 18 months, one can predict the wide availability of 8-GHz CPUs by 2008.

SIDEBAR

Moore's Law

Gordon Moore, the cofounder of Intel, observed in 1965 that the number of transistors that could be put on a chip was doubling every year. In the 1970s, that pace slowed slightly, to a doubling every 18 months, but has been remarkably uniform since then, to the surprise of almost everyone, including Dr. Moore himself. Only in the past few years has the pace weakened.

The implications of smaller transistors (and increasing transistor density) are profound. First, the cost per square inch of a silicon chip itself has been relatively steady by comparison, so doubling the density will approximately halve the cost of a chip. Second, smaller transistors react faster, and components can be placed closer together, so that they can communicate with each other faster, vastly increasing the speed of the chip. Smaller transistors also consume less power, meaning longer battery life and lower cooling requirements, avoiding the need for climate-controlled rooms and bulky fans. Because more transistors can be placed on a chip, less soldering is needed to connect chips together, with an accordingly reduced chance of solder breakage and correspondingly greater overall reliability. Finally, the fact that the chips are smaller means that computers themselves can be made smaller, enough to make things like embedded controller chips and/or personal digital assistants (PDAs) practical. It is hard to overestimate the effect that Moore's law has had on the development of the modern computer. Moore's law by now is generally taken to mean, more simply, that the power of an available computer doubles every 18 months (for whatever reason, not just transistor density). A standard, even low-end, computer available off the shelf at the local store is faster, more reliable, and has more memory than the original Cray-1 supercomputer of 1973.

The problem with Moore's law is that it will not hold forever. Eventually, the laws of physics are likely to dictate that a transistor can't be any smaller than an atom (or something like that). More worrisome is what's sometimes called Moore's second law, which states that fabrication costs double every three years. As long as fabrication costs grow more slowly than computer power, the performance/cost ratio should remain reasonable. But the cost of investing in new chip technologies may make it difficult for manufacturers such as Intel to continue investing in new capital.

CPUs can usually be described in families of technological progress; the Pentium 4, for example, is a further development of the Pentium, the Pentium II, and the Pentium III, all manufactured by the Intel corporation. Before that, the Pentium itself derived from a long line of numbered Intel chips, starting with the Intel 8088 and progressing through the 80286, 80386, and 80486. The so-called "x86 series" became the basis for the best-selling IBM personal computers (PCs and their clones) and is probably the most widely used CPU chip. Modern Apple computers use a different family of chips, the PowerPC G3 and G4, manufactured by a consortium of Apple, IBM, and Motorola (AIM). Older Apples and Sun workstations used chips from the Motorola-designed 68000 family.

The CPU itself can be divided into two or three main functional components. The **Control Unit** is responsible for moving data around within the machine For example, the Control Unit takes care of loading individual program instructions from memory, identifying individual instructions, and passing the instructions to other appropriate parts of the computer to be performed The **Arithmetic and Logical Unit** (ALU) performs all necessary arithmetic for the computer; it typically contains special-purpose hardware for addition, multiplication, division, and so forth. It also, as the name implies, performs all the logical operations, determining whether a given number is bigger or smaller than another number or checking whether two numbers are equal. Some computers, particularly older ones, have special-purpose hardware, sometimes on a separate chip from the CPU itself, to handle operations involving fractions and decimals. This special hardware is often called the **Floating Point Unit** or FPU (also called the Floating Point Processor or FPP). Other computers fold the FPU hardware onto the same CPU chip as the ALU and the Control Unit, but the FPU can still be thought of as a different module within the same set of circuitry.

Memory

Both the program to be executed and its data are stored in memory. Conceptually, memory can be regarded as a very long array or row of electromagnetic storage devices. These array locations are numbered, from 0 to a CPU-defined maximum, and can be addressed individually by the Control Unit to place data memory or to retrieve data from memory (figure 1.3). In addition, most modern machines allow high-speed devices such as disk drives to copy large blocks of data without needing the intervention of the Control Unit for each signal. Memory can be broadly divided into two types: **Read-Only Memory** (ROM), which is permanent, unalterable, and remains even after the power is switched off, and **Random Access Memory** (RAM), the contents of which can be changed by the CPU for temporary storage but usually disappears when the power does. Many machines have both kinds of memory; ROM holds standardized data and a basic version of the operating system that can be used to start the machine. More extensive programs are held in long-term storage such as disk drives and CDs, and loaded as needed into RAM for short-term storage and execution.

This simplified description deliberately hides some tricky aspects of memory that the hardware and operating system usually take care of for the user. (These issues also tend to be hardware-specific, so they will be dealt with in more detail in later chapters.) For example, different computers, even with identical CPUs, often have different amounts of memory. The amount of physical memory installed on a computer may be less than the maximum number of locations the CPU can address or, in odd cases, may even be more. Furthermore, memory located on the CPU chip

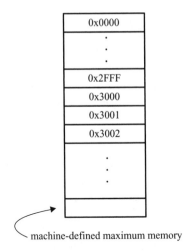

Figure 1.3   Block diagram of a linear array of memory cells

itself can typically be accessed much more quickly than memory located on separate chips, so a clever system can try to make sure that data is moved or copied as necessary to be available in the fastest memory when needed.

Input/Output (I/O) Peripherals

In addition to the CPU and memory, a computer usually contains other devices to read, display or store data, or more generally to interact with the outside world. These devices vary from commonplace keyboards and hard drives through more unusual devices like facsimile (FAX) boards, speakers, and musical keyboards to downright weird gadgets like chemical sensors, robotic arms, and security deadbolts. The general term for these gizmos is **peripherals**. For the most part, these devices have little direct effect on the architecture and organization of the computer itself; they are just sources and sinks for information. A keyboard, for instance, is simply a device to let the computer gather information from the user. From the point of view of the CPU designer, data is data, whether it came from the Internet, from the keyboard, or from a fancy chemical spectrum analyzer.

In many cases, a peripheral can be physically divided into two or more parts. For example, computers usually display their information to the user on some form of video monitor. The **monitor** itself is a separate device, connected via a cable to a video adapter board located inside the computer's casing. The CPU can draw pictures by sending command signals to the video board, which in turn will generate the picture and send appropriate visual signals over the video cable to the monitor itself. A similar process describes how the computer can load a file from many different kinds of hard drives via a SCSI (Small Computer System Interface) controller card, or interact via an Ethernet card with the millions of miles of wire that comprise the Internet. Conceptually, engineers draw a distinction between the device itself, the device cable (which is often just a wire), and the device controller, which is usually a board inside the computer—but to the programmer, they're usually all one device. Using this kind of logic, the entire Internet, with its millions of miles of wire, is just "a device." With a suitably well-designed system, there's not much difference between downloading a file off the Internet or loading it from a hard drive.

Interconnections and Buses

In order for the data to move between the CPU, memory, and the peripherals, there must be connections. These connections, especially between separate boards, are usually groups of wires to allow multiple individual signals to be sent in a block. The original IBM-PC, for example, had eight wires to allow data to pass between the CPU and peripherals. A more modern computer's PCI (Peripheral Component Interconnect) bus has 64 data wires, allowing data to pass eight times as fast, even before increased computer speed is taken into account. These wires are usually grouped into what is called a **bus**, a single wire set connecting several different devices. Because it is shared (like an early party-line telephone), only one device can transmit data at a time, but the data is available to any connected device. Additional wires are used to determine which device should listen to the data and what exactly it should do when it gets it.

In general, the more devices attached to a single bus, the slower it runs. This is true for two main reasons. First, the more devices, the greater the possibility that two devices will have data to transmit at the same time, and thus that one device will have to wait its turn. Second, more devices usually means longer wires in the bus, which reduces the speed of the bus due to delays in propagation—the time it takes a signal to get from one end of the wire to the other. For this reason, many computers now have a multiple-bus design, in which, for example, the local bus connects the CPU with high-speed memory stored on the CPU's motherboard (often on the CPU chip itself). The system bus connects the memory board, the CPU motherboard, and an "expansion bus" interface board. The expansion bus, in turn, is a second bus that connects to other devices such as the network, the disk drives, the keyboard, and the mouse.

On particularly high-performance computers (such as the one in figure 1.4), there may be four or five separate buses, with one reserved for high-speed, data-intensive devices such as the network and video cards, while lower-speed devices such as the keyboard are relegated to a separate, slower bus.

Support Units

In addition to the devices mentioned already, a typical computer will have a number of components that are important to its physical condition. For example, inside the case (itself crucial for the physical protection of the delicate circuit boards) will be a power supply that converts the AC line voltage into an appropriately conditioned DC voltage for the circuit boards. There may also be a battery, particularly in laptops, to provide power when wall current is unavailable and to maintain memory settings. There is usually a fan to circulate air inside the case and to prevent components from overheating. There may also be other devices such as heat sensors (to control fan speed), security devices to prevent unauthorized use or removal, and often several wholly internal peripherals such as internal disk drives and CD readers.

1.2 Digital and Numeric Representations

1.2.1 Digital Representations and Bits

At a fundamental level, computer components, like so many other electronic components, have two stable states. Lights are on or off, switches are open or closed, and wires are either carrying current or not. In the case of computer hardware, individual components such as transistors and

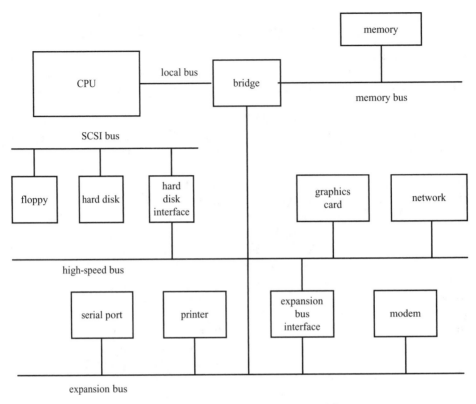

Figure 1.4 Block architecture of a high-speed, multibus computer

resistors are either at 0 volts relative to ground or at some other voltage (typically 5 volts above ground). These two states are usually held to represent the numbers 1 and 0, respectively. In the early stages of computer development, these values were hand-encoded by flipping mechanical switches. Today, high-speed transistors serve much the same purpose, but the representation of data in terms of these two values remains unchanged since the 1940s. Every such 1 or 0 is usually called a **bit**, an abbreviation for "binary digit." (Of course, the word "bit" is itself a normal English word, meaning "a very small amount"—which also describes a "bit" of information.)

S I D E B A R

How Transistors Work

The single most important electrical component in the modern computer is the transistor, first invented by Bardeen, Brattain, and Shockley in 1947 at Bell Telephone Labs. (These men received the Nobel Prize for Physics in 1956 for this invention.) The fundamental idea involves some fairly high-powered (well, yes, Nobel-caliber) quantum physics, but it can be understood in terms of electron transport, as long as you don't need the actual equations. A transistor consists mostly of a type of material called a **semiconductor**, which occupies an uneasy middle ground between good conductors (like copper) and bad conductors/good insulators (like glass). A key aspect of semiconductors is that their ability to transmit electricity can change dramatically with impurities (**dopants**) in the semiconductor.

For example, the element phosphorus, when added to pure silicon (a semiconductor), will donate electrons to the silicon. Since electrons have a negative charge, phosphorus is termed an **n-type** dopant, and phosphorus-doped silicon is sometimes called an **n-type semiconductor**. Aluminum, by contrast, is a **p-type** dopant and will actually remove—actually, lock up—electrons from the silicon matrix. The places where these electrons have been removed are sometimes called "holes" in the p-type semiconductor.

When you put a piece of n-type next to a piece of p-type semiconductor (the resulting widget is called a **diode**; figure 1.5), an interesting electrical effect occurs. An electrical current will not typically be able to pass through such a diode; the electrons carrying the current will encounter and "fall into" the holes. If you apply a **bias voltage** to this gadget, however, the extra electrons will fill the holes, allowing current to pass. This means that electricity can pass in only one direction through a diode, which makes it useful as an electrical **rectifier**.

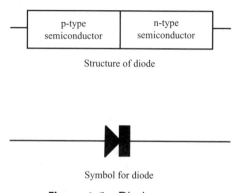

Structure of diode

Symbol for diode

Figure 1.5 Diodes

A modern transistor is made like a semiconductor sandwich; a thin layer of p-type semiconductor between two slices of n-type semiconductor, or sometimes the reverse. (Yes, this is just two diodes back to back; figure 1.6). Under normal circumstances, current can't pass from the **emitter** to the **collector** as electrons fall into the holes. Applying a **bias voltage** to the **base** (the middle wire) will fill the holes so that electricity can pass. You can think of the base as a gate that can open or shut to allow electricity to flow or not. Alternatively, you can think of it as a valve in a hosepipe to control the amount of water it lets through. Turn it one way, and the electrical signal drops to a trickle. Turn it the other way, and it flows without hindrance.

The overall effect of the transistor is that a small change in voltage (at the base) will result in a very large change in the amount of current that flows from the emitter to the collector. This makes a transistor extremely useful for amplifying small signals. It also can function as a binary switch, the key advantage being that it has no moving parts and thus nothing to break. (It's also much, much faster to throw an electrical switch than a mechanical one.) With the invention of the IC, for which Jack Kilby also won the Nobel Prize, engineers gained the ability to create thousands, millions, or billions of tiny transistors by doping very small areas of a larger piece of silicon. To this day, this remains the primary way that computers are manufactured.

(*continued*)

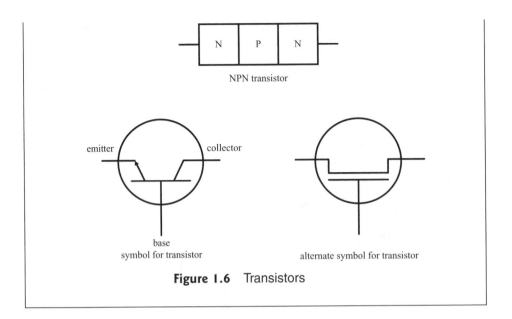

Figure 1.6   Transistors

1.2.2   Boolean Logic

Modern computers operate using a logic based on **bits**. A bit is the smallest unit that can be said to carry information, as in the children's game "Twenty Questions," where each yes or no question yields an answer that could be encoded with a single bit (for example, 1 represents a "yes" and 0 a "no"). If you are familiar with the old Milton Bradley board game, "Guess Who," the same principle applies. By asking yes/no questions, you gradually learn which person your opponent has chosen—and by recording the answers to your questions, you can recreate that learning at any point. A bit is therefore the smallest unit that can be operated upon—stored, transmited, or manipulated—using logic. The conventional way of performing logic on bit quantities is called **Boolean** logic, after the nineteenth-century mathematician George Boole. He identified three basic operations—AND, OR, and NOT—and defined their meaning in terms of simple changes on bits. For example, the expression X AND Y is true (a "yes," or a 1) if and only if, independently, X is a "yes" and Y is a "yes." The expression X OR Y, conversely, is a "yes" if either X is a "yes" or Y is a "yes." An equivalent way of stating this is that X OR Y is false (a "no," or a 0) if and only if X is a "no" and Y is a "no." The expression NOT X is the exact opposite of X: "yes" if X is a "no" and "no" if X is a "yes" (figure 1.7). Because a bit can be in only one of two states, there are no other possibilities to consider. These operations(AND, OR, and NOT) can be nested or combined as needed. For example, NOT (NOT X)) is the exact opposite of the exact opposite of X, which works out to be the same as X itself. These three operations parallel their English lexical equivalents fairly well: if I want a cup of coffee "with milk and sugar," logically what I am asking for is a cup of coffee where "with milk" is true AND "with sugar" is true. Similarly, a cup of coffee "without milk or sugar" is the same as a cup "with no milk and no sugar." (Think about it for a bit.)

In addition to these three basic operations, there are a number of other operations that can be defined from them. For example, NAND is an abbreviation for NOT-AND. The expression

AND	no	yes
no	no	no
yes	no	yes

OR	no	yes
no	no	yes
yes	yes	yes

NOT	
no	yes
yes	no

Figure 1.7 Truth tables for AND, OR, and NOT

X NAND Y refers to NOT (X AND Y). Similarly, X NOR Y refers to NOT (X OR Y). Another common expression is exclusive-OR, written XOR. The expression X OR Y is true if X is true, Y is true, or both. By contrast, X XOR Y is true if X is true or Y is true, but not both. This difference is not captured cleanly in English but is implicit in several different uses: for example, if I am asked if I want milk or sugar in my coffee, I'm allowed to say "yes, please," meaning that I want both. This is the normal (inclusive) OR. By contrast, if I am offered coffee or tea, it wouldn't make much sense for me to say "yes," meaning both. This is an exclusive XOR; I can have either coffee XOR tea, but not both at the same time.

From a strictly theoretical point of view, it doesn't matter much whether 1/"yes"/"true" is encoded as ground voltage or as 5 volts above ground as long as 0/"no"/"false" is encoded differently and the difference is consistently applied. From the point of view of a computer engineer or system designer, there may be particular reasons (such as power consumption) to choose one representation over another. The choice of representation can have profound implications for the design of the chips themselves. The Boolean operations described above are usually implemented in hardware at a very low level on the chip itself. For example, one can build a simple circuit with a pair of switches (or transistors) that will allow current to flow only if both switches are closed. Such a circuit is called an AND gate, because it implements the AND function on the 2 bits represented by the switch state. This tiny circuit and others like it (OR gates, NAND gates, and so forth), copied millions or billions of times across the computer chip, are the fundamental building blocks of a computer. (See Appendix A for more on how these blocks work.)

1.2.3 Bytes and Words

For convenience, 8 bits are usually grouped into a single block, conventionally called a **byte**. There are two main advantages to doing this. First, writing and reading a long sequence of 0s and 1s is, for humans, tedious and error prone. Second, most interesting computations require more data than a single bit. If multiple wires are available, as in standard buses, then electrical signals can be moved around in groups, resulting in faster computation.

The next-largest named block of bits is a **word**. The definition and size of a word are not absolute, but vary from computer to computer. A word is the size of the most convenient block of data for the computer to deal with. (Usually, though not always, it's the size of the bus leading to main memory—but see the Intel 8088, discussed later, for a counterexample.) For example, the Zilog Z-80 microprocessor (the chip underlying the Radio Shack TRS-80, popular in the mid-1970s) had a word size of 8 bits, or 1 byte. The CPU, memory storage, and buses had all been optimized to handle 8 bits at a time (for example, there were eight data wires in the system bus). In the event that the computer had to process 16 bits of data, it would be handled in two separate halves, while if the computer had only 4 bits of data to process, the CPU would work as though it had 8 bits of data, then throw away the extra 4 (useless) bits. The original IBM-PC, based on the

Intel 8088 chip, had a word size of 16 bits. More modern computers such as the Intel Pentium 4 or the PowerPC G4 have word sizes of 32 bits, and computers with word sizes of 64 bits or even larger, such as the Intel Itanium and AMD Opteron series, are available. Especially for high-end scientific computation or graphics, such as in home video game consoles, a large word size can be key to delivering data fast enough to allow smoothly animated, high-detail graphics.

Formally speaking, the word size of a machine is defined as the size (in bits) of the machine's **registers**. A register is the memory location inside the CPU where the actual computations, such as addition, subtraction, and comparisons, take place (figure 1.8). The number, type, and organization of registers vary widely from chip to chip and may even change significantly within chips of the same family. The Intel 8088, for example, had four 16-bit general-purpose registers, while the Intel 80386, designed seven years later, used 32-bit registers instead. Efficient use of registers is key to writing fast, well-optimized programs. Unfortunately, because of the differences between different computers, this can be one of the more difficult aspects of writing such programs for various computers.

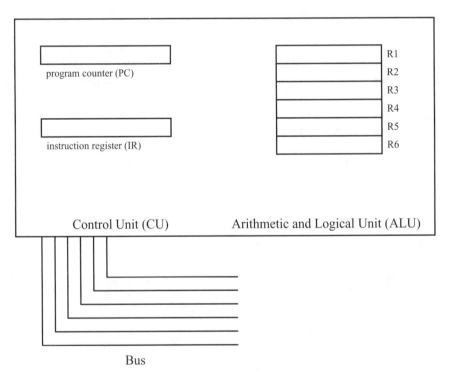

Figure 1.8   Typical internal structure of a CPU

1.2.4   Representations
Bit Patterns are Arbitrary
Consider, for a moment, one of the registers in an old-fashioned 8-bit microcomputer chip. How many different patterns can it hold? Other ways of asking the same question are to consider how

many different ways you can arrange a sequence of 10 pennies in terms of heads and tails or how many strings can be made up of only 8 letters, each of which is a 0 or a 1.

There are two possibilities for the first bit/coin/letter/digit, two for the second, and so on until we reach the eighth and final digit. There are thus $2 \cdot 2 \cdot 2 \cdot 2 \cdot 2 \cdot 2 \cdot 2 \cdot 2$ possibilities. This works out to 2^8 or 256 different storable patterns. Similar reasoning shows that there are 2^{32} or just over 4 billion storable patterns in a 32-bit register. (All right, for the pedants, $2^{32} = 4,294,967,296$. A handy rule of thumb for dealing with large binary powers is that 2^{10}, really 1024, is close to 1000. Remember that to multiply numbers, you add the exponents: $a^b \cdot a^c = a^{b+c}$. Thus, 2^{32} is $2^{2+10+10+10}$, or $2^2 \cdot 2^{10} \cdot 2^{10} \cdot 2^{10}$, or about $4 \cdot 1000 \cdot 1000 \cdot 1000$.)

Yes, but what do these patterns mean? The practical answer is: whatever you as the programmer want them to mean. As you'll see in the next subsection, it's fairly easy to read the bit pattern 00101101 as the number 77. It's also possible to read it as a record of the answers to eight different yes/no questions. ("Are you married?"—No. "Are you older than 25?"—No. "Are you male?"—Yes. And so forth.) It could also represent a key being pressed on the keyboard (in this case, the pattern represents the ASCII value for a capital M). The interpretation of bit patterns is arbitrary, and computers can typically use the same patterns in many ways. Part of the programmer's task is to make sure that the computer interprets these arbitrary and ambiguous patterns correctly at all times.

Natural Numbers

A common way to interpret bit patterns involves using **binary** arithmetic (in base 2). In conventional, or **decimal** (base 10) arithmetic, there are only ten different number symbols, 0 through 9. Larger numbers are expressed as individual digits times a power of the base value. The number four hundred eighty-one (481), for instance, is really $4 \cdot 10^2 + 8 \cdot 10^1 + 1$. Using this notation, we can express all natural numbers up to nine hundred ninety-nine in only three decimal digits. Using a similar notation, but adding up powers of 2, we can express any number in binary using only 0s and 1s.

Taking as an example the (decimal) number 85, simple arithmetic shows that it is equivalent to $64 + 16 + 4 + 1$, or (in more detail) to $1 \cdot 2^6 + 0 \cdot 2^5 + 1 \cdot 2^4 + 0 \cdot 2^3 + 1 \cdot 2^2 + 0 \cdot 2^1 + 1$. In binary, then, the number would be written as 1010101. In an 8-bit register, this could be stored as 01010101, while in a 32-bit register, it would be 00000000000000000000000001010101.

It's possible to do arithmetic on these binary numbers using the same strategies and algorithms that elementary students use for solving base 10 problems. In fact, it's even easier, as the addition and multiplication tables are much smaller and simpler! Because there are only two digits, 0 and 1, there are only four entries in the tables, as can be seen in figure 1.9. Just remember that, when adding in binary (base 2), every time the result is a 2, it generates a carry (just as every 10 generates a carry in base 10). So the result of adding $1 + 1$ in base 2 is not 2, but 0 carry the 1 or 10.

Inspection of the tables reveals the fundamental connection between binary arithmetic and Boolean algebra. The multiplication table is identical to the AND of the two factors. Addition, of course, can potentially generate two numbers: a one-digit sum and a possible carry. There is a carry if and only if the first number is a 1 and the second number is a 1; in other words, the carry is simply the AND of the two addends, while the sum (excluding the carry) is 1 if the first number is 1 or the second number is 1, but not both: the XOR of the two addends. By building an

$$
\begin{array}{c|cc}
+ & 0 & 1 \\
\hline
0 & 0 & 1 \\
1 & 1 & 10
\end{array}
\qquad
\begin{array}{c|cc}
\cdot & 0 & 1 \\
\hline
0 & 0 & 0 \\
1 & 0 & 1
\end{array}
$$

Figure 1.9   Addition and multiplication tables for binary (base 2) arithmetic

appropriate collection of AND and XOR gates, the computer can add or multiply any numbers within the expressive power of the registers.

How large a number, then, can be stored in an 8-bit register? The smallest possible value is obviously 00000000, representing the number 0. The largest possible value, then, would be 11111111, the number 255. Any integer in this range can be represented easily as an 8-bit quantity. For 32-bit registers, the smallest value is still 0, but the largest value is just over 4.2 billion.

Although computers have no difficulty interpreting long binary numbers, humans often do. For example, is the 32-bit number 00010000000000000000100000000000 the same as the number (deep breath here) 00010000000000000001000000000000? (No, they are different. There are sixteen 0s between the 1s in the first number and only fifteen in the second.) For this reason, when it is necessary (rarely, one hopes) to deal with binary numbers, most programmers prefer to use **hexadecimal** (base 16) numbers instead. Since $16 = 2^4$, every block of 4 bits (sometimes called a **nybble**) can be represented as a single base 16 "digit." Ten of the 16 hexadecimal digits are familiar to us as the numbers 0 through 9, representing the patterns 0000 through 1001. Since our normal base 10 uses only 10 digits, computer scientists have co-opted the letters A through F to represent the remaining patterns (1010, 1011, 1100, 1101, 1110, 1111; see table 1.1 for the complete conversion list). Nowadays, this is about the only use that people have for hexadecimal numbers: to specify and abbreviate long lists of bitstring values such as might be used in cryptography or networking. The two numbers above are clearly different when converted to base 16:

$$
\left.
\begin{array}{cccccccc}
0001 & 0000 & 0000 & 0000 & 0000 & 1000 & 0000 & 0000 \\
1 & 0 & 0 & 0 & 0 & 8 & 0 & 0
\end{array}
\right| = 0\mathrm{x}10000800
$$

$$
\left.
\begin{array}{cccccccc}
0001 & 0000 & 0000 & 0000 & 0001 & 0000 & 0000 & 0000 \\
1 & 0 & 0 & 0 & 1 & 0 & 0 & 0
\end{array}
\right| = 0\mathrm{x}10001000
$$

Hex	Binary	Hex	Binary	Hex	Binary	Hex	Binary
0	0000	4	0100	8	1000	C	1100
1	0001	5	0101	9	1001	D	1101
2	0010	6	0110	A	1010	E	1110
3	0011	7	0111	B	1011	F	1111

Table 1.1   Hexadecimal ↔ binary digit conversions

By convention in many computer languages (including Java, C, and C++), hexadecimal numbers are written with an initial "0x" or "0X." We follow that convention here, so the number 1001 refers to the decimal value one thousand one. The value 0x1001 would refer to $16^3 + 1$, the decimal value four thousand ninety-seven. (Binary quantities will be clearly identified as such in the text. Also, on rare occasions, some patterns will be written as **octal**, or base 8, numbers. In C, C++, or Java, these numbers are written with a leading 0, so the number 01001 would be an octal value equivalent to 513. This is a rather unfortunate convention, since almost no one uses octal for any reason, but the tradition continues.) Note that 0 is still 0 (and 1 is still 1) in any base.

Base Conversions

Converting from a representation in one base to another can be a tedious but necessary task. Fortunately, the mathematics involved is fairly simple. Converting from any other base into base 10, for example, is simple if you understand the notation. The binary number 110110, for instance, is defined to represent $2^5 + 2^4 + 2^2 + 2^1$, $32 + 16 + 4 + 2$, or 54. Similarly, 0x481 is $4 \cdot 16^2 + 8 \cdot 16^1 + 1$, $1024 + 128 + 1$, or (decimal) 1153.

An easier way to perform the calculation involves alternating multiplication and addition. The binary number 110110 is, perhaps obviously, twice the binary value of 11011. (If this isn't obvious, notice that the base 10 number 5280 is 10 times the value of 528.) The binary number 11011 is, in turn, twice 1101 plus 1. Thus, one can simply alternate multiplying by the base value and adding the new digit. Using this system, binary 110110 becomes

$$(((((((((1 \cdot 2) + 1) \cdot 2) + 0) \cdot 2) + 1) \cdot 2) + 1) \cdot 2) + 0)$$

which simple arithmetic will confirm is 54. Similarly 0x481 is

$$((((4 \cdot 16) + 8) \cdot 16) + 1)$$

which can be shown to be 1153.

If alternating multiplication and addition will convert to base 10, then it stands to reason that alternating division and subtraction can be used to convert from base 10 to binary. Subtraction is actually implicit in the way we will be using division. When dividing integers by integers, it's rather rare that the answer is exact; normally there's a remainder that must be implicitly subtracted from the dividend. These remainders are exactly the base digits. Using 54 again as our example, the remainders generated when we repeatedly divide by 2 will generate the necessary binary digits.

$$54 \div 2 = 27r\mathbf{0}$$
$$27 \div 2 = 13r\mathbf{1}$$
$$13 \div 2 = 6r\mathbf{1}$$
$$6 \div 2 = 3r\mathbf{0}$$
$$3 \div 2 = 1r\mathbf{1}$$
$$1 \div 2 = 0r\mathbf{1}$$

The boldface numbers are, of course, the bits for the binary digits of 54 (binary 110110). The only tricky thing to remember is that, in the multiplication procedure, the digits are entered in the normal order (left to right), so in the division procedure, unsurprisingly, the digits come out in right-to-left order, backward. The same procedure works for base 16 (or indeed for base 8, base 4, or any other base):

$$1153 \div 16 = \mathbf{72r1}$$

$$72 \div 16 = 4r\mathbf{8}$$

$$4 \div 16 = 0r\mathbf{4}$$

Finally, the most often used and perhaps the most important conversion is direct (and quick) conversion between base 2 and base 16, in either direction. Fortunately, this is also the easiest. Because 16 is the fourth power of 2, multiplying by 16 is really just multiplying by 2^4. Thus, every hexadecimal digit corresponds directly to a group of 4 binary digits. To convert from hexadecimal to binary, as discussed earlier, simply replace each digit with its 4-bit equivalent. To convert from binary to hexadecimal (hex), break the binary number into groups of 4 bits (starting at the right) and perform the replacement in the other direction. The complete conversion chart is (re)presented as table 1.2.

Hex	Binary	Hex	Binary	Hex	Binary	Hex	Binary
0	0000	4	0100	8	1000	C	1100
1	0001	5	0101	9	1001	D	1101
2	0010	6	0110	A	1010	E	1110
3	0011	7	0111	B	1011	F	1111

Table 1.2   Hexadecimal ↔ binary digit conversions (copy of table 1.1)

So, for example, the binary number 100101101100101 would be broken up into 4-bit nybbles, starting from the right, as 100 1011 0110 0101. (Please note that I cheated: the number I gave you has only 15 bits, so one group of 4 isn't complete. This group will always be on the far left and will be padded out with 0s, so the "real" value you will need to convert will be 0100 1011 0110 0101.) If you look these four values up in the table, you will find that they correspond to the values 4, B, 6, and 5. Therefore, the corresponding hexadecimal number is 0x4B65.

Going the other way, the hexadecimal number 0x18C3 would be converted to the four binary groups 0001 (1), 0100 (8), 1100 (C) and 0101 (3), which are put together to give the binary quantity 0001010011000101.

A similar technique would work for octal (base 8) with only the first two columns of table 1.1 and using only the last 3 (instead of 4) bits of the binary entries, as shown in table 1.3. Using these notations and techniques, you can represent any nonnegative integer in a sufficiently large register and interpret it in any base we've discussed. With a bit of creativity and flair, you can even adapt these techniques to oddball bases like base 3 or base 7.

Hex	Binary	Hex	Binary
0	000	4	100
1	001	5	101
2	010	6	110
3	011	7	111

Table 1.3 Octal ↔ binary digit conversions

Signed Representations

In the real world, there is often a use for negative numbers. If the smallest possible value stored in a register is 0, how can a computer store negative values? The question, oddly enough, is not one of storage but of interpretation. Although the maximum number of storable patterns is fixed (for a given register size), the programmer can decide to interpret some patterns as meaning negative values. The usual method for doing this is to use an interpretation known as **two's complement notation**.

It's a common belief (you can even see it in the film *Ferris Beuller's Day Off*) that if you drive a car in reverse, the odometer will run backward and apparently take miles off the engine. I don't know if it works or not—it didn't work for Ferris—but Howstuffworks.com[1] says that it should have. Imagine for a moment that it did. Suppose I took a relatively new car (say, with 10 miles on it) and ran it in reverse for 11 miles. What would the odometer say?

Well, the odometer *wouldn't* say −1 miles. It would probably read 999,999 miles, having turned over at 000,000. But if I then drove another mile forward, the odometer would turn over (again) to 000,000. We can implicitly define the number −1 as the number that, when 1 is added to it, results in a 0.

This is how two's complement notation works; negative numbers are created and manipulated by counting backward (in binary) from a register full of 0s, as in figure 1.10. Numbers in which the first bit is a 0 are interpreted as positive numbers (or 0), while numbers in which the first bit is a 1 are interpreted as negative. For example, the number 13 would be written in (8-bit) binary as 00001101 (hexadecimal 0x0D), while the number −13 would be 11110011 (0xF3). These patterns are called **signed** numbers (integers, technically) as opposed to the previously defined **unsigned** numbers. In particular, the pattern 0xF3 is the **two's complement notation** representation of −13 (in an 8-bit register).

How do we get from 0xF3 to −13? Beyond the leading 1, there appears to be no similarity between the two representations. The connection is a rather subtle one based on the above definition of negative numbers as the inverses of positive numbers. In particular, 13 + −13 should equal 0. Using the binary representations above, we note that

```
  00001101              13
+ 11110011              -13 in two's-complement notation
  -----------
  100000000             0 plus an overflow/carry
```

---

[1] http://auto.howstuffworks.com/odometer1.htm

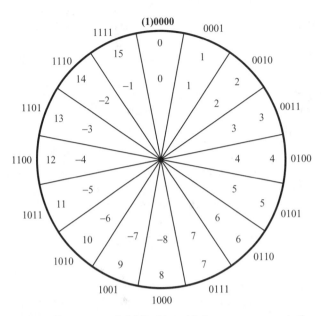

Figure 1.10   Structure of 4-bit signed integer representation

However, the 9-bit quantity 100000000 (0x100) cannot be stored in only an 8-bit register! Like a car odometer that rolls over when the mileage becomes too great, an 8-bit register will **overflow** and lose the information contained in the ninth bit. The resulting stored pattern is therefore 00000000 or 0x00, which is the binary (and hex equivalent of 0. Using this method, we can see that the range of values stored in an 8-bit register will vary from -128 (0x80) to $+127$ (0x7F). Approximately half of the values are positive and half are negative, which in practical terms is about what people typically want. Figure 1.10 shows that, in general, there is one more negative number than positive number, because the number opposite 0 on the figure is negative.

This demonstration relies critically on the use of an 8-bit register. In a 32-bit register, a much larger value is necessary to produce overflow and wrap around to 0. The 32-bit two's complement representation of -13 would not be 0xF3, but 0xFFFFFFF3. In fact, viewed as a 32-bit number, 0xF3 would normally be interpreted as 0x000000F3, which isn't even negative, since the first bit isn't a 1.

Calculating the two's complement representation of a number (for a given fixed register size) by hand is not difficult. Notice first that the representation of -1, for any register size, will always be a register containing all 1s. Adding 1 to this number will produce overflow and a register full of 0s. For any given bit pattern, if you reverse every individual bit (each 1 becomes a 0, each 0 becomes a 1, while preserving the original order—this operation is sometimes called the **bitwise** NOT, because it applies a NOT to every individual bit) and add the resulting number to the original, the result will always give you a register full of 1s. (Why?) This inverted pattern (sometimes called the "one's complement" or just the "complement"), added to the original pattern, will yield a sum of -1. And, of course, adding one more will give you a $-1 + 1$, or 0. This inverted pattern plus 1, then, will give you the two's complement of the original number.

```
  00001101   (= 13)
  11110010   (inverted)
+        1
-----------
  11110011   (= -13)
```

Note that repeating the process a second time will negate the negation.

```
  11110011   (= -13)
  00001100   (inverted)
+        1
-----------
  00001101   (= 13)
```

This process will generalize to any numbers and any (positive) register size. Subtraction will happen in exactly the same way, since subtracting a number is exactly the same as adding its negative.

Floating Point Representation

In addition to representing signed integers, computers are often called upon to represent fractions or quantities with decimal points. To do this, they use a modification of standard scientific notation based on powers of 2 instead of powers of 10. These numbers are often called **floating point** numbers because they contain a "decimal" point that can float around, depending upon the representation.

Starting with the basics, it's readily apparent that any integer can be converted into a number with a decimal point just by adding a decimal point and a lot of 0s. For example, the integer 5 is also $5.000\ldots$, the number -22 is also $-22.0000\ldots$, and so forth. This is also true for numbers in other bases (except that technically the "decimal" point refers to base 10; in other bases, it would be called a "radix" point). So the (binary) number 1010 is also $1010.0000\ldots$, while the (hexadecimal) number 0x357 is also $0x357.0000\ldots$.

Any radix point number can also be written in scientific notation by shifting the point around and multiplying by the base a certain number of times. For example, Avogadro's number is usually approximated as $6.023 \cdot 10^{23}$. Even students who have forgotten its significance in chemistry should be able to interpret the notation—Avogadro's number is a 24-digit $(23 + 1)$ number whose first four digits are 6, 0, 2, 3, or about 602,300,000,000,000,000,000,000. Scientific notation as used here has three parts: the **base** (in this case, 10), the **exponent** (23), and the **mantissa** (6.023). To interpret the number, one raises the base to the power of the exponent and multiplies by the mantissa. Perhaps obviously, there are many different mantissa/exponent sets that would produce the same number; Avogadro's number could also be written as $6023 \cdot 10^{20}$, $60.23 \cdot 10^{22}$, or even $0.6023 \cdot 10^{24}$.

Computers can use the same idea, but using binary representations. In particular, note the patterns in table 1.4. Multiplying the decimal number by 2 shifts the representation 1 bit to the left, while dividing by 2 shifts it 1 bit to the right. Alternatively, a form of scientific notation applies where the same bit pattern can be shifted (and the exponent adjusted appropriately), as in table 1.4.

Decimal	Binary integer	Binary radix	Scientific notation
5	00000101	00000101.0000...	1.01 (binary) $\cdot 2^2$
10	00001010	00001010.0000...	1.01 (binary) $\cdot 2^3$
20	00010100	00010100.0000...	1.01 (binary) $\cdot 2^4$
40	00101000	00101000.0000...	1.01 (binary) $\cdot 2^5$

Table 1.4   Exponential notation with binary numbers

We extend this to represent noninteger floating point numbers in binary the usual way, as expressed in table 1.5. The number 2.5, for example, being exactly half of 5, could be represented as the binary quantity 10.1 or as the binary quantity 1.01 times 2^1. 1.25 would be (binary) 1.01 or 1.01 times 2^0. Using this sort of notation, any decimal floating point quantity has an equivalent binary representation.

Decimal	Binary	Binary real	Scientific notation
5	101	00101.000...	1.0100 (binary) $\cdot 2^2$
2.5		00010.100...	1.0100 (binary) $\cdot 2^1$
1.25		00001.010...	1.0100 (binary) $\cdot 2^0$
0.6125		00000.101...	1.0100 (binary) $\cdot 2^{-1}$

Table 1.5   Exponential notation with binary fractions

The Institute for Electrical and Electronic Engineers (IEEE) has issued a series of specification documents describing standardized ways to represent floating point numbers in binary. One such standard, IEEE 754-1985, describes a method of storing floating point numbers as 32-bit words as follows (and as illustrated in figure 1.11:

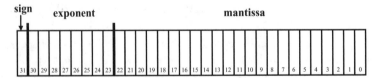

Figure 1.11   IEEE 32-bit floating point storage: sign, exponent, mantissa

Number the 32 bits of the word starting from bit 31 at the left down to bit 0 at the right. The first bit (bit 31) is the **sign** bit, which (as before) tells whether the number is positive or negative. Unlike two's complement notation, this sign bit is the only way in which two numbers of equal magnitude differ.

The next 8 bits (bits 30–23) are a "biased" **exponent**. It would make sense to use the bit pattern 0000000 to represent 2^0 and 0000001 to represent 2^1, but then one couldn't represent small values like 0.125 (2^{-3}). It would also make sense to use 8-bit two's complement notation, but that's not what the IEEE chose. Instead, the IEEE specified the use of the unsigned numbers 0..255, but the number stored in the exponent bits (the representational exponent) is a "biased" exponent, actually 127 higher than the "real" exponent. In other words, a real exponent of 0 will be stored as a representational exponent of 127 (binary 01111111). A real exponent of 1 would be stored as 128 (binary 10000000), and a stored exponent of 00000000 would actually represent the tiny quantity 2^{-127}. The remaining 23 bits (bits 22–0) are the mantissa with the decimal point—technically called the **radix point**, since we're no longer dealing with base 10— placed conventionally immediately after the first binary digit. This format, using a fixed number of positions in front of the radix point, is sometimes called **normalized form**.

Thus, for normal numbers, the value stored in the register is the value

$$(-1)^{sign\ bit} \cdot mantissa \cdot 2^{realexponent\ +\ 127}$$

A representational exponent of 127, then, means that the mantissa is multiplied by 1 (a corresponding real exponent of 0, hence a multiplier of 2^0), while an exponent of 126 means that the fraction is multiplied by 2^{-1} or 0.5, and so forth.

Actually, there is a micro-lie in the above formula. Because the numbers are in binary, the first nonzero digit has to be a 1 (there aren't any other choices that aren't 0!). Since we know that the first digit is a 1, we can leave it out and use the space freed up to store another digit whose value we didn't know beforehand. So the real formula would be

$$(-1)^{sign\ bit} \cdot 1.mantissa \cdot 2^{realexponent\ +\ 127}$$

As a simple example, the decimal number 2.0 in binary is $1.0 \cdot 2^1$. Representing this as an IEEE floating point number, the sign bit would be 0 (a positive number), the mantissa would be all 0s (and an implicit leading 1), while the exponent would be $127 + 1$, or 128, or binary 10000000. This would be stored in the 32-bit quantity

```
  0      10000000     00000000000000000000000
sign     exponent            mantissa
```

This same bit pattern could be written as the hexadecimal number 0x40000000.

The number -1.0, on the other hand, would have a sign bit of 1, an exponent of $127 + 0$, or binary 01111111, and a mantissa of all 0s (plus an implicit leading 1). This would yield the following 32-bit quantity :

```
  1      01111111     00000000000000000000000
sign     exponent            mantissa
```

Another way of writing this bit pattern would be 0xBF800000.

There's a little problem with this. What do you do if the number is to be stored exactly (0.000...)? There is no "implicit leading 1" anywhere in a string of all 0s. The IEEE defined as a special case that a bit pattern of all 0s (sign, exponent, and mantissa) would represent the number 0.0. There are also a number of other special cases, including representations of both positive and negative infinity, and the so-called NaN (not a number, the number that results when you try an illegal operation such as taking the logarithm of a negative number) and "denormalized numbers," which are used, rarely, to represent extremely tiny numbers with greater accuracy. The IEEE has also defined standard methods for storing numbers more accurately in 64-bit and larger registers. These additional cases are similar in spirit, if not in detail, to the 32-bit standard described above, but the details are rather dry and technical and not necessarily of interest to the average programmer.

One problem that comes up in any kind of radix-based representation is that of numbers that are not represented exactly. Even without worrying about irrational numbers (like π), some simple fractions can't be represented exactly. In base 10, for example, the fraction 1/7 has the approximate value 0.14285714285714... but never comes to an end. The fraction 1/3 is similarly 0.33333.... In base 2, the fraction 1/3 is 0.010101010101010101.... But there's no way to fit an infinite sequence into only 23 mantissa bits. So the solution is: we don't.

Instead, the number is represented as closely as possible. Converting to radix point, we see that 1/3 is about equal to $1.01010101010101010101010 \cdot 2^{-2}$, represented as

```
0       01111101   01010101010101010101010
sign    exponent            mantissa
```

This isn't a perfect representation, but it's close. But "close" may not be good enough in all contexts; small errors (called **roundoff error**) will inevitably creep into calculations involving floating point numbers. If I multiplied this number by the value 3.0 ($1.1 \cdot 2^1$), I'd be very unlikely to get the exact value 1.0. Programmers, especially those who handle big numerical problems like matrix inversion, spend a lot of time trying to minimize this sort of error. For now, all we can do is to be aware of it.

Performing operations on floating point numbers is tricky (and often slow). Intuitively, the algorithms are understandable and very similar to those you already know for manipulating numbers in scientific notation. Multiplication is relatively easy, since we know that 2^x times 2^y is just 2^{x+y}. Therefore, the product of two floating point numbers has as its sign bit the product or XOR of the two signs, as its mantissa the product of the two mantissae, and as its exponent the sum of the two exponents.[2] Thus we have the following:

$3.0 =$ (0) (10000000) (10000000000000000000000) [0x40400000]

$2.5 =$ (0) (10000000) (01000000000000000000000) [0x40200000]

The sign bit of the result of $3.0 \cdot 2.5$ would be 0. The mantissa would be $1.100... \cdot 1.010...$, or $1.111...$ (do you see why?). Finally, the exponent would be $1 + 1$, or 2, represented as 1000001. Thus we see that the product would be

(0) (10000001) (11100000000000000000000) [0x40F00000]

as expected, which converts to 7.5.

---

[2] But remember to account for both the exponent bias and the unexpressed 1 bit at the head of the mantissa!

Addition is considerably more difficult, as addition can happen only when the exponents of the two quantites are the same. If the two exponent values are the same, then adding the mantissae is (almost) enough:

3.0 = (0) (10000000) (10000000000000000000000) [0x40400000]

2.5 = (0) (10000000) (01000000000000000000000) [0x40200000]

The binary quantities 1.01 and 1.1 add up to 10.11, so the answer would be 10.11 times the common exponent: $10.11 \cdot 2^1$. Of course, this isn't legal, but it's easy enough to convert by shifting to a legal equivalent: $1.011 \cdot 2^2$. This yields

(0) (10000001) (01100000000000000000000) [0x40B00000]

which converts, as expected, to 5.5.

However, when the two exponents are not the same (for example, when adding 2.5 and 7.5), one of the addends must be converted to an equivalent form, but with a compatible exponent.

2.5 = (0) (10000000) (01000000000000000000000) [0x40200000]

7.5 = (0) (10000001) (11100000000000000000000) [0x40F00000]

Let's convert 7.5: $1.111 \cdot 2^2$ is the same as $11.11 \cdot 2^1$. Adding $11.11 + 1.01$ yields 101.00; $101.00 \cdot 2^1$ is the same as $1.01 \cdot 2^3$. The final answer is thus

(0) (10000010) (01000000000000000000000) [0x41200000]

which, again, is the expected value, in this case 10.0.

Character Representations

Nonnumeric data such as characters and strings are also treated as binary quantities and differ only in interpretation by the programmer/user. The most common standard for storing characters is the **ASCII** code, formally the American Standard Code for Information Interchange. ASCII code assigns a particular character value to every number between 0 and 127.

This is a slight oversimplification. Technically speaking, ASCII provides an interpretation for every 7-bit binary pattern between (and including) 0000000 and 1111111. Many of these patterns are interpreted as characters; for example, the pattern 100001 is an uppercase 'A.' Some binary strings, especially those between 0000000 and 0011111, are interpreted as "control characters," such as a carriage return, or a command to a peripheral such as "start of header" or "end of transmission." As almost all computers are byte-oriented, most store ASCII characters not as 7-bit patterns but as 8-bit patterns, with the leading bit being a 0. The letter A would be, for example, (binary) 01000001, or (hexadecimal) 0x41, or (decimal) 65. Using 8-bit storage allows computers to use the additional (high-bit) patterns for character set extensions; in Microsoft Windows, for example, almost every character set has different display values in the range 128–255. These display values may include graphics characters, suits (of cards), foreign characters with diacritical marks, and so forth.

The chief advantage of the ASCII encoding is that every character fits comfortably into a single byte. The chief disadvantage of ASCII is that, as the *American* standard code, it does not well reflect the variety of alphabets and letters in use worldwide. As the Internet continued to connect people of different nationalities and languages together, it became obvious that some method of encoding non-English (or at least, non-U.S.) characters was necessary. The result was **UTF-16** encoding, promulgated by the **Unicode** consortium.

UTF-16 uses 2 bytes (16 bits) to store each character. The first 128 patterns are almost identical to the ASCII code. With 16 bits available, however, there are over 65,000 (technically, 65,536) different patterns, each of which can be assigned a separate (printable) character. This huge set of characters allows uniform and portable treatment of documents written in a variety of alphabets, including (U.S.) English, unusual characters such as ligatures (e.g., æ) and currency symbols, variations on the Latin alphabet such as French and German, and unusual (from the point of view of American computer scientists) alphabets such as Greek, Hebrew, Cyrillic (used for Russian), Thai, Cherokee, and Tibetan. The Greek capital psi (Ψ), for example, is represented by 0x803A, or in binary by 1000000000111010. Even the Chinese/Japanese/Korean ideograph set (containing over 40,000 characters) can be represented (see figure 1.12 for an example).

Machine Operation Representations

In addition to storing data of many different types, computers need to store executable program code. As with all other patterns we have discussed, at its most basic level the computer can only interpret binary activation patterns. These patterns are usually called **machine language** instructions. One of the major roles of a register in the CPU is to fetch and hold an individual bit pattern where that pattern can be decoded into a machine instruction and then executed as that instruction.

Interpretation of machine language is difficult in general and varies greatly from computer to computer. For any given computer, the **instruction set** defines which operations the computer can execute. The Java Virtual Machine (JVM), for example, has a relatively small instruction set, with only 256 possible operations. Every byte, then, can be interpreted as a possible action to take. The value 89 (0x59) corresponds to the dup instruction, causing the machine to duplicate a particular piece of information stored in the CPU. The value 146 (0x92) corresponds to the i2c instruction, which converts a 32-bit quantity (usually an integer) to a 16-bit quantity (usually a Unicode character). These number-to-instruction correspondences are specific to the JVM and would not work on a Pentium 4 or a PowerPC, which have their own idiosyncratic instruction sets.

The task of generating machine code to do a particular task is often extremely demanding. Computers usually provide a large degree of programmed support for this task. Programmers usually write their programs in some form of human-readable language. This language is then converted into machine code by a program such as a compiler, in essence a program that converts human-readable descriptions of programs into machine code.

Interpretation

In light of what we have seen in the preceding sections, it is clear that any given bit pattern can almost certainly be interpreted in several different ways. A given 32-bit pattern might be a floating point number, two UTF-16 characters, a few machine instructions, two 16-bit signed integers, an unsigned 32-bit integer, or many other possibilities (see figure 1.12). How does the computer distinguish between two otherwise identical bitstrings?

Interpreted as...	0011 1110	0010 0000	0111 0010	0011 0111
Hexadecimal numbers	3E	20	72	37
Signed 32-bit integer	1042313783			
Signed 16-bit integers	15904		29239	
Signed 32-bit float	0.156686			
8-bit characters	>	space	r	7
16-bit characters	桃		爷	
JVM machinei nstructions	istore_3	lstore_2	frem	lstore

Figure 1.12 Bit pattern with multiple interpretations

The short and misleading answer is that it can't. A longer and more useful answer is that the distinction between the bitstrings is provided by the context of the program instructions. As will be discussed in the following chapter, most computers (including the primary machine discussed, the JVM) have several different kinds of instructions that do, broadly speaking, the same thing. The JVM, for example, has separate instructions to add 32-bit integers, 64-bit integers, 32-bit floating point numbers, and 64-bit floating point numbers. Implicit in these instructions is that the bit patterns to be added will be treated as though they were the appropriate type. If your program loads two integers into registers and then tells the computer to add two floating point numbers, the computer will naively and innocently treat the (integer) bit patterns as though they were floating point numbers, add them, and get a meaningless and error-ridden result. (Figure 1.12 illustrates this, since the instructions implicit in that pattern are type-illegal.) Similarly, if you tell the computer to execute a floating point number as though it were machine code, the computer will attempt to carry out, to the best of its ability, whatever silly instruction(s) that number corresponds to. If you're lucky, this will merely cause your program to crash. If you're not lucky,... well, that's one of the major ways that hackers can break into a computer: by overflowing a buffer and overwriting executable code with their own instructions.

It's almost always an error to try to use something as though it were a different data type. Unfortunately, this is an error that the computer can only partially compensate for. Ultimately, it is the responsibility of the programmer (and the compiler writer) to make sure that data is correctly stored and that bit patterns are correctly interpreted. One of the major advantages of the JVM is that it can catch some of these errors.

1.3 Virtual Machines

1.3.1 What is a "Virtual Machine"?

Because of differences between instruction sets, the chances are very good (warning: that's quite an understatement!) that a program written for one particular platform (CPU type and/or operating system) will not run on a different one. This is why software vendors sell different versions of programs for Windows computers using Pentium 4 CPUs and Macintosh computers using PowerPC CPUs, and also why many programs have "required configurations," stating that a particular computer must have certain amounts of memory or certain specific video cards to work properly. In the extreme case, this would require that computer programmers write related programs (such as the Mac and Windows versions of the same game) independently from scratch, a process that would essentially double the time, effort, and cost of such programs. Fortunately, this is rarely necessary. Most programming is done in so-called **high-level languages** such as C, C++, or Java, and then the (human-readable) program source code is converted to executable machine code by another program such as a compiler. Only small parts of programs—for example, embedded systems, graphics requiring direct hardware access, or device drivers controlling unusual peripherals—need be written in a machine-specific language.

The designers of Java, recognizing the popularity of the Web and the need for program-enabled Web pages to run anywhere, have taken a different approach. Java itself is a high-level language. Java programs are typically compiled into **class files**, with each file corresponding to the machine language for a program or part of a program. Unlike normal executables compiled from C, Pascal, or C++, the class files do not necessarily correspond to the physical computer on which the program is written or running. Instead, the class file is written using the machine language and instruction set of the **Java Virtual Machine** (JVM), a machine that exists only as a software emulation, a computer program pretending to be a chip. This "machine" has structure and computing power typical of—in some cases, even greater than–a normal physical computer such as an Intel Pentium 4, but is freed from many of the problems and limitations of a physical chip.

The JVM is usually a program running on the host machine. Like any other executable program, it runs on a physical chip using the instruction set of the local machine. This program, though, has a special purpose: its primary function is to interpret and execute class files written in the machine language of the JVM. By running a specific program, then, the physical chip installed in the computer can pretend to be a JVM chip, thereby being able to run programs written using the JVM instruction set and machine code.

The idea of a "virtual machine" is not new. In 1964, IBM began work on what would be known as VM/CMS, an operating system for the System/360 that provided time-sharing service to a number of users simultaneously. In order to provide the full services of the computer to every user, the IBM engineers decided to build a software system and user interface that gave the user the impression that he or she was alone and had the entire system to himself or herself. Every person or program could have an entire virtual S/360 at his or her disposal as needed, without worrying about whether this program would cause another person's program to crash. This also allowed engineers to upgrade and improve the hardware significantly without forcing users to relearn or rewrite programs. More than twenty years later, VM/CMS was still in use on large IBM mainframes, running programs designed and written for a virtual S/360 on hardware almost a million times faster. Since then, virtual machines and emulators have become a standard part of many programming tools and languages (including Smalltalk, an early example of an object-oriented language).

SIDEBAR

The .Net Framework

Another example of a common virtual machine is the .NET Framework, developed by Microsoft and released in 2002. The .NET Framework underlies the current version of Visual Studio and provides a unified programming model for many network-based technologies such as ASP.NET, ADO.NET, SOAP, and .NET Enterprise Servers. Following Sun's example of the JVM, .NET incorporates a **Common Language Runtime** (CLR), a virtual machine to manage and execute code developed in any of several languages. The underlying machine uses a virtual instruction set called **Microsoft Intermediate Language** (MSIL) that is very similar in spirit to JVM bytecode. Even the detailed architecture of the CLR's execution engine is similar to that of the JVM; for example, they're both stack-based architectures with instruction set support for object-oriented, class-based environments. Like the JVM, the CLR was designed to have most of the advantages of a virtual machine: abstract portable code that can be widely distributed and run without compromising local machine security. Microsoft has also followed Sun's example in the development and distribution of a huge library of predefined classes to support programmers using the .NET Framework who don't want to reinvent wheels. Both systems were designed with Web services and mobile applications in mind. Unlike the JVM, MSIL was designed more or less from the start to support a wide variety of programming languages, including J#, C#, Managed C++, and Visual Basic. Microsoft has also established a standard assembler **Ilasm**. In practical terms, the CLR is not as common or as widely distributed a computing environment as the JVM, but the software market is extremely dynamic and its final verdict has not yet been returned.

One key issue that will probably have a significant impact is the degree of multiplatform support that Microsoft provides. In theory, MSIL is as platform-independent as the JVM, but substantial parts of the .NET Framework libraries are based on earlier Microsoft technologies and will not run successfully on UNIX systems or even on older Windows systems (such as Windows 98). Microsoft's track record of supporting non-Microsoft (or even older Microsoft) operating systems does not encourage third-party developers to develop cross-platform MSIL software. Java, by comparison, has developed a strong group of developers on all platforms who both rely on and support this portability. If Microsoft can follow through on its promise of multiplatform support and develop a sufficient customer base, .NET might be able to replace Java as the system of choice for developing and deploying portable Web-based applications.

1.3.2 Portability Concerns

A primary advantage of a virtual machine, and the JVM in particular, then, is that it will run anywhere that a suitable interpreter is available. Unlike a Mac program that requires a PowerPC G4 chip to run (G4 emulators exist, but they can be hard to find and expensive), the JVM is widely available for almost all computers and for many kinds of equipment such as PDAs. Every major Web browser such as Internet Explorer, Netscape, or Konqueror has a JVM (sometimes called a "Java runtime system" built in to allow Java programs to run properly).

Furthermore, the JVM will probably continue to run anywhere, as the program itself is relatively unaffected by changes in the underlying hardware. A Java program (or JVM class file) should behave in the same way, except for speed, on a JVM emulator written for an old Pentium computer as for a top-end Power G7—a machine so new that it doesn't exist yet. However, if/when Motorola makes one, someone will almost certainly write a JVM client for it.

1.3.3   Transcending Limitations

Another advantage that virtual machines (and the JVM in particular) can provide is the ability to transcend, ignore, or mask limitations imposed by the underlying hardware. The JVM has imaginary parts corresponding to the real computer components discussed above, but because they consist only of software, there's little or no cost to making them. As a result, they can be as large or numerous as the programmer needs. Every (physical) register on a chip takes up space, consumes power, and costs significant amounts of money; as a result, registers are often in somewhat short supply. On the JVM registers are essentially free, and programmers can have and use as many as they like. The system bus, connecting the CPU to memory, can be as large as a programmer wants or needs.

A historical example may make the significance of this point clear. The original IBM-PC was based on the Intel 8088 chip. The 8088 was, in turn, based on another (earlier) chip by Intel, the 8086, almost identical in design but with a 16-bit bus instead of an 8-bit bus. This implicitly limits the data transfer speed between the CPU and memory (of an 8088) by about 50% relative to an 8086, but IBM chose the 8088 to keep its manufacturing costs and sales prices down. Unfortunately, this decision limited PC performance for the next 15 years or so, as IBM, Intel, and Microsoft were required to maintain backward compatibility with every succeeding generation of chips in the so-called Intel 80x86 family. Only with the development of Windows was Microsoft finally able to take full advantage of cheaper manufacturing and wider buses. Similar problems still occur, with most major software and hardware manufacturers struggling to support several different chips and chipsets in their products, and a feature available on a high-end chipset may not be available at the low end. Appropriately written Java runtime systems can take advantage of the feature where available (on a JVM written specifically for the new architecture) and make it useful to all Java programs or JVM class files.

The JVM also has the advantage of having, fundamentally, a better and cleaner design than most physical computer chips. This is due in part to its being designed from scratch in 1995 instead of inheriting several generations of engineering compromises from earlier versions. But the simplicity that results from not having to worry about physical limitations such as chip size, power consumption, or cost meant that the designers were able to focus their attention on producing a mathematically tractable and elegant design that allows the addition of useful high-level properties. In particular, the JVM design allows for a high degree of security enhancements, something discussed briefly below and in greater detail in chapter 10.

1.3.4   Ease of Updates

Another advantage of a virtual machine is the ease of updating or changing it compared to the difficulty of upgrading hardware. A well-documented error with the release of the Pentium chip in 1994 showed that the FPU in the Pentium P54C didn't work properly. Unfortunately, fixing this flaw required consumers to send the old chips back to Intel and to receive/install a complete physical replacement. By contrast, a bug in a JVM implementation can be repaired in software by the writers, or even possibly by a third party with source-code access, and distributed via normal channels, including simply making it available on the Internet.

Similarly, a new and improved version of the JVM, perhaps with updated algorithms or a significant speed increase, can be distributed as easily as any other updated program, such as a new video card driver or a security upgrade to a standard program. Since the JVM is software only, a particularly paranoid user can even keep several successive versions so that in case a new version has some subtle and undiscovered bug, she can revert to the old version and still run programs. (Of course, you only think this user is paranoid until you find out she's right. Then you realize she's just careful and responsible.)

1.3.5   Security Concerns

A final advantage of virtual machines is that, with the cooperation of the underlying hardware, they can be configured to run in a more secure environment. The Java language and the JVM were designed specifically with this sort of security enhancement in mind. For instance, most Java applets don't require access to the host computer's hard drive, and providing them with such access, especially with the ability to write on the hard drive, might leave the computer open to infection by a computer virus, theft of data, or simply deletion or corruption of crucial system files. The virtual machine, being software only, is in a position to vet attempted disk accesses and to enforce a more sophisticated security policy than the operating system itself may be willing or able to enforce.

The JVM goes even further, being designed not only for security but for a certain degree of verifiable security. Many security flaws in programs are created accidentally—for example, by a programmer attempting to read in a string without making sure that enough space has been allocated to hold it, or even attempting to perform an illegal operation (perhaps dividing a number by an ASCII string), with unpredictable and perhaps harmful results. JVM bytecode is designed to be verifiable and verified via a computer program that checks for this sort of accidental error. Not only does this reduce the possibility of a harmful security flaw, but it also improves the overall quality and reliability of the software. Software errors, after all, don't necessarily crash the system or allow unauthorized access. Many errors will, instead, quietly and happily—and almost undetectably—produce wrong answers. Catching these errors before the answers are produced, sometimes even before the program is run, substantially reduces this source of wrong answers and significantly increases the reliability of programs. The JVM security policy will be discussed extensively in chapter 10.

1.3.6   Disadvantages

So, if virtual machines are so wonderful, why aren't they more common? The primary answer, in one word, is "speed." It usually takes about 1000 times longer to do a particular operation in software instead of hardware, so performing hard-core computations (matrix multiplications, DNA sequencing, and so forth) in Java on a JVM may be significantly slower than performing the same computations in (chip-specific) machine language compiled from C++.

The practical gap, fortunately, does not appear to be anywhere near 1000 times, mainly because there have been some very smart JVM implementers. A properly written JVM will take advantage of the available hardware where practical and will do as many operations as possible using the available hardware. Thus, the program will (for example) use the native machine's circuitry for addition instead of emulating it entirely in software. Improvements in compiler technology have made Java run almost as fast as natively compiled code, often within a factor of 2, and sometimes almost imperceptibly slower. A February 1998 study by *JavaWorld* ("Performance tests show Java as fast as C++") found that, for a set of benchmark tasks, high-performance JVMs with high-efficiency compilers typically produced programs that ran, at worst, only slightly (about 5.6%) more slowly than their C++ equivalents, and for the most part ran identically to the limits of measurement. Of course, comparing computers and languages for speed is a notoriously difficult process, much like the standard apples and oranges comparison, and other researchers have found other values.

In some regards, speed comparisons can be a nonissue; for most purposes other than hard-core number crunching, Java or any other reasonable language is fast enough for most people's purposes. Java, and by extension the JVM, provide a powerful set of computation primitives including extensive security measures that are not found in many other languages, such as C++. It's not clear that the ability to crash a computer quickly is a tremendous advantage over being able to run a program to completion but somewhat more slowly.

A more significant disadvantage is the interposition of the JVM interpreter between the programmer and the actual physical hardware. For many applications demanding assembly language programming (games, high-speed network interfacing, or attaching new peripherals), the key reason that assembly language is used is to allow direct control of the hardware (especially of peripherals) at a very low level, often bit by bit and wire by wire. A badly written JVM prevents this direct control. This is becoming less and less of an issue with the development of silicon implementations of the JVM such as the aJile Systems' aJ-100 microcontroller or the Zucotto Systems' Xpresso family of processors. Both of these companies are producing controller chips suitable for hand-held Internet devices that use a chip-based implementation of JVM bytecode as machine code. In other words, these chips do not require any software support to translate JVM bytecode into native instruction sets and therefore can run at full hardware speeds, with full control over the hardware at a bit-by-bit level. With the development of Java chips, the JVM has come full circle from a clever mathematical abstraction to allow portable and secure access to a wide variety of processors to a physical chip of interest in its own right.

1.4   Programming the JVM

1.4.1   Java: What the JVM Isn't

Java, it must be stressed, is not the same as the Java Virtual Machine, although they were designed together and often are used together. The Java programming language is a high-level programming language designed to support secure platform-independent applications in a distributed network-ing environment such as the Internet. Perhaps the most common use of Java is to create "applets," to be downloaded as part of a Web page and to interact with the browser without cluttering up the server's network connection. The Java Virtual Machine, on the other hand, is a shared virtual computer that provides the basis for Java applications to run.

Much of the design of Java strongly influenced the JVM. For example, the JVM is a virtual machine precisely because Java should be a platform-independent language, so it cannot make any assumption about what kind of computer the viewer uses (figure 1.13). The JVM was designed around the notion of a security verifier so that Java programs could run in a secure environment. Networking support is built into the JVM's standard libraries at a relatively low level to ensure that Java programs will have access to a standardized and useful set of networking operations. There is, however, no necessary connection between the two products. A Java compiler could in theory be written to compile to native code for the PowerPC (the hardware underlying older Macintosh computers) instead of to JVM bytecode, and a compiler for any other language could be written to compile to JVM code.

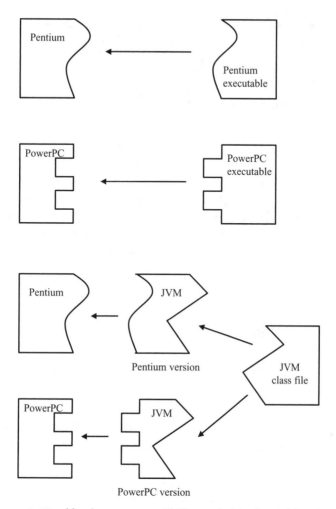

Figure 1.13   Hardware compatibility and virtual machines

In particular, consider the program written in figure 1.14. This is a simple example of a Java program that outputs a given fixed string to the default system output, usually the currently active window. This, or a very similar program, is often the standard first example in any elementary programming class, although sometimes one is shown instead a program that opens a new window and displays a message. When examined in more detail, however, the Java program itself is found to do nothing of the sort. The Java program, by itself, does nothing. In order to be executed, it must first be run through a translation program of some sort (the compiler) in order to produce an executable class file. Only this can be run to produce the desired output.

Java, or any programming language, is better viewed as a structure for specifying computations to be performed by the computer. A program in any language is a specification of a particular computation. In order for the computer to do its thing, the specification (program) must

```
public class JavaExample {
      public static void main(String [] args) {
            System.out.println("This is a sample program.");
      }
}
```

Figure I.14   Sample program in Java

be translated into the machine code that the computer ultimately recognizes as a sequence of program steps.

1.4.2   Translations of the Sample Program

There are usually many ways of specifying a given computation. A very similar program can be written in many other languages. For example, figures 1.15, 1.16, and 1.17 show programs with identical behavior written in C, Pascal, and C++. These programs also show great similarity in overall structure. The core of the program is written in a single line that somehow accesses a

```
#include <stdio.h>

int main()
{
      (void) printf("This is a sample program.\n");
}
```

Figure I.15   Sample program in C

```
Program PascalExample(output);

begin
      writeln ('This is a sample program.');
end.
```

Figure I.16   Sample program in Pascal

```
using namespace std;
#include <iostream.h>
int main()
{
      cout << "This is a sample program." << endl;
}
```

Figure I.17   Sample program in C++

fixed string (of ASCII characters) and calls a standard library function on it to pass it to a default output device. The differences are subtle and in the details; for example, the Pascal program has a name (PascalExample), while the C and C++ versions do not. In both C and C++, the program must explicitly represent the end-of-line carriage return, while Java and Pascal have a function that will automatically put a return at the end of the line. These differences, however, are relatively small when compared with the tremendous amount of similarity, especially when one considers the differences between this and machine-level code.

In light of the preceding discussion of the architecture and organization of a typical computer, consider the following: Few, if any, CPUs have enough registers within the ALU or Control Unit to allow storing an entire string. (This is especially true since there is no necessary upper limit to the length of a string in the abstract. Instead of printing a mere sentence, the programs could have printed an entire textbook.) No CPU has a single instruction to print a string to the screen. Instead, the compiler must break the program down into sufficiently small steps that are within the computer's instruction set.

1. The string itself must be stored somewhere in main memory, and
2. the CPU must determine where that storage location is.
3. The CPU must also determine which output peripheral should print the message, and possibly
4. what type it is. Finally,
5. it must pass the appropriate instructions to the peripheral, telling it
6. where the string is stored,
7. that the string is a string (and not an integer or a floating point number), and
8. that the appropriate action to take is to print it (possibly while automatically appending a return).

A single line of code may translate into eight or more individual operations that the computer must perform. In fact, there's no limit to the number of operations that might be performed in a single line of code; a line in Java like

$$i = 1 + 2 + 3 + 4 + 5 + 6 + 7 + 8 + 9 + 10;$$

requires an operation for every addition, in this case nine separate calculations. Since there's no limit to the theoretical complexity of a mathematical formula, there's no limit to the complexity of a single Java statement.

1.4.3   High- and Low-Level Languages

This encapsulation of many machine language instructions in a single line of code is typical of what are called **high-level** languages. Java, Pascal, and so forth are typical examples of one style of such languages. The task of a Java compiler is to take a complicated statement or expression and produce an appropriate series of machine instructions to perform the task.

By contrast, a **low-level** language is characterized by a very close relationship between operations in machine language and statements in the program code. Using this definition, machine language is, of course, a very low-level language, since there is always a 1:1 relationship between a machine language program and itself. **Assembly language** is a slightly more human-readable, but still low-level, language designed to promote total control over the machine and the machine code instructions but still be readable and understandable by the programmer. Assembly language is also characterized by a 1:1 relationship between assembly language instructions and machine code instructions.

In machine language, every element of the instruction (also called **opcode**, an abbreviation for "operation code") is, like everything else in the computer, a number. An earlier section

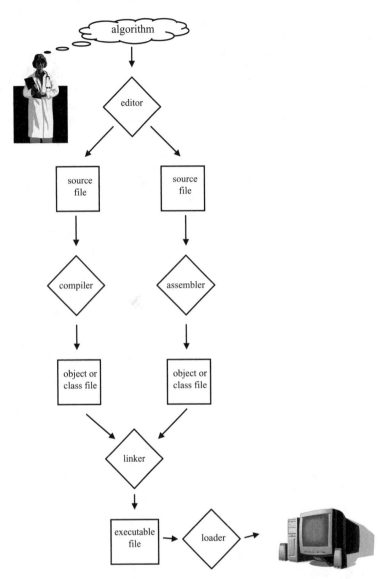

Figure 1.18   The programming process

mentioned in passing, for instance, that the opcode 89 (0x59) is meaningful to the JVM and causes it to duplicate a particular piece of information. In assembly language, every opcode is also given a **mnemonic** (pronounced "num-ON-ik," from the Greek word for memory) that explains or summarizes exactly what it does. The corresponding mnemonic for opcode 89 is dup, short for "duplicate." Similarly, the mnemonic iadd, short for "integer add," corresponds to the machine opcode used to perform an integer addition. The task of the translation program, in this case called an **assembler**, is to translate each mnemonic into its appropriate binary opcode and to gather the appropriate pieces of data that the computer needs (figure 1.18).

1.4.4 The Sample Program as the JVM Sees It

The JVM machine code version of the sample program(s) above would thus be a long and mostly unreadable binary string. A version of the program that corresponds to the machine code is presented in figure 1.19. This program was written (by hand) in a (low-level) JVM assembly language called jasmin, but could also have been written by a compiler starting from one of the original sample programs. Notice that the program is much longer—almost 30 lines instead of only 3 or 4—and much more difficult to understand. This is because many of the things that you take

```
; defines the class file associated with this as jasminExample.class
.class public jasminExample
; defines jasminExample as a subclass of Object
.super java/lang/Object

; boilerplate needed for object creation
.method public <init>()V
    aload_0

    invokespecial java/lang/Object/<init>()V
    return
.end method

.method public static main([Ljava/lang/String;)V
    ; we need two stack elements, for System.out and the string
    .limit stack 2

    ; find System.out (an object of type PrintStream)
    ; and put it on the stack
    getstatic java/lang/System/out Ljava/io/PrintStream;

    ; find the string (characters) to be printed
    ; and put it on the stack
    ldc "This is a sample program."

    ; invoke the PrintStream/println method
    invokevirtual java/io/PrintStream/println(Ljava/lang/String;)V

    ; ... and that's it!
    return
.end method
```

Figure 1.19 Sample program in JVM assembly language

Java code	`jasmin` code	JVM machine code
$x = 1 + 2 + 3 + 4 + 5;$	`bipush 1`	0x10
		0x01
	`bipush 2`	0x10
		0x02
	`iadd`	0x60
	`bipush 3`	0x10
		0x03
	`iadd`	0x60
	`bipush 4`	0x10
		0x04
	`iadd`	0x60
	`bipush 5`	0x10
		0x05
	`iadd`	0x60
	`istore_1`	0x3c

Figure 1.20   Sample expression in Java, `jasmin`, and JVM machine code (see the next chapter for details)

for granted in writing high-level programs must be specified exactly and explicitly. For example, in Java, every class is implicitly a subclass of type Object unless specified otherwise. The JVM requires, instead, that every class define its relationship to other classes explicitly. The comments (beginning with semicolons) in figure 1.19 present a more detailed, line-by-line description (for the human reader) of exactly how the (implicit) operations are defined and carried out.

Notice, though, that although the notions of class, subclass, and so forth are explicitly supported and used in Java, there is nothing especially Java-specific about the JVM low-language program presented in this section. In fact, just as it is the task of a Java compiler to convert the high-level Java code to something akin to JVM machine code, it is the task of a C++ or Pascal compiler to do the same with its program code for a specific platform. There is no reason that a Pascal compiler couldn't be written that produces JVM code as its final (compiled) output instead of PowerPC or Pentium machine code; the program would then run on a JVM (for instance, on a JVM emulator, inside a Web browser, or on a special-purpose chip like those mentioned earlier) instead of on the specific chip hardware (figure 1.20).

1.5 Chapter Review

- Computers are simply high-speed algorithmic devices; the details of their construction as electronic devices are less important than the details of how they work as information processing devices.
- The main part of a computer is the Central Processing Unit (CPU), which in turn contains the Control Unit, Arithmetic and Logical Unit (ALU), and Floating Point Unit (FPU). This is where all computations actually happen and programs actually run.

- Memory and peripherals are connected to the CPU through a collection of electrical buses that carry information to and from the CPU.
- All values stored in a conventional computer are stored as binary digits or bits. These are grouped for convenience into larger units such as bytes and words. A particular bit pattern may have several interpretations as an integer, a floating point number, a character or sequence of characters, or even a set of instructions to the computer itself. Deciding what types of data a given bit patterns represents depends on the context and is largely the programmer's responsibility.
- Different CPU chips have different instruction sets representing different things that they can do and ways that they do things. Every CPU, then, needs a different executable program written in a different kind of machine language even to run the same program.
- A virtual machine is a program that runs atop a real CPU and interprets machine instructions as though it itself were a CPU chip. The Java Virtual Machine (JVM) is a common example of such a program, and can be found on almost every computer and in every Web browser worldwide.
- Virtual machines have many advantages over conventional silicon-based CPUs, such as portability, fewer hardware limitations, ease of updates, and security. Virtual machines may have a big disadvantage in speed.
- Java is an example of a high-level language that can combine many machine-code instructions into a single statement. C, Pascal, and C++ are similar high-level languages. These languages must be compiled to convert their code into a machine-executable format.
- Low-level languages like assembly language have a tight, typically 1:1 relationship between program statement and machine instructions.
- There is no necessary connection between Java and the JVM; most Java compilers compile to JVM executable code, but a C, Pascal, or C++ compiler could do this as well. Similarly, a Java compiler could compile to Pentium 4 native code, but the resulting program would not run on a Macintosh computer.

1.6 Exercises

1. What is an algorithm?
2. Is a recipe as given in a cookbook an example of an algorithm?
3. Name the part of the computer described by each of the following phrases:

   - The heart and ultimate controller of the computer, the place where all calculations are performed
   - The part of the computer responsible for moving data around within the machine
   - The part of the computer responsible for all computations, such as addition, subtraction, multiplication, and division
   - A set of wires used to interconnect different devices for data connectivity
   - A device for reading, displaying, or storing data
   - A place for short-term storage for data and executing programs

4. How many different patterns could be stored in a 16-bit register? What is the largest value that could be stored as a (two's complement) signed integer in such a register? What is the

smallest value? How about the largest and smallest values that could be stored as unsigned integers?

5. Convert the following 16-bit binary numbers into hexadecimal and signed decimal numbers (no, you don't get to use a calculator!):

- 1001110011101110
- 1111111111111111
- 0000000011111111
- 0100100010000100
- 1111111100000000
- 1100101011111110

6. Convert the following 32-bit IEEE floating point numbers from hexadecimal into standard decimal notation.

- 0x40200000
- 0x41020000
- 0xC1060000
- 0xBD800000
- 0x3EAAAAAB
- 0x3F000000
- 0x42FA8000
- 0x42896666
- 0x47C35000
- 0x4B189680

7. Convert the following decimal numbers into 32-bit IEEE floating point notation.

- 2.0
- 45.0
- 61.01
- −18.375
- −6.68
- 65536
- 0.000001
- 10000000.0

8. Are there any numbers that can be represented exactly as a 32-bit integer but not as a 32-bit IEEE floating point number? Why or why not?

9. Using a standard ASCII table (check the Internet or appendix E), what 4 hexadecimal bytes would represent the string "Fred"?

10. What ASCII character string would correspond to the hexadecimal number 0x45617379?

11. True or false: the more 1s there are in a binary number, the larger it is. Why or why not?

12. Why won't executables created for a Windows Pentium IV run on a PowerPC-based Macintosh (without special software support)?

13. What is the most important advantage of a virtual machine over a chip-based architecture?

14. What is the most important disadvantage?
15. What languages can be used to write programs for the Java Virtual Machine (JVM)?
16. How many low-level machine instructions correspond to the following statement?

$$x = a + (b^*c) + (d^*e);$$

1.7 Programming Exercises

1. Write a program (in any language approved by the instructor) to read in a 32-bit (binary) signed integer and to output its decimal equivalent.
2. Write a program (...) to read in a 32-bit (binary) floating point number and to output its decimal equivalent.
3. Write a program (...) to read in a decimal floating point number and output its IEEE 64-bit hexadecimal equivalent. (Note: this may require additional reading.)
4. Write a program (...) to read two 32-bit floating point numbers (in hexadecimal IEEE format) A and B and to output their product $A \cdot B$ in hexadecimal. Do not convert internally to decimal floating point numbers and multiply using the language's multiply operation.
5. Write a program (...) to read two 32-bit floating point numbers (in hexadecimal IEEE format) A and B and to output their sum $A + B$ in hexadecimal. Do not simply convert to decimal and add.
6. Write a program (...) to read a 32-bit floating point number A (in hexadecimal) and to output its reciprocal $\frac{1.0}{A}$ in both hexadecimal and decimal. Can you use this program in conjunction with program 4 to perform floating point division? How?

2

Arithmetic Expressions

2.1 Notations

2.1.1 Instruction Sets

Two central problems—indeed, perhaps the two central problems—with computers are their lack of imagination and the limited set of things that they can do. Consider trying to work out the following story problem (figure 2.1) on a typical pocket calculator:

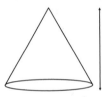

Figure 2.1   A conical mountain

What is the volume of a circular mountain 450 m in diameter at the base and 150 m high? A few minutes of searching through geometry textbooks will give you the formulas you need: the volume of a cone is one-third the product of the area of the base and the height. The area of the (circular) base is π times the square of the radius. The radius is half of the diameter. The value of π, of course, is 3.14 and a bit. Putting it all together, the answer would be

$$\frac{1}{3} \cdot \left[\pi \cdot \left(\frac{450}{2} \right)^2 \right] \cdot 150$$

So how do you work with this mess?

Here is where the issue of the computer's—or in this case, the calculator's—instruction set rears its head. This formula cannot be entered as is into a typical calculator. It will need to be broken down into bite-sized pieces that the calculator, or computer, can work with. Only a sequence of such pieces will allow us to extract the final answer. This is no different from traditional computer programming, except that the pieces used by such a calculator are much smaller than the-pieces used in higher-level languages such as Java.

Depending upon the specific calculator used, there are several sequences of keystrokes that would work to solve this problem. On a typical high-end calculator, the following sequence would calculate $(\frac{450}{2})^2$:

$$\boxed{(}\ \boxed{4}\ \boxed{5}\ \boxed{0}\ \boxed{\div}\ \boxed{2}\ \boxed{)}\ \boxed{x^2}$$

or, alternately,

$$\boxed{4}\ \boxed{5}\ \boxed{0}\ \boxed{\div}\ \boxed{2}\ \boxed{=}\ \boxed{x^2}$$

The entire calculation can be performed by

$$\boxed{1}\ \boxed{\div}\ \boxed{3}\ \boxed{\cdot}\ \boxed{\pi}\ \boxed{\cdot}\ \boxed{(}\ \boxed{4}\ \boxed{5}\ \boxed{0}\ \boxed{\div}\ \boxed{2}\ \boxed{)}\ \boxed{x^2}\ \boxed{\cdot}\ \boxed{1}\ \boxed{5}\ \boxed{0}$$

2.1.2 Operations, Operands, and Ordering

Implicit in this are a few subtle points. First, notice that the "instruction set" of this calculator includes an $\boxed{x^2}$ button, so that a number can be squared with a single press. It also has a $\boxed{\pi}$ button. Without these conveniences, more keystrokes and greater complexity would be needed. In fact, few people know what the right sequence of keystrokes would be to replace the $\boxed{\sqrt{x}}$ button.

Second, notice that ordering is important in this sequence. Just as there is a difference between 450 and 540, there is also a difference between $450 \div 2$ and $450\ 2 \div$. The first yields the value 225, while the second does not even make sense (under conventional notation). In general, most of the mathematical operations people think of are **binary**; that is, they take two numbers (arguments, formally called **operands**)) and produce a third. Add 3 and 4, get 7. A few advanced mathematical operations, such as $\sin x$, $\cos x$, and $\log x$, are **unary**, meaning that they take only one argument. In order to process an operation, a computer needs both the **operator**, defining which operation is to be performed, and the values of all necessary operands, in a very strict format.

In conventional chalkboard mathematics, for example, binary operations are written in so-called **infix** notation, meaning that the operator is written in the middle, between the two operands (as in $3 + 4$). Trig functions such as sin are written in **prefix** notation, where the operator preceeds the operand(s) (as in $\sin \frac{\pi}{2}$). Some high-end calculators such as the Hewlett-Packard HP 49G also support **postfix** notation (also called "**reverse Polish notation**"), where the operator comes last, after the operands. On such a calculator, the sequence of buttons to press to divide 450 by 2 would be

$$\boxed{4}\ \boxed{5}\ \boxed{0}\ \boxed{\text{ENTER}}\ \boxed{2}\ \boxed{\div}$$

Although this notation may appear confusing at first, many people come to prefer it, with a little bit of experience, for reasons we shall explore later.

2.1.3 Stack-Based Calculators

This kind of calculator (RPN-using) can be easily modeled by the use of a data structure called a **stack**. The term derives from the image of a stack of trays in a cafeteria or of styrofoam cups at a fast-food restaurant (figure 2.2). Such cups are typically stored in spring-loaded containers, where the weight of the trays pushes the entire pile down so that the top cup is always at a uniform height. At any point, only the top cup can be removed (causing the rest of the stack to pop up

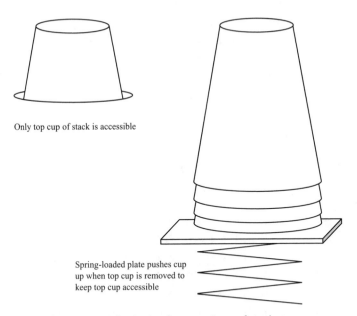

Only top cup of stack is accessible

Spring-loaded plate pushes cup
up when top cup is removed to
keep top cup accessible

Figure 2.2   A stack of cups at a cafeteria

slightly and expose a new tray) or an additional cups can be placed on top, causing the additional weight to push the trays down slightly. In slightly more abstract terms, only the top object is available for access.

A stack is a collection of numeric or data objects with similar access properties. Only the "top" object is available for processing, but it can be removed ("popped") at any time or another object can be added ("pushed") to the stack, displacing the previous top one (to the second position in the stack, and so forth). Stack-based calculations work particularly well in conjunction with postfix notation. Items are pushed onto the stack in order. Unary operations, such as sin and log, can simply pop the top item off the stack for an operand, perform the operation, and push the answer. For binary operations such as addition, the top two stack items are popped, the operation is performed, and the answer is pushed back.

The following sequence of operations, then, would perform the calculation described above:

$$1\ 3 \div \pi \cdot 450\ 2 \div 450\ 2 \div \cdot 150 \cdot$$

Unpacking this sequence, first the numbers 1 and 3 are pushed onto the stack; then they are popped and the quotient $\frac{1}{3}$ or 0.3333 is calculated. The value π is pushed, and then both 0.3333 and π are multiplied, yielding about 1.047, and so forth. Calculations can be performed quickly, in sequence, without the need for extensive parentheses and structures. In particular, note that there is no possible ambiguity about the order of operations, as there would be with an infix expression such as $1 + 3 \cdot 4$. The two possibly equivalent expressions $1\ 3\ 4 \cdot +$ and $1\ 3 + 4 \cdot$ are clearly and obviously distinct.

2.2 Stored-Program Computers

2.2.1 The fetch-execute Cycle

Computers, of course, do not require direct interaction with the operator (via button presses) in order to do their calculations. Instead, every possible operation is stored (as described in the previous chapter) as a bit pattern; the sequence of operations is stored as a program containing the sequence of bit patterns. The computer gets its instructions by reading them from memory (into the control unit) and interpreting each bit pattern as an operation to be performed. This is usually called the **fetch-execute cycle**, as it is performed cyclically and endlessly, millions or billions of times per second within the computer (figure 2.3).

Inside the Control Unit are at least two important storage locations. The first, the **instruction register** or IR, holds the bit pattern that has just been fetched from memory so that it can be

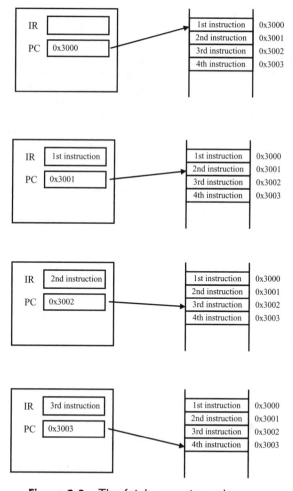

Figure 2.3 The fetch-execute cycle

SIDEBAR

Stored-Program Computers and "Von Neumann Architectures."

The first computers were outgrowths of ballistic calculators and code-breaking machines built for the Second World War. It's almost incorrect to call them computers, as they were really just complicated special-purpose electrical machinery. Most importantly, to change what they did required changes in the physical circuitry of the machinery; the program, if you will, was "hard-wired" into the computer. If you needed to solve a different problem, you needed to rewire the machine and build new circuits.

The great mathematician John Von Neumann recognized this as a major limitation and proposed ("Preliminary Discussion of the Logical Design of an Electronic Computing Instrument," written with Arthur Burks and Hermann Goldstine in 1946) a revolutionary concept for producing "general-purpose" computing machines. He identified four major "organs" involved in computing, related respectively to arithmetic, memory, control, and connection to the outside world (and the human operator). The key, in his view, to building a general-purpose computer was that it should be able to store not only the intermediate results of arithmetic calculations, but also the orders (instructions) that created those calculations. In other words, the "control organ" should be able to read patterns from memory and act upon them. Furthermore, the storage of the control patterns should be as flexible as the storage of numeric data. Why not, therefore, store instructions as binary patterns, just like numeric data? The design of the control organ thus becomes a kind of selector: when this pattern is read from memory, energize that circuit. Von Neumann further pointed out that control patterns and data patterns could even reside in the same memory if there were some way of telling them apart. Alternatively (the approach taken by modern computers), they are distinguished not by patterns, but by use. Any pattern loaded into the control unit is automatically treated as an instruction. (A competing proposal, the **Harvard architecture**, uses separate storage for code and for data. We'll see this architecture later in the discussion of the Atmel microcontroller.) This also implies that instructions can be used as data or even overwritten, allowing the possibility of **self-modifying code**. This allows the computer to reprogram itself, for example, by copying a program (as data) from storage into main memory and then executing the program (as code).

Von Neumann's computer operates by repeatedly performing the following operations:

1. Get an instruction pattern from the memory organ.
2. Determine and get any data required for this instruction from memory.
3. Process the data in the arithmetic organ.
4. Store the arithmetic results into the memory organ.
5. Go back to step 1.

Von Neumann thus laid most of the theoretical foundations for today's computers. His four organs, for example, can easily be seen to correspond to the ALU, system memory, control unit, and peripherals defined earlier. His method of operation is the fetch-execute cycle. Researchers have been exploring the implications of Von Neumann's architecture for decades and in some ways have been able to generalize beyond the limitations of his model. For example, multiprocessor systems, in general, replace the single control organ with several CPUs, each able to operate independently. A more radically non–Von Neumann architecture can be seen in the various proposals for neural networks and connectionist systems, in which "memory" is distributed among dozens or thousands of interlocking "units" and there is no control organ. (In particular, see footnote 1 on the Connection Machine in chapter 50.) Today, however, the term "Von Neumann computer" is rather rare, for the same reason that fish don't often talk about water. This kind of computer is so omnipresent that it's usually assumed that any given machine follows the Von Neumann/stored-program architecture.

interpreted The second, the **program counter** or PC, holds the location from which the next instruction will be fetched. Under normal circumstances, every time an instruction is fetched, the PC is incremented so that it points to the next word in memory. If, for example, the PC contains the pattern 0x3000, the next instruction will be fetched from that location (interpreted as a memory address). This means that the bit pattern stored at location 0x3000 (not 0x3000 itself) will be placed into the IR. The PC will then be updated to contain the number 0x3001. On successive cycles, the PC will contain 0x3002, 0x3003, 0x3004, and so forth. At each of these cycles, the IR will contain some instruction which the computer will dutifully follow. Typical examples of instructions include data transfers (where data is moved between the CPU and either memory or an I/O peripheral), data processing (where data already in the CPU will have some arithmetic or logical operation performed upon it), or control operations that affect the control unit itself.

Interpreting the instructions is itself a task of moderate complexity, in part because some instructions are actually instruction groups that need further specification. For example, an instruction to store information in memory is incomplete. What information needs to be stored, and where in memory should it be placed? In addition, many machines need further details, such as the "addressing mode" (does this bit pattern refer to a memory location or just a number?), the size (number of words) of the data to be stored, and so forth. For this reason, many machine language instructions are actually complexes of related bits (like the detailed structure of floating point numbers in the previous chapter).

An example of this for the IBM-PC (Intel 8086 and later machines) is the simple ADD instruction. This can be encoded in 2 bytes where the first 8 bits hold the number 0x04 and the second hold an (unsigned) 8-bit number from 0 to 255. This number will be added, implicitly, to the number already stored in a particular location (the AL register, a specific 8-bit register in the CPU). If you need to add a number larger than 255, there is a different machine instruction, with the first byte 0x05, and the next 16 bits defining a number from 0 to 65525. If you want to add to the number stored somewhere other than the AL register, then the machine instruction would begin with the opcode byte 0x81, define exactly where the number is stored in a second byte, and then define the number to be added.

Because of the design chosen for the JVM architecture (in particular, all addition is done in one place, the stack), the corresponding interpretation task on the JVM is easier (figure 2.4). As will be discussed in the following section, this reflects as much on the fundamental design philosophies of the builders as it does on the power of the JVM itself. For example, all addition is done on the stack (as in an RPN calculator). This means that the computer doesn't need to worry about where the addends come from (since they always come from the stack) or where the sum

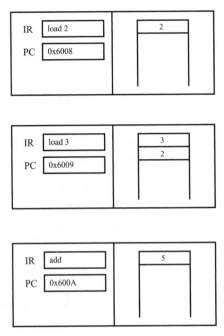

Figure 2.4   Illustration of stack-based computation on the JVM

goes (since it always goes back to the stack). The instruction to add two integers is thus a single byte of value 0x60—no mess or kerfluffle.

2.2.2   CISC vs. RISC Computers

Perhaps obviously, the more different things the CPU needs to do, the more different opcodes and machine instructions there will be. Less obviously, the more different opcodes there are, the more unique bit patterns will be needed and the longer they will need to be (on average) in order to make sure that the computer can tell them apart. (Imagine the disaster that would occur if the number 0x05 meant not only "add two numbers" but also "halt the computer"! How could the computer tell which was meant?) Longer opcodes, however, mean a larger IR, a larger bus connecting the computer to program memory, and a more complicated (and expensive) set of circuitry to interpret the instructions. Such a complex instruction set will also require a lot of circuitry to perform the various operations, since every operation might need a different set of wiring and transistors. This means that such a complex CPU chip is likely to be expensive, require expensive support, and perform more slowly on each instruction than a more streamlined design. (It will also require a bigger chip, run hotter [and therefore need better cooling], and burn more power, reducing battery life.)

Does this mean that a smaller instruction set is better? Not necessarily, for while a CPU with a reduced instruction set may be able to perform certain tasks faster (every CPU, for example, needs the ability to add two numbers together), there will be many tasks that the smaller CPU can only do by combining several steps. For example, a complex instruction set computing (**CISC**) chip may be able to move a large block of data, perhaps a string consisting of several thousand bytes, from one memory location to another without using any of the CPU's internal storage. By contrast, a reduced instruction set computing (**RISC**) chip might have to move each byte or word into the CPU (from memory) and then back into memory. More importantly, at every step, the instruction to move a particular byte would have to be fetched and interpreted. So, although the overall fetch-execute cycle may run faster (and usually does), the particular program or application may need to use many instructions to do (slowly) what the CISC computer could do in a single, although long and complex, machine instruction. Another advantage claimed by RISC proponents is a resistance to "creeping featurism," the tendency of equipment and programs to add complexity in the form of new features. A RISC chip will typically have a small, clean, simple design (by definition) that will remain small, clean, and simple in future versions, while newer versions of CISC chips will typically add more instructions, more features, and more complexity. Among other effects, this will hinder backward compatibility, because a program written for a later CISC chip will often take advantage of features and instructions that didn't exist six months earlier. On the other hand, of course, the new features added to the chip are probably features that the engineers found useful.

The two major CPU chips on the market today provide a good example of this difference. The Pentium 4 is a CISC chip with a huge instruction set (34 different ways alone of expressing ADD, even before taking into account which register or memory location contains the data), while the PowerPC is a RISC chip, tuned to perform common operations quickly while taking much longer on rare or complex tasks. For this reason, when comparing processor speeds between the CPUs, one can't just look at numbers like clock speeds. A single clock cycle on a RISC chip is likely to correspond to a single machine instruction, while a CISC chip is likely to take at least two or three clock cycles to accomplish anything. On the other hand, the larger instruction in the CISC chip may be able to do a more complicated calculation in those few clock cycles, depending on the application. The performance difference thus depends more on the type of program being run and the exact operations than on clock speed differences. In particular, Apple's sales documentation claims that the (RISC) 865 MHz Power Mac G4 will perform approximately 60% faster than the (CISC) 1.7 GHz Pentium 4 (and "3 to 4 times faster ... in graphics and sound manipulation") simply by getting more work done per clock cycle. Whether you believe Apple's sales literature or not, their central point—that clock speed is a poor way to compare different CPUs and that computers can be tuned to different sorts of tasks in the instruction set—remains almost irrefutable, irrespective of which side of the CISC/RISC debate you take.

2.3 Arithmetic Calculations on the JVM

2.3.1 General Comments

The Java Virtual Machine is an example of a stack-based RISC processor, but with a few twists reflecting the fact that physically it doesn't exist. As with most computers, the direct arithmetic abilities of the JVM are limited to common and simple operations for efficiency reasons. Few if any machines—and the JVM is not one of them—offer trig functions, but all support elementary arithmetic, including operations such as addition, subtraction, multiplication, and division. The JVM goes beyond most computers, however, by using stack-based computations, like the high-end calculator described earlier. This makes it very easy to emulate on other computers in a way that a fixed set of registers could not be emulated. The JVM itself maintains a stack of binary patterns, holding elements previously pushed and the results of prior computations. The operands of any given operation are taken from the top elements on the computation stack, and the answer is returned to the top of the stack. To calculate $7 \cdot (2 + 3)$, then, would require pushing the 7, 2, and 3 (in that order), then executing first an addition and then a multiplication.

This procedure is made slightly more tricky because the JVM (and Java in general) use **typed** calculations (in this regard, it's a little different from most RISC machines but offers much greater security). As discussed in the previous chapter, the same bit pattern can represent several different items, and the same number may be represented by several different bit patterns. In order to process these properly, any computer needs to be informed of the the data types represented by the bit patterns. The JVM is unusual only in how strictly this type system is enforced in an effort to prevent program errors.

As a result, there are, for example, several different ways to express addition, depending upon the types to be added. (This, it could be argued, puts the JVM somewhere in the middle of the CISC/RISC debate.) In general, the first letter of the operation name reflects the type(s) that it expects as arguments and the type of the answer. To add two integers, one uses the operation with mnemonic iadd, while to add two floating point numbers, one uses fadd. This pattern is followed by other arithmetic operations, so the operation to subtract one integer from another is isub, while the operation to divide two double-precision numbers is ddiv.

In detail, the JVM stack is a collection of 32-bit numbers with no fixed maximum depth. For data types that can fit within a 32-bit register, there is no problem with storing data elements in a single stack location. Longer types are typically stored as pairs of 32-bit numbers, so a 64-bit "double" at the top of the stack actually occupies two positions.

How many positions are there on the JVM stack? In theory, because the JVM is not hardware-limited, there are as many as you need. In practice, every program, method, or function that you write will define a maximum stack size. Similarly, there are no hardware-defined limitations on the amount of memory needed. Instead, every method defines a maximum number of local variables, not stored on the stack, that can be used to store values temporarily.

2.3.2   A Sample Arithmetic Instruction Set
Data Types
The JVM supports eight basic data types, most of which correspond closely to the basic data types of the JAVA language itself. These types are listed in table 2.1.The JVM also provides most of the standard arithmetic operations, including a few that students may not be familiar with. In the interests of reducing the instruction set, though, certain design simplifications have been made.

Notable for its absence from the collection of basic types is the **boolean** type found in Java but not in the JVM. Boolean variables, of course, can only hold the values *true* and *false*, and as such could be implemented in a single bit. In most computers, however, accessing a single bit is no more efficient—in fact, is much less efficient—than accessing a word. For this reason, in the JVM, boolean values are simply represented as the word-sized (32-bit) values 0 or 1, or in other words as integers.

Type	Code	Explanation
int	i	32-bit signed integer
float	f	32-bit IEEE 754 floating point number
long	l	64-bit integer stored in two successive stack locations
double	d	64-bit IEEE 754 floating point number (as above)
byte	b	8-bit signed integer
short	s	16-bit signed integer
char	c	16-bit unsigned integer or UTF-16 character
address	a	Java objects

Table 2.1   JVM basic types and their representations

The sub-word storage types byte, short, and char are also somewhat second-class types. Because in the JVM doing math on a 32-bit quantity takes no more time than doing math on smaller quantities, variables of this type are automatically promoted to 32-bit integers inside the CPU. On the other hand, there is an obvious difference when variables of this type are stored; for example, an array of a million bytes would take up a quarter of the space of a similar array of integers. For this reason, the JVM supports the operations of loading small types (byte, short, char, and even boolean) from memory and storing them into memory, particularly from and into arrays.

Basic Arithmetic Operations

With this collection of types, each of which requires special processing to support, almost every combination of type and operation needs a special opcode and mnemonic. To simplify the programmer's task, most mnemonics use a letter code to indicate the type of action. To add two ints, for example, the mnemonic is `iadd`. Adding two longs would use `ladd`, while floats and doubles would use `fadd` and `dadd`, respectively. For simplicity, this entire family will be abbreviated as `?add`, where the `?` stands for any of the legal type letters.

The basic arithmetic operations of addition (`?add`), subtraction (`?sub`), multiplication (`?mul`), and division (`?div`) are defined for each of the four major types (int, long, float, and double). All of these operations act by popping the first two elements off the stack (note: for the operation a long or double, the first two "elements" will each involve two stack locations, and hence four stack locations in total), computing the result, and then pushing the result back on the top of the stack. In addition, JVM provides the `?neg` operation which reverses the sign of the item at the top of the stack. This could also happen, of course, by pushing the value −1 and then executing a multiply instruction, but a special-purpose operation can do this commonly executed action faster.

One aspect of the `?div` operation requires special attention. Both `idiv` and `ldiv` operate on integers and produce integers (not fractions or decimals) as a result. Dividing 8 by 5, for instance, yields the answer 1, not the floating point number 1.6. To perform a floating point division, it is first necessary to convert both arguments to float or double types, as will be discussed later. Similarly, there is a special operation for int and long types, `?rem`, which takes the remainder or **modulus**. This operation does not exist for float/double types, as the division operation is defined to perform exact division—or as exact as the machine representation will allow.

Logical Operations

The JVM also provides the basic logical operations AND (?and), OR (?or), and XOR (?xor) for int and long types only (figure 2.5 and 2.6). These operate in what is called **bitwise** fashion, meaning that every bit of the first operand is individually compared with the corresponding bit of the second operand, and the result is the collection of the individual bit operations. When applied to boolean values, 0 and/or 1, the results are as one expects. The representation of 0 is 0x0000; the representation of 1 is 0x0001. For all locations except the last, the corresponding bits are 0 and 0; in the last location, the bits are, of course, 0 and 1. The value of 0x0000 OR 0x0001 would thus be, as expected, 0x0001; in other words, *false* OR *true* is *true*, as desired.

First value	1	1	0	0	1	0	1	0	= 0xCA
Second value	1	1	1	1	0	0	0	0	= 0xF0
AND result	1	1	0	0	0	0	0	0	= 0xC0

Figure 2.5   Illustration of bitwise AND

First value	1	1	0	0	1	0	1	0	= 0xCA
Second value	1	1	1	1	0	0	0	0	= 0xF0
XOR result	0	0	1	1	1	0	1	0	= 0x3F

Figure 2.6   Illustration of bitwise XOR

Shift Operations

In addition to these familiar operations, the JVM also provides some standard **shift** operations for changing bit patterns and specifically for moving bits around in a number. In Java/C/C++, these are represented as the $<<$ and $>>$ operators. The basic operation takes every bit in the number and moves it exactly one place to the right (or left). Using the binary pattern 0xBEEF as an example:

B	E	E	F	
1011	1110	1110	1111	becomes
0111	1101	1101	1110	when shifted one bit left and
0101	1111	0111	0111	when shifted one bit right.

Thus, a shift of 0xBEEF yields 0x7AAE when shifted left by one and 0x5F77 when shifted right by one. In both cases, the empty space at the right (left) side of the pattern is filled with a 0 bit This is sometimes called a **logical shift**, as opposed to an **arithmetic shift**. An arithmetic shift tries to preserve the sign of the number, so in an arithmetic right shift, the sign bit is duplicated and repeated in the empty space. (An arithmetic left shift does not duplicate the rightmost bit.)

B	E	E	F	
1011	1110	1110	1111	becomes
0101	1111	0111	0111	when logically shifted right or
1101	1111	0111	0111	when arithmetically shifted right.

Specifically in the case of signed quantities, a logical right shift will always give a positive result, because a 0 is inserted into the leftmost (sign) bit. By contrast, an arithmetic right shift will always give a negative result if and only if the initial value was negative, as the sign bit is duplicated in the operation. For unsigned values, a left shift is equivalent to multiplying the value by some power of 2, while the logical right shift is equivalent to dividing by some power of 2. Generally, however, these operations are used to put a known set of bits at a particular place in the patterns—for example, to use as an operand for later bitwise AND, OR, or XOR operations. The JVM provides three operations to perform such shifts: ?shl (shift left), ?shr (arithmetic shift right), and ?ushr (logical shift right—the mnemonic really stands for "unsigned shift right"), applicable both to ints (32-bit patterns) and to longs (64-bit patterns).

Conversion Operations

In addition to these basic arithmetic and logical operations, there are a number of unary conversion operations of the form ?2?—for example, i2f, which converts an int (i) to a float (f). Each of these, in general, will pop the top element off the stack, convert it to the appropriate (new) type, and push the result. This will usually leave the overall size of the stack unchanged except when the conversion is from a long to a short type (or vice versa). For example, the operation i2l will pop one word (32 bits) from the stack, convert it to 64 bits (two words), and then push the two-word quantity onto the stack, taking two elements. This will have the effect of increasing the depth of the stack by one; similarly, the d2i operation will decrease the depth of the stack by one.

As before, not all of the possible combinations of types are supported by the JVM for efficiency reasons. In general, it is always possible to convert to or from an integer. It is also always possible to convert between the basic four types of int, long, float, and double. It's not directly possible, however, to convert from a char to a float in a single operation, nor from a float to a char. There are two main reasons for this. First, as sub-word types are automatically converted to word-sized quantities, the operation that would be defined as b2i is, in a sense, automatic and cannot even be prevented. Second, conversion of integers to floating point numbers (for example, $2 \leftrightarrow 2.0$) will, as discussed earlier, involve not just selecting particular bits from a larger whole, but using an entirely different system of representation and changing the fundamental pattern of representation. If a person needs to convert between a floating point number and a character, this can be done in two steps (f2i,i2c). For analogical reasons, the output of the three operations i2s, i2c, and i2b is somewhat unusual. Instead of producing (and pushing) the second type named in the mnemonic, these operations produce an integer. However, the integer produced will have been truncated to the appropriate size and range. Thus, performing the i2b operation on 0x24581357 will yield the pattern 0x00000057, equivalent to the single byte 0x57.

2.3.3 Stack Manipulation Operations

Typeless Stack Operations

In addition to these type-specific operations, the JVM provides some general-purpose and untyped operations for routine stack manipulations. A simple and obvious example is the pop operation, which pops a single word from the stack. As the value is only to be thrown away, it doesn't matter if it's an int, a float, a byte, or whatever. Similarly, the pop2 operation removes two words or a single two-word entry, a long or a double, from the stack. Similar operations of this type include dup, which duplicates and pushes another copy of a single word entry at the top of the stack; dup2, which duplicates and pushes a doubleword entry; swap, which swaps the top two stack words; and nop, short for "no operation," which does nothing (but takes time and thus can be useful for causing the machine to wait for a microsecond or so).

In addition, there are a few unusual operations that perform rather specialized stack operations, such as dup_x1, which duplicates the top word of the stack and then inserts it beneath the second word; if the stack held, from the top down, (5 3 4 6), then executing dup_x1 would produce (5 3 5 4 6). These special operations are listed in appendix B and will not be discussed further in this book.

Constants and the Stack

Of course, in order to perform stack-based calculations, some method must be available to put (push) data onto the stack in the first place. The JVM has several such methods, depending upon the type of datum to be pushed and the location from which the datum comes.

The simplest case is where a single constant is to be pushed onto the stack. Depending upon the size of the constant, you can use the bipush instruction (which pushes a 1-byte signed integer), the sipush instruction (a 2-byte signed integer), the ldc instruction (a one-word constant, like an integer, a float, or an address), or the ldc2_w instruction (a two-word constant, like a long or a double). So, to put the numbers (integers) 3 and 5 onto the stack and then multiply them would require the following code:

```
bipush   5
bipush   3
imul
```

The variations

```
sipush   5        ldc 5
sipush   3        ldc 3
imul              imul
```

would accomplish the same thing but less efficiently. Because 5 (and 3) are such small numbers, they will both fit into a single byte and can be pushed using bipush. Also, note that because multiplication is commutative, it doesn't matter whether you push the 5 or the 3 first. This is not the case for subtraction and division. In these operations, the computer will subtract the second number pushed from the first (divide the first number pushed by the second). So, replacing imul in the above example by idiv would result in dividing 5 by 3. This will leave the value 1 on the stack (not 1.66667, because idiv specifies integer division, rounding down).

For efficiency, there are several special-purpose operations that will push commonly used constants onto the stack more quickly. For example, iconst_N, where N is one of 0, 1, 2, 3, 4, or 5, will push the appropriate one-word integer onto the stack. Since it is often necessary to initialize a variable to 1 or to add 1 to a variable, iconst_1 can be faster than the equivalent bipush 1. Thus, we can rewrite the example above to be slightly faster using

```
iconst_5
iconst_3
imul
```

Similarly, iconst_m1 pushes the integer value -1. There are equivalent shortcuts for floats (fconst_N for 0, 1, and 2), longs (lconst_N for 0 and 1), and doubles (dconst_N for 0 and 1).

Local Variables

In addition to loading constants, one can also load values from memory. Every JVM method has a set of memory locations associated with it that can be accessed freely, randomly, and in any order. As with the stack, the number of memory locations available is not limited by the hardware and can be set by the programmer. Also, as before, the type of pattern loaded determines the operation and mnemonic; to load an integer, use iload, but to load a float, use fload. Either of these will retrieve the appropriate variable and push its value onto the top of the stack

Variables are referred to by sequential numbers, starting at 0, so if a given method has 25 variables, they will have numbers from 0 to 24. Each variable stores a standard word-sized pattern, so there is no typing of variables. Storage of doubleword patterns (longs and doubles) is a little more tricky, as each pattern must occupy two adjacent variables. Loading a double from variable 4, for instance, will actually read the values from both variables 4 and 5. In addition, the JVM allows several shortcuts of the form ?load_N, so one can load an integer from local variable zero (#0) either by iload 0 or the shortcut iload_0. This shortcut exists for all four basic types, for and all variable numbers from 0 to 3.

Similarly, data can be popped from the stack to be stored in local variables for later use. The command in this case would be ?store, where the first character, as usual, is the type to be stored. As before, storing a long or a double will actually perform two pop operations and store the result in two adjacent variables, so the instruction dstore 3 would remove two elements, not one, from the stack and cause changes to both local variables #3 and #4. Also, as before, shortcuts exist of the form ?store_N for all types, with N varying between 0 and 3.

2.3.4   Assembly Language and Machine Code

Let's look, then, at a simple code fragment and see how the various conversions would take place. We'll start with a single, simple, high-level language statement (if this notion of "simple high-level language statement" isn't a contradiction in terms):

```
x = 1 + 2 + 3 + 4 + 5;
```

This statement (obviously?) calculates the sum of the constant numbers 1 through 5 and stores them in a local variable named x. The first problem is that the JVM doesn't understand the idea of named local variables, only numbered ones. The compiler needs to recognize that x is a variable and allocate a corresponding number (we'll assume that we're using #1 and that it's an int). One way of writing code to perform this task (there are lots of others) is the sequence of operations shown in figure 2.7.

This is the main task of the compiler: to convert a high-level statement into several basic operations. At this point, it is the task of the assembler (or of a different part of the compiler) to convert each operation mnemonic into the corresponding machine code byte. The full correspondences are given in appendices B and C. For simplicity, we note that the iadd used in this program corresponds to the machine instruction 0x60. Converting the entire program would result in the instructions listed in table 2.2.

```
; x = 1 + 2 + 3 + 4 + 5;
; translate to: 1 2 + 3 + 4 + 5 +, then load into #1
iconst_1          ; load constant value 1
iconst_2          ; load constant value 2
iadd              ; add
iconst_3          ; load constant value 3
iadd              ; add
iconst_4          ; load constant value 4
iadd              ; add
iconst_5          ; load constant value 5
iadd              ; add
istore_1          ; store in x
```

Figure 2.7   jasmin program fragment #1

Mnemonic	Machine Code Byte
iconst_1	0x04
iconst_2	0x05
iadd	0x60
iconst_3	0x06
iadd	0x60
iconst_4	0x07
iadd	0x60
iconst_5	0x08
iadd	0x60
istore_1	0x3c

Table 2.2   Translation of program fragment #1 into bytecode

The corresponding machine code would thus be the byte sequence 0x04, 0x05, 0x60, 0x06, 0x60, 0x07, 0x60, 0x08, 0x60, 0x3c, which would be stored on disk as part of the executable program.

Translation is not always this simple, because some operations may take more than 1 byte. For example, the bipush instruction pushes a byte onto the stack (just as iconst_0 pushes the value 0). But which byte? The bipush instruction itself has the value 0x10, but it is always followed by a single byte telling what needs to be pushed. To push the value 0, the compiler could also use bipush 0, but this would assemble to two successive bytes: 0x10, 0x00. We thus have an alternate version of the program, as given in table 2.3. Notice, however, that this second version is about 50% longer and therefore less efficient.

2.3.5   Illegal Operations

Because both the stack and the local variables only store bit patterns, there the programmer can easily be confused. This can heppen especially with pushing constants, because types of constants are not explicitly marked in the mnemonic. The command to place the (integer) value 10 into the stack is ldc 10. The command to place the floating point value 10.0 into the stack is ldc 10.0.

Revised Mnemonic	Machine Code Byte
bipush 1	0x10
	0x01
bipush 2	0x10
	0x02
iadd	0x60
bipush 3	0x10
	0x03
iadd	0x60
bipush 4	0x10
	0x04
iadd	0x60
bipush 5	0x10
	0x05
iadd	0x60
istore_1	0x3c

Table 2.3   Translation of program fragment #2 into bytecode

Because most JVM assemblers are smart enough to figure out that 10 is an integer and 10.0 is a floating point number, the correct bit pattern will be pushed in either case. However, these bit patterns are not the same. Attempting to push 10.0 twice and then execute an imul instruction will not give you the value 100.0 (or even 100). Trying to perform arithmetic on a float as though it were an integer, or on an integer as though it were a float, is an error. In the best case, the machine will complain. In the worst case, the machine won't even notice and will give answers that are completely, mysteriously, and untraceably wrong.

It's equally an error to attempt to access the top (or bottom) half of a doubleword variable, a long or a double, as though it were a single word. If you've stored a double into local variables #4 (and #5), you can't then load an integer from local variable #5 (or #4). Again, at best the machine will complain, and at worst it will silently give meaningless and horribly wrong results. It's also an error to attempt to pop from an empty stack, to load from (or store into a variable that doesn't exist, and so forth).

One of the chief advantages of the JVM is that it has been designed (as will be discussed in chapter 3) to catch these sorts of errors as they occur in a running program, or even as the program is written, so that the programmer cannot get away with them. This has the effect of increasing the security and reliability of JVM programs tremendously. However, a good programmer should not rely on the ability of the computer to catch her errors. Careful planning and careful writing of code is a much better way to make sure that the computer gives you correct answers.

2.4 An Example Program

2.4.1   An Annotated Example

Returning to the cone problem that opened the chapter, the question becomes not only what the answer is, but how it can be implemented on the machine under discussion (the JVM). To briefly recap, the problem was:

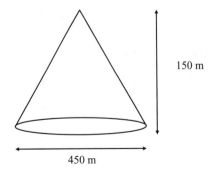

Figure 2.8   A conical mountain

What is the volume of a circular mountain 450 m in diameter at the base and 150 m high (figure 2.8)? The formula as it would be written on a chalkboard looks like this:

$$\frac{1}{3} \cdot \left[\pi \cdot \left(\frac{450}{2} \right)^2 \right] \cdot 150$$

What sequence of JVM instructions would solve this problem?

First, we need to calculate the floating point value 1/3. Integer division will not work, since 1/3 is 0, while 1.0/3.0 is 0.333333. Thus, we push the two elements 1.0 and 3.0 and execute a division.

```
ldc 1.0
ldc 3.0
fdiv
```

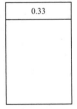

                        after `ldc 3.0`   after `fdiv`

We then push the known value of pi.

```
ldc 3.141593
```

                        after `ldc 3.141593`

To calculate the radius, we simply push 450, push 2, and then divide. Note that 450 is too big to store in a single byte (which only goes up to the integer value 127), so we have to use `sipush`.

2
450
3.141593
0.33

```
sipush 450
bipush 2
idiv
```

after `bipush 2`

To square the radius, we can either recalculate $\frac{450}{2}$ or, more efficiently, use the dup instruction to copy the top of the stack and multiply.

```
dup
imul
```

225
225
3.141593
0.33

after `dup`

50625
3.141593
0.33

after `imul`

Next, push the height of 150 and multiply.

```
sipush 150
imul
```

150
50625
3.141593
0.33

after `sipush 150`

7593750
3.141593
0.33

after `imul`

The integer value at the top of the stack must be converted to a floating point number

```
i2f
fmul
fmul
```

7593750.0
3.141593
0.33

after `i2f`

and then two (floating point) multiplications will calculate the final answer and leave it at the top of the stack.

This process will be stored as a sequence of machine code instructions Each instructions will be fetched individually (from memory) and executed. As the statements are in sequence, the instruction fetched next will be the next instruction in the sequence—and thus this complex series of statements will do as expected and desired. A similar process can be used to perform any calculation within the basic operations available in the instruction set.

2.4.2   The Final JVM Code

```
; calculate 1/3
ldc     1.0
ldc     3.0
fdiv

; push pi
ldc     3.141593

; calculate radius
sipush 450
bipush 2
idiv

; and square it
dup
imul

; push height
sipush 150

; multiply height times radius-squared
imul

; convert to floating point
i2f
; and multiply times pi and 1/3 previously calculated
fmul
fmul
```

2.5 JVM Calculation Instructions Summarized

```
Arithmetic Operations:
```

	int	long	float	double	short	char	byte
add	iadd	ladd	fadd	dadd			
subtract	isub	lsub	fsub	dsub			
multiply	imul	lmul	fmul	dmul			
divide	idiv	ldiv	fdiv	ddiv			
remainder	irem	lrem					
negate	ineg	lneg	fneg	dneg			

```
Logical (Boolean) operations:
             int     long
logical AND  iand    land
logical OR   ior     lor
logical XOR  ixor    lxor

Shift operations:
left shift (arithmetic)
               int     long
               ishl    lshl
right shift (arithmetic)
               ishr    lshr
right shift (logical)
               iushr   lushr

Conversion operations:
from:        to:
             int    long    float   double   short   char   byte
int                 i2l     i2f     i2d      i2s     i2c    i2b
long         l2i            l2f     l2d
float        f2i    f2l             f2d
double       d2i    d2l     d2f

(conversion of short, char, and byte types to int is implicit and automatic)
```

2.6 Chapter Review

- Computers are like calculators in that they can only do the few actions allowed by their hardware. Complex calculations that cannot be done in a single operation or button press must be done as a sequence of several elementary steps within the allowed actions.
- Conventional math, as written on the blackboard, uses infix notation, where operations like division are written between their arguments. Some calculators and computers, the JVM among them, use postfix notation instead, where the operation comes after the arguments.
- Postfix notations can be easily described and simulated using a standard data structure called a stack.
- The basic operation of any computer is the fetch-execute cycle, during which instructions are fetched from main memory, interpreted, and executed. This cycle is repeated more or less without end.
- The CPU holds two important pieces of information for the fetch-execute cycle: the instruction register (IR), which holds the currently executing instruction, and the program counter (PC), which holds the location of the next instruction to be fetched.
- There are two major philosophies of computer design: Complex Instruction Set Computing (CISC) and Reduced Instruction Set Computing (RISC). These are typified by the Intel Pentium and the Apple/IBM/Motorola Power architecture, respectively.
- The JVM uses typed stack-based computations to perform most of its arithmetic operations. Mnemonics describe both the operation to be performed and the type of data used. It is an error to perform an operation on a piece of data of the wrong type.

- The JVM also provides some shortcut operations for commonly used operations, such as loading a value of 0 into the stack.
- Simple sequencing of elementary mathematical operations can nonetheless perform very complex computations.

2.7 Exercises

1. What are the advantages to having a $\boxed{\sqrt{x}}$ button on a calculator? What are the disadvantages?
2. What sequence of operations would be used to calculate $(7 + 1) \cdot (8 - 3)$ on a normal (infix notation) calculator? How about on a RPN (postfix) calculator?
3. Is there a corresponding sequence of operations using prefix notation to perform the calculation above. If yes, what is it? If no, why not?
4. Is the fetch-execute cycle more complex on a CISC or a RISC computer? Why?
5. What is the difference between typed and untyped calculations? Give two examples of each.
6. What are the advantages and disadvantages of typed arithmetic calculations?
7. Why doesn't the instruction `cadd` exist?
8. Which of the following are illegal and why?

   - `bipush 7`
   - `bipush -7`
   - `sipush 7`
   - `ldc -7`
   - `ldc2 -7`
   - `bipush 200`
   - `ldc 3.5`
   - `sipush -300`
   - `sipush -300.0`
   - `ldc 42.15`

9. How can a shift operation be used to multiply an integer by 8?
10. Describe two ways to get (only) the smallest 8 bits of a 64-bit-long integer.
11. Is there any basic operation that will work on both an int and a float? On both an int and a long?
12. In the `?div` instruction, is the number divided by stored at the top of the stack or is it the second element?
13. The surface area of a sphere is four times the area of a circle of equivalent radius. Write a postfix expression to calculate the surface area of a hemispherical dome of radius R.
14. Write a postfix expression for the arithmetic mean of the five numbers a, b, c, d, and e.
15. Prove that for every infix expression there is an equivalent postfix expression and vice versa.

2.8 Programming Exercises

1. Write a program to interpret a postfix expression and to print the resulting value.
2. Write a program to read in an infix expression and to write out the correcponding equivalent postfix expression.

3. Write a program to read a sequence of JVM instructions and to determine the maximum stack height that would result if they were executed, starting from an empty stack.

4. Write a program to read a sequence of JVM instructions and to determine if any of them will ever attempt to pop from an empty stack. (Note: this is actually one of the tasks performed by the **verifier** in a real system.)

3

Assembly Language Programming in jasmin

3.1 Java, the Programming System

As discussed in chapter 1, there is no reason in theory why a program written in Java would need to be run on the JVM or why a JVM program could not have been written in any high-level language such as C++. In practical terms, though, there is a strong connection between the two, and the design of the Java, language has strongly influenced the designs both of the Java Virtual Machine and of the assemblers for that machine.

In particular, Java strongly supports and encourages a particular style of programming and design called **object-oriented programming** (OOP). As one might suspect from the name, OOP is a programming technique that focuses on objects—individual active elements of the world (or a model of the world), each with its own set of actions that it can perform or that can be performed upon it. Objects, in turn, can be grouped into **classes** of similarly typed objects that share certain properties by virtue of their types. For example, in the real world, "cars" might be a natural class, and with very few exceptions, all cars share certain properties: they have steering wheels, gas pedals, brakes, and headlights. They also share certain actions: I can turn a car left or right (by turning the wheel), make it slow down (by pressing the brake), or make it stop altogether (by running out of gas). More strongly, if someone said that he had just bought a new car, you would assume that this car came with a steering wheel, brake, gas tank, and so forth.

Java supports this style of programming by forcing all functions to be attached to classes and by forcing all executable program code to be stored as separate (and separable) "class files." These class files correspond fairly closely to Linux executable files or Windows .EXE files, except that they are not necessarily guaranteed to be complete, functional programs in their own right. Instead, a particular class file contains only those functions necessary for the operation of that particular class; if it, in turn, relies on the properties and functions of another kind of object, then those would be stored in a class corresponding to the second kind of object.

The other main difference between a Java class file and a typical executable is that the Java class file is supposed to be portable between different machine types. As such, it's written not in the machine language of the host machine, but in the machine language of the JVM. This is sometimes called **bytecode** to distinguish it as specifically not tied to a particular machine. As such, any class file, compiled on any machine, can be freely copied to any other machine and will still run. Technically, the JVM bytecode will only run on a copy of the JVM (just as a Windows executable will usually only run on a Windows computer), but the JVM is enabled, via software, on almost every hardware platform.

When a bytecode file is to be executed, the computer is required to run a special program to **load** the class from disk into the computer's memory. In addition, the computer will usually perform other actions at this time, such as loading other classes that are needed to support the class of interest, verifying the structural soundness and safety of the class and its methods, and initializing static and class-level variables to the appropriate values. Fortunately, from the point of view of a user or programmer, these steps are all built into the JVM implementation, so the user doesn't need to do anything.

Running Java programs is thus a three-step process. After the program source code is written, it must be compiled or converted into a class file. The user must then create a (software) instance of the JVM in order to execute the bytecode. The exact commands to do this will vary from system to system. On a typical Linux system, for instance, the command to execute the JVM would look like this:

```
java TheClassOfInterest
```

This command will look for a file named `TheClassOfInterest.class` and will then load, verify, and initialize it. It will then look for a specific method in that class called `main()` and attempt to invoke that method. For this reason, any standalone Java application class must contain a "main" method. On many other systems (Windows and MacOS, for example), just clicking on the icon corresponding to the **.class** file will launch a JVM and run the class file. In addition, certain kinds of class files can be run directly from a Web browser such as Microsoft's Internet Explorer or Netscape Communications' Navigator.

However, none of these programs will actually run Java programs, only JVM bytecode. There are a number of compilers that will convert high-level Java code into JVM bytecode, and, perhaps unsurprisingly, there are also programs that will convert languages other than Java into JVM bytecode. Here, we will focus on one particular kind of language, in which each bytecode statement is uniquely associated with a single statement in the program source code. As discussed in chapter 1, this kind of language (where source code statements and machine instructions have a 1:1 relationship) is usually called **assembly language**, and the program to convert from one language to the other is called an **assembler**. (The corresponding conversion program for a high-level language is usually called a **compiler**.)

3.2 Using the Assembler

3.2.1   The Assembler

As might be expected, the conversion process between assembly language and machine code is fairly straightforward. As a result, the program itself is also fairly easy to write. The task of an `assembler` is simple enough that there are usually several to choose from, often with very slight differences between them. Sun has not established an official, standard assembler for the JVM, so in this book the example programs have been written specifically for the `jasmin` assembler. This program was written in 1996 by Jon Meyer and Troy Downing of the NYU Media Research Laboratory.[1] It is available for free download at `http://jasmin.sourceforge.net/` and has become a defacto standard format for assembly language for the JVM. The jasmin program is also available at the companion Web site to this book: `http://prenhall.com/juola`. The first step, then, is to get and install `jasmin` on the machine you are working on. For simplicity, since "Java Virtual Machine assembly language" is such a mouthful, we'll call this language `jasmin` as well.

3.2.2   Running a Program

In order to execute the program in figure 1.19, duplicated here as figure 3.1, it must first be typed into a machine-readable form (like a text file). You can use any editing program for this, from simple editors like Notepad to complicated and feature-laden publishing packages. Bear in mind, though, that assemblers can almost never handle fancy formatting or font changes, so save the program as plain text. By authorial tradition, programs written in `jasmin` are usually saved with a `.j` extension, so the program above would have been written and saved as `jasminExample.j` to the disk.

In order to run the program, the same steps used in executing a Java program must be followed. After the program has been written in text format, it must first be converted from (human-readable) `jasmin` syntax into JVM machine code. Second, the JVM (Java run-time engine) must be run to allow the JVM code to be executed. To do the first (for an appropriately configured Linux machine), simply type

```
jasmin jasminExample.j
```

at the appropriate command prompt. This will execute the assembler (`jasmin` on the file and produce a new file, named `jasminExample.class`, which contains JVM executable code).

This `.class` file is a standard part of the Java run-time system and can be run by any of the usual means; the simplest is to type

```
java jasminExample
```

which will create a JVM process and execute the `jasminExample.class` file (specifically, the main method defined in that file) on this virtual machine.

---

[1] Jon Meyer's Web site, as I write, is `http://www.cybergrain.com/`. Meyer and Downing also have an excellent, if unfortunately out-of-print, book describing the JVM and `jasmin`: Meyer, J. & T. Downing. (1997). *Java Virtual Machine*. Cambridge, MA: O'Reilly.

```
; defines the class file associated with this as jasminExample.class
.class public jasminExample
; defines jasminExample as a subclass of Object
.super java/lang/Object

; boilerplate needed for object creation
.method public <init>()V
     aload_0

     invokespecial java/lang/Object/<init>()V
     return
.end method

.method public static main([Ljava/lang/String;)V
     ; we need two stack elements, for System.out and the string
     .limit stack 2

     ; find System.out (an object of type PrintStream)
     ; and put it on the stack
     getstatic java/lang/System/out Ljava/io/PrintStream;

     ; find the string (characters) to be printed
     ; and put it on the stack
     ldc "This is a sample program."

     ; invoke the PrintStream/println method
     invokevirtual java/io/PrintStream/println(Ljava/lang/String;)V

     ; ... and that's it!
     return
.end method
```

Figure 3.1   Sample program in JVM assembly language

This or a similar process will work on most machines and on all examples in this book (except for the ones containing deliberate errors, of course).

3.2.3   Display to the Console vs. a Window

Running the program as described in section 3.2.2 uses a rather old-fashioned and unpopular style of interfacing. Most modern programmers prefer to use windows interfaces and interact with their computer via mouse presses than to use a command-line and text-based interface. A primary reason for the popularity of Java is the extensive support it provides for windowed and networked applications. However, there are slight differences in the way these kinds of applications interact with the outside world.

The most popular kind of Web application for Java is called an applet. As the name suggests, this is a small, rather lightweight application specifically designed for interoperation with Web browers, and as such, all major browsers support Web pages incorporating JVM applets. Figure 3.2 shows a very simple example of a Web page, the only contents of which are an <APPLET> tag. The effect of this page is that, when it is displayed on a browser, the browser will also download and run the applet. The exact methods of running the applet differ. Instead of invoking the "main" method, the browser will invoke a "paint" method as the starting point for the code. In addition, the output instructions (such as println) are replaced by graphics-specific instructions such as drawstring that take not only a particular string to be drawn, but also parameters such as the location (in the window) at which to display the string.

```
<HTML>
<HEAD> <TITLE>A Sample JVM Applet</TITLE> </HEAD>
<BODY>
<APPLET code = "jasminAppletExample" width = 300 height = 100>
</APPLET>
</BODY>
</HTML>
```

Figure 3.2   Web page for applet invocation

Applet programming is a fine art and requires some knowledge of applet-specific functions. Using these functions, a skilled programmer can create detailed pictures, or text in any font, size, shape, and orientation she desires. As shown in figure 3.3, the overall structure of a jasmin program does not change much, regardless of whether it was written as an applet, to output to a window, or written as a standalone application to output to the console.

As before, the program (jasminAppletExample.j) would be assembled using the jasmin program to produce a class file.

```
jasmin jasminAppletExample.j
```

Once the class file jasminAppletExample.class has been created, the applet can be run by simply opening the Web page shown in figure 3.2. This can be opened in any Web browser—for example, in Internet Explorer or Netscape—or using a special program such as appletviewer supplied with the Java system by Sun. Using technology such as this, Java (and jasmin) programs can be supplied as executable code to be used by any JVM on a machine anywhere in the world.

3.2.4   Using System.out and System.in

When programming in any assembly language, getting the computer to read and write data can be among the most challenging tasks. This is related to the more general problem of simply interacting with I/O peripherals; because of the wide variety of peripheral types (reading from the network is very different from reading from the keyboard) and, even more annoyingly, the wide variety within a given peripheral type (does your keyboard have a numeric keypad or not?), every device may have to be approached on an individual basis.

```
; defines jasminAppletExample as a subclass of Applet
.class public jasminAppletExample
.super java/applet/Applet

; boilerplate needed for Applet creation
; note similarity to Object creation in previous example
.method public <init>()V
   aload_0
   ; this isn't an Object, so we have to invoke the Applet <init>
   invokespecial java/applet/Applet/<init>()V
   return
.end method


; Note that Applets start at paint() method instead of main()
; also notice the subtly different definition
.method public paint(Ljava/awt/Graphics;)V
   ; we need 4 stack elements :
   ;          the Graphics object
   ;          the string to be printed
   ;          the x-coordinate of print location
   ;          the y-coordinate of print location
   .limit stack 4

   ; Graphics object stored in local #1
   .limit locals 2

   ; This boilerplate is a little unusual as it's harder to draw
   ; text in an Applet than on System.out
   ; load the four parameters
   aload_1         ; this is the Graphics object passed as a parameter
   ldc "This is a sample applet" ; a string to be printed
   bipush 30       ; the coordinates at which this string prints
   bipush 50

   ; and invoke the drawString method
   invokevirtual java/awt/Graphics/drawString(Ljava/lang/String;II)V

   ; ... th'th'th'that's all, folks!
   return
.end method
```

Figure 3.3   A sample applet in `jasmin`

The Java class system somewhat mitigates this problem. Just as one can steer an unfamiliar car, because all cars have steering wheels and all of them work about the the same way Java defines a PrintStream class that includes methods named print and println. The JVM always defines a particular PrintStream named System.out, which is attached to a default print-capable device.

This provides a relatively simple method of generating output using either the print or println method. This has already been demonstrated in the sample program (figure 3.1) for printing String types, but it can be extended to print any type supported by the method (with a few changes). The necessary steps are presented here largely without explanation—you are not necessarily expected to understand them right now. To understand them fully will require a deeper investigation of both the JVM type and the class system and how they are represented; we'll return to this simple example, at length, in chapter 10.

First, the System.out object must be pushed onto the stack from its static and unchanging location in the system.

```
getstatic java/lang/System/out Ljava/io/PrintStream;
```

Second, the data to be printed must be loaded onto the stack using any of the usual ways presented in chapter 2.

```
iload_2    ; this loads local variable #2 AS AN INTEGER!
```

Third, the println method must be invoked, including a representation of the type pushed onto the stack in the second step. Since the statement iload_2 pushes an integer, the command would be

```
invokevirtual java/io/PrintStream/println(I)V;
```

If, instead, we had pushed a float (perhaps with fload_2), the command would be modified to include an F instead of an I as follows:

```
invokevirtual java/io/PrintStream/println(F)V;
```

For printing out a character string, the complex line given in the sample program is needed.

```
invokevirtual java/io/PrintStream/println(Ljava/lang/String;)V;
```

If you find this confusing, don't worry about it for now. Classes and class invocation will be discussed at length in chapter 10. For now, these statements can be treated as a kind of legal boilerplate or black magic. Any time you want to generate output, just use the appropriate version. A similar but more complicated set of boilerplate can be used to get input from a similarly constructed System.in object, but this discussion will also be deferred until we have a better understanding of classes in general. At this point, understanding the basic statements is more important in developing working jasmin programs.

With the newest version of Java (Java 1.5), an entirely new method of doing console input and output has become available using newly defined classes such as **Scanner** and **Formatter** and a newly structured `printf` method for formatted output. From the perspective of the underlying assembly language, these are treated simply as new functions/methods to be invoked; they do not involve any radical changes in technology.

3.3 Assembly Language Statement Types

3.3.1 Instructions and Comments

Assembly language statements can be divided roughly into three types (In particular, this is also true of `jasmin` statements.) The first, **instructions**, correspond directly to instructions in the computer's machine language or bytecode. In many cases, these are produced by looking them up in a table stored in the assembler; the bytecode corresponding to the mnemonic `iconst_0` is the bit pattern 0x03. In addition, most assemblers allow the use of comments so that programmer can insert reminders and design notes to help themselves understand later what they are doing today. In `jasmin`, any part of the line that follows a semicolon (;) is a comment, so the first two lines in figure 3.1 are, in their entirety, comments. The assembler is programmed to ignore comments as though they weren't there, so their content is skipped in the assembly process, but they are visible in the source code (for the benefit of human readers, like the professor who will no doubt be grading your programs).

The `jasmin` program is a little unusual among assemblers in the freedom of formatting it permits its programmers. Assembly language program statements usually have a very stereotyped and inflexible format that looks something like this:

```
Label:
        mnemonic     parameter(s)      ; Comment
```

The mnemonic/parameter combination has already been seen, for example, in statements like `iload 2`. Depending upon the type of mnemonic, there may be any number of parameters from zero on up, although zero, one, and two are the most common. The label will be discussed in detail in chapter 4; for now, suffice to say that it marks a part of the program so that you can go back and repeat a section of code. Finally, this stereotyped statement contains a comment. Technically, the computer will never require you to comment programs. On the other hand, your teacher almost certainly will—and good programming practice demands comments. Most assembly language programming standards, in particular, usually demand at least one comment per line.

This book, and `jasmin`, take a slightly nonstandard view of comments. Because many of the arguments used in `jasmin` programs can be long, especially string arguments and the locations of standard objects such as the system output, there may not be room on a line to put comments related to that line. A more serious problem with the one- comment-per-line standard is that it can encourage poor and uninformative commenting.

As an example, consider the following line:

```
bipush    5      ; load the int value 5 onto the stack
```

This comment tells the programmer little or nothing. The statement `bipush 5`, after all, means "load the int value 5 onto the stack." Any programmer reading the statement, even in isolation, would know this. In order to understand the program, she probably needs to know the answers to broader questions. Why does the particular value 5 need to be pushed onto the stack at this particular step (and why should it be loaded as an int)? By focusing on the large-scale roles of statements and the meanings of blocks and groups of statements, comments are rendered (more) useful and informative:

```
bipush  5    ; load number of pentagon sides to measure
```

or even

```
bipush  5    ; load number of pentagon sides
             ; to calculate perimeter
bipush  8    ; load length of sides 1-5 in sequence
bipush 13
bipush  9
bipush  7
bipush  2
             ; now add individual side lengths together
```

For this reason, I recommend not a slavish devotion to an artificial standard like "one comment per line," but instead a reasoned and respectful devotion to the idea that comments should be explanatory—and that assembly language programs, in particular, need a lot of explanation.

3.3.2 Assembler Directives

The third kind of statement, called a `directive`, is an instruction to the assembler itself telling it how to perform its task. In `jasmin`, most directives begin with a period (`.`), as does the third line (or first noncomment line) of the sample program. This directive (`.class`), for example, informs the assembler that this file defines a particular class named `jasminExample`, and therefore (among other things) that the name of the class file to be created is `jasminExample.class`. This doesn't directly affect the process of converting program instructions to bytecode (and doesn't correspond to any bytecode instructions), but it does directly inform `jasmin` how to interact with the rest of the computer, the disk, and the operating system.

Many of the directives may not have a particularly clear meaning at this point. This is because the JVM and the class files themselves are tied directly to the object-oriented structure and the class hierarchy. For example, all classes must be tied to the class hierarchy and must, in particular, be subtypes of another class. (A Mercedes, for example, is a subtype of car, while a car is a subtype of vehicle, and so on.) The Java language enforces this by making any class that does not explicitly mention its relationship in the hierarchy, by default, a subtype of Object (`java/lang/Object`). The `jasmin` assembler enforces a similar requirement in that any `jasmin`-defined class must contain a `.super` directive defining the superclass of which the new class is a subtype. The programmer can often, without harm, simply copy this same line:

```
.super java/lang/Object
```

from one `jasmin` program to another.

Other directives (.method, .end method) are used to define the interactions between this class and the rest of the universe. In particular, the OOP model enforced by the JVM demands that calls to functions from outside classes be explicitly defined as "public methods" and strongly encourages that all functions be so defined. The details of this sort of definition will be explored in greater detail in chapter 10.

3.3.3 Resource Directives

The most important directive, from the point of view of the jasmin programmer, is the .limit directive. This is used to define the limits, and by extension the availability, of resources for computation within a single method. It is one of the unique and very powerful aspects of the JVM's status as a virtual machine, since methods can use as many or as few resources as they need.

In particular, a typical stack-based microprocessor or controller (the old Intel 8087 math coprocessor chip, later incorporated into the 80486 and beyond as part of the main CPU, is an archetypical example) holds only a few elements (eight in this case). A complex computation that needed more than eight numbers would need to store some of them in the CPU stack and some elsewhere, such as in main memory. The programmer would then have to make sure that data was moved in and out of memory as necessary, with the price of failure usually being a buggy or entirely dysfunctional program. Increasing the amount of stack space available inside the CPU could solve this problem, but only by making each CPU chip larger, hotter, more power-hungry, and more expensive. Furthermore, changing fundamental chip parameters between versions will introduce incompatibilities, so that newer programs cannot run on legacy hardware.

The corresponding solution on the JVM is characteristically clean. The directive

```
.limit stack 14
```

as a statement immediately inside a defined method (using the .method directive) will set the maximum size of the stack to 14 int- or float-sized elements. (It will also store seven long or double-sized double elements, or five long/double and four int/float elements, or any appropriate combination.) Similarly, the maximum number of (int-sized) local variables in a method can be set to 12 by use of the related directive

```
.limit locals 12
```

If either of these directives is omitted, then a default limit of one item, enough for a single int or float and not enough for a larger type, will be applied.

3.4 Example: Random Number Generation

3.4.1 Generating Pseudorandom Numbers

A common but mathematically sophisticated task that computers are often called upon to perform is the generation of apparently "random" numbers. For example, in computer games, it may be necessary to shuffle a deck of cards into apparently random order. Because of several fundamental limitations of present-day computer hardware, computers are not actually capable of generating random data (in the strict sense that a statistician would insist upon). Instead, computers generate deterministic pseudorandom data that, although predictable, technically speaking, appears to be naively unpredictable.

We focus here on the task of generating integers uniformly over the range of 0 to n. If, for some reason, the user wishes to generate random floating point numbers, this can be done by simply dividing the random integer by $n + 1$. If n is large enough, this will give a good approximation of a uniform distribution of reals over the interval [0,1). (For example, if n is 999, the floating point number will be one of the set $\{0.000, 0.001, 0.002, \ldots, 0.999\}$. If n is a billion, the final number will look pretty random.)

Mathematically, the computer takes a given number (the seed) and returns a related but apparently unpredictable number. The usual method of doing this, which is followed here, is to use a so-called linear congruential generator. With this method, the number to be returned is generated by an equation of the form

$$newvalue = (a \cdot oldvalue + c) \bmod m$$

for particular values of a, c, and m. The parameter m, for example, determines the maximum size of the returned random number, as computations mod m will give the highest answer of $m - 1$; hence $n = m - 1$. There is a lot of theoretical research behind the selection of the "best" values for a and c, and to investigate this fully would take us too far afield. The value of $oldvalue$ must be selected anew every time the generator is run, as the value of $newvalue$ strictly depends upon it. However, this generator can be used repeatedly to generate a sequence of (pseudo)random numbers, so it needs to be seeded only once per program. Typical sources for the initial seed include truly random (to the program) values such as the current time of day, the process ID number, the most recent movements of the mouse, and so forth.

3.4.2   Implementation on the JVM

In order to implement this algorithm on the JVM, a few design decisions need to be made. For practical reasons, the value of $oldvalue$ will probably be stored in a local variable, as it is likely to change from call to call, but the values of a, c, and m can be stored and manipulated as constants. For simplicity, the values of both $oldvalue$ and $newvalue$ will be stored as ints in a single stack element, but the intermediate values, especially if a and c are large, may overflow a single stack element and will have to be stored as the long type. Without explanation, we use the largest prime value that can be stored as a (signed) int (2147483647) as our value for m and select the prime values $2^{16} + 1(= 65537)$ for a and 5 for c.

The calculations themselves are straightforward. The expression above

$$(a \cdot oldvalue + c) \bmod m$$

can be expressed in JVM (reverse Polish) notation

$$a \; oldvalue \cdot c + m \bmod$$

Therefore, appropriate JVM instructions would be

```
; compute a * oldvalue
ldc2_w   65537   ; a is 2^16 + 1, stored as a long
iload_1          ; oldvalue is (assumed) stored as local variable #1
i2l              ; convert oldvalue to a long
lmul             ; and multiply

; add c
ldc2_w 5   ; c is 5, stored as a long
ladd       ; and add to a*oldvalue

; and take the remainder mod m
ldc2_w 2147483647 ; load value for m
lrem       ; calculate modulus
l2i        ; convert back to integer

; newvalue is now left at top of stack
```

SIDEBAR

Parameter Passing, Local Variables, and the Stack

Most programs need input to be useful. In fact, most functions and methods need input to be useful. The normal method of getting information into a method is by passing parameters; for example, the usual definition of sine takes a single **formal parameter**. When the sine function is used, the corresponding **actual parameter** is passed to the function and used for computation.

The JVM has a rather odd way of handling this process. In traditional (chip-based) architectures, the computer uses a single shared "stack" in memory to separate memory areas used by different programs or functions. The JVM, in contrast, provides a unique private stack for every method. This keeps one method from running amok and destroying data sacred to other parts of the program (which enhances security tremendously) but makes it difficult for one function to pass data to another function. Instead, when a function/method is invoked, the parameters are placed (by the JVM) in local variables available to the method. In general, the first parameter will be placed in local variable #1, the second in #2, and so forth.

There are three exceptions to this general rule. First, if a parameter is too big to fit in a single stack element (a long or a double), then it will be placed in two successive elements (and all the later elements will be shifted down an additional element). Second, this rule leaves local variable #0 free. Normally (with **instance methods**), a reference to the current object will be passed in #0. Methods defined as **static** have no current object and thus pass the first parameter in local #1, #0, and so forth.

Finally, Java 1.5 defines a new parameter-passing method to use when you have a variable number of arguments. In this case, the variable arguments will be converted to an array and passed as a single array argument (probably in #1); the called method will be responsible for determining how many arguments were actually passed and operating on them properly.

The use of the stack for parameter passing on machines other than the JVM will be described in detail in the later chapters dealing with specific machines.

By inspection, the maximum depth of the stack needed in these calculations is two long-sized (double) stack elements, so this could be executed in any method with a stack limit of four or more. Similarly, the code as presented assumes that *oldvalue* is stored in local variable #1. Because variables are numbered starting at zero, this means that the program will require two local variables. (The reason *oldvalue* is stored in variable #1 is that in some cases, local variable #0 is reserved by the Java class environment.)

In order for this program to run properly, the method containing this code would need the two directives

```
.limit stack 4
.limit locals 2
```

There are several variations on this code that would also work; like most programming problems, there are several correct solutions. Most obviously, the two directives could be reversed, defining the local variables first and the stack size second. A more sophisticated change would have the calculation performed using a different order of operations, perhaps pushing c first, doing the muliplication, and then adding. Technically, this would be an implementation of the equivalent but different RPN expression

$$c \; a \; oldvalue \cdot +m \bmod$$

If this implementation is chosen, though, the maximum depth of the stack will be three (long) elements, requiring a `.limit stack 6` directive.

Similarly, there are equivalent ways to perform many of the smaller steps. Instead of pushing the value 5 as a long directly (using `ldc2_w 5`), the programmer could push the int value 5 (`iconst_5`) and then convert it to a long (`i2l`). This would exchange one instruction for two, but the two operations replaced may be shorter and quicker to execute. Rarely, however, do minor changes like this have substantial effects on the size and running speed of a program; more often, they are simply different ways to perform the same task, at the risk of confusing a novice programmer who expects a single solution to a given problem.

3.4.3   Another Implementation

Not only are there multiple solutions to the random number generator problem presented above, but there are also many different algorithms and parameters that can solve the problem. A detailed examination of the representation scheme used by the JVM can allow a streamlined and more sophisticated random number generator. In particular, because mathematics involving ints is always performed using 32-bit quantities, taking numbers mod 2^{32} is automatic. By setting m to be (implicitly) 2^{32}, the programmer can avoid the part of the computation involving taking the modulus. Furthermore, there is no need to use long-sized storage or stack elements if all computations will be done implicitly in this modulus.

One proposed set of numbers that may produce a good random number generator using this modulus is setting a to 69069 and c to 0. (These numbers are actually part of the "Super-Duper" generator proposed by the researcher George Marsaglia.) By setting c to 0 in particular, this will also simplify the code because no addition needs to be done. The resulting code

```
; compute a * oldvalue
ldc2_w   69069    ; proposed for Super-Duper as a's value
iload_1           ; oldvalue is (assumed) stored as local variable 1
imul              ; and multiply (implicitly taking mod 2^32)

; newvalue is now left at top of stack
```

is short, simple, and elegant.

So, which random number generator is better? Comparing generators can be very difficult and can involve fairly high-powered statistics. In additions, depending upon your application, linear congruential generators, in general, may have some very bad properties. Also, depending upon how the generator is used, some bits of the answer may be more random than others. The second generator, for instance, will always generate an odd number if *oldvalue* is odd and an even number otherwise. Using only the high-order bits will give much better results than using the low-order ones. The easiest way to compare the quality of the numbers produced by these generators would be to program both into a computer, run them for several thousand, million, or billion numbers, and subject them to statistical tests based on the desired use.

From the perspective of speed (and, more importantly, from the perspective of a course on computer organization and assembly language), it should be apparent that the second random number generator will run faster. Not only does it involve fewer operations, but the operations themselves will run using integer mathematics and therefore might be faster than the long operations of the first generator.

3.4.4 Interfacing with Java Classes
(This section may be skipped without loss of continuity and assumes some Java programming knowledge.)

So, why assume that the seed (*oldvalue*) is stored in local variable #1? This is related directly to how methods are implemented in Java and how the JVM handles object and method interactions between classes. Specifically, whenever an object's method is invoked, the JVM passes the object itself (as a reference type variable; hence, the leading a in the operation mnemonic) in local variable #0, and the various method parameters are passed in local variables #1, #2, #3, and so forth (for as many variables/parameters as are needed).

In order to run properly, the second generator described above would need to be placed in a method with at least two stack elements and at least two local variables (one for the object, one for the seed value). A sample complete jasmin program that defines a particular class (jrandGenerator.class) and defines two methods, one for object creation and one for generating random numbers using the second method above, is presented as figure 3.4.

The structure of this program closely mirrors that of the previous program for printing a string. Unlike the previous program, however, no main () method is defined (the jrandGenerator class is not expected to be a standalone program), It requires multiple local variables (as defined

```
; defines jrandGenerator as a subclass of Object
; also defines the class file associated with this as jrandGenerator.class
.class public jrandGenerator
.super java/lang/Object

; boilerplate, same as before
.method public <init>()V
   aload_0

   invokespecial java/lang/Object/<init>()V
   return
.end method

; define a Generate() method that takes an int and returns an int
.method public Generate(I)I
   ; we need two stack elements for calculations
   .limit stack 2

   ; we also need two local variables, of which #1 holds the argument
   ; since this is a normal method, #0 will be set by Java itself
   .limit locals 2

   ; compute a * old_value (and store at top of stack)
   ldc    69069      ; proposed for Super-Duper as a's value
   iload_1            ; old_value is (assumed) stored as local variable 1
   imul               ; and multiply (implicitly taking mod 2^32)

   ; new_value is stored at top of stack, return as int
   ireturn

.end method
```

Figure 3.4 Complete RNG in jasmin

in the .limit directive), and the argument and return types of the Generate method have been changed to reflect their use as a random number generator.

When assembled using the jasmin program, the result will be a Java class file named jrandGenerator.class. Objects of this class can be created and used like any other within a Java programming environment, as seen in figure 3.5. This simple program merely creates an instance of a jrandGenerator and invokes the Generate method on it 10 times in rapid succession, thus generating 10 random numbers

A similar program could be written to generate 10 million random numbers or to call a different generator written to implement the first RNG described above.

```
public class jrandExample {
    public static void main(String args[]) {
        int i;
        int old_value = 1;
        jrandGenerator g = new jrandGenerator();

        for (i=0;i<10;i++) {
            old_value = g.Generate(old_value);
            System.out.println("Generated: " + old_value);
        }
        return;
    }
}
```

Figure 3.5 Java program to call `jrandGenerator`

3.5 Chapter Review

- The JVM was designed together with the (high-level) programming language Java, and thus supports a similar style of object-oriented programming (OOP). Although it's not necessary to use OOP in `jasmin` programming, it's often a good idea.
- Java programs and `jasmin` programs must both be converted to `.class` files before they can be executed by the JVM.
- The command to convert `jasmin` programs to class files (that is used in this book) is usually named `jasmin`. At the time of writing, it is available without charge at Jon Meyer's Web site or at the companion Web site `http://prenhall.com/juola`.
- Input and output are typically difficult problems because of the large number of devices. Java and the JVM simplify this problem by using the class system. By memorizing the three correct `jasmin` statements, a programmer can send data (of any type) to the standard output at any time.
- Assembly language statements can be divided into three major types: instructions (which are converted to bytecode machine instructions), comments (which are ignored by the computer), and directives (which affect the conversion/assembly process itself).
- Directives are used to define how class files fit into the standard Java class hierarchy.
- Directives, and specifically the `.limit` directive, are also used to control the amount of resources available to a given method or function. In particular, `.limit stack X` will set the maximum stack size, and `.limit locals Y` will set the maximum number of local variables.

3.6 Exercises

1. What is the difference between a compiler and an assembler?
2. List at least five instructions (mnemonics) that take exactly one argument.
3. How can the computer tell if a given line contains a directive, a comment, or an instruction?
4. Will your `jasmin` program still work if you forget the `.limit` directive?

3.7 Programming Exercises

1. Write a jasmin program to display the following poem on a Web page:

   There once was a lady named Nan
   Whose limericks never would scan
   When she was asked why
   She replied, with a sigh,
   "It's because I always try to put as many syllables into the last line as I possibly can."

2. Write a jasmin program to display a triangular pattern of capital O's as follows:

```
         0
        0 0
       0   0
      0     0
     0       0
     00000000000
```

3. Write a jasmin program to display today's date in the following format: Today is Monday, 9/19/2008.

4. Write a jasmin program to calculate and print the wages due me in the following circumstances: This month, I worked 80 hours at a job paying $25.00/hour, 40 hours at a job paying $15.50/hour, and 45 hours at a job paying $35.00/hour.

5. The Boeing 777-300 has airplane a maximum passenger capacity of 386. Write a program to determine how many planes I would need to charter in order to take N people on a round-the-world trip. You may assemble a specific value of N into your program. (Note: planes are chartered one at at time; chartering three-fifths of a plane doesn't make sense.)

6. The date February 29 only occurs once every four years—for example, in 2000, 2004, and 2008. If a friend of mine was born on February 29, 1980, and the current year is Y_1, write a program to tell me how many times he has actually been able to celebrate his birthday. (You can assume, if you like, that he's been able to celebrate this year if appropriate.)

7. Unlike Christmas (which is always December 25), the date of Easter varies from year to year. An anonymous correspondent to *Nature*[2] published this algorithm to determine the date upon which Easter falls. (It was later proven correct by Samuel Butcher, Bishop of Meath, and is thus called *Butcher's Algorithm*.) All values are integers, all division is integer division, and mod means the integer modulus (the remainder after division):

   - Let y be the relevant year
   - Let a be y mod 19
   - Let b be $y/100$
   - Let c be y mod 100
   - Let d be $b/4$
   - Let e be b mod 4
   - Let f be $(b+8)/25$

---

[2] *Nature*, April 20, 1876, vol. 13, p. 487.

- Let g be $(b - f + 1)/3$
- Let h be $(19 \cdot a + b - d - g + 15) \bmod 30$
- Let i be $c/4$
- Let k be $c \bmod 4$
- Let l be $(32 + 2 \cdot e + 2 \cdot i - h - k) \bmod 7$
- Let m be $(a + 11 \cdot h + 22 \cdot l)/451$
- Let p be $(h + l - 7 \cdot m + 114) \bmod 31$
- The Easter month is $(h + l - 7 \cdot m + 114)/31$. (3 = March, 4 = April).
- The Easter day is $p + 1$.

Implement this algorithm and determine the date of the next 10 Easters.

4

Control Structures

4.1 "Everything They've Taught You Is Wrong"

4.1.1 Fetch-Execute Revisited

In chapters 2 and 3, we explored how to write and evaluate fairly complex mathematical expressions using the JVM's stack-based computations. By pushing arguments onto the calculation stack and performing an appropriate sequence of elementary operations, one can more or less get the computer to do one's bidding. Once. From a practical standpoint, the real advantage of a computer is its ability to perform tasks over and over again without boredom or error.

Reviewing the representation structure of the JVM, it's not difficult to see how the computer could be made to execute the same block of code repeatedly. Program code, remember, consists of successive machine instructions stored as sequential elements of a computer's memory. In order to execute a particular statement, the computer first "fetches" the current instruction from memory, interprets and "executes that" instruction, and then updates its notion of the "current instruction." The current instruction is, formally, a number stored in the program counter (PC) referring to a location in the bytecode of the current method. Every time the fetch-execute cycle occurs, the value stored in the PC goes up by 1 or more bytes so that it points to the next instruction to be executed.

Why 1 "or more" bytes? Shouldn't the PC go up by one each time? Not really, since some operations need more than 1 byte to define. For example, basic arithmetic operations such as irem only require 1 byte to define. However, operations such as bipush are underspecified. The bipush operation specifies that a byte should be pushed onto the stack (and promoted to a 32-bit integer) but does not, by itself, specify which byte this should be. Whenever this instruction is used, the opcode for bipush (0x10) is followed by a single byte-to-be-pushed. The sipush instruction (0x11), as one might expect, is followed by not 1 but 2 bytes (a short) to be pushed. Similarly, the iload instruction is followed by 1 or 2 bytes describing the local variable to be loaded. By contrast, the iload_1 shortcut operation (0x1B) automatically loads local variable #1 and can be expressed in a single byte.

Because operations are variably sized, the fetch-execute cycle needs to be smart enough to fetch (possibly) several bytes, either at the same time or in sequence, in order to fetch the entire instruction and all of its arguments; the PC must be updated to reflect the size of the instruction fetched. Once these difficulties are dealt with, setting the PC to the appropriate location will cause the JVM automatically to execute the sequence of instructions. If, therefore, there were some way to force the PC to contain a particular value, one could cause the computer to execute that block of code over and over again. By controlling the PC, one directly controls what (and how many times) the computer does.

To summarize the next few sections, this kind of direct control is equivalent to the often vilified **goto** statement. Students are taught and indeed practically indoctrinated into an avoidance of such statements, as they can introduce more bugs than a shelf full of ant farms. In higher-level languages, students are taught programming methods to avoid them. At the level of assembly language, the gloves are off, and the best one can do is to understand them.

4.1.2 Branch Instructions and Labels

Any statement that might cause the PC to change its value is usually called a "branch" instruction. Unlike the normal fetch-execute cycle, a branch instruction might go anywhere. In order to define the target location, jasmin, like most other assembly languages, allows individual instructions to receive **labels** so that they can be referred to as individuals. Not all instructions will get such labels, but any statement can. To adjust the PC, one uses an appropriate statement and then gives the label of the target instruction.

So how is a branch statement created and stored? In more detail, what is a "label," and how can it be stored as a sequence of bits, like a number or a machine instruction? From the programmer's viewpoint, a label is just a line by itself holding an optional part of any instruction, a word (made up of letters and numbers, beginning with a letter, conventionally a capital letter, and followed by a colon [:]) that marks a particular instruction. To transfer control to a given location, use that label (without the colon) as the argument in an appropriate branch statement. For example,

```
goto Somewhere ; set value in PC to location of Somewhere
```

4.1.3 "Structured Programming"a Red Herring

From a machine design standpoint, the simplest way to control the PC is to treat it as a register or local variable and to assign appropriate values to it (see figure 4.1.) When a particular value is placed in the PC, the machine will "go to" that location and commence execution of code.

This, of course, is the infinitely abusable "goto" statement.

```
        ; do some computation
        ; do some more computation
        goto ALabel ; now transfer control directely to ALabel

        ; this statement is skipped
        ; as is this one

ALabel:
        ; but we pick up with whatever instruction is here
        ; and keep going on in normal fashion
```

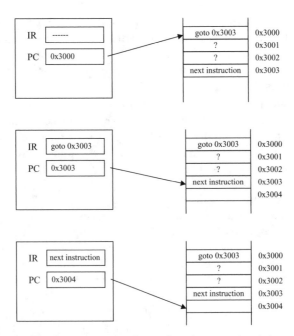

Figure 4.1   Fetch-execute cycle performing a goto statement

According to modern programming practice (since about 1970 and the very influential work of Dijkstra), programming using goto statements is subject to severe disapproval. One reason is that a naked goto can be dangerous. Placing a random location in the PC will cause the computer to begin executing whatever is stored at that location. If that location is computer code, fine. If that location happens to be (for instance) in the middle of the storage dedicated to a string variable, the computer will treat each byte of the string as though it were program code and begin executing. (In the JVM, for example, the ASCII character 65 (A) would correspond to `lstore_2` and cause the computer to try to pop a long int off the stack. If there is no such long int at the top of the stack, an immediate program crash will ensue.)

A potentially more serious problem is that programs written with goto statements can be confusing and (for that reason) error-prone. From the viewpoint of the statement which is the target of a goto, there is no obvious relationship between the visual structure of the program, the ordering of the program statements in bytecode, and the ordering of the program statements in execution. An apparently simple sequence of statements such as

```
        iload_1
        iload_2
Branch:
        iload_3
        iadd
        imul
```

may not mean what the casual reader thinks, because the code might be executed via a goto to the third iload_N statement. Thus, the value stored in local variable #3 is added to (and multiplied by) something nonobvious. In particularly bad cases, the control structure may be completely confusing (the usual metaphor is a plate of spaghetti), with all the usual problems that correspond with programmer confusion.

For this reason, modern "structured programming" recommends the use of high-order control structures such as block-structured loops and decision statements. However, at the level of the machine code, any change reflecting different computations must be expressed through changes to the PC, thus requiring an implicit goto.

Why, then, are programmers supposed to program without using goto statements? The idea behind structured programming is not to avoid using them altogether, but to restrict their use to contexts where they aren't confusing. In particular, as much of the program as possible should be modular (composed of logically divided code fragments that can be treated conceptually as single operations). These modules, as much as possible, should have a single defined starting point and a single defined exit point, ideally at the top and bottom of the physical code. (This is often formalized as the "single-entry/single-exit" principle as part of the definition of structured programming.) High-level languages will often prevent you from violating the single-entry/single exit rule by their design. The same principles can, and should, be applied to assembly language programming in general. Even though the language itself will give you the flexibility to do very silly and confusing things, a disciplined programmer will resist the temptation. Programmers familiar with the higher-level control structures such as if statements and loops will try to use similar easy-to-understand structures, even in jasmin, so that they and others who work with them will be able to figure out exactly what was intended.

4.1.4 High-Level Control Structures and Their Equivalents

A simple example may help to illustrate this. Figures 4.2 and 4.3 shows examples of similar loops in Java/C++ (and many other languages) and Pascal, respectively. In both cases, the computer counts from 100 down to 0, no doubt doing something clever each time through the loop. The block of clever stuff is most efficiently written as a continuous group of machine instructions. When the PC is loaded with the address of the first instruction in the group, the entire block will be executed.

In order to execute this block several times, the computer needs to decide at the beginning of each block whether or not the block needs to be executed (at least) one more time. In the case

```
for (i=100; i > 0; i--) {
    // do something clever 100 times
}
```

Figure 4.2 Sample loop in Java or C++

```
for i := 100 downto 1 begin
    { do something clever 100 times }
end
```

Figure 4.3 Equivalent sample loop in Pascal

of the loop in the figures, this decision is easy: if the counter is greater than 0, the block should be executed again. In this case, go to the beginning of the block (and decrement the counter). Alternatively, if the counter is less than or equal to 0, do not execute the loop again and go to the remainder of the program.

Informally, this can be expressed as a simple pop-and-if->0-goto. Formally, the mnemonic for this particular operation is `ifgt`. A formal translation of the loops into jasmin would be as in figure 4.4.

```
          ldc 100              ; load integer 100 (number of times)
          istore_1             ; store the index in #1 as an int
LoopTop:
          ; do something particularly clever using
          ; any needed local variables
          iload_1              ; reload loop index from #1
          iconst_m1            ; load -1 for subtraction
          iadd                 ; decrement loop index
          istore_1             ; store...
          iload_1              ; ... and reload loop index
          ifgt LoopTop         ; if top of stack > 0, put LoopTop into PC
                               ; and repeat
          ; otherwise, fall through
```

Figure 4.4 A (mostly) equivalent sample loop in jasmin

Actually, this isn't a perfectly accurate translation. As long as the initial value for the loop index is greater than 0, it will work. If, however, the programmer had specified a loop starting with a negative number (e.g., for (i=-1; i>0;i++)), the loop in Java or C++ would never have been executed. The jasmin version would still have been executed once, because the clever computations would have been performed before the computer had a chance to check whether or not the index was large enough. A more accurate translation would require smarter—or at least, more varied—decision and goto statements.

4.2 Types of Gotos

4.2.1   Unconditional Branches

The simplest form of a goto is an **unconditional branch** (or goto), which simply and always transfers control to the label designated as an argument. By itself, it can produce an infinite loop (a loop that runs forever), but not a loop that runs for a while and then terminates when something changes. For that purpose, the programmer needs **conditional** branches, branches that may or may not be taken.

4.2.2   Conditional Branches

The JVM supports six basic conditional branches (sometimes called "conditional gotos"), plus several shortcut operations and two more branches (to be described later, in conjunction with the class/object system). A basic conditional branch operates by popping an integer off the stack and determining whether the popped integer is greater than, less than, or equal to 0. If the desired condition is met, control is transferred to the designated label; otherwise, the PC is incremented as usual and control passes to the next statement. With three possible comparison results (greater than, less than, or equal to 0), all seven meaningful combinations can be designated. These are summarized in table 4.1. Note that the `goto` statement does not change the stack, while the `if??` operations all pop a single integer.

Mnemonic	top > 0	top = 0	top < 0	Interpretation
ifeq		X		Goto **if eq**ual
ifne	X		X	Goto **if n**ot **e**qual
iflt			X	Goto **if l**ess **t**han
ifge	X	X		Goto **if g**reater than or **e**qual
ifgt	X			Goto **if g**reater **t**han
ifle		X	X	Goto **if l**ess than or **e**qual
(goto)	X	X	X	(**Goto** always)

Table 4.1 Conditional and unconditional branch operations in `jasmin`

4.2.3 Comparison Operations

So, if the basic conditional branches only operate on integers, how does one compare other types? Comparing other types is performed explicitly by comparison operations that are defined to return integers. The operation `lcmp`, for example, pops two longs—as always, two longs will be stored as four stack elements—and pushes the integer value 1, 0, or −1, depending upon whether the first element pushed is greater than, less than, or equal to the second (the one at the top of the stack). For example, the following code fragment

```
lload_3        ; load local variable #3 (and #4)
lconst_1       ; push 1 (as long) for comparison
lcmp           ; compare magnitudes, push integer answer
ifgt  Somewhere ; go Somewhere if #3 > 1
; if we got here, #3 <= 1
```

compares the long value stored as local variable #3 against the number 1 and transfers control to Somewhere if, and only if, the stored value is larger.

There is a very important point to consider in stack ordering. The instruction sequence `lload_1`, `lload_3`, `lcmp` will first put local variables #1/#2, then #3/#4, and only then do the comparison. The comparison is order sensitive and would give a different result if #1/#2 were on top of the stack instead. To remember how order works, think of subtracting the top element of the stack from the second element. The result pushed is the sign (+1, 0, or −1) of the difference. See figure 4.5 for an example.

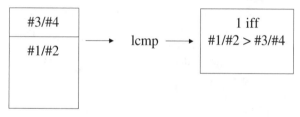

Figure 4.5 The `lcmp` instruction illustrated

Comparing floats and doubles is similar, but a bit trickier because of the sophistication of the IEEE representations. Specifically, IEEE 754 allows certain special bit patterns to represent "not a number," abbreviated as NaN. These special patterns, in essence, mean that a calculation somewhere previously went badly wrong (like trying to take the square root of a negative number or divide 0 by 0). It usually makes no sense to do comparisons against NaN, but the programmer sometimes has a special interpretation in mind.

For example, suppose a college defines the honors list as including all students with a grade point average (gpa) above 3.50. A brief program fragment (in Pascal) to determine whether or not a student is on the honors list would look like the following:

```
if (gpa > 3.50) then
       onhonorslist := true;
```

A student with no gpa (a first-semester student or a student who has taken an "incomplete" in every class for medical reasons, for example) would probably not be considered to be on the honors list. In other words, if a student has a gpa of NaN, then it should be treated as being less than 3.50. This same student, however, should probably not be expelled for having too low a gpa; NaN should be higher than the appropriate cutoff. The JVM and jasmin provide two separate comparison instructions to define these cases. The instruction fcmpg compares the two floating point numbers at the top of the stack and pushes 1, 0, −1 as expected, except that if either value is NaN, the result is 1. If either value is NaN, fcmpl returns −1. As expected, comparing doubles uses similarly named dcmpl and dcmpg with similar differences in behavior.

The jasmin equivalent of the Pascal fragment above, then, would look something like this:

```
fload_1        ; load gpa from #1 as float
ldc 3.50       ; load gpa cutoff (3.50)
fcmpl          ; compare gpa to cutoff, NaN being "below"
ifle  Skip     ; go to Skip gpa >= cutoff
iconst_1       ; push 1 (boolean : true)
istore_2       ; put "true" into #2 (as int/boolean
Skip:          ; do whatever else you needed to do with this student
```

4.2.4   Combination Operations

As before, the second-class types such as short and boolean are not directly supported and must be treated as int types in computation. More surprisingly, jasmin does not provide a way to compute the result of comparing two integers! Instead, integer comparison is done via shortcut operations that combine a comparison operation with built-in conditional branches (as in table 4.2.)

All of these operations work in mostly the same way. The CPU first pops two (int) elements off the stack and performs a comparison like the one that the icmp instruction would do if it existed. Instead of pushing the result of the comparison, though, the program immediately jumps (or not) to the appropriate location by modifying the program counter.

if_icmpeq	branch if second element is equal to top
if_icmpne	branch if second element is not equal to top
if_icmplt	branch if second element is less than top
if_icmpge	branch if second element is greater or equal to top
if_icmpgt	branch if second element is greater than top
if_icmple	branch if second element is less or equal to top

Table 4.2   Combination compare/branch instructions in jasmin

4.3   Building Control Structures

The main advantage of control structures in high-level languages is that they are relatively easy to understand. It's helpful in assembly language programming (on the JVM or any other computer) to keep this same ease of understanding to the greatest extent possible. One way to do this is to maintain a similar structure of logical blocks of code that are organized like high-order control structures.

4.3.1   If Statements

Expanding on the example from section 4.2.3 of how high-level control can be expressed in jasmin, the key to error-free and understandable code is to retain a similar block structure. A traditional if/then statement has up to three parts: a boolean expression, a set of statements to be executed if the expression evaluates as "true," and another set to be executed if the expression evaluates as "false." The C++ or Java block

```
if (a > 5) {
        // (if block)
        // do something
        // for several lines
} else {
        // (else block)
        // do something else
        // for several lines
}
        // do whatever other operations need doing
```

can be written equivalently in jasmin as (assuming that a is a long in #1)

```
        lload_1    ; if a is in #1
        ldc_2 5    ; load 5
        lcmp       ; compare a to 5
        ifle  Else
        ; if we got here, a > 5, hence perform the if-clause
        ; at the end of the if clause, skip over the else-clause
        ; via an unconditional goto
        ; ----  this corresponds to the if block above
        goto  Quit
```

```
Else:
     ; if we got here, then a <= 5, hence perform the else-clause
     ; ----  this corresponds to the else block above
Quit:
     ; do whatever additional operations need doing
     ; ----  this corresponds to the statement following the if statement
```

The block-structured similarity between this code and the high-level code above should be apparent. In particular, there are consecutive instructions in both code samples corresponding to the "if block" and to the "else block" that are always performed in sequence, starting at the top and continuing to the end. The `jasmin` code weaves in between these blocks to set the PC accordingly. In detail, note that the test in this example is slightly different; instead of branching directly to the if clause, this example skips over the if clause (to the else clause) if the reverse of the condition is true.

Complex boolean conditionals can be handled by appropriate use of the `iand`, `ior`, and other instructions or by repeated comparisons. For example, we can check that a is in the range between 5 and 10 (a > 5 and a < 10) as follows:

```
lload_1    ; if a is in #1
ldc_2 5    ; load 5
lcmp       ; compare a to 5
ifle  Else
; if we got here, a > 5
lload_1    ; if a is in #1
ldc_2 10   ; load 10
lcmp       ; compare a to 10
ifge  Else
; if we got here, a > 5 and a < 10
; and program continues as before
```

4.3.2   Loops
In many programming languages, there are two basic kinds of loops: those in which the program tests the condition at the beginning and those in which the program tests at the end. The second kind has already been illustrated. We retain the block structure of the interior of the loop, place a label at the top of the block, and then jump back to the top if the conditions are not right for loop exit. In broad terms, it looks something like this:

```
LoopTop:   ; do the stuff associated with the loop
           ; whatever operations are needed
           iload_1     ; load first operand of comparison
           iconst_m1   ; load second operand of comparison
           ifne LoopTop ; (this loops until #1 = -1)
           ; fall through
```

This performs what in Pascal would be a `repeat` loop and what in C, C++, or Java would be a do/while loop. For a more traditional `while` loop, the condition is placed before the loop body, the loop body is followed by an unconditional goto, and if the loop exit is met, control is transferred to the first statement outside the loop itself, as in the following:

```
Control:
        iload_1       ; load first operation of comparison
        iconst_m1     ; load second operand of comparison
        ifeq LoopOut ; (this loops until #1 = -1)
        ; do the stuff associated with the loop
        ; whatever operations are needed
        goto Control ; after the loop, jump to recheck condition
LoopOut: ; you can ONLY get here via the conditional branch above
```

This code fragment performs the equivalent of a loop akin to `while (i != 1)`. Alternatively, one can keep the do/while structure but enter the loop at the bottom via an unconditional branch, as in

```
        goto LoopEnd ; jump directly to loop test
LoopTop:  ; do the stuff associated with the loop
        ; whatever operations are needed
LoopEnd:
        iload_1       ; load first operand of comparison
        iconst_m1     ; load second operand of comparison
        ifne LoopTop ; (this loops until #1 = -1)
        ; fall through
```

This saves the execution of a single goto statement.

The equivalence of `while` and `for` loops is well known. A counter-controlled loop such as

```
for (i=0;i<10;i++)
        // do something
```

is equivalent to

```
i = 0;
while (i<10) {
        // do something
        i++;
}
```

and can be easily written using the framework above. The most significant change is the need to recruit a local variable as a counter; and otherwise the `while` structure is repeated almost exactly.

```
        bipush 0      ; using #1 as i, set it to zero initially
        istore_1

        goto LoopEnd ; jump directly to loop test
LoopTop:
        ; do the stuff associated with the loop
        ; whatever operations are needed

        ; increment #1
        iload_1       ; load i from #1
        iconst_1      ; load 1 for incrementing
        iadd          ; we've now done i++
        istore_1      ; ... and saved i in #1 (again)

        ; for efficiency demons, the four lines above could
        ; be replaced by a single operation : iinc 1 1
LoopEnd:
        iload_1       ; load first operand of comparison (i)
        bipush 10     ; load second operand of comparison (10)
        ifle LoopTop ; (this loops until #1 >= 10)
        ; fall through only when #1 >= 10
```

4.3.3   Details of Branch Instructions

From a programmer's point of view, using goto statements and labels is fairly simple. You make a label where you want control to go, and the program automatically jumps there. Under the hood, the picture is a bit more complex. Instead of storing labels, the computer actually stores **offsets**. For example, the goto instruction (opcode 0xA7) is followed in bytecode by a signed 2-byte (short) integer. This integer is used as a change to the program counter; in other words, after the instruction is executed, the value of the PC is changed to PC + offset. If the offset value is negative, this has the effect of moving control back to a previously executed statement (as in the repeat loop example above), while if the offset value is positive, the program jumps forward (as in the if/then/else example). In theory, there's nothing to prevent one from using an offset value of 0, but this would mean that the statement didn't change the PC and would create an infinite loop. An offset of zero would correspond to the jasmin statement

```
Self:
        goto Self
```

which is probably not what the programmer wanted.

So, how does the programmer calculate these offsets? Fortunately, she doesn't! That's the job, and one of the main advantages, of an assembler like jasmin. The programmer can simply use labels and find that it's the assembler's task to determine what the offsets should be. A potentially more serious problem (again from the programmer's point of view) with this implementation is that, with only 2 bytes of (signed) offset, no jump can be longer than approximately 32,000 bytes (in either direction). What happens in a really long program?

This is addressed in two ways in jasmin. First, jasmin provides, in addition to the goto instruction, a goto_w instruction (sometimes called a "wide goto" and implemented as opcode

```
              ; what I really want is "ifne DistantLocation," but
              ; that's too far to get in a single step.
              ; Unfortunately, ifne_w doesn't exist.
              ; The assembler will realize that and instead use

              ifeq Skip                ; notice the test is reversed
              goto_w DistantLocation   ; because we are branching AROUND
Skip:                                  ; the branch we don't want to take
              ; do something else
```

Figure 4.6   An example of a "branch around a branch" to jump conditionally to distant locations

0xC8). In most respects similar to a normal goto, it is followed by a full-sized integer, allowing programmers to jump forward or back up to 2 billion or so bytes. Since individual JVM methods are not allowed to be more than 2^{16} (about 64,000) bytes long, and since, if you find yourself writing a longer method than that, you probably should divide it into sections anyway, this new opcode solves the problem. Again, it's the assembler's job to decide which opcode is needed—technically, when it sees a statement like goto SomeWhere, it can use either the 0xA7 or 0xC8 instruction. If the necessary offset would be too large to fit into a short, then it will automatically translate the programmer's goto into a machine-internal goto_w.

A more serious problem is that there is no direct equivalent to ifne_w or other wide conditional branches. However, the assembler can (again) devise an equivalence without the programmer's knowledge or cooperation. A conditional (wide) branch to a distant location can be simulated by a branch around a branch, as in figure 4.6.

As with calculating branch sizes in the first place, a good assembler can always do the right thing in this instance.

The most serious problem with using branch statements is that they do not, in any way, provide the programmer with local block structures. Many programmers rely on the convenience of being able to redeclare local variables inside blocks, as in the following:

```
if (x > 0) {
    int x; // this is a new x, unrelated to the previous
    x = -1;
        ...
}
// here the old x reappears and reacquires its old value
```

No such convenience is available in assembly language; all local variables (and the stack) retain their values before, during, and after a jump. If an important variable is stored in location #2 before the jump and the next statement is fstore_2, then the important variable will be overwritten. Block structure is an important convenience for how to think about assembly language programs, but it does not provide any practical defense such as information hiding against mistakes and misuse.

4.4 Example: Syracuse Numbers

4.4.1 Problem Definition

As an example of how this can be put together, we'll explore the Syracuse number (or $3N + 1$) conjecture. It dates back to classical mathematics, when an early Greek noticed that a few simple arithmetic rules would produce surprising and unpredictable behavior. The rules are:

- If the number N you have is 1, stop.
- If the number N you have is odd, let N be $3N + 1$ and repeat.
- If the number N you have is even, let N be $\frac{N}{2}$ and repeat.

It was noticed early on that this procedure always seemed to end (to get to 1) when you started with any positive integer, but no one could actually prove that conjecture. Furthermore, no one could find a general rule for predicting how many steps it would take to get to 1. Sometimes it happens very quickly:

$$16 \to 8 \to 4 \to 2 \to 1$$

but close numbers can take different times:

$$15 \to 46 \to 23 \to 70 \to 35 \to 106 \to 53 \to 160 \to 80 \to$$

$$40 \to 20 \to 10 \to 5 \to 16 \to 8 \to 4 \to 2 \to 1$$

and sometimes it takes a very large number of steps. Even today, no one knows how many steps it takes or even whether it will always go to 1 (although mathematicians with computers have found that all numbers less than several billion will converge to 1 and thus end). Try it for yourself: how many steps do you think it will take to get to 1 starting from 81?

4.4.2 Design

Even better, don't try it yourself. Let the computer do the work. Figure 4.7 gives pseudocode for an algorithm that will start at 81 and count steps until the final value is 1. Implementing this algorithm in jasmin will get a quick answer to this conjecture.

```
(1)      count_of_steps <- 0
(2)      current_value <- 81
(3)      while (current_value != 1)
(4)            if (current_value is odd)
(5)                  current_value <- (current_value * 3) + 1
(6)            else
(7)                  current_value <- (current_value / 2)
(8)            endif
(9)            count_of_steps <- count_of_steps + 1
(10)     endwhile
(11)     final answer is count_of_steps
```

Figure 4.7 Test of Syracuse conjecture in pseudocode

```
        ; entry point for if/else
        iload_2      ; load current_value
        iconst_2     ; and the number 2, to determine if odd or even
        irem         ; calculate remainder
        iconst_0     ; compare remainder against zero
        if_icmpgt    CaseOdd  ; goto CaseOdd if it's odd

CaseEven:            ; technically speaking, we don't need this label
                     ; as we will never branch to this location

        ; divide #2 by 2 and resave
        iload_2      ; load current value
        iconst_2     ; push 2 for division
        idiv         ; do the division
        istore_2     ; and store the new value

        goto         Exit     ; and skip the Caseodd block

CaseOdd:
        ; multiply #2 by 3 and add one
        iload_2      ; load current value
        iconst_3     ; push 3 for multiplication
        imul         ; multiply  (value stored is now 3*N)
        iconst_1     ; push 1 for addition
        iadd         ; add (value stored is 3*N+1)
        istore_2     ; and store the new value

Exit:
        ; exit point for both branches of if/else
```

Figure 4.8 If/else structure for internal block of Syracuse number code

```
        ; entry point for while
LoopEntry:
        iload_2      ; load current_value from #2
        iconst_1     ; compare current_value against 1
        if_icmpeq    LoopExit    ; branch to LoopExit if equal

        ; do necessary statements for odd/even calculations

        ; do necessary statements for incrementing count_of_steps

        goto         LoopEntry   ; branch unconditionally to top of loop
                                 ; and recheck

LoopExit:
        ; exit point for while loop
```

Figure 4.9 While structure for main loop of Syracuse number code

The code in figure 4.7 calls for two integer variables, and for simplicity in calcuation, we'll keep them as int types (instead of long). In particular, count_of_steps can be stored as local variable #1 and current_value as #2. The arithmetic calculations in steps 1, 2, 5, 7, and 9 can be performed with techniques from chapter 2. Output, in line 11, can be done in any of several ways; again, we'll pick one of the simpler ones and just print the final results.

The if/else construction used in lines 4 to 8 can be modeled by the code block in section 4.3.1. Specifically, we can determine whether or not the current value is odd by taking the remainder (irem) when divided by 2; if the result is equal to 0 (if_icmpeq), then the number is even. The code in figure 4.8 illustrates this. As is typical of structured programming, this block as a whole has a single entry at the initial statement of the block and a single exit at the bottom (at the point labeled Exit:).

This entire block of code will in turn be used inside a while-loop structure, as in figure 4.9.

4.4.3   Solution and Implementation
The complete solution is presented here.

```
                                                            S I D E B A R

; boilerplate
.method public <init>()V
      aload_0
      invokespecial java/lang/Object/<init>()V
      return
.end method

.method public static main([Ljava/lang/String;)V
      .limit stack 2          ; no complex calculations here
      .limit locals 3         ; #0 is reserved (as usual)
                              ; #1 is a loop counter
                              ; #2 is the value of N

      iconst_0                ; #1 <- 0
      istore_1

      bipush 81               ; #2 <- 81
      istore_2

LoopEntry:
      iload_2                 ; load current_value  from #2
      iconst_1                ; compare current_value against 1
      if_icmpeq  LoopExit
                              ; branch to LoopExit if equal

      ; do necessary statements for odd/even calculations
; entry point for if/else
      iload_2                 ; load current_value
      iconst_2                ; and the number 2, to determine if odd
                              ; or even
```

```
        irem                    ; calculate remainder
        iconst_0                ; compare remainder against zero
        if_icmpgt CaseOdd       ; goto CaseOdd if it's odd

        ; we only get here if #2 is/was even
        ; divide #2 by 2 and resave
        iload_2                 ; load current value
        iconst_2                ; push 2 for division
        idiv                    ; do the division
        istore_2                ; store the new value

        goto Exit               ; and skip the Caseodd block
CaseOdd:
        ; multiply #2 by 3 and add one
        iload_2                 ; load current value
        iconst_3                ; push 3 for multiplication
        imul                    ; multiply  (value stored is now 3*N)
        iconst_1                ; push 1 for addition
        iadd                    ; add (value stored is 3*N+1)
        istore_2                ; and store the new value

Exit: ; do necessary statements for incrementing count_of_steps
        iinc 1 1                ; increment loop index

        goto        LoopEntry
                                ; branch unconditionally to top and recheck

LoopExit:
        ; print result to System.out (as usual)
        getstatic java/lang/System/out Ljava/io/PrintStream;
        iload 1                 ; load loop counter for printing
        invokevirtual java/io/PrintStream/println(I)V

        return                  ; and we're done
.end method
```

4.5 Table Jumps

Most high-level languages also support the concept of multiway decisions, such as would be expressed in a Java switch statement. As an example of these decisions in use, consider trying to figure out how many days there are in a month, as in figure 4.10.

Perhaps obviously, any multiway branch can be treated as equivalent to a set of two-way branches (such as if/else statements) and written accordingly. The JVM also provides a shortcut—in fact, two shortcuts—that can make the code simpler and faster to execute under certain conditions. The main condition is simply that the case labels (e.g., the numbers 1 to 12 in the example fragment) must be integers.

As before, there is no direct notion of block structure. What the machine offers instead is a multiway branch, where the computer will go to any of several destinations, depending upon

```
switch (monthno) {
    // 30 days hath September, April, June, and November
    case 9 :
    case 4 :
    case 6 :
    case 11 : days = 30; break;
    // ... all the rest have 31
    case 1 : case 3 : case 5 : case 7 : case 8 : case 10 : case 12:
            days = 31; break;
    // except February, alone (ignoring leap years)
    case 2 : days = 28; break;
    default : System.out.println("Error : Bad month!");
} // end switch
```

Figure 4.10   Multiway branch statement in Java (and C++)

the value at the top of the stack. The general format of a `lookupswitch` instruction consists of a set of value:Label pairs. If the value matches the top of the stack, then control is transferred to Label.

```
        iload_1              ; Assuming that "monthno" is stored in #1
        lookupswitch         ; begin multiway branch
            1    : Days31    ;
            2    : Days28    ;
            3    : Days31    ;
            4    : Days30    ;
            5    : Days31    ;
            6    : Days30    ;
            7    : Days31    ;
            8    : Days31    ;
            9    : Days30    ;
            10   : Days31    ;
            11   : Days30    ;
            12   : Days31    ;
        default : ERROR      ;
Days28:
        bipush 28            ; Load 28 days
        istore_2             ; and assign to days (#2)
        goto ExampleEnd
Days30:
        bipush 30            ; Load 30 days
        istore_2             ; and assign to days (#2)
        goto ExampleEnd
```

```
Days31:
        bipush 31          ; load 31 days
        istore_2           ; and assign to days (#2)
        goto ExampleEnd
Error:
        ; take appropriate error actions like getstatic .../System/out
        goto ExampleEnd
ExampleEnd:
        ; do whatever is needful
```

The dozen or so lines above that begin with `lookupswitch` and end with `default` are actually a single very complex machine instruction. Unlike the others that have been discussed, this instruction takes a variable number of arguments, and the task of the `jasmin` assembler (as well as the JVM bytecode interpreter) is correspondingly tricky. The default branch is mandatory in JVM machine code (unlike in Java). As with other branch statements, the values stored are offsets from the current program counter; unlike most other statements (except `goto_w`), the offsets are stored as 4-byte quantities, allowing for jumps to "distant" locations within the method.

SIDEBAR

Machine Code for `lookupswitch/` `tableswitch`

Both `lookupswitch` and `tableswitch` involve a variable number of arguments, and as such have a complex implementation in bytecode. Essentially, there is a "hidden" implicit argument about how many arguments there are, so that the computer knows where the next argument starts.

In the case of `lookupswitch`, the `jasmin` assembler will count the number of value:label pairs for you. The bytecode created involves not only the `lookupswitch` opcode (0xAB), but also a 4-byte count of the number of nondefault branches. Each branch is stored as a 4-byte integer (value) and then a corresponding 4-byte offset to be taken if the integer matches the top of the stack.

In the case of `tableswitch`, the values can be computed from the starting and ending values. A `tableswitch` statement is stored internally as the opcode byte (0xAA), as the low and high values (stored as 4-byte integers), and finally as a set of sequential 4-byte offsets corresponding to the values $low, low + 1, low + 2, \ldots high$. See appendix B for more details on both.

If, as in the above example, the values are not only integers but contiguous integers—meaning that they run from a starting value (1, January) to an ending value (12, December) without interruption or skips—then the JVM provides another shortcut operation for multiway decisions. The idea is simply that if the lowest possible value were (for example) 36, the next would have to be 37, then 38, and so forth. If the low and high ends of the spectrum are defined, the rest can be filled in as a table. For this reason, the operation is called `tableswitch`, and it's used as follows:

```
        iload_1                ; Assuming that "monthno" is stored in #1
        tableswitch 1 12       ; begin multiway branch, from 1 to 12
            Days31   ;
            Days28   ;
            Days31   ;
            Days30   ;
            Days31   ;
            Days30   ;
            Days31   ;
            Days31   ;
            Days30   ;
            Days31   ;
            Days30   ;
            Days31   ;
            default : Error    ;
Days28:
        bipush 28              ; Load 28 days
        istore_2               ; and assign to days (#2)
        goto ExampleEnd
Days30:
        bipush 30              ; Load 30 days
        istore_2               ; and assign to days (#2)
        goto ExampleEnd
Days31:
        bipush 31              ; load 31 days
        istore_2               ; and assign to days (#2)
        goto ExampleEnd
Error:
        ; take appropriate error actions like getstatic .../System/out
        ; and print an error message
        goto ExampleEnd
ExampleEnd:
        ; do whatever is needful
```

The only different operation in the `tableswitch` example is the `tableswitch` itself; the rest of the code is identical. The important differences are related to the structure of the table. The programmer needs to define the low and high values that the variable of interest can legitimately take, and then to sort the labels into increasing order, but not to pair the labels explicitly with their corresponding values. This will be done automatically by the table structure; in the example above, the fourth label (Days30) is automatically attached to the fourth value. As before, a default case is mandatory.

Of course, whether or not these jump tables will aid program efficiency varies from situation to situation and from problem to problem. A switch statement can always be written as an appropriate collection of if statements with appropriately complex conditions; in some cases, it may be easier to calculate a boolean condition than to enumerate the cases.

4.6 Subroutines

4.6.1   Basic Instructions

One major limitation of branch-based control is that after a block of code is executed, it will automatically transfer control back to a single and unchangeable point. Unlike traditional procedures in high-level programming languages, it is not possible to set up a block of code that can be run from any point in the program and then return to the place from which it came. (See figure 4.11.) In order to do this, more information—and new control structures and operations—are needed.

```
Part1:  ; do something
        ; do something
        goto UtilityProcedure       ; do some basic utility (sub)routine
                                    ; like calculate a square root
Part1Return:
        ; do something with the returned value
        ...

Part2:  ; do something
        goto UtilityProcedure       ; same basic utility (sub)routine
Part2Return:
        ; and do something different with this returned value
        ....

UtilityProcedure:
        ; take value(s) from the stack
        ; and perform calculations
        ...
        ; (sub)routine now finished
        goto ??????                 ; Where? Part1Return or Part2Return?

             ; There is no way to make this decision!
```

Figure 4.11   Subroutine return problem

The main piece of information needed is, of course, the location from which control was passed so that the program can use the same location as a point of return. This requires two basic modifications—first, that there be a branch instruction that also stores (somewhere) the value of the PC before the jump and, second, that there be another kind of branch instruction that will return to a variable location. A block of code written using these semantics is usually referred to as a **subroutine**.

The JVM provides a jsr (Jump to SubRoutine) instruction—all right, technically it provides two instructions, jsr and jsr_w, analogous to goto and goto_w—to fill this need. When the jsr instruction is executed, control is immediately passed (as with a goto) to the label whose offset is stored in the bytecode. Before this happens, though, the machine calculates the value $(PC + 3)$, the address of the next instruction that immediately follows the jsr instruction itself. This value is pushed onto the stack as a normal 32-bit (4-byte) quantity, and only then is control passed to the label.

SIDEBAR

Machine Language for `jsr`

To understand exactly how this works, let's look at the detailed machine code for the `jsr` instruction The `jsr` mnemonic corresponds to a single byte (0xA8). It is then followed by a 2-byte **offset**, stored as a signed short integer. Assume that memory locations 0x1000–0x1003 hold the pattern as shown in table 4.3.

Location	0x1000	0x1001	0x1002	0x1003
Byte value	0xA8	0x00	0x10	0x3b
Interpretation	`jsr`	Integer : 0x0010 = 16		istore_0

Table 4.3   Bytecode structure of `jsr` instruction

When the `jsr` instruction is executed, the PC will have the value 0x1000 (by definition). The next instruction in memory (`istore_0`) is stored at location 0x1003.

All machines that provide calls to subroutines also provide instructions for **returning** from subroutines. It is fairly easy to see how this could be accomplished on a stack-based computer; the return instruction would examine the top of the stack and use the value stored there, which we piously hope was pushed by a `jsr` instruction, as the location to which to return. This location becomes the target of an implicit branch, control returns to the main program, and computation proceeds merrily on its way.

Things are slightly more complicated on the JVM, primarily for security reasons; the `ret` instruction does not examine the stack for the location to return to, but instead accepts as an argument the number of a local variable. The first task any subroutine must perform, then, is to store the value (implicitly) pushed by the `jsr` instruction into an appropriate local variable—and once that is done, to leave this location untouched. Trying to perform computations on memory addresses is at best dangerous, usually misleading, and in Java and related languages, outright illegal. Again, this is something that the security model and verifier will usually try to prevent.

4.6.2   Examples of Subroutines

Why Subroutines?

One common use for a subroutine is as something akin to a Java method or C++ procedure: to perform a specific fixed task that may be needed at several points in the program. An obvious example would be to print something. As has been seen in earlier examples, something as simple as printing a string can be rather tricky and take several lines. To make the program easier and more efficient, a skilled programmer can make those lines into a single subroutine block accessed via `jsr` and `ret`.

Subroutine Max(int A int B)

Let's start with a simple example of a subroutine to do arithmetic calculations. An easy example would calculate (and return) the higher of two integers.[1] Let's assume that the two numbers are on the stack (as integers), as in figure 4.13.

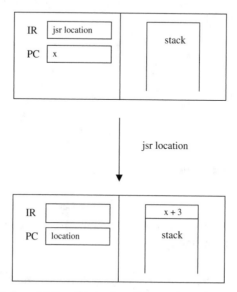

Figure 4.12   `jsr` instruction and stack

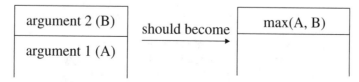

Figure 4.13   Stack structure for max (A,B)

The `if_icmp??` instruction will do the appropriate comparision for us but will pop (and destroy) the two numbers. So before doing this, we should duplicate the top two words on the stack using `dup2`. Before doing that, though, any subroutine must handle the return address. For simplicity, we will store that in local variable #1.

---

[1] When the `jsr` instruction is executed, the value 0x1003 is pushed (as an address) onto the stack, and the value of the PC is changed to 0x1000 + 0x0010, or 0x1010. This implies that the program will jump 16 bytes forward and begin executing a new section of code. When the `ret` instruction is executed, transfer will return to location 0x1003 and the `iconst_0` instruction. The `jsr_w` instruction is similar, except that it involves a 4-byte offset (thus possibly a longer jump) and the value PC+5 is pushed. (See figure 4.12.)

```
      ; assume that this is called via jsr Max, with
      ; the two integers already on the stack
Max:
      astore_1                ; stores return (a)ddress in #1

      dup2                    ; copy two arguments for later use
      if_icmpgt Second        ; branch if A < B
First:
      ; A >= B, so need to delete B from stack
      pop
      goto Exit
Second:
      ; A < B, so need to swap A to top and delete it
      swap
      pop
Exit:

      ret 1     ; return to the location stored in #1
```

Subroutine Printstring (String s)

For a second example, we'll write (and use) a subroutine to output a fixed string pushed on the stack. Let's write the subroutine first:

```
      ; assume that this is called via jsr Printstring, with
      ; the string to be printed already pushed onto the stack
      ; (below the return address
PrintString:
      astore_1 ; stores return (a)ddress in #1

      ; assume that the string to be printed is already on the stack

      ; you should already know the next three lines
      getstatic java/lang/System/out Ljava/io/PrintStream
      swap       ; put the arguments in the right order
      invokevirtual java/io/PrintStream/println(Ljava/lang/String;)V

      ret 1     ; return to the location stored in #1
```

The new instruction `astore_1` is just another example of the `?store_N` instruction, but it stores an address (type 'a') instead of a float, double, int, or long. The `getstatic` and `invokevirtual` lines should already be familiar. The code assumes that the calling environment pushed the string prior to executing the jump-to-subroutine call—and thus merely pushes the System.out object and invokes the necessary method. Once this is done, the `ret` instruction uses the value newly stored in #1 as the location to return to Notice, however, that there is still very little "information hiding" or block structure and that, in particular, this subroutine will irretrievably destroy any information that had been stored in local variable #1. If a programmer wants to use this particular code block, she needs to should be aware of this behavior. More generally, for any subroutine, it is important to know what local variables are and aren't used by the subroutine, since they're in the same set of local variables used by the main program.

Using Subroutines

The main program can be as complex as we like and may involve several calls to this subroutine. How about some poetry?

```
; push the first string/line to be printed
ldc "'Twas brillig, and the slithy toves"
; call the subroutine beginning at PrintString
jsr PrintString  ; return to immediately after this line
                 ; note that no label is needed

; and continue in similar fashion
ldc "Did gyre and gimble in the wabe."
jsr PrintString

ldc "All mimsy were the borogroves"
jsr PrintString

ldc "And the mome raths outgrabe."
jsr PrintString

; never forget to cite your sources
ldc "(from Jabberwocky, by Lewis Carroll)"

return   ; quit the method, since we've printed the poem
```

A complete version of this program is presented in Figure 4.14. (Actually, there is a deliberate error in this figure. One line will not be printed. Can you figure out which line it is and why? More importantly, do you know how to correct this error?)

4.7 Example: Monte Carlo Estimation of π

4.7.1 Problem Definition

Today, everyone knows the value of π (3.14159 and a bit). How did mathematicians figure out its value? Many approaches have been tried over the centuries, including one notable not for its mathematical sophistication, but instead for its simplicity. We present here a modification of this method, which was originally used by Georges de Buffon.

Consider throwing darts (randomly and uniformly) at the diagram shown in figure 4.15. We assume that the darts can land anywhere within the square; in particular, some of them will land inside the circle and some won't. Since the square is 2 units on a side, it has a total area of 4. The circle, having area πr^2, has an area of π. Thus, we expect that the proportion of darts that land inside the circle will be $\frac{\pi}{4}$.

In other words, if we threw 10,000 darts at the diagram, we would expect about 7,854 of them to land inside the circle. We can even restrict our attention to the upper-right-hand quadrant and expect the same result.

```
; program to print first verse of Lewis Carroll s _Jabberwocky_

.class public jabberwocky
.super java/lang/Object

; the usual boilerplate
.method public <init>()V
    aload_0

    invokespecial java/lang/Object/<init>()V
    return
.end method

.method public static main([Ljava/lang/String;)V
    .limit stack 2
    .limit locals 2

    ; push the first string/line to be printed
    ldc " Twas brillig, and the slithy toves"
    ; call the subroutine beginning at PrintString
    jsr PrintString  ; return to immedately after this line
                     ; note that no label is needed

    ; and continue in similar fashion
    ldc "Did gyre and gimble in the wabe."
    jsr PrintString

    ldc "All mimsy were the borogroves"
    jsr PrintString

    ldc "And the mome raths outgrabe."
    jsr PrintString

    ; never forget to cite your sources
    ldc "(from Jabberwocky, by Lewis Carroll)"

    return   ; quit the method, since we've printed the poem

    ; assume that this is called via jsr Printstring, with
    ; the string to be printed already pushed onto the stack
    ; (below the return address)

PrintString:
    astore_1 ; stores return (a)ddress in #1

    ; assume that the string to be printed is already on the stack

    ; you should already know the next three lines
    getstatic java/lang/System/out Ljava/io/PrintStream;
    swap     ; put the arguments in the right order
    invokevirtual java/io/PrintStream/println(Ljava/lang/String;)V

    ret 1    ; return to the location stored in #1
.end method
```

Figure 4.14   Complete program (with one error) as a subroutine example

This method of exploration is often called **Monte Carlo simulation**. It can be a very powerful way of exploring a large probability space when you're not sure of the exact parameters of the space. It's also the sort of task at which computers excel, since the simple calculations (Where did the dart land? Is it inside or outside the circle?) can be repeated thousands or millions of times until you have an accurate enough answer.

4.7.2   Design

Section 3.4.1 discussed a bit of the theory and practice of random number generation. The code developed in that section can provide random integers for us, with a few changes. The main change

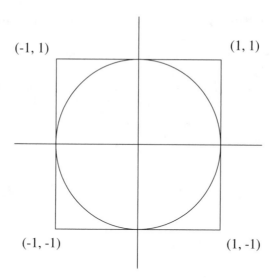

Figure 4.15 Diagram for Monte Carlo π estimation

```
(1)     total_hits <- 0
(2)     for (total_darts := 1 up to 10000)
(3)             generate (x,y) position for new dart
(4)             if ( (x,y) inside circle )
(5)                     total_hits <- total_hits + 1
(6)             endif
(7)     endfor
(8)     final answer is (total_hits / 10000)
(9)     FINAL final answer is (total_hits / 10000) * 4
```

Figure 4.16 Monte Carlo calculation of π in pseudocode

will be that every location (in the unit square) is defined by exactly two numbers, and hence we will need to call the generator from two separate places. This implies a subroutine.

Other than that, the program will need two counters, one for the number of darts thrown and one for the number of darts that land inside the circle. For any dart, if the position where it lands is (x,y), then it's inside the circle if and only if $x^2 + y^2 \leq 1$.[2]

The pseudocode for solving this problem might look something like Figure 4.16. The structure of the problem itself, involving repeated generation of random points and then totaling successes and failures, suggests some sort of loop. The actual decision concerning success or failure (inside or outside the unit circle) will be implemented with an if/then-equivalent structure. In summary, this program can be approached and designed using the same higher-order constructions that would be appropriate for other programming languages such as Java or Pascal.

---

[2] Use the distance formula if you're not sure why that works.

After this block has been executed enough times, the ratio of successes to total executions should approximate $\frac{\pi}{4}$.

For variables, we will need at least two integers to serve as counters, another location to hold the current value of the seed of the random number, two more to hold the (x,y) coordinates of the current dart, and a sixth to hold the return location from the random number generation subroutine. The necessary control structures have all been developed in earlier sections.

In particular, if variables #4 and #5 hold (as floats) the x and y coordinates, respectively, then the following block of code will increment the counter in #1 only if the dart is inside the circle:

```
        fload_4          ; load x coordinate from #4
        dup              ; square it
        fmul
        fload_5          ; load y coordinate from #5
        dup              ; square it
        fmul
        fadd             ; calculate x^2 + y^2
        fconst_1         ; push 1 for comparison
        fcmpg            ; compare
        ifgt Skip        ; go to Skip if outside the circle
        iinc 1 1         ; increment the counter in #1
Skip:    ; do whatever is needed
```

We can modify the first random number generator from section 3.4.2 to generate floating point numbers fairly easily, as in the following code fragment:

```
; compute a * oldvalue
ldc2_w    65537      ; a is 2^16 + 1, stored as a long
iload_3              ; oldvalue is stored as local variable #3
i2l                  ; convert oldvalue to a long
lmul                 ; and multiply

; add c
ldc2_w 5             ; c is 5, stored as a long
ladd                 ; and add to a*oldvalue

; and take the remainder mod m
ldc2_w 4294967291 ; load value for m
lrem                 ; calculate modulus
l2i                  ; convert back to integer
dup                  ; duplicate for storage
istore_3             ; store new value for next time

i2f                  ; convert to floating point number
ldc 4294967291.0   ; load m as floating point
fdiv                 ; divide to get number in [0,1)

; floating point is left on top of the stack
```

This fragment, in turn, will become the core of a subroutine to generate both x and y coordinates.

4.7.3 Solution and Implementation
The complete solution is presented here.

```
; program to calculate pi via Monte Carlo simulation

.class public pi
.super java/lang/Object

; boilerplate
.method public <init>()V
      aload_0
      invokespecial java/lang/Object/<init>()V
      return
.end method

.method public static main([Ljava/lang/String;)V
      .limit stack 4
      .limit locals 7

      iconst_0          ; number of darts thrown so far is 0
      istore_1          ; number of darts is in #1

      iconst_0          ; number of darts inside so far is 0
      istore_2          ; number of darts inside is in #2

      iconst_1          ; seed the random number generator with 1
      istore_3          ; RNG seed in #3

Head:
      iload_1           ; load number of darts thrown
      ldc 10000         ; compare to 10,000 darts
      if_icmpgt End     ; if more than 10,000, exit the loop

      jsr Random        ; get random float for x coordinate
      fstore 4          ; and store in #4

      jsr Random        ; get random float for y coordinate
      fstore 5          ; and store in #5

      fload 4           ; load x coordinate from #4
      dup               ; square it
```

```
      fmul
      fload 5          ; load y coordinate from #5
      dup              ; square it
      fmul
      fadd             ; calculate x^2 + y^2
      fconst_1         ; push 1 for comparison
      fcmpg            ; compare
      ifgt Skip        ; go to Skip if outside the circle
      iinc 2 1         ; increment number of darts inside in #2

Skip:
      iinc 1 1         ; increment total darts thrown in #1
      goto Head        ; and go to top of loop

Random:
      astore 6         ; store return value

      ; compute a * oldvalue
      ldc2_w   65537   ; a is 2^16 + 1, stored as a long
      iload_3          ; oldvalue is stored as local variable #3
      i2l              ; convert oldvalue to a long
      lmul             ; and multiply

      ; add c

      ldc2_w 5         ; c is 5, stored as a long
      ladd             ; and add to a*oldvalue

      ; and take the remainder mod m
      ldc2_w 2147483647 ; load value for m
      lrem             ; calculate modulus
      l2i              ; convert back to integer
      dup              ; duplicate for storage
      istore_3         ; store new value for next time

      i2f              ; convert to floating point number
      ldc 2147483647.0 ; load m as floating point
      fdiv             ; divide to get number in [0,1)
      ret 6            ; return to calling environment stored in #6

End:
      iload_2          ; load total darts inside
      i2f              ; calculate ratio in floating point
      iload_1          ; load total darts
      i2f              ; calculate ratio in floating point
```

```
        fdiv                ; divide for ratio (pi/4)
        ldc 4.0             ; multiply by 4
        fmul                ; to get final answer

        ; and print it
        getstatic java/lang/System/out Ljava/io/PrintStream;
        swap                ; arguments in correct order
        invokevirtual java/io/PrintStream/println(F)V
        return
.end method
```

4.8 Chapter Review

- The location of the instruction currently being executed is stored in the program counter (PC) inside the CPU. Under normal circumstances, every time an instruction is executed, the PC is incremented to point to the immediately following instruction.
- Certain instructions can alter the contents of the PC and thus cause the computer to change its execution path. These statements are often called branch statements or goto statements.
- Any statement that is the target of a branch must have a **label**; this is just a word, usually beginning with a capital letter, that marks its location in the code.
- The goto statement executes an unconditional branch; control is immediately transferred to the point marked by its argument.
- The if?? family of conditional branches may or may not transfer control to their target. They pop an integer off the stack and, depending upon the size and sign of that integer, will either branch or continue the normal fetch-execute cycle.
- The ?cmp family of statements are used to compare types other than integers. They pop two members of the appropriate type off the stack and push an integer with value 1, 0, or -1, depending on whether the first argument is greater than, equal to, or less than the second. This integer can then be used by a following if?? instruction.
- The if_icmp?? instructions combine the functions of an icmp statement with the conditional branches of the if?? family into a single instruction.
- Higher-order control structures such as if/else statements and while loops can—in fact, must—be implemented at the assembly language level using conditional and unconditional branches.
- The lookupswitch and tableswitch statements provide a way to execute multiway branch statements that may be more efficient ways of implementing case or switch statements than a series of if/else statements.
- Subroutines work by pushing the current value on the PC onto the stack and then returning to the previously saved location at the end of the subroutine. In jasmin, these correspond to the jsr and ret instructions, respectively. Unlike most other machines, the ret instruction expects to find its return location in a local variable for security reasons. Therefore, the first operation in a subroutine is usually the astore operation to store the (pushed) return location from the stack to a local variable.

4.9 Exercises

1. Why won't the JVM let you load an integer into the PC directly?
2. How can structured programming concepts be implemented in assembly language?
3. Is a "branch if greater than 0 or less than 0" instruction available in the JVM instruction set? If not, how would you implement it?
4. Is NaN (not a number) greater or less than 0.0?
5. How do you build an if/else-if/else-if/else control structure in `jasmin`?
6. What's the difference between `goto` and `goto_w`? Is there a corresponding `ifne_w`?
7. The code in Figure 4.8 uses `irem` to determine if a number is odd or even. Juola's law of multiple cat skinning states that there's always at least one more way to do anything. Can you find a way to use `iand` to determine if a number is odd or even? How about using `ior`?
8. How about using shift operations?
9. What is the error in Figure 4.14? What is the solution?
10. (For advanced programmers) Do the semantics of `jsr` and `ret` as presented in this chapter support recursion? Explain.

4.10 Programming Exercises

1. Write a program to determine the largest power of 2 less than or equal to N.
2. There are (at least) two different approaches to writing the previous problem, one using shift instructions and one using multiplication/division. Which one runs faster on your machine?
3. Write a program to determine the largest power of N that will fit into an integer local variable. In addition, determine the largest power of N that will fit into a long local variable. How can you tell when an overflow occurs?
4. Write a program to implement RSA encryption and decryption (you'll probably have to look this up on the Web) using the key N = 13*17 and e = 11.
5. a. Write a program to test how good the random number generator is. In particular, it should produce all outputs with about the same frequency. Generate 100,000 numbers (randomly) from 1 to 10. The least frequent number should be at least 90% as frequent as the most frequent one. How good is your generator?
   b. Find values of a, c, and m that produce a good generator.
   c. Find values of a, c, and m that produce a bad generator.
   d. (For advanced programmers) Run a chi-squared test on the output of your generator to determine how good it is.

Part the Second:
Real Computers

5

General Architecture Issues: Real Computers

5.1 The Limitations of a Virtual Machine

As a virtual machine, the JVM has been designed to be cleanly and simply implementable on most real computers. In some ways, the designers have succeeded brilliantly—the JVM is a very simple and easily understandable architecture, and one of the best machines for teaching computer organization and architectures. However, this simplicity is achieved, in part, by ignoring some of the real-world limitations of actual computer chips. For example, every method in the JVM is presumed to run in its own self-contained environment; changing a local variable in one method will not affect any other method. By contrast, on a physical computer, there is normally only one CPU and one bank of main memory, which means that two functions running at the same time within the CPU might compete for registers, memory storage, and so forth. You can imagine the chaos that might result if a check-writing program started picking up the data from, say, a computer game and started printing out checks payable to Starfleet Academy for the number of remaining photon torpedoes.

Similarly, issues of machine capacity are not issues for the JVM or similar virtual machines; the JVM machine stack has, for all practical purposes, an unlimited depth and an unlimited capacity for local variables. By contrast, the PowerPC (the chip inside a gaming console and until recently inside a Macintosh) has only 32 registers in which to perform calculations, and a Pentium-based Windows PC has even fewer.

Another major issue that the JVM can safely ignore is speed. To run a JVM program faster, you just run a copy of the JVM on a faster physical chip. Building a faster physical chip, by comparison, requires a difficult (and fiercely competitive) job of engineering. Engineers at Intel and Advanced Micro Devices (or any other chip manufacturing company) are always looking for edges that will let their chips run faster. Of course, with some of the most highly trained engineers in the world working on this problem, the details of how to do this are beyond the scope of this textbook, but the following sections will explore some ways of optimizing the components of a computer to improve its performance.

5.2 Optimizing the CPU

5.2.1 Building a Better Mousetrap

The most obvious way to get more performance out of the computer is simply to increase the overall performance numbers—for example, increasing the word size of the computer from 16 bits to 32 bits. Adding two 32-bit numbers can be done in a single operation on a 32-bit machine but will take at least two operations (and possibly more) on a 16-bit one. Similarly, increasing the clock speed from 500 MHz to 1 GHz should result in every operation taking half as long, or a 100% increase in machine performance

In practical terms, this is rarely as effective as one might think. For one thing, almost all machines today have 32 bits, and a 32-bit register is accurate enough for most purposes. Using a 64-bit register would let the programmer do operations involving numbers in the quadrillions more quickly—but how often do you need a quadrillion of anything? In addition, making a faster CPU chip might not be helpful if the CPU can now process data faster than the memory and bus can deliver it.

More seriously, though, increasing performance this way is expensive and difficult. The arithmetic hardware of a chip, for example, is limited by how fast it can be driven by the physical and electrical response characteristics of the transistors; trying to run them too fast will simply break them. Even if it were physically possible to make faster transistors (which it often isn't), the cost might be prohibitively high. This is particularly the case if one is trying to make a 64-bit machine at the same time, which requires not only making extremely expensive transistors, but also making twice as many of them. So, engineers have been forced to look for performance improvements that can be made within the same general technological framework.

5.2.2 Multiprocessing

One way to make computers more useful is to allow them to run more than one program at a time. (This way, you can be writing a paper for homework and pause to load a Web page and check some information at the same time that the computer is automatically receiving e-mail your roommate sent you and someone else is downloading your home page to see your latest pictures.) With only one CPU (and therefore only one instruction register), how does the computer juggle the load?

Aside from buying another CPU—which is possible, but expensive and technically demanding—a usual choice is **time-sharing**. As with time-sharing a vacation condominium, time is divided into slices (weeks for the condo, perhaps milli- or microseconds for the CPU), and you are allowed to use the equipment for one slice. After that slice of time ends, someone else comes in and spends his or her week in the condo or on the CPU. In order to make this work, the computer must be prepared to stop the program at any point, copy all the program-relevant information (the state of the stack, local variables, the current PC, etc.) into main memory, and then load another program's relevant information from a different area. As long as the time slices and the memory areas are kept separate (we'll see how both are done a bit later), the computer appears to be running several different programs at once.

For security reasons, each program must be able to run independently, and each program must be prevented from influencing other programs. On the other hand, the computer needs to have a programmatic way to swap user programs in and out of the CPU at appropriate times.

Rather than relying on the good citizenship of each user program, the solution is to create a special überprogram called the **operating system**, whose primary job is to act as a program control program, as in "program to control [other] programs," and enforcer of the security rules. The operating system (abbreviated OS, as in "MacOS," "OS X," and even "MS-DOS") is granted privileges and powers not permitted to normal user-level programs, including the ability to interrupt a running program (to stop it or shut it down), the ability to write to an area of memory irrespective of the program using it, and so forth—these powers are often formalized as **programming models** and define the difference between **supervisor**- and **user**- level privileges and capacities.

5.2.3   Instruction Set Optimization

One way to speed up a computer is to make the individual instructions faster. A particular instruction that occurs very frequently, for example, might be "tuned" in hardware to run faster than the rest of the instruction set would lead you to expect. This kind of optimization has already been seen on the JVM, for example, with the special-purpose iload_0 instruction. This instruction is both shorter (1 byte vs. 2) and faster than the equivalent iload 0 instruction. (Of course, almost every method can be expected to use local variable #0, but relatively few will need, say, local variable #245.) Depending upon the programs that are expected to be run, there may also be kinds of instructions that are expected to be very common, and the designers can optimize for that.

For example, on the multiprogramming system described above, "save all local variables to main memory" might be a commonly performed action. A more accessible example of a common and demanding application type is a graphics-heavy computer game. Good graphics performance, in turn, demands a fast way of moving data (bitmaps) from main memory to the graphics display peripheral. Loading data one word at a time into the CPU and then storing it (one word at a time) to the graphics card is probably not as fast as a hypothetical instruction to move a large block of data directly from memory to the graphics card. It shouldn't surprise you to learn that this kind of **Direct Memory Access** is supported by many modern computers as a primitive instruction type. Similarly, the ability to perform arithmetic operations on entire blocks of memory (for example, to turn the entire screen orange in a single operation) is part of the basic instruction set of some of the later Intel chips. "Doing the same operation independently on several different pieces of data" is a fundamental increase in processing power. By permitting **parallel** operations to proceed at the same time (this kind of parallel operation is called **SIMD** parallelism, an acronym for "Single Instruction, Multiple Data"), the effective speed of a program can be greatly increased.

5.2.4   Pipelining

Another way to try to make a CPU work faster is somehow to pack more instructions into a given microsecond. One possibility that suggests itself is to try to do more than one instruction at a time. In order to do this, the CPU must have a much more complex, **pipelined**, fetch-execute cycle that allows it to process several different instructions at once.

Wait a minute! How is this even possible? The trick is that, although the operations themselves have to be processed in sequence, each operation takes several steps, and the steps can be processed in an assembly-line fashion. As a physical example, consider the line of people involved in a bucket brigade for carrying water. Rather than carrying water the 40 feet from the well to the

	2 p.m.	3 p.m.	4 p.m.	5 p.m.	6 p.m.	7 p.m.
Wash	load 1			load 2		
Dry		load 1			load 2	
Fold			load 1			load 2

Figure 5.1   Unpipelined laundry: two loads in six hours

	2 p.m.	3 p.m.	4 p.m.	5 p.m.	6 p.m.	7 p.m.
Wash	load 1	load 2	load 3	load 4		
Dry		load 1	load 2	load 3	load 4	
Fold			load 1	load 2	load 3	load 4

Figure 5.2   Pipelined laundry: four loads in six hours

fire (a task that might take a minute), I instead accept a bucket from my neighbor and hand it off, moving the bucket perhaps 4 feet. Although the bucket is still 36 feet from the fire, my hands are now free to accept another bucket. It still takes each bucket a minute to get from the well to the fire, but 10 buckets can be moving at once, so 10 times as much water per unit time gets to the fire. A car assembly line is another good example; instead of putting cars together one at a time, every worker has a single well-defined job and thousands of cars are put together in small steps. More prosaically, if I have a lot of laundry to do, I can put one load in the washer; then, when it's done, I move that load to the dryer, place another load in the washer, and run both machines at once.

This kind of task breakdown occurs in a modern high-end CPU. For example, while part of the CPU (the dryer) is *executing* one instruction, a different part (the washer) of the CPU already be *fetching* a different instruction. By the time the instruction finishes executing, the next instruction is here and available to be executed. This procedure is sometimes called **instruction prefetch**; an instruction is fetched before the CPU actually needs it, so it's available at once. Essentially, the CPU is working on two instructions at once and, as a result, can perform twice as many instructions in a given time, as shown in figures 5.1 and 5.2. This doesn't improve the **latency**—each operation still takes the same amount of time from start to finish—but can substantially improve the **throughput**, the number of instructions that can be handled per second by the CPU as a whole.

The number of stages in a typical pipeline can vary from computer to computer in general, newer, faster computers have more stages in their pipeline. As an example, a typical mid-range PowerPC (model 603e, for example) uses a four-stage pipeline and so can handle up to four instructions at once. The first stage is the **fetch** stage, in which an instruction is loaded from program main memory and the next instruction to be performed is determined. Once an instruction has been fetched, the **dispatch** stage analyzes it to determine what kind of instruction it is, gets the source arguments from the appropriate locations, and prepares the instruction for execution by the third, **execute** stage of the pipeline. Finally, the **complete/writeback** phase transfers the results of the computation to the appropriate registers and updates the overall machine state as necessary (figure 5.3).

	$1\,\mu s$	$2\,\mu s$	$3\,\mu s$	$4\,\mu s$	$5\,\mu s$	$6\,\mu s$
fetch	instruction 1	instruction 2	instruction 3			
dispatch		instruction 1	instruction 2	instruction 3		
execute			instruction 1	instruction 2	instruction 3	
writeback				instruction 1	instruction 2	instruction 3

Figure 5.3   PowerPC-like pipeline

In order for this process to work as efficiently as possible, the pipeline must be full at all times, and data must continue to flow smoothly. First, a pipeline can only run as fast as its slowest stage. Simple things, like fetching a particular instruction, can be done as quickly as the machine can access memory, but the execution of instructions, especially long, involved ones, can take much more time. When one of these instructions needs to be executed, it can cause a blockage (sometimes called a "bubble") in the pipeline as other instructions pile up behind it like cars behind a slow-moving commuter. Ideally, each pipeline stage should consistently take the same amount of time, and designers will do their best to make sure that this happens.

The other easy way to break a pipeline is by loading the wrong data, fetching from the wrong location in memory. The worst offenders in this regard are conditional branches, such as "jump if less than." Once this instruction has been encountered, the next instruction will come either from the next instruction in sequence or from the instruction at the target of the jump—and we may not know which one. Often, in fact, we have no way of telling which, because the condition depends on the results of a computation ahead of us in the pipeline and therefore unavailable. Unconditional branches are not too bad if the computer has a way of identifying them quickly enough (usually in the first stage of the pipeline). Returns from subroutines create their own problems, because the target of the return is stored in a register and again may not be available. In the worst case, the computer may have no choice but to stall the pipeline until it is empty (which can seriously affect performance, since branch instructions are very common). For this reason, a lot of research has focused on the ability to predict the target of a branch well enough to continue and keep the pipeline full. **Branch prediction** is the art of guessing whether or not the computer will take a given branch (and to where). The computer will continue to execute instructions based upon this guess, producing results that may or may not be valid. These results are usually stored in special locations within the pipeline and then later copied to registers if the guess is confirmed correct. If the guess is wrong, these locations (and the pipeline) are flushed and the computer restarts with an empty pipeline. If you think about it, even the worst-case scenario is no worse than having to stall the pipeline—and if the computer guesses right, then some time has been saved.

Even a poor algorithm should be able to guess right about 50% of the time, since a branch is either taken or not taken. However, it's often possible to guess much more accurately by inspecting the program as a whole. For example, the machine code corresponding to a for loop usually involves a block of code and a (backward) branch at the end to the start of the loop. Since most such loops are executed more than once (often hundreds or thousands of times), the branch will be taken many, many times and not taken once. A guess of "take the branch" in this case could be accurate 99.9% of the time without much effort. A more sophisticated analysis would look at the history of each individual branch instruction. If the branch instruction has been executed twice and has not been taken in either case, then it might be a good bet that it won't be taken this time, either. By adapting the amount and kind of information available, engineers have become very accurate (well above 90%) at guessing, enough to make pipelining a crucial aspect of modern design.

5.2.5   Superscalar Architecture

The other technique concerning multiple different instructions involves duplication of pipeline stages or even entire pipelines. One of the difficulties in pipelining is keeping the stages balanced; if it takes substantially longer to execute a particular instruction than it did to fetch it, the stages behind it may back up. The idea underlying superscalar processing is to perform multiple different instructions at once in the same clock cycle. To fully understand this, we have to generalize the fetch-execute cycle somewhat and pretend that instead of just loading one instruction at a time, we have a queue of instructions waiting to be processed. (For obvious reasons, this is sometimes called an **instruction queue**—and there's no pretense involved.) A typical CPU will have separate modules duplicating possibly time-consuming operations. A good analogy involves adding a lane to a busy highway, allowing more traffic to flow. Alternatively, think of the way a typical bank operates, with several tellers each taking the next customer. If one customer has a serious problem, requiring more time than expected, then other tellers can take up the slack. Unlike the SIMD parallelism described earlier, this is an example of **MIMD** (Multiple Instruction, Multiple Data) parallelism. While one pipeline is performing one instruction (perhaps a floating point multiplication) on a piece of data, another pipeline can be doing an entirely different operation (perhaps loading a register) on different data.

SIDEBAR

The Connection Machine

If you want to see a really scary version of parallel operations, check out the architecture of the Connection Machine, built by Thinking Machines Corporation in the late 1980s. The CM-1 (and the later, faster CM-2) model incorporates up to 65,536 different "cells," each a 1-bit individual processor. All cells are connected to a central unit called the "microcontroller," which issues the same "nanoinstructions" to each one. The CM-5 model can only handle 16,384 different processors, but each one is as powerful as a Sun workstation. These processors run individually but are connected to a very fast, flexible internetwork to allow high-speed parallel computation.

The original CM-1 involved a custom cell architecture manufactured in groups of 16 cells to a chip. These chips, in turn, were connected to each other in the form of a 12-way **hypercube** to create a very dense network fast enough to keep all the cells informed about each other. Conceptually, the Connection Machines were an attempt to explore the possibilities of massive parallelism, as exemplified by the human brain, and to transcend some of the traditional limits of the Von Neumann architecture. A typical neuron isn't capable of very powerful computations, but the 10^{12} neurons in a normal human can do amazing things. In practical terms, the CM-1 can be seen as an example of 64K-way SIMD parallelism. Unfortunately, the cost of the special-purpose chips was prohibitive, so the CM-5 switched to a smaller number of commercial SPARC chips, thereby abandoning SIMD processing (like the human brain) in favor of MIMD. The descendants of the CM-5 are very active today—for example, in the kind of parallel processing done by a Beowulf cluster.

5.3 Optimizing Memory

To make sure that the computer runs as quickly and smoothly as possible requires two things. First, the data the computer needs should be available as quickly as possible so that the CPU doesn't need to waste time waiting for it. Second, the memory should be protected from accidental rewriting so that, for example, the user mail agent doesn't misread data from a Web browser and mail the contents of the page you're looking at to someone else.

5.3.1 Cache Memory

On a computer with a 32-bit word size, each register can hold 2^{32} (about 4 billion) patterns. In theory, this allows up to about 4 gigabytes of memory to be used by the processor. In practice, the amount installed on any given machine is usually much less, and the amount actually used by any given program is usually smaller yet. Most importantly, the program generally uses only a small fraction of the total program size at any given instant (for example, the code in a Web browser to download a page is used only when you actually click a button).

Memory comes in many different speeds; that is, the amount of time that it takes to retrieve a bit from memory varies from chip to chip. Because speed is valuable, the fastest memory chips also cost the most. Because most programs use a relatively small amount of memory at a time, most real computers use a multilevel memory structure. Although the CPU chip itself may be running at 2 or 3 GHz, (executing one instruction every 300 to 500 trillionths of a second), most memory chips are substantially slower, sometimes taking 50 or 100 billionths of a second (a twentieth to a tenth of a microsecond) to respond. This may still seem fast, but it is about 400 times slower than the CPU chip itself. To reduce this memory access bottleneck, the computer will also have a few chips of very-high-speed memory but with much smaller capacity (usually a few megabytes at most) called **cache memory**. (The word is pronounced "CASH" memory, from the French verb *cacher*, meaning "to hide.") The basic idea is that frequently and recently used memory locations are copied into cache memory so that they are available more quickly (at CPU speeds!) when the CPU needs them. The proper design and use of cache memory can be a tricky task, but the CPU itself takes care of the details for you, so the programmer doesn't need to worry about it. Most computers support two different kinds (levels) of cache: level one (L1) cache is built into the CPU chip itself and runs at CPU speed, while level two (L2) cache is a special set of high-speed memory chips placed next to the CPU on the motherboard. As you might expect,

L1 cache is faster and more expensive, which means that it is the smallest but can provide the greatest performance boost.

5.3.2 Memory Management

With this same 32-bit word size, a computer can write to a set of 2^{32} different memory locations. (On the 64-bit computer, of course, there are 2^{64} different addresses/locations.) These define the **logical memory** available to the program. Of course, the amount of physical memory available on any computer depends on the chips attached, which in turn depends at least partly on how much money the computer's owner is able and willing to spend. Rather than referring to specific physical locations in memory, the program refers to a particular logical address which is reinterpreted by the **memory manager** to a particular physical location, or possibly even on the hard disk.

Normally, memory management is considered to be a function of the operating system, but many computers provide hardware support in the interests of speed, portability, and security. Security concerns, though, make it almost essential that the user-level programs not have access to this hardware. This means that most of the interesting parts of the memory system are invisible to the user and are available only to programs operating in **supervisor** mode. As far as the user is concerned, memory is simply a flat array the size of logical memory, any element of which can be independently accessed. There is little fuss or complexity involved. This is important enough to be worth repeating: user-level programs can assume that logical addresses are identical to physical addresses and that any bit pattern of appropriate length represents a memory location somewhere in physical memory, even if the real physical memory is considerably larger or smaller than the logical address space.

Under the hood, as it were, is a sophisticated way of converting (and controlling the conversion of) logical memory addresses into appropriate physical addresses. This conversion allows the computer to access memory locations that directly correspond to the machine's physical (real) memory layout This process uses a set of address substitutions to convert one address space (logical memory) into another (physical memory). The resulting memory process and memory address space is thus usually called **virtual memory**. For simplicity of explanation, we'll focus on a somewhat abstracted memory manager taken broadly from a 32-bit PowerPC. There are several different methods of performing this sort of conversion, as detailed here.

5.3.3 Direct Address Translation

The simplest method of determining the physical address, **direct address translation**, occurs when hardware address translation has been turned off (only the supervisor can do this, for obvious reasons). In this case, the physical address is bit for bit identical to the logical address, and only 4 gigabytes of memory can be accessed. If two processes try to access the same logical address, there's no easy way to prevent it. This is usually done only in the interests of speed on a special-purpose computer expected to run only one program at a time; otherwise, most operating systems enforce some kind of address transtation.

5.3.4 Page Address Translation

To prevent two processes from accessing the same physical address (and if address translation is enabled), the memory management system of the CPU actually expands logical address space into a third space, called **virtual address space**. For example, we could define a set of 24-bit **segment registers** to extend the value address. In our case, the top 4 bits of the logical address will define and select a particular segment register. The value stored in this register defines a particular **virtual segment identifier** (VSID) of 24 bits (plus a few extra fields). The **virtual address** is obtained by concatenating the 24-bit VSID with the lower 28 bits of the logical address, as shown in figure 5.4. This creates a new 52-bit address capable of handling more memory and thereby prevent collisions.

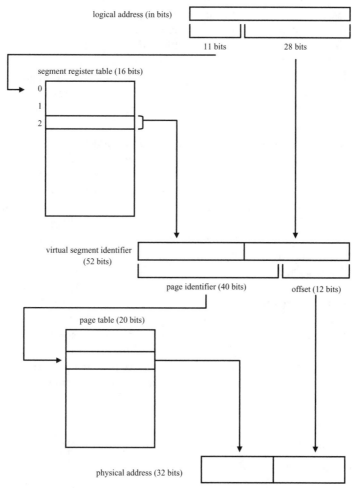

Figure 5.4 Diagram of idealized PowerPC-like virtual memory structure

For example, let's say that the computer wants to access memory location 0x13572468 (a 32-bit address). The top 4 bits (0x1) indicate that the computer should look at segment register #1. Suppose further that this register contains the (24-bit) value 0xAAAAAA. Concatenating this to the original memory location yields the 52-bit VSID 0xAAAAAA3572468. On the other hand, if another program wanted to access the same *logical* address, but the value in the segment register were instead 0xBBBBBB, the VSID for this second program would be 0xBBBBBB3572468. Thus, two different programs, accessing the same logical location, would nevertheless get two separate VSIDs. This explains how local variable #1 could be in two different memory locations (VSIDs) for two different programs.

Of course, no machine yet built has had 2^{52} bytes of memory (that would be about 4,000,000,000,000,000 bytes, 4 million gigabytes, or 4 *peta*bytes—now there's a word to drop into dinner conversations!). What physical memory is present is actually addressed through yet another table. Physical memory is divided into **pages** of 4196 (2^{12}) bytes each. Each 52-bit virtual address can be thought of as a 40-bit page identifier (this is the 24-bit VSID and a 16-bit page identifier extracted from the original logical address), plus a 12-bit offset within a given page. The computer stores a set of "page tables," in essence a hash table that stores the physical location of each page as a 20-bit number. The 40-bit page identifier is thus converted, via a table lookup, to a 20-bit physical page address. At the end of this process, the final 32-bit physical address is simply the page address plus the offset.

It's not quite as confusing as it sounds, especially if you look at figure 5.4. It involves, however, a potentially large amount of work. So, why does the computer go through such an involved process? There are several advantages. First, not every page in virtual memory need be stored in physical memory. When pages are not often used, it may be possible to "swap them out" and store them on a long-term storage device such as a peripheral. (This is the original reason for talking about "virtual memory," the idea that the computer can access "memory" that isn't really there, but instead is on the hard drive. This lets the computer run programs that are much larger than would physically fit into memory at the expense of speed.) Another advantage is that the same logical address can be made to refer to different physical addresses by changing the value in the segment registers. Finally, this allows a certain degree of security to be added on a page-by-page basis. A given page (in the page table) can be labeled "supervisor-only," meaning that only supervisor-level programs can read or write to locations on that page. A page can similarly be labeled "read-only" (programs can load data from locations on that page but not save to locations on that page); "supervisor write-only" (user-level programs can load, but only supervisor-level programs can save); or the most inclusive, "read/write" (where any program can load or save). This will keep user-level programs from, for instance, scribbling over crucial operating system data.

5.4 Optimizing Peripherals

5.4.1   The Problem with Busy-Waiting

To get the best performance out of peripherals, they must not be permitted to prevent the CPU from doing other useful stuff. Computers are so fast that they can usually outrun almost any other physical process. As a simple example, a good human typist can type about 120 words per minute, which means approximately one character every tenth of a second. A 1 GHz computer can add 100,000,000 numbers together between two keystrokes. Thus, a computer should be able to do lots and lots of number crunching while still keeping up with the word processing program. But how does the computer respond to (infrequent, by its standards) keystrokes in a timely fashion while still doing its job?

A dumb method of handling this involves **polling**, checking to see if anything useful has happened at periodic intervals. In high-level pseudocode, the operation would look like this:

```
while (no key is pressed)
    wait a little bit
figure out what the key was and do something
```

Polling is an inefficient use of the CPU, because the CPU has to spend a lot of time repeatedly checking to determine whether or not something has happened. For this reason, it's sometimes called **busy-waiting**, because the computer is "busy" waiting for the key to be pressed and can't do any other useful work.

5.4.2   Interrupt Handling

A more intelligent way of dealing with an expected future event is to set up a procedure to follow when the event occurs and then to do whatever else needs doing in the meantime. When the event happens, one will **interrupt** the current task to deal with it, using the previously established procedure.

This is more or less how most computers deal with expected but unpredictable events. The CPU establishes several different kinds of **interrupt** signals that are generated under preestablished circumstances such as the press of a key. When such an event occurs, the normal fetch-execute cycle is changed slightly. Instead of loading and executing the next instruction (defined in the PC), the CPU will consult a table of **interrupt vectors** that contains a program location for each of the possible interrupts. Control is then transferred (as though through a `call` or `jsr` to a subroutine) to that location, and the special **interrupt handler** will be executed to do whatever is needful. (On computers with official programming modes, this also usually marks the point at which the computer switches from user to supervisor mode.) At the end of the interrupt handler, the computer will return (normally, as from a subroutine) to the main task.

On most computers, the possible interrupts for a given chip are numbered from 0 to a small value (like 10). These numbers also correspond to locations programmed into the interrupt vector. When interrupt number 0 occurs, the CPU will jump to location 0x00 and execute whatever code is stored there. Interrupt number 1 would jump to location 0x01, and so forth. Usually, all that is stored at the interrupt location itself is a single branch instruction to transfer control (still inside the interrupt handler) to a larger block of code that does the real work.

This interrupt handling mechanism can be generalized to handle system-internal events as well. For example, the time-sharing aspect of the CPU can be controlled by setting an internal **timer** (a detailed discussion of how such timers might work will be presented in chapter 9). When the timer expires, an interrupt will be generated, causing the machine, first, to switch from user to supervisor mode and, second, to branch to an interrupt handler that swaps the programming context for the current program out and the context for the next program in. The timer can then be reset and computation resumed for the new program.

5.4.3   Communicating with the Peripherals: Using the Bus

As discussed in chapter 1, data must move between the CPU, memory, and peripherials using one or more **buses**. This is analogous to traveling from your house to the store using one or more roads; depending upon the quality of the roads, the skill of the drivers, and the amount of traffic, the trip can be faster or slower. Whether you're a computer or a shopper, you would like the trip to be as fast as possible.

There are two key issues involved in the typical use of a bus. The first is that, electrically, a bus is usually just a set of wires connecting all the components together at the same time. This means that a bus acts as a small-scale broadcast medium, where every peripheral gets the same message at the same time. The second is that only one device can use the bus at one time; if the keyboard and hard drive both try to send data, neither will succeed. To use a bus successfully requires discipline from all parties involved. This discipline usually takes the form of a strict protocol involving communication in a stylized, formal way. A typical bus protocol might involve the CPU sending a START message and then an identifier for a particular device. Every device will receive both of these messages, but only the specific device will respond (typically with some sort of ACKNOWLEDGE) message. All other devices have been warned by this START message not to attempt to communicate until the CPU finishes and sends a similar STOP message. Only the CPU and the specific device are allowed to use the bus during this time, which reduces contention and traffic flow problems.

5.5   Chapter Review

- As a virtual machine, the JVM is freed from some practical limitations that affect the design and performance of physical chip-based architectures.
- With the chip market as competitive as it is, engineers have developed many techniques to squeeze better performance out of their chips. These tend to involve improvements in both security and speed.
- One way to get better user-level performance is to improve the basic numbers—size, speed, latency—of the chip, but this is usually a difficult and expensive process.
- Another way to improve the performance of the system (from the user's perspective) is to allow it to run more than one program at a time. Computers can do this via **time-sharing**, where the program runs in very short spurts and programs are swapped in and out.
- When engineers know what sorts of programs will be run on a to-be-designed computer, they can create special-purpose instructions and hardware specifically to support those programs. An example of such a program would be computer games, which place specific demands on the graphics processing capability of a computer. The Pentium processor provides basic machine-level instructions to speed up graphics performance.
- Performance can also be increased by **parallelism**, the execution of more than one instruction at a time. **SIMD parallelism** differs from **MIMD parallelism** in the kinds of instructions that can be simultaneously executed.
- Significant performance enhancement can be obtained by a form of parallelism called **pipelining**, in which the fetch-execute cycle is broken down into several stages, each of which is independently (and simultaneously) executed. For example, by executing one instruction while fetching the next, the computer can get 100% speedup in **throughput**, even while **latency** remains the same.

- **Superscalar architecture**, in which entire pipeline stages are replicated several times, provides another way to speed up processing by doing the same thing several times simultaneously.
- Memory access time can be reduced by using **cache memory** to speed up access to frequently used items.
- Memory management techniques such as **virtual memory** and **paging** can provide computers with access to greater amounts of memory more quickly and securely.
- By preventing the computer from wasting time checking to determine if an expected event has happened, **interrupts** can achieve substantial performance increases.
- A suitably designed bus protocol can speed up the movement of data within the computer by reducing competition for traffic slots.

5.6 Exercises

1. What kinds of storage limitations does a physical computer have that the JVM stack can ignore?
2. a. What advantages would a 128-bit CPU have over a 64-bit CPU?
   b. How significant are these advantages?
3. Would a special-purpose instruction to store the entire contents of the stack in memory and retrieve the contents from memory be helpful to the JVM?
4. What enhancement(s) would you make to the JVM architecture if you were in charge? Why?
5. Give two real-world examples of pipelining in addition to those mentioned in the text.
6. How would you apply branch prediction to the `lookupswitch` instruction?
7. Give two real-world examples of superscalar processing in addition to those given in the text.
8. How should a cache determine what items to store and what items to discard?
9. Explain how memory management allows two programs to use the same memory location at the same time without conflict.
10. How would **memory-mapped I/O** interact with a virtual memory system?

6

The Intel 8088

6.1 Background

In 1981, IBM released the first generation of its Personal Computer, later known to all and sundry as the IBM-PC. As a relatively low-cost computer produced by a company whose name was a household word (Apple already existed but was only known to the hobbyist market, and few other computer companies you have heard of even existed at the time), it was a runaway success, dominating business purchases of "microcomputers" almost instantly.

At that time the computer was sold with only 64K of RAM and no hard drive (people loaded programs onto the computer from ($5^{1/4}$-inch floppy disks). The chip inside this machine, manufactured by the Intel corporation, was designated model number 8088. Today, the legacy of the 8088 persists in computers all over the world that are still based on the original 8088 design.

Technically, the 8088 was a second-generation chip based on the earlier 8086 design. The differences between the two chips were subtle; both were 16-bit computers with a segmented memory architecture. The big difference between them was that the 8086 had a 16-bit data bus, so the entire contents of a register could be flushed to memory in a single bus operation. The 8088 had only an 8-bit data bus, so it took a little longer to load or store data from the CPU into memory, but the chip was also a little cheaper to produce, which reduced the overall price of the IBM-PC (and hence improved its marketability).

With the success of the 8088-based IBM-PC, Intel and IBM had a ready market for later and improved chips. The 80286 (the 80186 was designed but never sold well as the base for a personal computer) incorporated security features into an otherwise laughably insecure 8088, as well as running much more quickly. This chip was the basis for the IBM-PC/Advanced Technology, also known as the PC/AT.

The 80386 increased the number of registers and made them substantially larger (32 bits each), making the chip even more powerful. Further improvements followed with the 80486 and the Pentium (a renamed 80586), which will be discussed in detail in chapter 8. These later chips, plus the original, are sometimes called the **80x86 family**.

To a certain extent, the 8088 is of historical interest only; even as a low-cost microcontroller (for example, the kind of chip that figures out how brown your toast should be or which floor to stop the elevator on), it competes with many other architectures based on more modern principles and technology. However, later generations of the Intel 80x86 family have all adhered to the principle of **backward compatibility** in the interest of preserving their existing customer base. For example, in 1995, when the Pentium was introduced, millions of people were running software on their existing 80486 systems. Rather than force people to buy new software as well as new hardware (which might have caused them to buy software and hardware from another company, like Apple), the designers made sure that programs written for the 486 would still run on the Pentium. Since this decision was made at every stage, programs written in 1981 for the IBM-PC should still run on a modern P4. Of course, they won't be able to take advantage of modern improvements such as increased speed (the original PC ran at 4 *Megahertz*, while a modern system runs 1000 times faster), improved graphics resolution, and even modern devices such as mice, USB keychain drives, and so forth. But because of backward compatibility, an understanding of the 8088 is important to comprehand the modern Pentium architecture.

6.2   Organization and Architecture

6.2.1   The Central Processing Unit

At the grossest possible level of abstraction, the CPU of the Intel 8088 closely resembles that of most other processors, including the JVM (figure 6.1). Data is stored in a set of general-purpose registers, operated on by the instructions fetched and decoded inside the control unit, in keeping with the laws of arithmetic as defined by the circuitry of the ALU. There are, however, a few subtle but significant differences.

The first difference is that because the 8088 is a physical chip, its capacities (for example, the number of registers) are fixed and unchangeable. The 8088 contains eight so-called "general-purpose" registers. Unlike the JVM stack, these are not organized in any particular way, and they are given names instead of numbers. These registers are named

    AX   BX   CX   DX
    SI   DI   BP   SP

Although these are called "general-purpose" registers, most of them are tuned with additional hardware to make specific operations run faster. For example, the CPU has special-purpose instructions tuned to use CX as a loop counter, and the AX/DX pair is the only pair optimized for integer multiplication and division. The SI and DI registers support special high-speed memory transfers (SI and DI stand for **source index** and **destination index**, respectively), and the BP register is usually used for stack instructions for local function variables and function parameters.

In addition to these registers, the 8088 has several special-purpose registers that can't be used for general computation. The most important of these is probably the IP (**instruction pointer**) register, which holds the location of the next instruction to be executed. (On other machines, this register might be called the **program counter** or PC, as they're synonymous.) Four **segment registers** (CS, SS, DS, and ES) are used to enable access to more memory and to structure memory access. Finally, the FLAGS register holds a set of individual bits that describe the result of the current computation, such as whether or not the last operation resulted in a zero, a positive, or a negative number.

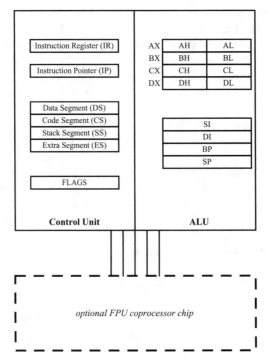

Figure 6.1   Block diagram of the 8088 CPU

All of these registers are 16 bits wide. This means that the 8088 has a 16-bit word size and that most operations (can) deal in 16-bit quantities. If for some reason a programmer wants to use smaller representations, she can use fractions of the general-purpose registers. For example, the AX register can be subdivided and used as two 8-bit registers, called the AH (**high**) and AL (**low**) registers (figure 6.2). There are all just (sections of) the same register, so changes in one will effect changes in all. If you loaded the value 0x5678 into the AX register, this would, as a side effect, set the value in AL to 0x78 and the value in AH to 0x56. Similarly, clearing the AL register at this point would set the value in the AX register to 0x5600. This kind of subdivision is valid for all general-purpose registers; the BX register can be divided into the BH and BL registers, and so on.

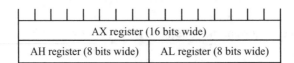

Figure 6.2   Register subdivision in the 8088

Almost all values in the 8088 registers are stored in 16-bit (or smaller) signed two's complement notation. Unlike the JVM, the 8088 also supports unsigned integer notation. In most operations (for example, moving data around, comparing whether two bit patterns are the same, or even adding two patterns), it doesn't matter whether or not a given bit pattern is supposed to be a signed or an unsigned quantity, but for the few in which it is important, there are two different operations to handle the two cases. As an example, to multiply two unsigned quantities uses the mnemonic MUL; to multiply two different signed quantities, one uses the mnemonic IMUL.

The registers defined above handle most of the work that a 8088 computer might perform, from memory accesses, to control structures and loops, to high-speed integer processing. For high-speed floating point processing, a separate section of the chip is designed to be a logically separate Floating Point Unit (FPU). This FPU has its own set of eight registers, each 80 bits wide for high-precision operations, structured like a stack. The data stored in these registers uses a different, and specialized, kind of floating point representation, similar to standards discussed earlier, but with more bits for both the mantissa and the exponent. There are also a few additional registers, both as part of the FPU (for example, the FPU has its own instruction register) and for certain special-purpose operations.

6.2.2 The Fetch-Execute Cycle

The fetch-execute cycle on the 8088 is almost identical to that on the JVM; the value stored in the IP register is used as a memory location, and the value stored in that location (the one pointed to by the IP register) is copied ("fetched") into the instruction register. Once the instruction value has been fetched, the value in the IP register is incremented (to point to the next instruction) and the fetched instruction is executed by the CPU.

The only limitation is the size of the IP register itself. With only 16 bits, the IP register can access only about 65,000 different locations, and hence only (at most) about 65,000 different instructions. This would appear to place stringent limits on the size of programs; in particular, no program could be larger than 64K. Fortunately, the memory management techniques described in the next section increase this limit somewhat, essentially by recruiting extra bits from other registers to increase the address space.

6.2.3 Memory

On a computer with a 16-bit word size, each register can hold 2^{16} (about 65,000) patterns. This means that any register holding a memory address (for example, the IP) can point to only 65,000 different locations, which by modern standards is hardly enough to be worth the effort. (A quick reality check: the text processing software used to typeset this book takes up 251,864 locations, excluding the editing and printing software. Eeek.) Even in 1981, 64Kbytes of memory was regarded as a very small amount.

There are several solutions to this problem. The easiest one is to make each pattern/location refer not to a single byte of memory, but to a word (or even a larger unit). This reduces efficiency when storing data items smaller than a word (such as characters in a string) but makes it possible to address more memory.

The designers of the 8088 used a slightly more complex approach. The memory of the 8088 was divided into **segments** of 64 Kbytes each. Each segment contains exactly as many memory bytes as can be addressed by a normal 16-bit register, but these addresses are interpreted *relative to a base address defining a particular segment.* As you might expect from the name, the segment definitions are stored in the so-called **segment registers**.

Unfortunately, the math at this point gets a little tricky. The segment registers themselves are 16 bits wide. The actual (sometimes called the **absolute**) address used is calculated by multiplying the value in the relevant segment register by 16 (equivalent to shifting its value to the left by four binary places, or one hexadecimal place) and then adding it to the value in the appropriate general-purpose register or IP (called the **offset**). For example, if the value stored in the segment register were 0xC000, this would define a segment starting value of 0xC0000. An offset of 0x0000 would correspond to the (20-bit) location 0xC0000, while an offset of 0x35A7 would correspond to the absolute location 0xC35A7. Each of these locations corresponds to exactly 1 byte.

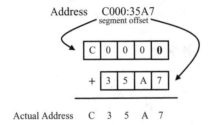

Figure 6.3   Segment: offset calculations illustrated

There is no particular reason that a segment must start at an even multiple of 64K. Loading a value of 0x259A would define a segment starting at the value of 0x259A0. In fact, any location ending with a hexadecimal value of 0 is a possible starting location for a segment. In the segment defined above, the segment value of 0x259A plus a hypothetical offset 0x8041 would yield an absolute address of (0x259A0+0x8041) or location/byte 0x2D9E1. For simplicity, such address pairs are often written in the form **segment:offset**, such as 259A:8041. In this scheme, legitimate addresses run from 0x00000 (0000:0000) to 0xFFFFF (F000:FFFF). It should also be noted that there are usually many segment:offset pairs that refer to a given location. The location F000:FFFF is also the location FFFF:000F, as well as F888:777F (figure 6.3).

In common practice, the four segment registers are used in conjunction with different offset registers to define several different types and uses of memory. They correspond (roughly) to

- CS (code segment): The code segment register is used in conjunction with the IP (instruction pointer) to define the location in memory of the executable machine instructions (the program **code**).
- DS (data segment): The data segment register is used in conjunction with the general-purpose registers AX, BX, CX, and DX to control access to global program data.
- SS (stack segment): The stack segment register is used in conjunction with the stack registers (SP and BP) to define stack frames, function parameters, and local variables, as discussed below.
- ES (extra segment): The extra segment register is used to hold additional segments—for example, if a program is too large to fit into a single code segment.

Even with this segmented memory model, the computer could still access only 2^{20} different locations, or 1 megabyte. Even this much memory wasn't available in practice, since (by design) some of this megabyte was reserved as video memory instead of general-purpose program memory. In practical terms, programmers could only access the first 512K of memory for their programs. Fortunately, by the time computers with more than 1 megabyte of memory became financially practical, the design of the 8088 had been superseded by later generations of the same family, including the Pentium. Memory access on the Pentium is substantially different, in part to avoid this 1-megabyte restriction.

6.2.4   Devices and Peripherals

The modern computer can be attached to a bewildering array of peripherals, ranging from simple keyboards and monitors through business accessories such as scanners and fax machines through truly unusual specialist devices such as vending machines, toasters, and medical imaging devices. Because 80x86-based machines are so common, it's not unusual to see almost any device being designed and built to interface with a 8088.

From the computer's (and computer designer's) point of view, however, the task is simplified somewhat by the use of standardized interface designs and ports. For example, many computers come with an IDE controller chip built into the motherboard and attached directly to the system bus. This controller chip, in turn, is attached to a set of cables that will plug into any IDE-style drive. When the controller gets the appropriate signals (on the system bus), it interprets these signals for the drive. Any manufacturer of hard drives can simply make sure that they follow the IDE specifications and work with (almost) any PC. The PCI (Peripheral Component Interconnect) provides similar standardization, connecting main memory directly to a variety of devices. Perhaps the most widely used connection out there is the USB (Universal Serial Bus) connection. This provides a standardized high-speed connection to any USB-supported device, ranging from a mouse to a printer. The USB controller itself will query any new gadgets attached to figure out their names, their types, and what they do (and how they do it). The USB port can also provide power, as well as communicate with these devices at almost network speeds. From the programmer's point of view, however, the advantage is that one need only write a program to communicate with the USB controller, greatly simplifying the task of device communication.

6.3 Assembly Language

6.3.1   Operations and Addressing

The 8088 is considered to be a textbook example of CISC (Complex Instruction Set Computing) at work. The set of possible operations that can be performed is large, and the possible operations are themselves correspondingly powerful. One side effect of the CISC design is that some simple operations can be performed in several different ways using different machine operations; this usually means that Intel's designers decided to provide a shortcut optimization for some specific uses of registers.

Because registers are named, instead of numbered or indexed (as in the JVM), the basic operation format is a little different. On the JVM, it is enough to simply say "add"; the two numbers to be added (addends) are automatically on the top of the stack, and the result is automatically left at the top of the stack when the addition is complete. On the 8088, things are different; the programmer must specify where the addends are stored and where the sum should be kept.

For this reason, most 8088 instructions use a two-argument format as follows:

```
MNEMONIC      operand1, operand2    ; possible comment
```

Usually the first operand is called the **destination operand** (sometimes abbreviated **dst**), and the second operand is called the **source operand** (abbreviated **src**). The fundamental idea is that data is taken from the source (but the source is otherwise left unchanged), while the computation result is left in the destination. So, to add (mnemonic: ADD) the value in CX to the value in AX (and leave the resulting sum in AX), the 8088 assembly language instruction would be

```
ADD    AX, CX            ; really means AX = AX + CX
```

Because there are eight general-purpose 16-bit registers, there are 64 (8 · 8) different ADD instructions. But in fact, there are more, since one can also add 16-bit or 8-bit values, as in

```
ADD    AH, BL            ; AH = AH + BL
```

The 8088 also supports several different **addressing modes** or ways of interpreting a given register pattern to refer to different storage locations. In the simplest examples, given above, are the values stored in a register are the values used in the computation. This is sometimes called **register mode** addressing. By contrast, one can also use **immediate mode** addressing, in which the data to be used is written into the program itself, as in

```
ADD    AX, 1             ; AX = AX + 1
```

Note that this makes sense only if the 1 is the second (src) operand. Trying to use immediate mode addressing for the destination operand will result in an error. Also note that this is an example of the power of CISC computing, since this operation would take two separate instructions on the JVM—one to load the integer constant 1 and another to perform the addition.

Either immediate data or register values can also be used as memory addresses, telling the computer not what the value is but where it can be found. For example, if location BX held the address of a particular 8-bit value, we could add that value to the current value held in CL with the following statement. The square brackets ([ ]) show that the register BX holds a value to be used in **indirect mode** (we'll get to direct mode presently) as the address of a location in memory:

```
ADD    CL, [BX]          ; CL = CL + whatever value is
                         ; stored in the location indexed
                         ; by BX
```

This is a tricky concept, so let's explore it a little bit more. Notice that these two statements do different things:

```
ADD     BX, 1              ; increment BX
ADD     [BX], 1            ; increment the value pointed to
                           ; by BX
```

How do they differ? Let's assume that the value stored in BX is 4000. Performing the first operation would increment the value in BX itself, making it equal to 4001. By contrast, the second operation would leave the value in BX alone (it stays 4000) but try to increment the value stored at memory location 4000, whatever that value was. (Actually, there would be an error here, for reasons we will discuss in section 6.4.1. But basically, although we know that there is a value at location 4000, we don't know whether it's a byte, word, doubleword, or something else. So how can the computer increment something whose size is unknown?) Similarly, executing

```
ADD     AX, [4000h]        ; add the value stored in 4000h to AX
```

looks at memory location 0x4000 (the number in brackets is automatically interpreted as a hex-adecimal quantity because of the trailing h) to figure out what the 16-bit quantity stored there is and then adds that quantity—not 0x4000—to whatever is stored in AX. In this case, where no register is involved and a defined constant memory location is used, we refer to it as **direct mode**.

These addressing modes can be used with the ADD operation in almost any combination, with two exceptions. It's legitimate, for example, to add one register to another, to add a memory location to a register or a register to a memory location, or to add an immediate value to either a register or memory. However, it's not legal to add one memory location directly to another memory location; one addend or the other must be placed in a register first. It's also illegal, and rather silly, to try to use an immediate value as the destination of an addition. So, in the following list of operations, the first five are legal but the last two are not.

```
ADD     AX, BX             ; register-to-register
ADD     AX, [4000]         ; memory-to-register
ADD     AX, 4000           ; immediate-to-register
ADD     [4000], AX         ; register-to-memory
ADD     [4000], 4000       ; immediate-to-memory
ADD     [3000],[4000]      ; illegal!  memory-to-memory
ADD     4000, AX           ; illegal!  ANYTHING-to-immediate
```

Each of these operations and addressing modes is expressed using slightly different machine code. In machine code, the complexity is increased by the existence of special-purpose (and faster) instructions for the 8088 to be used when the destination is specifically the AX register. Armed with this kind of instruction, an intelligent programmer (or compiler) can make the program faster and shorter by putting data to be added into AX rather than any other register. (We've already seen this kind of instruction on the JVM with examples like iload_1 as a shortcut for the more general iload instruction. Confusingly, most assemblers don't use different mnemonics for the high-speed AX instructions; instead, the assembler program itself will recognize when a special-purpose instruction can be used and automatically generate it. This means that the assembly language programmer doesn't need to worry about these instructions if the assembler is smart enough.) This kind of register designed for high-speed arithmetic is sometimes called an **accumulator**, and the 8088 technically has two different ones—or at least two parts of the same register used as accumulators. The AX register serves as a 16-bit accumulator and the AL register as an 8-bit accumulator.

6.3.2   Arithmetic Instruction Set

This two-operand format is common for most arithmetic operations. For example, instead of adding two numbers, one can subtract them using the SUB instruction:

```
SUB    BX, AX            ; BX = BX - AX
```

The 8088 also recognizes a MOV instruction for moving to and from memory or registers, using the same two-argument conventions in which the first is the destination and the second is the source. It also recognizes AND, OR, and XOR instructions of the same format; these all also have the special accumulator shortcuts.

There are also a number of one-argument instructions, such as INC (increment), DEC (decrement), NEG (negate—that is, multiply by -1), and NOT (toggle/reverse all bits in the argument, equivalent to doing an XOR operation with a second argument of all 1s). The format is fairly simple:

```
DEC    AX                ; AX = AX - 1
```

Multiplication and division are more complicated. The reason is simple: when you add (for instance) two 16-bit integers, you get more or less a 16-bit result, which will still fit into the 16-bit register. When you multiply these numbers, the result can be up to 32 bits long (which will not fit). Similarly, integer division actually produces two results, the quotient and the remainder (example: $22/5 = 4$ remainder 2, just like in elementary school). The 8088 chip thus coopts additional registers for the results of multiplication and division—and because of the complexity of the necessary hardware, it can only use a few specific register sets for these operations.

To multiply two numbers, the first number must already be present in the accumulator (of whatever bit size is appropriate). The multiplication instruction itself (MUL) takes one argument, which is the second number to multiply. The product is then placed in a pair of registers, guaranteeing that multiplication will never overflow. Table 6.1 shows how and where information flows in multiplication operations

(The DX-AX register pair is sometimes abbreviated as DX:AX; the AH:AL pair is usually abbreviated as the AX register.)

Multiplier	Multiplicand	High half of product	Low half of product
AL	argument	AH	AL
AX	argument	DX	AX

Table 6.1   Information flow in 8088 multiplication

To multiply the numbers 59 and 71 as 16-bit values, the code fragment below could be used. First, the (decimal) value 59 is loaded into the AX register via a MOV instruction, and the value 71 is similarly loaded into the BX register. Then the value in the accumulator (AX) is multiplied by the value in BX. The result will be left in DX:AX. Specifically, AX will hold the lowest 16 bits of the results (the decimal value 4189, stored as 0x105D), while DX holds the highest 16 bits, which in this specific case would be all 0s.

```
MOV     AX, 59          ; AX gets multiplicand
MOV     BX, 71          ; BX gets multiplier
MUL     BX              ; DX:AX = AX * BX
```

There are actually two different multiplication instructions, one for unsigned integer multiplication (MUL) and one for signed integers (IMUL). The register use in both cases is the same; the only difference is whether the highest bit in the multiplicand and multiplier is treated as a sign bit or a data bit. For example, the value 0xFF (as an 8-bit quantity) is either -1 (as a signed quantity) or 255 (as an unsigned quantity). MULtiplying 0xFF by itself would result in storing 0xFF01 in the AX register, while the IMUL instruction would produce 0x0001 (since -1 times itself is, of course, 1).

Division uses the same rather complicated register sets, but in reverse. The dividend (the number to be divided) is put into a pair of registers, either the AH:AL pair or the DX:AX pair. The argument to the division is used as the divisor. The quotient is stored in the low half of the original register pair and the remainder in the high half. Using a previous example:

```
MOV DX, 0               ; clear DX
MOV AX, 22              ; DX:AX = 22
MOV BX, 5               ; divisor is 5
DIV BX                  ; perform division
                        ; DX now holds 2
                        ; AX now holds 4
```

As with multiplication, there are two instructions, DIV and IDIV, performing unsigned and signed integer division, respectively.

6.3.3   Floating Point Operations

The 8088 FPU is almost a separate, self-contained computer with its own registers and its own idiosyncratic instruction set specifically for performing floating point operations. Actually, it *is* a separate, self-contained chip, sold under the model number 8087 as a **math coprococessor**. Data is transported as necessary from the main CPU of the 8088 to the coprocessor and back. The unnamed 8087 registers are a stack (yes, just like the JVM) of eight 80-bit-wide storage locations, and again, just like the JVM, the instruction set is structured to address the operation type as well as the representation type.

The FPU can store and process three different types of data: standard IEEE floating point numbers, integer values, and a special format called **binary-coded decimal (BCD)**, where each 4-bit group represents the binary encoding of a single base-10 digit. This format was often used by IBM mainframe computers, because it was easy for engineers to reinterpret the binary patterns as (intuitive) decimal numbers and vice versa. Inside the 8087, all these formats are converted to and stored in an 80-bit format that is substantially more precise than the standard format defined by the IEEE.

Operations for the FPU all begin with the letter F (again, this should be familiar to JVM programmers) and operate as one might expect on the top of the stack, like the JVM or a reverse Polish calculator. The FADD instruction pops the top two elements of the FPU stack, adds them together, and then pushes the result. Other arithmetic operations include FSUB, FMUL, and FDIV, which perform as expected. There are two additional operations: FSUBR and FDIVR, which perform subtraction (division) in "reverse," subtracting the top of the stack from the second element instead of subtracting the second element from the top.

SIDEBAR

Other FPU Argument Formats

Although the FPU always manipulates data using an internal 80-bit "extended precision" format, data can be loaded/stored in main memory in a variety of formats. Conversion happens at load/store time, depending upon the operation mnemonic used. There are many different instructions, most of which have several interpretations, as follows:

- Integers: Integer data, either 16- or 32-bit, is loaded with the FILD instruction. On later machines, 64-bit quantities can also be loaded with this instruction.
- BCD integers: Integer data in 80-bit **Binary-Coded Decimal** format is loaded with the FBLD instruction.
- Floating point numbers: Floating point numbers, in 32-bit, 64-bit, and 80-bit lengths, are loaded with the FLD instruction

Once these quantities are loaded, they are treated identically by the FPU. To store a value, replace "LD" with "ST" in the mnemonics above.

There are also special-purpose instructions like FSQRT to handle common math functions like square roots and trigonometric functions.

Data can be pushed (loaded) into the FPU stack via the FLD instruction. This actually comes in three flavors: FLD loads a 32- or 64-bit IEEE floating point number from a given memory location, FILD loads a 16- or 32-bit integer from memory (and converts it to an internal floating point number), and FBLD loads an 80-bit BCD number from memory (and converts it). There are a few special-purpose operations for commonly used constants: FLD1 loads the value 1.0, FLDZ loads 0.0, FLDPI loads an 80-bit representation of π, and a few other instructions specify quantities like commonly used logarithms, such as the natural log of 2. To move data from the FPU to storage, use some variation of the FST instruction—again, there are variations for integer (FIST) and BCD (FBST) storage. Some operations have additional variations, marked with a trailing -P, to pop the stack when the operation is complete (for example, FISTP STores the Integer at the top of the stack, and then Pops the stack). One limitation of the FPU is that data can only be loaded/stored from memory locations, not directly from ALU registers. So a statement like

```
FILD    AX                      ; Illegal! can't use register
```

is illegal; the value stored in AX must first be MOVed to a memory word and then loaded from that location as follows:

```
MOV     Location,AX             ; Move AX to memory
FILD    Location                ; Load from memory to FPU
```

6.3.4   Decisions and Control Structures
Like most assembly languages, the 8088 control structures are built on unconditional and conditional jump instructions, in which control is transferred to a label declared in the source code. As with the JVM, this is actually handled by computing an offset and adding/subtracting that offset to the current location in the program counter. The format of the jump instruction (mnemonic: JMP) is also familiar to us:

```
LABEL: JMP    LABEL                     ; silly infinite loop
```

Conditional jumps use a set of binary **flags** grouped together in the **FLAGS register** in the CPU. These flags hold single-bit descriptors of the most recent result of computation; for example, the zero flag **ZF** is **set** if and only if the result of the most recent operation (in the ALU) was a zero. The sign flag **SF** contains a copy of the highest bit (what would be the sign bit if the result is a signed integer) and is set if-and-only-if the result of the last number is negative. The carry bit **CF** is set if-and-only-if the most recent computation generated a carry out of the register, which (when unsigned calculations are being performed) signals a result too large for the register. The overflow bit **OF** handles similar cases, where when signed calculations are performed, the result is too large (or too small) for the register. There are several other flags, but these are the main ones used.

A conditional jump has a mnemonic of of the form "Jcondition," where "condition" describes the flag setting that causes the jump to be taken. For example, JZ means jump-if-zero-flag-set, while JNZ means jump-if-zero-flag-not-set. We can use this to test whether two values are equal:

```
    SUB    AX, BX                  ; AX = AX - BX
                                   ; set ZF if AX now == 0
    JZ     ISEQUAL
    ; if we got here, AX didn't equal BX
    JMP    OUTSIDE                          :
```

```
ISEQUAL:
        ; if we got here, AX did equal BX
OUTSIDE:
        ; rejoin after if/else statement
```

Other conditional jumps include JC/JNC (jump if CF set/clear), JS/JNS (jump if SF set/clear), JO/JNO (jump if OF set/clear), and so forth. Unfortunately, not all of the flags have nice, clear arithmetic interpretations, so a second set of conditional jumps are available to handle proper arithmetic comparisons such as "greater than," "less than or equal to," and so forth. These instructions interpret flags in combination as appropriate to the arithmetic relationship.

In more detail, these additional jumps expect that the flags register contains the result of SUBtracting the first number from the second, as in the example fragment immediately above. (This is a micro-lie; wait a bit for a more detailed explanation of the CMP instruction.) To determine whether one signed integer is greater than another, the JG (Jump if Greater) mnemonic can be used. Other mnemonics include JL (Jump if Less), JLE (Jump if Less than or Equal), and JGE (Jump if Greater or Equal). These also exist in negative form—JNGE (Jump if Not Greater or Equal) is, of course, identical to JL—and are in fact implemented as two different mnemonics for the same instructions. Similarly, JE exists, and is equivalent to the previously defined JZ, and JNE is the same as JNZ.

For comparison of unsigned integers, a different set of instructions is needed. To understand why, consider the 16-bit quantity 0xFFFF. As a signed integer, this represents −1, which is less than 0. As an unsigned integer, this represents the largest possible 16-bit number, a shade over 65,000—and this, of course, is greater than 0. So the question "is 0xFFFF > 0x0000?" has two different answers, depending upon whether or not the numbers are signed. The 8088 provides, for this purpose, a set of conditional branch instructions based on Above and Below (i.e., JA, JB, JAE, JBE, JNA, JNB, JNAE, JNBE) for comparing unsigned numbers. So, to determine if the value stored in AX would fit into an 8-bit register, the following code fragment is used:

```
        ; version one of 8-bit safety test
        SUB    AX, 100h                    ; subtract 2^8 from AX
        JAE    TOOBIG                       ; unsigned compare
        ; If it gets here, the number is fine
        JMP    OUTSIDE
TOOBIG:
        ; if it gets here, AX is bigger than 8 bits
OUTSIDE:
        ; continue doing what's needed
```

One problem with this code fragment is that in order to set the flags properly, the value of AX must be modified. One possible solution is to store the value of AX (MOV it to a memory location) and reload it after setting the flags. This would work, and the MOV instruction has been specifically set up to leave the flags register alone and to preserve the previous settings. So, we can rewrite our 8-bit safety test, with slightly less space and time efficiency, as

```
        ; version two of 8-bit safety test
        MOV     SOMEWHERE, AX                   ; store AX SOMEWHERE
        SUB     AX, 100h                        ; subtract 2^8 from AX
        MOV     AX, SOMEWHERE                   ; restore AX, leave flags
        JAE     TOOBIG                          ; unsigned compare
        ; If it gets here, the number is fine
        JMP     OUTSIDE
TOOBIG:
        ; if it gets here, AX is too big
OUTSIDE:
        ; continue doing what's needed
```

The Intel instruction set provides a better solution with a special-purpose command. Specifically, the CMP mnemonic performs a nondestructive subtraction. This instruction calculates the result of subtracting the second argument from the first (as has been done in the examples above), and sets the flags register accordingly, but does not save the subtraction result anywhere. So, rewriting the first version as

```
        ; version three of 8-bit safety test
        CMP     AX, 100h                        ; compare 2^8 to AX
        JAE     TOOBIG                          ; unsigned compare
        ; If it gets here, the number is fine
        JMP     OUTSIDE
TOOBIG:
        ; if it gets here, AX is bigger than 16 bits
OUTSIDE:
        ; continue doing what's needed
```

preserves the efficiency of the first version while not destroying the value stored in the registers.

In addition to these fairly traditional comparison and branch instructions, Intel provides a few special-purpose instructions (this is getting repetitive, isn't it?) to support efficient loops. The register tuned for this purpose is the CX register. Specifically, the computer can be told to jump if the value of CX is 0 with the JCXZ instruction. Using this instruction, one can set up a simple counter-controlled loop with

```
        MOV     CX, 100                         ; loop 100 times
BEGIN:
        ; do something interesting
        DEC     CX                              ; subtract 1 from counter
        JCXZ    LOOPEXIT                        ; quit if done (CX==0)
        JMP     BEGIN                           ; return to BEGIN
LOOPEXIT:
        ; now outside of loop
```

Even more tersely, the LOOP instruction handles both the decrementing and the branch—it will decrement the loop counter and branch to the target label if the counter has not yet reached 0. Thus, we can simplify the loop above to a single statement of interest:

```
        MOV    CX, 100                              ; loop 100 times
BEGIN:
        ; do something interesting, quit when CX == 0
        LOOP  BEGIN                         ; return to BEGIN
        ; now outside of loop
```

Using the results of floating point comparisons can also be tricky. The basic problem is that the flags register is located in the main CPU (in the Control Unit), which also handles branch instructions through the PC in the Control Unit. At the same time, all the floating point numbers are stored in the FPU in a completely separate section of silicon. The data must be moved from the FPU into the normal flags registers, using a set of special-purpose instructions perhaps beyond the scope of this discussion.

SIDEBAR

Oh, all right. If you insist. The FPU provides both an FCOM instruction, which compares the top two elements on the stack, and an FTST instruction, which compares the top element to 0.0. This comparison is stored in a "status word," the equivalent of the **flags register**. To use the information, the data must be moved, first to memory (because the FPU cannot access CPU registers directly), then to a register (because the flags register cannot access memory directly), and finally to its eventual destination. The instruction to do the first is FSTSW (STore Status Word, which takes a memory location as its single argument); for the second, an ordinary MOV into the AX register suffices; and for the third, the special-purpose SAHF (Save AH in Flags) instruction is used. Ordinary unsigned conditional jumps will then work properly. The complexity of this process explains and illustrates in part why it can be so much faster to use integer variables when writing a computer program.

6.3.5   Advanced Operations

The 8088 provides many more operations, of which we will only be able to touch on a few. Many of them, perhaps most, are shortcuts to perform (common) tasks with fewer machine instructions than would be needed using the simpler instruction(s). An example is the XCHG (eXCHanGe) instruction, which swaps the source and destination arguments around. Another example is the XLAT instruction, which uses the BX register as a table index and adjusts the value in AL by the amount stored in the table. Essentially, this is a one-operation abbreviation for AL = [[AL] + BX], which would take several steps to perform using the primitive operations described earlier. (It's useful, for example, if you need to convert a string to UPPERCASE quickly, but it doesn't make possible anything previously impossible.)

The 8088 also supports operations on string and array types, using (yet another set of) special-purpose instructions. We'll see these in action a little in section 6.4.4, since strings and arrays generally have to be be stored in memory (registers aren't big enough).

As we will see, this tendency to use additional operations becomes much more pronounced in later members of the family, and the instruction set becomes substantially larger and more complex, to the point where almost no human programmer today knows all of the Pentium 4 instructions in detail. (This is one reason that writing a good compiler is both tricky and important. The smarter you make the compiler, the dumber the programmer can be.)

6.4 Memory Organization and Use

6.4.1 Addresses and Variables

The segmented organization of the 8088's memory has already been described. Every possible register pattern represents a possible byte location in memory. For larger patterns (a 16-bit word or a 32-bit "double," or even an 80-bit "tbyte," containing 10 bytes and holding an FPU value), one can coopt two or more adjacent byte locations. As long as the computer can figure out how many bytes are in use, accessing memory of varying sizes is fairly simple.

Unfortunately, this information is not always available to the computer. An earlier micro-lie suggested that

```
ADD     [BX], 1             ; increment the value pointed to
                            ; by BX
```

was legal. Unfortunately, the value stored in BX is a location; therefore, there is no easy way of knowing whether the destination is a 16-bit or an 8-bit quantity. (Similarly, we don't know whether we need to add 0x0001 or 0x01.) Depending upon these sizes, this statement could be interpreted/assembled as any of three different machine instructions. The assembler (and we) need a hint to know how to interpret [BX]. This would also apply when a specific memory address is used directly, as in

```
ADD     [4000h], 1          ; increment the value at 0x4000
```

There are two ways of giving the computer such a hint. The simpler, but less useful, is to explain exactly what is meant in that line, and in particular, that [4000h] should be interpreted as the address of ("pointer to") a word (16 bits) by rewriting the line:

```
ADD     WORD PTR [4000h], 1  ; increment the 16-bit value at 0x4000
```

By contrast, using BYTE PTR would force an 8-bit interpretation, and using DWORD PTR (double word) a 32-bit one.

A more general solution is to notify the assembler in advance of one's intention to use a particular memory location and of the size one expects to use. The name of this memory location can then be used as shorthand for the contents of the location as a direct mode operation. This has approximately the same effect as declaring a variable in a higher-level language such as Java, C++, or Pascal. Depending upon the version and manufacturer of the 8088 assembly, either of the following will work to define a 16-bit variable (with names selected by the programmer):

```
example1    WORD    1000   ; 1000
example2    DW      2000h  ; 2000h == 0x2000
```

The values can now be used in direct mode more or less at will:

```
MOV    AX, example1        ; AX is now 1000
ADD    example2, 16        ; example2 is now 2010h
CMP    AX, example2        ; is AX > example2? (no)
```

This statement serves several purposes. First, the computer now knows that two 16-bit chunks of memory have been reserved for program data. Second, the programmer has been relieved of the burden of remembering exactly where these chunks are, since she can refer to them by meaningful names. Third, the assembler already knows their sizes and can take them into account in writing the machine code. That's not to say that the programmer can't override the assembler

```
exple3 WORD    1234h         ; define 16-bit space
ADD    BYTE PTR exple3, 1    ; legal but silly
```

but it is very likely to result in a bug in the program. (By contrast, of course, the JVM gets very annoyed if you try to access only part of a stored data element and generally won't let you do it.)

Assemblers will accept a wide variety of types for memory reservation, including some types so big that they can't be handled easily in registers. Using the more modern syntax, any of the following are legal definitions:

```
Tiny   BYTE   12h                  ; single byte
Small  WORD   1234h                ; two bytes
Medium DWORD  12345678h            ; four bytes
Big    QWORD  1234567812345678h
                                   ; eight bytes
Huge   TBYTE  12345678901234567890h
                                   ; ten bytes
                                   ; (used by FPU)
```

Floating point constants can be defined with either REAL4 (for 32-bit numbers), REAL8 (for 64-bit) or REAL10 (for 80-bit). The number values themselves are usually written either normally or in exponential notation:

```
Sqrt2  REAL4  1.4143135    ; real number
Avogad REAL8  6.023E+23    ; exponential notation
```

Memory locations can be defined without initializing them by using ? as the starting value. Of course, in this case the memory will still hold some pattern, but it's not predictable just what it is, and if you try to use that value, bad things will probably happen.

6.4.2   Byte Swapping

How does storage in memory compare with storage in registers? Specifically, if the 16-bit pattern 0100 1001 1000 0101 is stored in the AX register, does it have the same value as the same 16-bit pattern stored in memory?

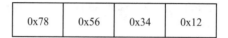

| 0x78 | 0x56 | 0x34 | 0x12 |

Figure 6.4   Memory storage of 0x12345678, illustrating byte swapping

The answer, surprisingly, is "no." (Perhaps it's not that surprising, since if it really were that simple, this section of the book probably wouldn't exist.) Again, as a legacy of older machines, the 8088 has a rather odd storage pattern.

When writing down numbers, people usually use so-called **big-endian** notation. The so-called **most significant** numbers (the ones corresponding to the highest powers of the base) are written (and stored) first, and the smaller, less significant numbers trail afterward. Quick check for clarification: numbers are traditionally written on paper in big-endian format; the first digit written involves the largest power of the base. The 8088 CPU similarly stores values in registers in big-endian order. The value written above (0x4985) would thus represent the decimal value 18821. Data stored in memory, however, are actually stored in **little-endian** format by bytes. The byte with the smaller address (0x49, 0100 1001) is the **least significant byte**; the second is the most. (Miss Williams, my seventh-grade English teacher, would have insisted that, with only 2 bytes, one can't have a "most" significant byte, only a "more" significant one. This is one area where specialized jargon trumps traditional English grammar.) So, this pattern in memory would represent 0x8448, almost twice as large. This pattern continues with larger numbers, so the 32-bit quantity 0x12345678 would be stored as 4 separate memory bytes, as in figure 6.4.

Fortunately, the programmer rarely needs to remember this. Any time data is moved to or from memory, byte swapping happens automatically at the hardware level. Unless the programmer explicitly overrides the assembler's knowledge of data sizes (as in the previous section), the only time this might become important is in dealing with large groups of data such as **arrays** and their extension, strings, or in moving data from one type of machine to another. (Of course, "rarely" doesn't mean "never," and when it does become important, this can be a source of the sort of error that can make you pound your head against a wall for a week.)

6.4.3   Arrays and Strings

The same notation used to reserve a single memory location can also be used to reserve large, multilocation blocks of memory. Values can be set using either a comma-separated list of values or a shorthand DUP notation for repeated values. For example,

```
Greet  BYTE   48h,45h,4Ch,4Ch,4Fh  ; ASCII "HELLO"
Thing  DWORD  5 DUP  0x12345678     ; 5 identical values
Empty  WORD   10 DUP (?)            ; 10 empty slots
```

define, respectively, Greet as a 5-byte array of the letters (H, E, L, L, and O), Thing as a set of doublewords, and Empty as an array of ten 2-byte values, none of which are initialized.

To access elements of these arrays, the programmer needs to index or offset from the named array base. If the 'H' in Greet were stored at 3000h, then the 'E' would be stored at 3001h, the first 'L' at 3002h, and the 'O' at 3004h. Of course, we don't know where Greet happens to be stored, but wherever it is, the location of the 'H' is one less than the location of the 'E.' By convention, the array name itself refers to the location of the initial value of the array. So, to load the first three letters into the AH, BH, and CH (byte) registers, we can use

```
MOV     AH, [Greet]              ; Load H
MOV     BH, [Greet + 1]          ; Load E
MOV     CH, [Greet + 2]          ; Load L
```

This is actually a new (to this book, at least) addressing mode called **index mode**. As before, the notation [X] means "the contents of memory stored at location X," but the X in this case is a rather complex value that the computer calculates on the fly. It should be intuitive that [Greet] is the same as [Greet + 0] and Greet itself, while [Greet + 1] is the next byte over. And because the computer knows that Greet holds bytes (as defined by the memory reservation statement), it will assume that [Greet + 1] is also a byte.

How do we access elements of the Empty array? The initial element is simply [Empty], or [Empty + 0], or even Empty itself. In this case, though, Empty holds WORD objects, so the next entry is not [Empty + 1] but [Empty + 2]! Unlike most high-level languages, where arithmetic on indices automatically takes the kind of elements involved into account, index mode addressing on the 8088 requires the programmer to handle size issues.

Index mode addressing has more general uses involving registers. In high-level languages, for example, one of the most common array actions is to use a variable index—for example, accessing element a[i] inside a loop involving an integer variable i. The assembly language equivalent uses a general-purpose register as part of the index expression. The expression [Greet + BX] would refer to the "BX-th" (if that word even makes sense) element of the array Greet. By adjusting the value in BX (say, from 0 to 4), the expression [Greet + BX] will sequentially select each element. Similarly, by adjusting the value in BX by 2, the size of a word, each time, we can initialize the entire Empty array to 0 with

```
        MOV     CX, 10           ; 10 elements in Empty
        MOV     BX, 0            ; start at [Empty + 0]
BEGIN:
        MOV     [Empty+BX], 0    ; zero out this element
        ADD     BX, 2            ; move to next WORD
        LOOP    BEGIN            ; loop until CX == 0
```

Only a few of the 16-bit registers can legally be used as an index in this sort of expression, and none of the 8-bit ones are legal. Only the BX, BP, SI, and DI registers can be used; and, bluntly, one shouldn't mess with the BP register for this purpose, as bad things are likely to occur. The BP register is already used by the operating system itself for its own nefarious purposes, as discussed later in section 6.4.7.

Experienced C and C++ programmers may already be chafing at the bit for a faster and more efficient way. Instead of calculating [Empty + BX] at each pass through the loop, why not set BX itself to the spot where [Empty + 0] is stored and then just use [BX]? This suggests code something like

```
        ; warning, doesn't work!
        MOV    CX, 10             ; 10 elements in Empty
        MOV    BX, Empty          ; start at [Empty+0] (WRONG!)
BEGIN:
        MOV    [BX], 0            ; zero out this element
        ADD    BX, 2             ; move to next WORD
        LOOP   BEGIN             ; loop until CX == 0
```

Although the idea is good, the execution falters, mostly because MOV BX, Empty doesn't actually mean what we hoped it would. The assembler treats Empty as a simple byte variable in direct mode and tries to move the first byte of Empty (the 'H') into BX. This isn't what we want. In fact, it isn't even legal, since we're trying to move a single byte into a 4-byte register, which results in a size conflict. To explicitly get a pointer variable, we use the OFFSET keyword, which produces the memory location instead of its contents.

```
        ; improved, functional version
        MOV    CX, 10             ; 10 elements in Empty
        MOV    BX, OFFSET Empty   ; start at [Empty + 0]
BEGIN:
        MOV    [BX], 0            ; zero out this element
        ADD    BX, 2             ; move to next WORD
        LOOP   BEGIN             ; loop until CX == 0
```

Of course, the actual time/space improvement gained may be marginal, since the index addition is still performed within a single machine operation on the 8088. But every little improvement may help, especially in a tight, small, often executed loop.

6.4.4 String Primitives

Strings can be implemented as arrays of characters (most often as bytes, but sometimes larger), as with the Greet example. The 8088 also provides some so-called **string primitive operations** for performing common string functions quickly and easily. These basic operations all use SI, DI, or both—that's the special purpose to which SI and DI are optimized—for these operations.

We'll focus, for the moment, on the simple task of copying or moving a string from one location to another. Depending upon the size of the string elements, there are two basic operations: MOVSB (MOVe a String of Bytes) and MOVSW (MOVe a String of Words). This twofold division based on size holds for all string primitives; there are also (for example) two variations for doing comparisons, ending with B and W, respectively. So, for simplicity of explanation, we'll fold these similarly behaving operations together under the name MOVS?.

The MOVS? operation copies data from [SI] to [DI]. By itself, it will copy only a single element, but it's easy to put it in a simple loop structure. The advantage of the string primitives is that the CPU supports automatic looping in the machine instruction, expressed at the assembly language level as a prefix to the mnemonic. The simplest example would be the REP prefix, as in

```
REP    MOVSB
```

This acts rather like the LOOP? instruction in that the CX register is used as a counter. Every time this instruction is performed, the values of SI and DI will be adjusted, the value of CX will be decremented, and the instruction will repeat until CX drops to 0.

There are two main variations in the way SI and DI are adjusted. First, the amount of the update automatically corresponds to the size of the element specified in the MOVS? command, so SI/DI will be changed by 1 for a Byte instruction or by 2 for a Word instruction. Second, a special flag in the flags register (the Direction flag) controls whether the addresses are adjusted from low to high (by adding to SI/DI) or from high to low (by subtracting). This flag is controlled by two instructions, as in table 6.2.

Instruction	Flag Status	SI/DI Operation	Address sequence
CLD	clear (=0)	addition	low to high
STD	set (=1)	subtraction	high to low

Table 6.2   Direction flag operations for string primitives

To see how this works, let's make a couple of arrays and copy them.

```
Arr1    WORD    100 DUP (-1)    ; source array : 100 words
Arr2    WORD    100 DUP (?)     ; dest array : also 100 words

MOV     SI, OFFSET Arr1         ; set source address
MOV     DI, OFFSET Arr2         ; set destination address
CLD                             ; clear direction flag
                                ; so goes from Arr1[0] to Arr1[99]
MOV     CX, 100                 ; loop over 99 words
REP     MOVSW                   ; .. and do the copy
```

Another common operation is to compare two strings for equality. This can be done with the CMPS? operation, which performs an implicit subtraction of the destination from the source. Important safety tip: this is the reverse of the CMP instruction, which subtracts the source from the destination! More importantly, this instruction sets the flags such that normal unsigned conditional jumps will do The Right Thing.

Another variant of the REP prefix is particularly useful in this context. REPZ (alternatively, REPE) loops as long as CX is **not** 0 and the zero flag is set. This actually means "as long as we haven't hit the end of the string and the strings so far have been identical," since the zero flag is set only when the result of the subtraction is 0, meaning that the last two characters are the same. Using this, we can perform general string comparison operations with

```
MOV     SI, OFFSET Astring      ; set source address
MOV     DI, OFFSET Bstring      ; set destination address
CLD                             ; clear direction flag
MOV     CX, 100                 ; loop over (up to) 99 words
REPE    CMPSW                   ; .. and compare
```

After this code fragment has run, one of two possible things has happened. Possibility one: CX hit 0 with the Z flag still set, in which case the two word strings are identical. So, a simple statement like

```
JE      STRINGSEQUAL           ; the strings were equal
```

can branch to the appropriate section of code.

Alternatively (possibility two), the Z flag was cleared when two elements were compared and found to be different. The detailed results of the difference (was the byte in SI greater or less than the byte in DI?) are stored in the flags register, like the result of a CMP operation. By examining the other flags with JB, JA, JAE, and so on, we can figure out whether the source (SI) or destination (DI) register pointed to the smaller string. The main difficulty is that the SI and DI registers are left pointing to the wrong spot. Specifically, the value in SI (DI) is the location just *past* the place where the strings were found to differ—or alternatively, one slot past the end of the strings.

```
JB      SOURCESMALLER          ; SI held smaller string
; if we get here, DI < SI
```

A third useful operation looking for the occurrence (or lack) of a particular value within a string. (For example, a string that holds a floating point number will have a '.' character; otherwise, it would be an integer.) This is handled by the SCAS? (SCAn String) instruction. Unlike the previous instructions, this only involves one string and hence one index register (DI). It compares the value in the accumulator (AL or AX, depending upon the size) with each element, setting flags and updating DI appropriately. Again, if the appropriate REP? prefix is used, it will stop either when CX hits 0 at the end of the string or when the Z flag hits the correct value, in any case leaving DI pointing one slot past the location of interest.

Using the REPZ prefix, we can use this operation to skip leading or trailing blanks from a string. Assume that Astring contains an array of 100 bytes, some of which (at the beginning or end) are space characters (ASCII 32). To find out where the first nonblank character is located, we can use this code fragment:

```
MOV     DI,Astring             ; load string
MOV     AL, 32                 ; load byte accumulator with ' '
MOV     CX, 100                ; 100 characters in Astring
CLD                            ; clear direction flag
REPE    SCASB                  ; scan for mismatch
JE      ALLBLANKS              ; if Z flag set, no mismatch found
; otherwise, DI points 1 byte past first nonblank character
        DEC   DI               ; back DI up
```

To skip trailing blanks, we simply start at the end (at Astring+99) and set the direction flag so that the operation goes from right to left in the string

```
MOV     DI,Astring          ; load string
ADD     DI, 99              ; jump to end of string
MOV     AL, 32              ; load byte accumulator with ' '
MOV     CX, 100             ; 100 characters in Astring
STD                         ; set direction flag
REPE    SCASB               ; scan for mismatch
JE      ALLBLANKS           ; if Z flag set, no mismatch found
; otherwise, DI points 1 byte past first nonblank character
INC     DI                  ; back DI up
```

A similar prefix, REPNZ (or REPNE), will repeat as long as the Z flag is not set, which is to say, as long as the elements differ. So, to find the first '.' (ASCII 44) in a string, we use a slight variation on the first example:

```
MOV     DI,Astring          ; load string
MOV     AL, 44              ; load byte accumulator with '.'
MOV     CX, 100             ; 100 characters in Astring
CLD                         ; clear direction flag
REPNE   SCASB               ; scan for match
JNE     NOPERIOD            ; if Z flag clear, no match found
; otherwise, DI points 1 byte past first '.'
DEC     DI                  ; back EDI up
```

Finally, the last commonly useful string primitive will copy a particular value over and over again into a string. This can be useful to quickly zero out an array, for example. The STOS (STOre String) copies the value in the accumulator to the string. To store all 0s in the Empty array previously defined (an array of 10 doublewords), we can simply use

```
MOV     DI, Empty           ; store destination string
MOV     CX, 10              ; 10 elements to store
MOV     AX, 0               ; value to store is 0
REP     STOSD
```

Unfortunately, this is the only support that the 8088 provides for user-defined **derived types**. If the programmer wants a multidimensional array, for example, she must figure out herself how to tile/parcel the memory locations out. Similarly, a structure or record would be represented by adjacent memory locations alone, and no support is provided for object-oriented programming. This must be addressed at a higher level through the assembler and/or compiler.

6.4.5   Local Variables and Information Hiding

One problem with the memory structure defined so far is that every memory location is defined implicitly for the entire computer. In terms common to higher-level language programming, every example of a variable we've seen is global—meaning that the Greet array (previously defined) could be accessed or changed from anywhere in the program. It also means that there can only be one variable in the entire program named Greet. Better programming practice calls for the use of local variables, which provides some privacy and security as well as the ability to reuse names.

Similarly, as discussed in regard to the JVM, having only jump instructions available limits the programmer's ability to reuse code.

6.4.6 System Stack

The solution, for both the JVM and the 8088, is to support subroutines (or subprograms). Like the JVM's jsr instruction, the 8088 provides a CALL instruction in conjunction with a hardware stack. This instruction pushes the current value of the instruction pointer (IP) and executes a branch to the location given as an argument. The corresponding RET instruction pops the top value from the stack, loads it into the instruction pointer, and continues execution at the saved location.

The 8088 also recognizes standard PUSH and POP instructions for moving data to and from the machine stack. For example, good programming practice suggests that one shouldn't wantonly destroy the contents of registers inside subroutines, since there's no way to be sure that the calling environment didn't need that data. The easiest way to make sure this doesn't happen is to save (PUSH) the registers that one plans to use at the beginning of the subroutine and to restore (POP) them at the end. Both the PUSH and POP statements will accept any register or memory location; both PUSH AX and PUSH SomeLocn are legal. To push a constant value, one must first load it into memory or a register—and, of course, POP-ping something into a constant doesn't make much sense.

Most assemblers discourage the practice of using the same labels for both subroutine calls and jump statements, although the CPU doesn't care (after all, both of them are just numeric values to be added to the program counter!) However, if this is not done extremely carefully, the programmer will violate stack discipline and end up either leaving extra stuff on the stack (resulting in filling it up and getting some sort of overflow-based error) or popping and using garbage from an empty stack. In other words, don't do that. For this reason, a subroutine in 8088 assembly language looks slightly different than the labels we've already seen:

```
MyProc PROC
        PUSH   CX                       ; push CX to save it
        ; do something extremely clever
        MOV    CX, 10
MyLabel:
        ; do something clever inside a loop 10 times
        LOOP   MyLabel
        POP    CX                       ; restore CX
        RET
MyProc ENDP
```

There are a few points to pay attention to here. First, the declaration of the label MyProc looks different from the label MyLabel (there's no colon, for instance) to help both you and the assembler keep track of the difference. Second, the procedure begins and ends with PROC/ENDP. These aren't mnemonics, merely directives, as they don't translate into machine instructions. They just (again) help you and the assembler structure the program. The last machine instruction is RET, which is not only typical but required for a subroutine. Third, the CX register is used for a loop index inside the routine, but since the value is PUSHed at the top and POP-ped at the

bottom of the routine, the calling environment will not see any change in CX. It would be legal
(and even typical) to invoke this routine from another routine as follows:

```
Other   PROC
        MOV    CX, 50                      ; call MyProc 50 times
LoopTop:
        CALL   MyProc                      ; execute MyProc subroutine
        LOOP   LoopTop                     ; ... in a loop (50 times)
        RET
Other   ENDP
```

The "Other" procedure uses the same loop structure, including CX, to call MyProc 50
times, but since the CX register is protected, no errors will result. Of course, the Other procedure
itself clobbers the CX register, so someone calling Other must be careful. (A better version of
Other—the sort expected of a professional programmer—would similarly protect CX before using
it, using the same PUSH/POP instructions.)

6.4.7 Stack Frames

In addition to providing temporary storage for registers, the stack can be used to provide temporary
storage for local variables in memory. To understand how this works, we'll first consider how the
stack itself works (figure 6.5).

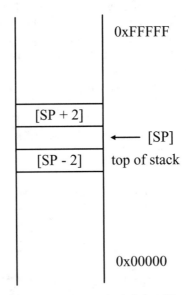

Figure 6.5 The CPU stack (simplified)

One of the "general-purpose" registers of the 8088, the SP register, is for all practical intents
reserved by the CPU and operating system to hold the current location of the top of the machine
stack. At the beginning of any program, the value of SP is set to a number somewhere near the top
of main memory—the part of main memory that has relatively high addresses while the program

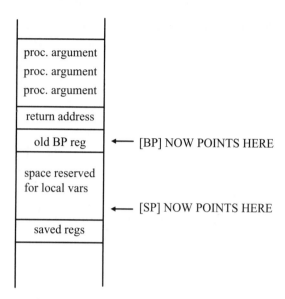

Figure 6.6 An 80x86 stack frame

itself is stored in much lower locations. Between the program and the top of the stack is a large no-man's-land of unused and empty memory.

Whenever data must be placed on the stack (typically via a PUSH or a CALL), the SP register is decremented by the appropriate amount, usually 2. This pushes the top of the stack 2 bytes closer to the rest of the program into no-man's-land. The value to be pushed is stored in these "new" 2 bytes. Another PUSH would bring SP down another 2 bytes and store another piece of data. Counterintuitively, this means that the "top" of the stack is actually the part of the stack with the lowest (smallest) address. Contrariwise, when data is POP-ped from the stack, the value at [SP] is copied into the argument; then SP is incremented by 2, setting it to the new "top." (This also applies when you execute RET and have to take [pop] the old program counter from the stack.)

However, the stack also provides a perfect location to store local variables, since every time a procedure is called, it results in a new top of the stack. In fact, any information that needs to be local to the procedure, such as function arguments, local variables, saved registers, and data, can be put on the stack. Since this is such a common task, especially in high-level languages, there's a standard way of structuring the stack so that different complex procedures can "play nice" with each other.

The basic idea is called a **stack frame** (figure 6.6). As usually implemented, it involves two registers, SP and BP. This is why the programmer shouldn't mess with the BP register for general-purpose indexing; it's already being used in the stack frames. But because BP works as an index register, expressions like MOV AX, [BP + 4] are legal and can be used to refer to memory locations near BP.

With this in mind, a stack frame looks like this (starting at the top of memory, or the "bottom" of the stack):

```
public static int further(int x, int y)
{
        int i,j;
        i = x;
        if (i < 0)
                i = -x;
        j = y;
        if (y < 0)
                j = -y;
        if (i < j)
                i = j;
        return i;
}
```

Figure 6.7   Function *further* (int x, int y) in Java

```
int further(int x, int y)
{
        int i,j;
        i = x;
        if (x < 0)
                i = -x;
        j = y;
        if (y < 0)
                j = -y;
        if (i < j)
                i = j;
        return i;
}
```

Figure 6.8   Function *further* (int x, int y) in C/C++

- Any arguments to the procedure/subprogram
- Return address
- Old value of BP (pointed to by BP)
- Space for local variables (top pointed to by SP)
- Saved registers

How does this work? We'll use a somewhat contrived example: I want to write the assembly language equivalent of a function or method `further()` that takes two arguments and returns the absolute value of the one more distant from 0. In Java, this method would be written as in figure 6.7; in C/C++, it would look more like figure 6.8.

The code for the comparison itself is simple; assuming that we can move the data into AX and BX, we can simply compare the two, and if BX is larger, move it into AX. Similarly, by comparing the function parameters (x and y) to 0, we can either use a NEG instruction or not on their local variables. However, to access these properly, we need enough space on the stack to hold these local variables.

The following code will solve that problem nicely:

```
Further      PROC
        PUSH  BP              ; save old BP
        MOV   BP, SP          ; BP now points to old BP
        SUB   SP, 4           ; make two 16-bit local
                              ; variables
        PUSH  BX              ; save BX

        MOV   AX,[BP+2]       ; get 1st argument
        MOV   [SP+2], AX      ; and store in 1st local
        CMP   [SP+2],0        ; compare to 0
        JGE   Skip1           ; if >= don't negate
        NEG   [SP+2]          ; otherwise negate
Skip1:

        MOV   AX,[BP+4]       ; get 2nd argument
        MOV   [SP+4], AX      ; and store in 2nd local
        CMP   [SP+4], 0       ; compare to 0
        JGE   Skip2           ; if >= don't negate
        NEG   [SP+4]          ; otherwise negate
Skip2:
        MOV   AX, [SP+2]      ; load 1st local
        MOV   BX, [SP+4]      ; load 2nd local
        CMP   AX, BX          ; if 1st local >= 2nd local
        JGE   Skip3           ; .. then don't ...
        MOV   BX, AX
Skip3:                        ; answer now in AX

        POP   BX              ; restore old BX value
        ADD   SP, 4           ; destroy local vars
        POP   BP              ; restore old BP value
        RET                   ; still need to pop args
Further ENDP
```

Figure 6.9 shows the stack frame as built by this procedure. Note particularly the two arguments passed and the locations where the old register values are stored. Finally, there are two words of memory corresponding to the local variables i and j. At the end of the procedure, the stack is essentially unbuilt in reverse order. Why didn't we save and restore the value in AX? Because AX is the register that is being used to hold the return value, and as such it will have to be clobbered.

How does this work? We'll use a somewhat contrived example: I want to write the assembly language equivalent of further (−100,50) (which should, of course, return 100). In order to invoke this procedure, the calling environment must first push two integers on the stack; then it must find a way to get rid of those two values after the function returns. An easy way to do this involves the following code:

```
X       DW      -100        ; first variable
Y       DW      50          ; second variable
PUSH    X                   ; er, PUSH X
PUSH    Y                   ; um,...
CALL    FURTHER             ; check it out
; AX darn well better hold 100 at this point
ADD     SP, 4               ; remove X, Y from stack
; AX still better hold 100
```

The full stack frame built thus looks like figure 6.9.

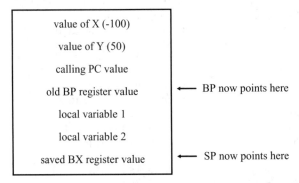

Figure 6.9   Stack frame for *further (X,Y)*

6.5   Conical Mountains Revisited

As a worked-out example of how arithmetic on the 8088 looks, let's resolve the earlier problem concerning the volume of a given mountain. As given in chapter 2, the original problem statement is:

> What is the volume of a circular mountain 450 m in diameter at the base and 150 m high?

Because the answer involves using π, at least part of the computation must be in the FPU. We assume (for clarity) that the name/identifier "STORAGE" somehow refers to a 16-bit memory location (as in 6.4.1; this can either be a global variable somewhere or on the stack as a local variable), and we can use that location to move data in and out of the FPU. For simplicity, we'll use 16-bit integers and registers for our calculations. We assume (for clarity) integer calculations; since none of the numbers involved are very large, this should present few problems.

First, we calculate the radius:

```
MOV     AX, 450             ; diameter = 450m
MOV     BX, 2               ; can't divide by a constant
DIV     BX                  ; AX = 450 / 2, DX is still 0
```

The area of the base is the radius squared times π. In order to use π, we need to initialize the FPU and move the computation there.

```
                              ; AX holds radius
MUL     AX                    ; square AX, result in DX:AX
FINIT                         ; initialize FPU
MOV     STORAGE, AX           ; move r^2 to memory (as integer
FILD    STORAGE               ; ... and move to FPU
FLDPI                         ; load pi = 3.1415...
FMUL                          ; and calculate base area
```

At this point, we could move the base area from the FPU back into the main ALU, but by doing so, we lose everything to the right of the decimal point (and thus accuracy). A better solution is to continue our calculations in the FPU, using memory location STORAGE as a temporary location for integer data. To recap: the volume of a cone is one-third of the volume of a corresponding cylinder, and the volume of the cylinder is the base area (already calculated) times the height (150 m). So, the final stage of the calculations looks like this:

```
MOV     STORAGE, 150          ; get height into the FPU
FILD    STORAGE               ;
FMUL                          ; cylinder volume = base * height
MOV     STORAGE, 3            ; get 3 into the FPU for division
FILD    STORAGE               ;
FDIV                          ; ... and divide by 3
                              ; for cone volume
; the result is now at the top of the FPU stack
FISTP   STORAGE               ; 'P' means pop the stack after
                              ; performing operation (storing)
; STORAGE now holds the final answer, rounded to an integer
FWAIT                         ; Wait for FPU to finish before
                              ; doing anything in the ALU
```

6.6 Interfacing Issues

Code like the previous example is one way in which assembly language programs can interface with the outside world; these stack frames also allow code generated from high-level languages (with a few minor variations, so be careful) to operate. So, if you have a large Pascal or C++ program, you can code a small section (one or a few functions) in assembly language to make sure that you have total control over the machine—to get that tiny extra burst of speed for the animations in your game, for example.

When most people consider interfacing, though, they usually think about interfacing with devices and peripherals. For example, how do I get data from the keyboard (where the user typed it) to the CPU and then to the screen (where it can be seen)? The unfortunate answer is ,"it depends."

It depends, in fact, on many things, starting with the type of gadget you want to use, the kind of machine you have, and the kind of operating system you're running. Any operating system

(Windows, Linux, MacOS, FreeBSD, etc.) is actually a special kind of computer program, one that's always running and tries to interpose itself between the other programs on the system and the device hardware. It both provides and controls access to the input and output devices—which means that if you want to do something with a device, you have to call an appropriate function (provided by the operating system) by putting the correct arguments on the stack and then doing a CALL on the right location. The details of these functions vary from system to system. Linux works one way, using one set of functions. Microsoft Windows does the same thing, using a different set of functions that need different arguments and calls. So, to interface with most normal devices, the secret is to figure out how your operating system does it and then use the magic handshake to get the OS to do what you want.

There are two other major approaches to interfacing with devices. Some devices, such as the video controller, can be attached directly to the computer's memory and automatically update themselves whenever the appropriate memory changes. Obviously, this memory is not available for other purposes (like storing programs). On the original PC (running MS-DOS), for example, "video memory" (VRAM) started at 0xA0000, which meant that programs couldn't use anything beyond 0x9FFFF. However, this also meant that a clever program could cause (data to appear on the screen by putting the right values in the right locations beyond) 0xA0000. This technique, called **memory-mapped I/O**, could be easily implemented, for example, by setting the ES segment register to 0xA000 and then using register pairs like ES:AX instead of the more normal DS:AX as the destination argument to a MOV instruction.

The other way devices commmunicate is through various ports (such as the serial port, a UDP port, and so forth). This is usually called **port-mapped I/O**. Each of these ports (as well as various internal data values, such as the video color palette) can be independently addressed using a 16-bit port identification number. The OUT instruction takes two arguments, a 16-bit port and an 8-bit data value, and simply transmits that data value to that port and thus to the device attached at that port. What the device does with that value is up to it. A IN instruction will read a byte of data from a specific port. Obviously, programming in this fashion requires very detailed knowledge both of the port numbering system and of the types and meanings of data. But with this kind of control, if you had to do so, you could hook up your fish tank to a 8088's printer port and, instead of printing, automatically control the temperature and aeration of the tank.

6.7 Chapter Review

- The Intel 8088 is the forerunner of a family of chips that comprise the best-known and best-selling CPU chips the world. Specifically, as the chip inside the original IBM-PC, it rapidly became the most common chip on the business desktop and established IBM and Microsoft as the dominant industrial players for most of the rest of the 20th century.
- The 8088 is a classic example of CISC chip design, a complex chip with a very large, rich instruction set.
- The 8088 has eight named 16-bit "general-purpose" registers (although many of these are optimized for different special purposes), as well as a number of smaller (8-bit) registers that are physically part of the 16-bit registers and a logically (and often physically) separate Floating Point Unit (FPU).

- Most assembly language operations use a two-argument format where the operation mnemonic is followed by a destination and a source argument like this:

```
OP      dest,src           ; dest = dest OP src
```

- Available operations include the usual arithmetic operations (although multiplication and division have special formats and use special registers), data transfers, logical operations, and several other special-purpose operational shortcuts.
- The 8088 supports a variety of addressing modes, including immediate mode, direct mode, indirect mode, and index mode.
- Floating point operations are performed in the FPU using stack-based notation and a special set of operations (most of which begin with the letter F).
- The 8088 supports normal branch instructions as well as special loop instructions using the CX register as loop counters.
- As a result of legacy support, the 8088 stores data in memory in a different format than it stores it in registers, which can be confusing to novice programmers.
- Arrays and strings are implemented using adjacent memory locations; there are also special-purpose **string primitive** operations for common string/array operations.
- The SP and BP registers are normally used to support a standardized machine stack with standard **stack frames**; this makes it easy to merge assembly language code with code written in a higher-level language.

6.8   Exercises

1. What does the idea of "a family of chips" mean?
2. Why does the 8088 have a fixed number of registers?
3. What is the difference between the BX and BL registers?
4. What is the actual address corresponding to the following segment:offset pairs?
   a. 0000:0000
   b. ABCD:0000
   c. A000:BCD0
   d. ABCD:1234
5. What is an example of a CISC instruction not found on the JVM?
6. How is the MUL instruction different from the ADD instruction?
7. What is the difference between JA and JG?
8. What is the difference between ADD WORD PTR [4000h], 1 and ADD BYTE PTR [4000h], 1?
9. How would the 8088 handle string operations in a language (like Java) where characters are 16-bit UNICODE quantities?
10. How could so-called global variables be stored in a computer program for the 8088?
11. Does it matter to the 8088 whether parameters to a function are pushed onto the stack in left-to-right or right-to-left order?

7

The Power
Architecture

7.1 Background

The single biggest competitor to Intel-designed chips as a CPU for desktop hardware is probably the Power architecture. Until mid-2005, the PowerPC chip was the chip used in Apple Macintosh computers. Although Apple has switched to Intel-based chips, the Power architecture still dominates in many application areas. As of November 2005, half of the 20 fastest supercomputers in the world used Power-based chips, and all three main gaming platforms (Sony, Microsoft, and Nintendo) plan to use Power chips for their consoles by the end of 2006. In embedded systems, about half of all 2006 car models use a Power-based microcontroller (manufactured by Freestyle).

If the Pentium is the definitive example of Complex Instruction Set Computing (CISC) architecture, the Power chip is the textbook version of Reduced Instruction Set Computing (RISC) architecture.

Historically, the Power architecture originated as a joint design project in 1991 between Apple, IBM, and Motorola. (Notice that Intel was not a player in this alliance. Why should it have been, when it already had a dominant market position with its CISC-based x86 series?) RISC, which IBM had been using for embedded systems (see chapter 9) for almost 20 years, was seen as a way to get substantial performance from relatively small (and therefore inexpensive) chips.

The key to RISC computing is that (as with so much in life) computer programs spend most of their time doing a few relatively common operations. For example, studies have found that about 20% of the instructions in a typical program are just load/store instructions that move data to/from the CPU from main memory. If engineers could double the speed at which only these instructions operated, then they could achieve about a 10% improvement in overall system performance! So, rather than spend time and effort designing hardware to do complicated tasks, their job was to design hardware to do simple tasks well and quickly. At the other extreme, adding a rarely used addressing mode (for example) reduces the performance of every instruction carried out, because the computer needs to inspect each instruction to see if it uses that mode, requiring either more time or expensive circuitry.

There are two particular aspects of a typical RISC chip architecture that usually speed up (and simplify) computing. First, the operations themselves are usually the same size (for the PowerPC, all instructions are 4 bytes long; on the Pentium, instruction length can vary from 1 to 15 bytes). This makes it easier and faster for the CPU to do the fetch part of the fetch-execute cycle, since it doesn't have to take the time to figure out exactly how many bytes to fetch. Similarly, decoding the binary pattern to determine what operation to perform can be done faster and more simply. And, finally, each of the instructions is individually simple enough that they can be done quickly (usually in the time it takes to fetch the next instruction—a single machine cycle).

The second advantage of RISC architecture has to do with groups of instructions. Not only is it usually possible to carry out each instruction more quickly, but the small number of instructions means that there usually aren't huge numbers of near-synonymous variations in how to carry out a given (high-level) computation. This makes it much easier for code to be analyzed, for example, by an optimizing compiler. Better analysis can usually produce better (read: faster) programs, even without the individual instruction speedup.

Of course, the down side to RISC architectures like Power is that most of the powerful operations (for example, the Pentium's string processing system, as described in chapter 6) don't exist as individual instructions and must be implemented in software. Even many of the memory access instructions and modes are typically unavailable.

One of the design goals of the Power alliance was to develop not only a useful chip, but a cross-compatible chip as well. Motorola and IBM, of course, already had well-established lines of individually designed chips (for example, IBM's RS/6000 chip and the Motorola 68000 series). By agreeing in advance on certain principles, the Power alliance could ensure that their chips interoperated with each other, as well as design in advance for future technological improvements. Like the 80x86/Pentium family, Power is a family of chips (including the PowerPC subfamily)—but unlike them, the family was designed in advance to be extensible.

This focus on flexibility has produced some odd results. First, unlike with the Intel family, the development focus has not been exclusively on producing newer, larger, machines. From the start, low-end desktops and even embedded system controllers have been part of the target market. (The marketing advantages should be obvious: if your desktop workstation is 100% compatible with the control chips used in your toaster oven factory, it is much easier to write and debug the control software for said toaster ovens. Thus, IBM could sell not only more toaster oven controller chips, but also more workstations.) At the same time, the alliance planned for eventual expansion to a 64-bit world (now typified by the PowerPC G5) and defined an extensible instruction set to handle 64-bit quantities as part of the original (32-bit) design. In addition, the PowerPC is equipped to handle a surprising amount of variation in data storage format, as will be seen below.

7.2 Organization and Architecture

As in most modern computers, there are at least two separate views of the system (formally called **programming models**, also often called **programming modes**) of the PowerPC in order to support multitasking. The basic idea is that user-level programs get limited-privilege access to part of the computer, while certain parts of the computer are off limits except to programs (typically the operating system) running with special **supervisor** privilege. (The lack of such a distinct programming model is one reason the 8088 is so insecure.) This keeps user programs from interfering either with each other or with critical system resources. This discussion will focus mostly on the user model, since that's the most relevant one for day-to-day programming tasks.

7.2.1   Central Processing Unit

Most of the features of the Power architecture CPU are familiar by this time (figure 7.1). There is a (relatively large) bank of 32 "general-purpose" registers 32 bits wide in early PowerPC models like the 601 (up to the G4) and 64 bits wide in the G5 and 970. There are also 32 floating point registers, designated at the outset as 64 bits. Both the ALU and the FPU have their designated status/control registers (CR and FPSCR), and there are a (relatively few) chip-specific special-purpose registers that you probably don't want to use to maintain compatibility among the PowerPC family. Or at least that's the story told to the users.

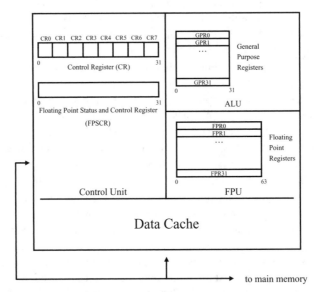

Figure 7.1   Block diagram of PowerPC CPU architecture

The actual underlying physical layout is a little more complicated, because there is some special-purpose hardware that is only available to the supervisor (that is, the operating system). For example, there is a **machine state register** (MSR) that stores critical system-wide supervisor-level information. (An example of such information is whether or not the system is currently operating at the user or supervisor level, perhaps responding to a supervisor-level event generated by an external peripheral. Another example of system-wide information is the memory storage format, whether **big-endian** or **little-endian**, as discussed later.) Separating the status of the current computation (stored in the CR and FPSCR) from the overall machine state makes it much easier for a multitasking environment to respond to sudden changes without interrupting the current computation. A more subtle advantage is that the chip designer can duplicate the CR and FPSCR and allow several different user-level programs to run at once, each using its own register set. This process could in theory be applied to the entire user-level register space. In particular, the PowerPC G5 duplicates both the integer and floating point processing hardware, allowing fully parallel execution of up to four instructions from up to four separate processes.

Another key distinction between the user's and supervisor's view of the chip concerns memory access. The operating system must be able to access (and indeed control) the entire available memory of the computer, while user-level programs are usually confined to their own space for security reasons. The PowerPC has a built-in set of registers to manage memory access at the hardware level, but only the supervisor has access to these. Their function is described in the following section.

7.2.2 Memory
Memory Management
At the user level, the memory of the PowerPC is simply organized (much more simply than that of the 8088). With a 32-bit address space, each user program has access in theory to a flat set of 2^{32} different memory locations. (On the 64-bit versions of the PowerPC, of course, there are 2^{64} different addresses/locations.) These locations define the **logical memory** available to the program. They can either be used as is in direct address translation (as previously defined) or as logical addresses to be converted by the memory management hardware. In addition, the PowerPC defines a third access method for speedy access to specific areas of memory.

Block Address Translation
If a particular block of memory must be frequently (and quickly) accessed, the CPU has another set of special-purpose registers, the **block address translation** (BAT) registers, that define special blocks of physical memory that perform a similar lookup task but use fewer steps. The BAT registers are most often used for areas in memory representing high-speed data transfers such as graphics devices and other similar I/O devices. If a logical address corresponds to an area of memory labeled by a BAT register, then the whole virtual memory process is skipped and the corresponding physical address is read directly from the BAT register.

Cache Access
The final step in memory access, irrespective of how it was achieved, is to determine whether the desired memory location has been accessed before (recently) or, more accurately, whether the data is stored in the CPU's cache memory or not. Since on-chip memory is much faster to access than memory stored off-chip in main memory, the PowerPC, like almost all modern chips, keeps copies of recently used data available in a small bank of very-high-speed memory.

7.2.3 Devices and Peripherals
Another feature of the memory management system defined earlier is that access to I/O devices can be handled easily within the memory management system. The use of the BAT registers to access high-speed I/O devices has already been mentioned. A similar method (**I/O controller interface translation**) can perform a similar task for memory addresses within the virtual memory

system. Each segment register contains information besides the VSID. Among that information is a field detailing whether this logical address refers to a peripheral. If it does, then page translation is skipped, and instead the logical address is used to generate a sequence of instructions and addresses for dealing with the appropriate device. This makes device access on the PowerPC as easy as (and in practical terms identical to) memory access, as long as the operating system has set values in the segment registers properly.

7.3 Assembly Language

7.3.1   Arithmetic

There are two obvious differences between the assemblys languages of the PowerPC and the systems we've already looked at. First, although the PowerPC has a register bank (like the x86 and Pentium), the registers are numbered instead of named. Second, Power architecture instructions have a rather unusual three-argument format. The instruction to add two numbers would be written as

```
add r3,r2,r1    # register 3 = register 2 + register 1
```

Notice that the second and third arguments (registers 1 and 2) remain unaffected in this calculation (this differs from any other CPU we've studied) and thus can be reused later as is. Of course, by repeating the arguments, we can get more traditional operations; for instance:

```
add r2,r2,r1    # is the equivalent of x86 ADD R2,R1
```

In general, any binary operation (arithmetic, logical, or even comparison) will be expressed this way. This three-argument format, combined with the relatively large number of registers available, gives the programmer or compiler tremendous flexibility in performing computations and storing intermediate results. It also allows the computer a certain amount of leeway in re-structuring computations on the fly as needed. If you think about the following sequence of instructions

```
add r3,r2,r1    # (1) register 3 = register 2 + register 1
add r6,r5,r4    # (2) et cetera
add r9,r8,r7    # (3)
add r12,r11,r10  # (4)
add r15,r14,r13  # (5)
add r18,r17,r16  # (6)
```

there's no reason that the computer to perform them in that particular order or even that a sufficiently capable computer couldn't perform them all at once.

A more interesting question is why the Power architecture works in this three-argument way. A simple answer is, "because it can." By design, the PowerPC uses a uniform and fairly large size for every instruction—32 bits. With a bank of 32 registers, it takes 5 bits to specify any given register, so specifying three registers takes about 15 of the 32 bits available, which still means that 2^{17} (about 128,000) *different* three-argument instructions could be available. Obviously, this is more than any sane engineer would be expected to design—but rather than making **add** instructions shorter than others, the engineers found a use for the extra space in providing extra flexibility.

However, one area they did not provide extra flexibility was memory addressing. In general, PowerPC arithmetic and logical operations cannot access memory. Formally speaking, there are only two addressing modes, **register mode** and **immediate mode**, as defined in previous chapters. These are distinguished by special opcodes and mnemonics; an unmarked mnemonic operates on three registers, while a mnemonic ending with -i operates on two registers and an immediate 16-bit quantity as follows:

```
add r3,r2,r1    # register 3 = register2 + register 1
addi r6,r5,4    # register 6 = register5 + 4
```

(In some assemblers, there is a potential for confusion here, as the programmer is allowed to refer to registers by number without using the r? notation. The statement add 2,2,1 would thus add the contents of register 1 to register 2; it would not add the number 1. Better yet, don't get careless with the code you write, even if the assembler lets you.)

Of course, with only a 16-bit immediate quantity available (why?), we can't do operations on the upper half of a 32-bit register. A few operations (add, and, or, and xor) have another variation with a -is an (immediate shifted suffix that will shift the immediate operand left by 16 bits, allowing the programmer to affect the high bits in the register directly). So the statement

```
andis r3,r3,FFFF    # r3 = r3 and 0xFFFF0000
```

would AND the contents of r3 with a 32-bit pattern of 0xFFFF0000, thus essentially setting the lower half to zero. Similarly,

```
andis r3,r3,0000    # r3 = r3 and 0x0000000
```

would zero out the entire register. Of course, the same effect could be obtained with register-to-register operations as follows:

```
xor r3,r3,r3    # XOR r3 with itself (zero it out)
subf r3,r3,r3    # SUBtract r3 From itself (zero it out)
```

(Even on a RISC chip, there are often several different ways to accomplish the same thing.)

Most of the arithmetic and logical operations that you would expect are present; there are operations for addition (add, addi), subtraction (subf, subfi), negation (arithmetic inverse, neg), and (and, andi), or (or, ori), xor (et cetera), nand, nor, multiplication, and division. There is also an extensive and powerful set of shift and rotate instructions. Not all of these have immediate forms in the interests of simplifying the chip logic a bit (*Reduced* Instruction Set Computing, after all), but few programmers will miss the convenience of an immediate-mode nand instruction. Some assemblers also provide mnemonic aliases—for example, the not instruction is not provided by the PowerPC CPU. It can be simulated as "nor with a constant zero" and thus doesn't need to be provided. Instead, a smart assembler will recognize the not instruction and output something equivalent without fuss. Multiplication and division, as usual, are a little more complicated. The classic problem is that the multiplication of two 32-bit factors generally yields a 64-bit product, which won't fit into a 32-bit register. The PowerPC thus supports two separate instructions mullw, mulhw, which return the low and high words, respectively, from the product. Each of these operations takes the usual three-argument format, so

```
mullw    r8,r7,r6
```

calculates the product r7 · r6 and then puts the low word into register 8. Division makes the usual separation between signed and unsigned divides: divw and divwu. The meaning of the 'w' in these mnemonics will hopefully become clear in a few paragraphs.

7.3.2   Floating Point Operations

Arithmetic instructions on floating point numbers are similar, but they use the (64-bit) floating point registers instead of the normal register bank, and the mnemonics begin with an f. The instruction to add two floating point numbers is thus fadd. By default, all floating point instructions operate on double-precision (64-bit) quantities, but a variation with an internal s (e.g., faddsx) specifies 32-bit values instead. Furthermore, the FPU is capable of storing and loading data in integer format, so conversion from/to integers can be handled within the FPU itself.

One danger of writing code on a PowerPC is that different registers share the same numbers. For example, the instructions

```
fmul   r7, r8, r9        # multiply something
add    r7, r8, r9        # add something
```

both appear to operate on the same registers. This is not true. The first statement operates on floating point registers, while the second operates on general-purpose registers. In some assemblers, a raw number will also be interpreted as a register number under the correct circumstances. This means that the statements

```
add    7, 8, 9          # add something
addi   7, 8, 9          # add something
```

are substantially different. The first adds the values in registers 8 and 9 together, while the second adds the value in register 8 to the immediate integer constant 9. *Caveat lector.*

7.3.3   Comparisons and Condition Flags

Most computers, by default, will update the condition register appropriately after every arithmetic or logical operation. The PowerPC is a little unusual in that regard. First, as already mentioned, there is no single condition register. More importantly, comparisons are performed only when explicitly requested (which helps support the idea of rearranging into a different order for speed). The simplest way to request a comparison is to append a period (.) to the end of most integer operations. This will cause bits in the condition register CR0 to be set according to whether the arithmetic result is greater than, equal to, or less than 0.

More generally, comparisons between two registers (or between a register and an immediate-mode constant) use a variation of the cmp instruction. This is arguably the most bizarre three-argument instruction, because it takes not only the two items to be compared (as the second and third arguments), but also the index of a condition register. For example

```
cmpw      CR1, r4, r5      # compare r4 to r5
                           # result will be in CR1
```

sets bits in the 4-bit condition register 1 to reflect the relative values of r4 and r5, as in table 7.1.

	meaning if bit set
bit 0	r4 < r5 (result < 0)
bit 1	r4 = r5 (result = 0)
bit 2	r4 > r5 (result > 0)

Table 7.1   Values in CR1 after cmpw CR1, r4, r5

7.3.4   Data Movement

To move data in and out of memory, there are special-purpose load and store instructions, as in the JVM. The general load instruction takes two arguments, the first being the destination register and the second being the logical address to be loaded (perhaps after undergoing memory management, as described above). As with the JVM, there are different instructions for different-sized chunks of data to move; the instructions to load data all begin with the letter l, while the next character indicates whether the data to be moved is a byte (b), halfword (h, 2 bytes), word (w, 4 bytes), or doubleword (d, 8 bytes; obviously available only on a 64-bit version of the PowerPC, since only that version could store such a large quantity in a register). The load instruction can also explicitly load both single precision (fs) and double precision (fd) floating point numbers. Of course, not all data is loaded from memory. The li instruction will load a constant using immediate mode.

When loading quantities smaller than a word, there are two different ways of filling the rest of the register. If the instruction specifies "zero loading" (using the letter z), the top part of the register will be set to 0s, while if the instruction specifies "algebraic" (a), the top part will be set by sign extension. Finally, there is an update mode available, specified with a u, that will be explained in the next section.

To understand the following examples, assume that (EA), an abbreviation of "effective address," is a memory location that holds a appropriately sized block of memory, currently storing a bit pattern of all 1s. The instruction wrl, (EA) would Load the Word at (EA) into register 1 and (on a 64-bit machine) zero out the rest of the register. On a 32-bit PowerPC, register 1 would hold the value 0xFFFFFFFF, while on a 64-bit machine, register 1 would hold the value 0x00000000FFFFFFFF. Table 7.2 gives some other examples of how load instructions work.

Instruction	32-bit register result	64-bit register result
lbz r1, (EA)	0x000000FF	0x00000000000000FF
lhz r1, (EA)	0x0000FFFF	0x000000000000FFFF
lha r1, (EA)	0xFFFFFFFF	0xFFFFFFFFFFFFFFFF
lwz r1, (EA)	0xFFFFFFFF	0x00000000FFFFFFFF
ld r1, (EA)	not allowed	0xFFFFFFFFFFFFFFFF

Table 7.2   Some sample PowerPC load instructions

There are a few caveats. Perhaps most obviously, there is no way to "extend" a 64-bit doubleword quantity even on a 64-bit machine. There is also no way to operate directly on doubleword quantities on a 32-bit PowerPC or for a 32-bit CPU to algebraically extend a word quantity. The instruction lwa is therefore not a part of the 32-bit PowerPC instruction set, and the lwz loads a 32-bit quantity but doesn't zero out anything on such a machine. Most annoyingly, the PowerPC architecture doesn't permit algebraic extension on byte quantities, so the instruction lba doesn't exist either. With these exceptions, the load instructions are fairly complete and reasonably understandable. For example, the instruction sur3, (EA) loads a single precision floating point number from memory using the as-yet undefined "update" and "index" modes.

The operations to store data from a register in memory are similar but begin with "st" and don't need to deal with issues of extension. The sth r6, (EA) instruction stores the lowest 16 bits of register 6 in memory at location EA, while the sthu, sthx, or sthux instructions do the same thing, but using update mode, index mode, or both, respectively.

7.3.5   Branches
The final elementary aspect of assembly language programming is the control/branch instructions. As we have come to expect, the PowerPC supports both unconditional and conditional branches. The mnemonic for an unconditional branch is simply b, with a single argument for the target address. The mnemonics for conditional branches (several variations, summarized as b?) include an argument for the condition register to look at as well:

```
bgt   CR0, address    # branch if bit 1 set in CR0
blt   CR1, address    # branch if bit 0 set in CR1
beq   CR2, address    # branch if bit 2 set in CR2
ble   CR3, address    # branch if bit 1 unset in CR3
bne   CR4, address    # branch if bit 2 unset in CR4
bge   CR5, address    # branch if bit 0 unset in CR5
```

The PowerPC does not support separate jump-to-subroutine instructions, but there is a dedicated **link register** that performs similar tasks. There is also a specialized **count register** for use in loops. Both of these registers have special-purpose instructions for their use.

Despite the simplicity of RISC design, there are many more instructions available than space permits us to look at. In particular, the supervisor-level registers such as the BAT and segment registers have their own instructions for access. If you need to write an operating system for a Power chip, then there are other books you'll need to read first.

7.4 Conical Mountains Revisited

Back to our old friend, the conical mountain, as a worked-out example. For simplicity of expression, this example assumes the availability of 64-bit operations. Also for simplicity, I assume that the value of π is available in memory, expressed as the location (PI). As given in chapter 2, the original problem statement is

What is the volume of a circular mountain 450 m in diameter at the base and 150 m high?

With the banks of registers available, the problem is fairly simple:

Step one is to calculate the radius, dividing the diameter (450) in half, and then to square it.

```
li    r3, 450        # load diameter into r3
li    r4, 2          # divide by 2 to get radius
divw  r3, r3, r4     # put radius into r3
mullw r3, r3, r3     # square the radius
```

Step two is to move the data (through memory) into the FPU.

```
std   (EA),r3        # store r^2 as 64-bit integer
ldf   r10, (EA)      # load value of r^2
fcfid r9, r10        # convert to float
```

Step three is to load pi and multiply by it.

```
ldf   r8, (PI)       # load value of pi for multiply
fmul  r7, r8, r9     # multiply
fcfid r9, r10        # load value of pi for multiply
```

And finally, the height (150) is loaded and multiplied, and then the final quantity is divided by 3. For clarity, we'll first load them as integers and then pass them to the floating point processor as before:

```
li    r5, 150        # load height
std   (EA),r5        # store as integer
ldf   r6, (EA)       # load height into FPU
fcfid r6, r6         # convert to float
fmul  r7, r6, r7     # multiply

li    r5, 3          # load constant 3
std   (EA),r5        # store as integer
ldf   r6, (EA)       # load 3 into FPU
fcfid r6, r6         # convert to float
fmul  r6, r6, r7     # multiply
```

Note that in this example, registers 3 to 5 are always used to hold integers and thus are always general-purpose registers, and registers 6 to 10 are always used to hold floating point numbers. This is for clarity of explanation only.

7.5 Memory Organization and Use

Memory organization on the PowerPC is easy once you get past the supervisor-level memory management. As discussed earlier, from the user's point of view, the PowerPC provides a simple, flat address space. The size of the memory space is a simple function of the word size of the CPU—2^{32} bytes (about 4 gigabytes) (GB) for a 32-bit CPU and 2^{64} bytes for its big brothers. Of course, no computer that could affordably be built would possess 16 exabytes of physical memory, but this size allows room for future breakthroughs in memory cost. A memory address is thus just a number of appropriate size; halfwords, words, and doublewords are stored at appropriately aligned intervals within memory space. (Actually, this is a lie. Bytes are bytes. But instructions such as ld r0, (EA) will only work when (EA) refers to an effective address whose value is a multiple of 8. Otherwise, an intelligent assembler/compiler needs to break down the doubleword load into up to eight partial load and shift instructions, which can slow your code down to a crawl. So, don't do it. Pretend instead that objects have to be stored at suitably aligned locations and you'll feel better for it.)

One key feature of the PowerPC is direct support for both big-endian and little-endian data storage built into the CPU instruction set. This feature was inherited from IBM and Motorola, which both had extensive product lines and a large body of code that needed to be supported but had (historically) made different choices in this regard. Data stored in the CPU is always stored in the same way, but it can be stored in memory in either normal or "byte-reversed" format.

Apart from these complexities, the operation of addressing memory is fairly simple. The PowerPC supports two basic addressing modes, indirect and indexed; the only difference is in the number of registers involved.

In indirect mode, the computer calculates the effective address as the sum of a 16-bit immediate offset and the contents of the single register specified. For example, if register 3 held the value 0x5678, then the instruction

```
lwz      r4, 0x1000(r3)
```

would load the lower 32 bits (w) of register 4 with the value stored at location 0x6678 (0x1000 + 0x5678). On a 64-bit machine, the high 32 bits are set to 0 because of the z. For most programs, the value 0x1000 would be compiler-defined and refer to a particular offset or size of a variable (as will be seen presently).

In indexed mode, the effective address is similarly calculated, but using two registers in place of a constant and a register. So, the effective address is the same in

```
lwzx      r4, r2, r3
```

only if the value stored in register 2 were already 0x1000. This provides a rather simple but useful two-step way of accessing memory; the second argument can be used to define a particular block of memory—for instance, the area where all the global program variables are stored—while the third argument is used to select a particular offset within that block. (This is similar in spirit to but much more flexible than the segment registers defined in the 8088.) If, for any reason, the block is shifted as a unit, only one register needs to be changed and the code will continue to work as designed.

For many applications, particularly those involving arrays, it is convenient to be able to change the register values as memory access occurs (Java programmers will already be familiar with the '++' and '--' operators). The PowerPC provides some of this functionality through **update mode**, represented by a u in the mnemonic. In update mode, the calculations of the effective address are performed as usual, as is the memory access, but the value stored in the controlling register is then (post)updated to the effective address.

As an example, consider the effect of the following statements, presumably in the middle of a loop:

```
lwzu    r4, 4(r3)          # access (r3+4) in update mode
add     r5, r5, r4         # maintain a running sum
```

Assuming that r3 held the value 0x10000 at the start of this block, the first statement would calculate an effective address of 0x10004 and load r4 with the word (4-byte) value stored at that address. So far, all is normal. After this load is complete, the value of **r3** will be updated to 0x10004, the effective address. The next time the next 4-byte memory location, probably the address of the next element in the word array is accessed r3 already points there. This may save substantial time and effort. This makes array processing, or more generally processing of any collection of items of similar size, very efficient.

Without special-purpose instructions for subroutines, there's no standardized, hardware-enforced notion of a system stack or a system stack pointer. Instead, the programmer (more likely, the operating system) will recruit one or more of the registers (normally r1) to serve as stack pointers and use normal register/memory operations to duplicate the push and pop operations. This is not only in keeping with the RISC philosophy (why create a special-purpose pop instruction when it can already be done?), but also allows different programs and systems to build different stack frames. Again, one can see the work of the design by committee in this decision, as Apple, IBM, and Motorola all had extensive code bases they wished to support, each with different and incompatible views of the stack.

7.6 Performance Issues

7.6.1 Pipelining

As with the other chips we have examined, performance of the computer is a crucial aspect of success. Each new instantiation of a computer needs to run faster than the previous ones. To accomplish this, the PowerPC provides an extensive pipelined architecture (see section 5.2.4). One easy way to make the JVM run faster is to execute it on a faster chip. In order to make a PowerPC chip run faster, one has to make the chip itself faster, or somehow to pack more computation into each tick of the system clock. In order to do this, the CPU has a much more complex, **pipelined**, fetch-execute cycle that allows it to process several instructions at once.

One feature of the RISC architecture is that it's designed to work well with pipelining. Remember that the two keys to good pipeline performance are to keep the pipeline moving and to keep the stages approximately uniform. The RISC instruction set is specifically designed so that all instructions take about the same amount of time and can usually be executed in a single machine cycle. So, in the time it takes to perform an instruction fetch, the machine can execute an add instruction and the pipeline remains clear. This also helps explain the limited number of address modes on a PowerPC; an instruction involving adding one memory location to another would require four load operations and a store operation besides the simple addition, and so would take four times as long (stalling the pipeline). Instead, the PowerPC forces this operation to be written as four separate instructions. Because of the pipelined operation, these instructions will still take place in the same amount of time, but will mesh more smoothly with the overall computation, giving better performance.

Instruction fetch is another area where this kind of optimization can happen. On the Pentium, instructions can vary in length from a single byte up to about 15 bytes. This means that it can take up to 15 times as long to load one instruction as another, and while a very long instruction is being loaded, the rest of the pipeline may be standing empty. By contrast, all instructions on the PowerPC are the same length and so can be loaded in a single operation, keeping the pipeline full.

Of course, some kinds of operations (floating point arithmetic, for example) still takes substantial time. To handle this, the execution stage for floating point arithmetic is itself pipelined (for example, handling multiplication, addition, and rounding in separate stages), so that it can still handle arithmetic at a throughput of one instruction per clock cycle. In cases where, delay is inevitable, there is a mechanism to stall the processor as necessary, but a good compiler can write code to minimize this as far as possible.

The other easy way to break a pipeline is by loading the wrong data, fetching from the wrong location in memory. The worst offenders in this regard are conditional branches, such as "jump if less than." Once this instruction has been encountered, the next instruction will come either from the next instruction in sequence or from the instruction at the target of the jump—and we may not know which. Often, in fact, we have no way of telling which instruction we will need because the condition depends on the results of a computation somewhere ahead of us in the pipeline and therefore unavailable. The PowerPC tries to help by making multiple condition registers available. If you (or the compiler) can perform the comparison early enough that the result is already available, having cleared the pipeline, when the branch instruction starts to execute, the target of the branch can be determined and the correct instructions loaded.

As we will see with the Pentium, the Power architecture also incorporates elements of **superscalar architecture**. Actually, superscalar design is more generally associated with RISC architectures than with CISC chips, but a good design idea is a good design idea and likely to be widely adopted. To review section 5.2.5, this design theory incorporates the idea of multiple independent instructions being executed in parallel in independent sections of the CPU. Again, the Power architecture's simplified instruction set aids in this—arithmetic operations are separated, for example, from load/store operations or from comparison operations, and the large number of registers makes it easy for a series of instructions to use nonoverlapping (and therefore parallelizable) registers.

A typical PowerPC CPU will have separate modules to handle different kinds of operations (like the distinction drawn earlier between the ALU and the FPU, only more so). Usually, a Power chip will have at least one "integer unit," at least one "floating point unit," and at least one "branch unit" (that processes branch instructions), possibly a "load/store unit," and so forth. The PowerPC 603 has five execution modules, separately handling integer arithmetic floating point arithmetic, branches, loads/stores, and system register operations. In higher-end versions, commonly used units are physically duplicated on the chip; the PowerPC G5, for example, has 10 separate modules on the chip:

- one permute unit (doing special-purpose "permute" operations)
- one logical arithmetic unit
- two floating point arithmetic units
- two fixed-point (register-to-register) arithmetic units
- two load/store units
- one condition/system register unit
- one branch unit

With this set of hardware, the CPU can execute up to 10 different instructions at the same time (within the same fetch-execute cycle). Within the size limits of the instruction queue, the first load/store instruction would be sent to the load/store unit, while the first floating point instruction would be sent to one of the floating point units, and so forth. You can see that there's no reason, in theory, that all the following instructions couldn't be done at the same time:

```
add    r3,r2,r1      # just some stuff
sub    r4,r2,r1      # another fixed-point operation
xor    r5,r5,r5      # zero out r5 using logical unit
faddx  r7,r6,r6      # add two floating point numbers
fsubx  f8,r6,r6      # zero out r8 using floating point unit
b      somewhere     # and branch to somewhere
```

Similarly, half of these instructions could be performed during this cycle and the other half next; alternatively, these instructions could be done one at a time, but in any order convenient to the computer, and not necessarily in the order written.

A few special properties are needed to allow this blatant, high-handed treatment of the program code. First, none of the instructions can depend on each other; if the second instruction changed the value in register 4 (it does) and the fifth instruction needed to use the new value, then the fifth instruction can't happen until at least the clock cycle after the second instruction. However, with 32 general-purpose registers available, an intelligent compiler can usually find a way to distribute the calculations among the registers to minimize this sort of dependency. Similarly, the instructions have to be of different types; with only one logical unit, logical instructions have to be executed one at a time. If part of the program consisted of 30 logical operations in a row, then that part would fill the instruction queue and it would only be able to dispatch one instruction at a time, basically slowing the computer down by a factor of up to 10. Again, an intelligent compiler can try to mix instructions to make sure that instructions of various types are in the queue.

7.7   Chapter Review

- The PowerPC, designed by a coalition including Apple, IBM, and Motorola, is the chip inside most Apple desktop computers. It is an example of the RISC (Reduced Instruction Set Computing) approach to CPU design, with relatively few instructions that can be executed quickly.
- The Power architecture is a flexible compromise among existing designs (mainly) from Motorola and IBM. Until recently, the PowerPC was the base chip for all Apple computers, and Power chips still dominate gaming consoles. As a result, the chip is actually a family of cross-compatible chips that differ substantially in architectural details. For example, the PowerPC exists in both 32- and 64-bit word size variants, and individual chips have tremendous flexibility in the way they interact with software (for example, any Power chip can store data in both big-endian and little-endian format).
- The Power CPU has a bank of 32 general-purpose registers and 32 floating point registers, plus chip-specific special-purpose registers, much more than a Pentium/x86. The chip also provides hardware support for memory management in several different modes, including direct (memory-mapped) access to the I/O peripherals.
- All Power instructions are the same size (32 bits) for speed and ease of handling.
- Power assembly language is written in a three-argument format. As with most RISC chips, there are relatively few addressing modes, and data movement in and out of the registers is handled by specific load/store instructions separate from the arithmetic calculations.
- The PowerPC has several different condition registers (CRS) that can be independently accessed.
- In order to speed up the chip, the PowerPC executes instructions using a **pipelined superscalar architecture**.

7.8   Exercises

1. What is an advantage of RISC chips over CISC chips? What is a disadvantage?
2. What are some examples of the flexibility of the Power architecture design?
3. Why does the power CPU have so many registers compared to the 8088 family?
4. What is an advantage of the three-argument format used by the PowerPC arithmetic instructions?
5. What is the difference between the and and andi instructions?
6. What is the difference between the and and andi. operations?
7. Why isn't there a standardized, hardware-supported stack frame format for the PowerPC?
8. For pipelining, why is it important that all instructions be the same size?
9. What is an instruction provided by the JVM that is not directly provided by the PowerPC? How could the PowerPC implement such an instruction?
10. How can rearranging the order of computations speed up a PowerPC program?

8

The Intel Pentium

8.1 Background

When was the last time you priced a computer? And what kind of computer did you price? For most people, in most of the world, the answer to the second question is probably "a Pentium." The Pentium computer chip, manufactured by Intel, is the best-selling hardware architecture in the world. Even competitors such as AMD usually very careful to make sure that their chips operate, at a bug-for-bug level, exactly as the Pentium does. Even most computers that don't run Windows (for example, most Linux machines) use a Pentium chip.

This means, among other things, that for the foreseeable future, if you have to write an assembly language program for a real (silicon-based) computer, it will probably be written on and for a Pentium. In order to take full advantage of the speed of assembly language, you have to understand the chip, its instruction set, and how it's used.

Unfortunately, this is a complicated task, both because the "Pentium" itself is a complicated chip and because the term "Pentium" actually refers to a family of slightly different chips. The original Pentium, manufactured in the early 1990s, has undergone continuous development, including the Pentium Pro, Pentium II, Pentium III, and the current Pentium 4 [P4]. Development is expected to continue, and no doubt Pentiums 5, 6, and 7 will follow unless Intel decides to change the name while keeping the systems compatible (as happened between the 80486 and the Pentium).

This successful development has made learning the architecture of the Pentium both easier and harder. Because of the tremendous success of the original Pentium (as well as that of the earlier x86 family that produced the Pentium), there are millions of programs out there, written for earlier chip versions, that people still want to run on their new computers. This produces pressure for backward compatibility, the ability of a modern computer to run programs written for older computers without a problem. So, if you understand the Pentium architecture, you implicitly understand most of the P4 architecture (and much of the x86 architecture). Conversely, every new step forward adds new features but eliminate the old ones. This makes the Pentium almost a poster child for CISC architecture, since every feature ever desired is still around—and every design decision made, good and bad, is still reflected in the current design. Unlike the designers of the JVM, who were able to start with a clean

175

slate, the Pentium designers at each stage had to start with a working system and improve it incrementally.

This makes the fundamental organization of the CPU chip, for example, rather complex, like a house that has undergone addition after addition after addition. Let's check it out...

8.2 Organization and Architecture

8.2.1   The Central Processing Unit

The logical abstract structure of the Pentium CPU is much like the previously described architecture of the 8088, only more so. In particular, there are more registers, more bus lines, more options, more instructions, and in general, more ways to do everything. As with the 8088, there is still a set of eight general-purpose named registers, but they have expanded to hold 32-bit quantities and have received new names. These registers are now

```
EAX   EBX   ECX   EDX
ESI   EDI   EBP   ESP
```

In fact, the EAX register (and in similar fashion the others) is simply an extension of the previous (16-bit) AX register. Just as the AX register is divided into the AH/AL **pair**, the lower 16 bits of the EAX register (called the **extended AX register**) are the AX register from the 8088. For this reason, old 8088 programs that use the 16-bit AX register will continue to run on a Pentium.

EAX (32 bits)		
not used	AX (16 bits)	
	AH (8 bits)	AL (8 bits)

Similarly, the 16-bit IP register has grown into the the EIP register, the **extended instruction pointer,** which holds the location of the next instruction to be executed. Instead of four, we now have six **segment registers** (CS, SS, DS, ES, FS, and GS) that are used to optimize memory access to often-used areas. Finally, the EFLAGS register holds 32 instead of 16 flags. All of these registers except the segment registers are 32 bits wide. This, in turn, implies that the Pentium has a 32-bit word size and that most operations deal in 32-bit quantities.

Beyond this, a major change between the 8088 and the Pentium is the creation of several different **modes** of operation to support multitasking. In the original 8088, any program had unfettered access to the entire register set, and by extension to the entire memory bank or to any peripherals attached—essentially, total control over the system and all its contents. This can be useful. It can also be dangerous; at the risk of indulging in old "war stories," one of the author's earliest professional experiences involved writing high-speed graphics programs for an original IBM-PC and, by mistake, putting graphics data in the part of system memory used by the hard drive controller The system didn't work quite right when it tried to boot using the "revised" parameters.

To prevent this problem, the Pentium can run in several different modes that control both the sort of instructions that can be executed and the way memory addresses are interpreted. Two modes of particular interest are **real mode**, essentially a detailed recreation of the 8088 operating environment (one program running at a time, only 1 megabyte of memory available, and no memory protection), and **protected mode**, which incorporates the memory management system described later (section 8.4.1) with support for multitasking. MS-DOS, the original IBM-PC operating system, runs in real mode, while MS-Windows and Linux both run in protected mode.

8.2.2 Memory

The Pentium supports several different structures and ways of accessing memory, but we'll ignore most of them here. First, they're complicated. Second, the complicated ones (from the programmer's point of view) are, for the most part, holdovers from the old 8088 architecture. If you have to write programs for a Pentium pretending to be an 8088 in real mode, they become relevant. When you write programs for a modern computer, the task is much simpler. Treating memory as a flat 32-bit address structure will handle almost everything necessary at the user level.

8.2.3 Devices and Peripherals

There are very few major differences between device interfacing on the Pentium and on the earlier 8088, again due to the Pentium's design for compatiblity. In practical terms, of course, this has been a tremendous advantage for the computer manufacturers, since consumers can buy a new computer and continue to use their old peripherals rather than having to buy a new printer and hard drive every time they upgrade a board.

However, as computers (and peripherals) have become more powerful, new methods of interfacing have come into common use that require the device and the I/O controller to do more of the work. For example, the direct **BIOS** control typical of MS-DOS programming requires a level of access to the hardware incompatible with protected-mode programming. Instead, a user-level program will request access to I/O hardware through a set of operating system to defined **device drivers** that control (and limit) access.

8.3 Assembly Language Programming

8.3.1   Operations and Addressing

Much of the Pentium instruction set is inherited directly from the 8088. In theory, in the name of compatibility, any program written for the 8088 will run on a Pentium. The Pentium uses the same two-argument format and even, in most cases, the same mnemonics. The only major change is that the mnemonics have been updated to reflect the possibility of using the extended (32-bit) registers; the instruction

```
ADD     EAX, EBX      ; ADD 32-bit register to 32-bit register
```

is legal and does the obvious thing.

Many new instructions have been created by obvious **analogy** to handle 32-bit quantities. For example, to the string primitives MOVSB and MOVSW (copy a string of bytes/words, defined in the previous chapter) has been added a new MOVSD that copies a string of doublewords (32-bit quantities) from one memory location to another.

8.3.2   Advanced Operations

The Pentium also provides many new-from-the-ground-up operations and mnemonics, more than can be described here. Many of them, perhaps most, are shortcuts to perform (common) tasks with fewer machine instructions than would be needed using the simpler instruction. For example, one instruction (BSWAP) swaps the end bytes in a 32-bit register (specified as an argument), a task that could be performed using basic arithmetic in a dozen or so steps. Another example is the XCHG (eXCHanGe) instruction, which swaps the source and destination arguments around. The idea behind these particular operations is that a sufficiently powerful compiler can produce highly optimized machine code to maximize system performance.

Another example of this sort of new instruction is the new set of control instructions, ENTER and LEAVE, which were included to support the semantics of functions and procedures in high-level languages such as C, C++, FORTRAN, Ada, Pascal, and so forth. As seen in section 6.4.7, local variables in such languages are normally made by creating temporary space on the system stack in a procedure-local frame. The new ENTER instruction largely duplicates the CALL semantics in transferring control to a new location while saving the old program counter on the stack, but at the same time, it builds the BP/SP stack frame and reserves space for a set of local variables, thus replacing a half-dozen simple instructions with a single rather complex one. It also provides some support for a nested declaration feature found in languages like Pascal and Ada (but not C, C++, or FORTRAN). The **LEAVE** instruction undoes the stack frame creation as a single instruction (although, again rather oddly, it doesn't perform the return from a subroutine, so a RET instruction is still needed). These instructions save a few bytes of program code, but (contrary to the wishes of the designers) they take longer to execute as a single slow instruction than the group of instructions they replace.

Another instruction added specifically to support high-level languages is the BOUND instruction, which checks that a value is between two specified upper and lower limits. The value to be checked is given as the first operand, and the second operand points to two (adjacent) memory locations giving the upper and lower limits. This allows a high-level language compiler to check that an array can be accessed safely. Again, this is something that could be done using more traditional comparison/branch instructions, but it would take a half-dozen instructions and probably would clobber several registers. Instead, the CISC instruction set lets the system do the operation cleanly, quickly, and with minimal fuss.

The various modes of operation and memory management need their own set of instructions. Examples of such instructions include VERR and VERW, which "verify" that a particular segment can be read from or written to, respectively. Another example is the INVD instruction, which flushes the internal cache memory to make sure that the cache state is consistent with the state of the system's main memory.

Finally, the continuing development of the Pentium, starting with the Pentium Pro and continuing through the PII, PIII, and P4, has added new capacities—but also new instructions and features—to the basic Pentium architecture. For example, the Pentium III (1999) added a set of special 128-bit registers, each of which can hold up to four (32-bit) numbers. Among the new instructions added were (special-purpose, of course) instructions to deal with these registers, including a set of SIMD (Single Instruction, Multiple Data) instructions that apply the same operation in parallel to four separate floating point numbers at once. Using these new instructions and registers, floating point performance can be increased substantially (by about four times), which means that math-heavy programs such as computer games will run substantially faster—or, alternatively, that a good programmer can pack graphics that are four times better into a game without slowing it down. Nice, huh?

At this point, you are probably wondering how you can possibly be expected to remember all these instructions. The answer, thank goodness, is that for the most part, you are not expected to do so. The Pentium instruction set is huge, beyond the capacity of most humans who don't work with it daily to remember. In practical terms, only the compiler needs to know the instructions so that it can select the appropriate specialized operation as needed.

8.3.3 Instruction Formats

Unlike other computers, most notably those with the Power architecture, and to a lesser extent the JVM, the Pentium does not require that all of its instructions take the same number of bits. Instead, simple operations—for example, a register-to-register ADD or a RETurn from subroutine—are stored and interpreted in only 1 or 2 bytes, making them quicker to fetch and taking up less space in memory or on the hard disk. More complicated instructions may require up to 15 bytes each.

What kind of information would go into a complicated instruction? The most obvious type is immediate-mode data, as (rather obviously), 32 bits of such data will add 4 bytes to the length of any such instruction. Similarly, an explicit (32-bit) named address for indirect addressing also adds 4 bytes, so the instruction

```
ADD   [EBX], 13572468H      ; add 32-bit quantity to memory
```

takes at least 4 bytes beyond the simple instruction. (In the previous chapter, we've seen how this issue is handled in a typical RISC chip, basically by breaking the instruction above into a half-dozen substeps.)

Beyond this, the complexity of the instruction requires more data. With so many addressing modes, the Pentium takes more bits (typically a full byte, sometimes two) to define which bit patterns are to be interpreted as registers, as memory addresses, and so forth. If an instruction is to use a nonstandard segment (one other than the default generated for that particular instruction type), another optional byte encodes that information, including the segment register to use. The various REP? prefixes used in string operations are encoded in yet another byte. These are a few examples of the complexities introduced in CISC architecture. Fortunately, these complexities are relatively rare and most instructions don't exercise them.

8.4 Memory Organization and Use

8.4.1 Memory Management

The simplest organization of the Pentium's memory is as a flat 32-bit address space. Every possible register pattern represents a possible byte location in memory. For larger patterns (for legacy reasons, a 16-byte pattern is usually called a "word," while an actual 32-bit word is called a "double"), one can coopt two or more adjacent byte locations. As long as the computer can figure out how many bytes are in use, accessing memory of varying sizes is fairly simple. This approach is also very fast, but has a substantial security weakness in that any memory address, including memory in use by the operating system or by other programs running on the machine, is available to be tampered with. (Remember my hard drive controller?), So, this simple organization (sometimes called **unsegmented unpaged memory**) is rarely used except for controller chips or other applications where the computer is doing one task and needs to do it really, really fast.

Under protected mode, additional hardware is available to prevent program tampering. The segment registers (CS, DS, etc.) inherited from the 8088 provide a solution of sorts. As with the 8088, each memory address in a general-purpose register will be interpreted relative to a given segment. However, the interpretation of the segment registers in the Pentium is a little different. Two of the 16 bits are interpreted as a protection level, while the other 14 define an extension to the 32-bit address, creating an effective 46-bit ($14 + 32$) virtual or **logical address**. This allows the computer to address much more than the 32-bit (4-gigabyte) address space and to mark large areas of memory as inaccessible to a particular program, thus protecting private data.

However, these 46-bit addresses may still need to be converted into physical addresses to be accessed over the memory bus (which has only 32 lines and hence takes 32-bit addresses). The task of converting from these **virtual addresses** to 32-bit **physical addresses** is handled by the **paging hardware**. The Pentium contains a directory of **page table entries** that act as a translation system for this conversion task. Use of the segmentation and/or paging hardware can be enabled or disabled independently, allowing the user of the system (or, more likely, the writer of the operating system) to tune performance to a particular application. From the user's point of view, much of the complexity is handled by the hardware, so you can write your program without worrying about it.

8.5 Performance Issues

8.5.1 Pipelining

A standard modern technique for improving the performance of a chip is **pipelining**. The Pentium, although less well suited in its instruction set to take advantage of pipelining than some other chips, nevertheless uses this technique extensively (figure 8.1).

Even before the Pentium was developed, the Intel 80486 had already incorporated a five-stage pipeline for instruction execution. The five stages are:

- *Fetch*: Instructions are fetched to fill one of two **prefetch buffers**. These buffers store up to 16 bytes (128 bits) each and operate independently of the rest of the pipeline.

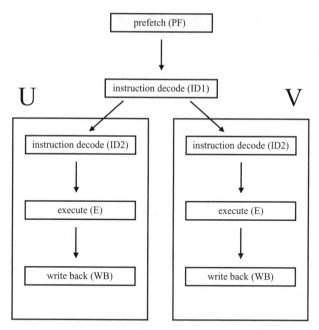

Figure 8.1 Illustration of the Pentium five-stage pipeline, including superscalar U and V pipelines

- *Decode stage 1*: Instruction decode is performed in two separate stages, with the first stage acting as a type of preanalysis to determine what sort of information must be extracted (and from where) in the full instruction. Specifically, the D1 stage extracts preliminary information about the opcode and the address mode, but not necessarily the full details of the address(es) involved.
- *Decode stage 2*: This completes the task of decoding the instruction, including identification of displacement or immediate data, and generates control signals for the ALU.
- *Execute*: This stage executes the instruction.
- *Write back*: This stage updates registers, status flags, and cache memory as appropriate given the results of the immediately previous stage.

This pipeline is more complicated than others we have seen (such as the Power chip), in part because of the complexity of the instruction set it needs to process. Remember that Pentium (and even 486) instructions can vary in length from 1 to 15 bytes. This is part of the reason that the instruction prefetch buffers need to be so large; they must be able to hold the next instruction completely. For similar reasons, it can take a long time to decode complicated instructions—sometimes as long as or even longer than it takes to execute simple ones. The number and complexity of the addressing modes are major factors, since they can add several layers of interpretation to an otherwise simple logical or arithmetic operation. For this reason, there are two separate decode stages to keep the pipeline flowing smoothly and quickly. The 80486 can perform most operations that do not involve memory loads at a rate of close to one operation per machine cycle. Even so, indirect addresses (where the value in a register is used as a memory address) and branches can slow the pipeline down.

This pipelining is considerably more extensive on the Pentium and later versions. Not only are there several pipelines (reflecting the superscalar architecture), but each pipeline may have more stages. The original Pentium had two pipelines with each of the five stages listed above. The Pentium II increased the number of pipelines and increased the number of stages per pipeline to 12, including a special stage to determine the length of each instruction. The Pentium III uses 14-stage pipelines and the P4 uses ones with 24 stages, pipelines that complicated to discuss in detail here. So despite not having an instruction set designed for efficient pipelines, the Pentium has taken to them with a vengeance.

8.5.2   Parallel Operations

The Pentium incorporates two other substantial architectural features to allow truly parallel operations—performing two instructions at the same time within the CPU. Starting with the Pentium II, the instruction set features a collection of **MMX instructions** specifically for multimedia applications, such as high-speed graphics (games) or sound (again, games). These implement a sort of **SIMD** (Single Instruction, Multiple Data) parallelism, whereby the same operation is performed on several independent pieces of data.

A typical multimedia application involves processing large arrays of relatively small numeric data types (for example, pixels in a screen image) and performing the same calculation on every data type rapidly enough to present the image without noticeable flicker. To support this operation, the Pentium II defines a set of MMX registers, each 64 bits long, holding either 8 bytes, four words, two doublewords, or less frequently an 8-byte quadword. A sample MMX instruction defines a single operation to be performed on all elements of the register simultaneously. For example, the PADDB (Parallel ADD Bytes) instruction performs eight additions on the 8 separate bytes, and the variant PAADW performs four simultaneous additions on four words. For a simple operation like displaying a simple byte-oriented image, this allows data to be processed up to eight times as fast as it would be using ordinary 8-bit operations.

8.5.3   Superscalar Architecture

As discussed before (section 5.2.5), the other major parallel instruction technique involves duplication of pipeline stages or even entire pipelines. One of the difficulties in pipelining is keeping the stages balanced; if it takes substantially longer to execute an instruction than it did to fetch it, the stages behind it may back up. The original Pentium used the 80486 five-stage pipeline but duplicated key stages to create two pipelines, called the **U** and **V** pipelines. Instructions can alternate between the two pipelines, or even execute two at a time, if both pipelines are clear. More generally, a **superscalar architecture** will have multiple pipelines or multiple execution units within specific stages of the pipelines to handle different kinds of operations (like the distinction drawn earlier between the ALU and the FPU, only more so).

Later models of the Pentium, starting with the Pentium II, extended this further. In particular, the Pentium II's decode 1 (ID1) stage is more or less replicated three times. In theory, this implies that the ID1 stage could take up to three times as long as other stages without slowing up the overall pipeline significantly. In practice, the situation is more complex. The first instruction decoder can handle instructions of moderate complexity, while the second and third decoders can only handle very simple instructions. The Pentium II hardware therefore includes a special instruction-fetch stage that will reorder instructions to align them with the decoder; therefore, if any one of the next three instructions in the instruction queue is complicated, it will be automatically placed in decoder 1. Since these instructions are rather rare, it wasn't considered necessary to add this (expensive) capacity to the second and third decoder. Finally, for extremely complex instructions, there's a fourth decoder, the microcode instruction sequencer (MIS).

There's also a duplication of hardware units at the execution stage. A special stage of the pipeline, the reorder buffer (ROB), takes instructions and dispatches them in groups of up to five among various execution units. These units handle, for instance, load instructions, store instructions, integer operations (divided into "simple" and "complex" types), floating point instructions (similarly divided), and several different kinds of MMX instructions.

8.6 RISC vs. CISC Revisited

Having spent several chapters dwelling on the differences between RISC and CISC architecture, you've probably notice that the practical differences are few—both the (RISC) Power chip and the (CISC) Pentium use many of the same techniques to get the greatest possible performance out of the machine. Part of the reason for this is competition is been enough that both groups are willing to figure out how to use each other's good ideas. More significantly, the lines themselves are blurring as technology improves. Moore's law indicated that transistor density, and hence the amount of circuitry that can be put on a reasonably sized microchip, has been getting larger and larger at a very fast rate. This, in turn, means that even "reduced" instruction set chips can have enough circuitry to include useful instructions, even if these are complicated.

At the same time, the hardware has gotten fast enough to allow extremely small-scale software emulation of traditional hardware functions. This approach, called **microprogramming**, involves the creation of a CPU within the CPU with its own tiny microinstruction set. A complicated machine instruction—for example, the 8088/Pentium MOVSB instruction that moves a string of bytes from one location to another—could be implemented at the microinstruction level by a sequence of individual microinstructions to move 1 byte each. The macroinstruction would be translated into a possibly large set of microinstructions which are executed one at a time from a microinstruction buffer invisible to the original programmer.

This kind of translation is the job of the various ID1 decoders in the Pentium superscalar architecture. The second and third decoders are only capable of translating instructions into a single microinstruction; the first decoder can handle more complicated instructions that produce up to four microinstructions. For even more complicated instructions, the MIS acts as a lookup table storing up to several hundred microinstructions for the really complicated parts of the Pentium instruction set.

At a more philosophical level, the irony is that the Pentium, as currently implemented, is a RISC chip. The individual microoperations at the core of the various execution units are the kinds of small-scale, fast operations at the heart of a strict RISC design. The major weakness of RISC—that it requires a sophisticated compiler to produce the right set of instructions—is handled instead by a sophisticated instruction compiler/interpreter, using the CISC instruction set as almost an intermediate expression stage. Programs written in a high-level language are compiled to the

CISC instructions of the executable file, and then each instruction, when executed, is reconverted into the RISC like microinstructions.

8.7 Chapter Review

- The Intel Pentium is a family of chips—the best-known and best-selling CPU chips in the world. Partly as a result of effective marketing, and partly as a result of the success of previous similar chips such as the x86 family, the Pentium (and third-party Pentium clones, made by companies such as Advanced Micro Devices) has been established as the CPU chip of choice for Windows and Linux-based computers.

- Partly as a result of the CISC design, and partly as a result of legacy improvements and backward compatibility, the Pentium is a complex chip with a very large instruction set.

- Available operations include the usual arithmetic operations (although multiplication and division have special formats and use special registers), data transfers, logical operations, and several other special-purpose operational shortcuts. The entire 8088 instruction set is available to provide backward compatibility.

- The Pentium includes a huge number of special-purpose instructions designed to support specific operations. For example, the ENTER/LEAVE instructions support the sorts of programs typically resulting from compiling high-level languages such as Pascal and Ada.

- The Pentium II offers a set of multimedia (MMX) instructions that provide instruction-level parallelism for simple arithmetic operations. The MMX instruction set allows SIMD operations—for instance, performing eight separate and independent additions or logical operations at once instead of one at a time.

- The Pentium also incorporates extensive pipelining and superscalar architecture to allow genuine MIMD parallelism.

- The implementation of the Pentium involves a RISC core where individual CISC instructions are implemented in a RISC-like microinstruction set.

8.8 Exercises

1. What are four major changes between the 8088 and the Pentium?
2. Name four instructions in the Pentium that the 8088 does not have.
3. Why are there two decode stages in the Pentium pipeline but only one execute stage?
4. How could SIMD parallelism smooth cursor/pointer movement on a computer screen?
5. What purpose is served by reordering the instruction fetches in the Pentium II?

9

Microcontrollers: The Atmel AVR

9.1 Background

A **microcontroller** is the kind of computer used for small-scale control operations inside devices that one doesn't usually think of as being computers. Classic examples of such devices include traffic lights, toasters, thermostats, and elevators, but better, more detailed types are the microcontrollers that are now installed in modern automobiles. Antilock braking, for instance, is only possible because of a microcontroller that monitors the braking system and cuts in when the wheels lock (and the car is about to skid). Other microcontrollers search for opportunities to fire the airbags, adjust fuel mixtures to reduce emissions, and so forth. According to Motorola, a microcontroller manufacturer, even a low-end 2002 model passenger vehicle contained about 15 microcontrollers; a luxury car, with much better entertainment and safety features, usually had 100 or more. These numbers have only gone up since then.

There is no formal accepted definition of microcontrollers, but they usually have three main characteristics. First, they are usually found in so-called **embedded systems**, running specialized single-purpose code as part of a larger system, instead of being general-purpose user-programmable computers. Second, they tend to be smaller, less capable. computers. (The Zilog Z8 Encore! microcontroller uses 8-bit words, runs at 20 MHz, can address only 64K of memory, and sells for about $4. By comparison, a Pentium 4 processor can easily cost $250 or more for the bare processor—without memory and therefore independently useless.). Third, as hinted at, microcontrollers are usually single-chip gadgets; their memory and most of their peripherial interfaces are located on the same physical chip. This is more usual now than it seems, since almost all modern computer architectures have cache memory located on the CPU chip. The important implication is that the memory available to a microcontroller is by definition all cache memory, and is therefore small but fast.

In this chapter, we'll look in detail at the AVR microcontroller manufactured by the Atmel Corporation. Of course, the AVR isn't by any stretch of the imagination the only such computer out there; microcontrollers are commodity items, sold by the billions. The field is fiercely competitive; other companies that make and sell microcontrollers include Microchip, Intel, AMD, Motorola, Zilog, Toshiba, Hitachi, and General Instrumentation. However, the AVR (or, more accurately, the AVR family, since there are several variants of the basic AVR design) is fairly typical in its capacities but differs in interesting ways from more main-stream chips such as the Pentium or Power chip (made by Intel and Apple/IBM/Motorola, respectively).

9.2   Organization and Architecture

9.2.1   Central Processing Unit

The Atmel AVR uses RISC design principles in the interests of both speed and simplicity. There are relatively few instructions, making those that do exist both short (2 bytes, compared to the PowerPC's 4 bytes or the Pentium's up to 15) and fast to execute. Each instruction is constrained to have a standardized length of 16 bits, including the necessary arguments. The instruction set is tuned specifically for the usual needs of a microcontroller, including a (relatively) large number of bit instructions for the manipulation of individual electrical signals. Despite this, there are still only about 130 different instructions (fewer than there are on the JVM). Even the AVR does not have the smallest instruction set; Microchip makes a relatively common tiny chip—used in toasters, as it happens—with fewer than 35 instructions.

The Atmel AVR contains 32 general-purpose registers (numbered from R0 to R31), as well as 64 **I/O registers**. Each of these registers is 8 bits wide, enough for a single byte or a number from 0 to 255 (or −128 to 127). As with the JVM, some registers can be used in pairs to permit larger numbers to be accessed. Unusually (at least compared with the computers we've already studied), these registers are physically part of memory instead of being separate from the memory chip (figure 9.1).

For all practical purposes, the AVR provides no support for floating point numbers; the ALU will only do operations on integer types, and on very small integers at that.

Operationally, the AVR is very similar to the computers we already know, having a special-purpose instruction register, PC, stack pointer, and so forth.

9.2.2   Memory

Because the AVR is a microcontroller, its memory on an AVR is quite limited. Unusually, its memory is divided into three separate banks that differ not only physically, but also in their

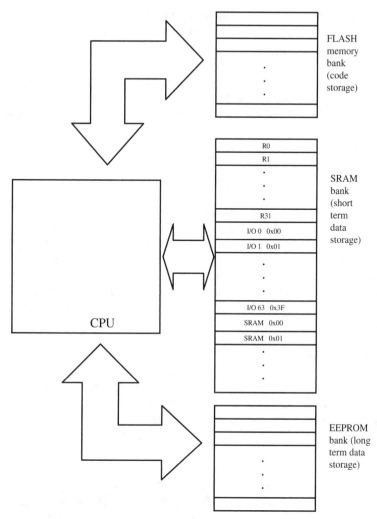

Figure 9.1 AVR block architecture. Note especially the Harvard architecture (multiple separate memory blocks) and general-purpose registers stored in memory, not in the CPU

sizes and capacities. The exact memory capacity differs from model to model, but the capacities of the AT90S2313 are representative. This machine, like most microcontrollers, is an example of the **Harvard architecture** design, where different physical storage banks (and different data buses) are available for transferring machine instructions and data. By using two separate paths, each memory bank can be independently tuned to maximize performance. Furthermore, the computer can load instructions and data at the same time (over the two buses), effectively doubling its speed. But for general-purpose computers, this would also ordinarily require two separate cache memories (one for instructions, one for data), which in turn would reduce the amount of cache available to each memory and seriously erode cache performance. On a microcontroller, where the memory is all cache anyway, it doesn't have as much of an impact.

On the AVR in particular, there are three separate banks of memory: a read-only bank for program code (since program code shouldn't change during the execution of a program), a read/write bank of high-speed memory for program variables, and a third bank for long-term storage of program data that must survive a power outage (for example, logging or configuration information). Unlike conventional architectures, where all memory is more or less created equal and a single virtual address space suffices to access anything, each of these three banks is independently structured and accessed with its own address space and instructions.

As discussed earlier, there is a fundamental distinction between **ROM** (Read-Only Memory), which can be read from but not written to, and **RAM** (Random Access Memory), which can be both read from and written to. This distinction is more fundamental in theory than it has become in practice, with the development of various types of memory that require extensive equipment to scribble on but are still writeable (in an abstract, Platonic, and expensive sense). In practical terms, the modern definition of the ROM/RAM distinction is a difference in use: whether or not the CPU is able to write to the memory (bank). On the AVR, the first bank of memory is made of FLASH ROM. Although FLASH memory is in theory read/write (it's the usual type of memory used in keychain drives), there are no circuits or instructions on the AVR to write to it. From the AVR's perspective, FLASH memory provides (on the AT90S2313, 2048 bytes of) **nonvolatile** memory, which does not lose information when the power is removed. This memory, for all practical purposes read-only, is organized into 16-bitwords and provides storage for the executable machine code. In particular, the value stored in the PC is used as a word address into this particular block of memory. The AVR chip itself cannot make any changes to the ROM, and so it can only be programmed (or reprogrammed) by someone with appropriate external equipment. (And, in all honesty, the equipment isn't that expensive.)

By contrast, the second bank of memory is specifically both readable and writable. This **data memory** is composed of **SRAM (static random access memory)**. As discussed in the sidebar, the primary difference between SRAM and **DRAM (dynamic random access memory)** is that dynamic RAM requires periodic "refresh" signals from the computer circuitry to retain its value. The AT90S2313 has fewer than 256 bytes of SRAM.

Since memory is composed of more or less the fastest data storage circuitry available, there is no need for a separate high-speed register bank, as in more typical computers. AVR data memory is organized as a sequence of 8-bit bytes divided into three subbanks. The first 32 bytes/words (0x00..0x1F, or $00..$1F, to use Atmel's notation) are used as the general-purpose registers R0..R31. The next 64 words (0x20..0x5F) are used as the 64 I/O registers, and the rest of the SRAM provides a bank of general-purpose memory storage registers for program variables and/or stack frames as necessary. These memory storage locations are addressed using addresses from 0x60 up to the amount of memory built into the chip (to 0xDF on our standard example, the AT90S2313).

Finally, the third bank uses another kind of memory, **EEPROM**. Like the Flash ROM, the EEPROM bank is nonvolatile, so the data persists after the power goes off. Like SRAM,

SIDEBAR

Kinds of Memory

A rose may be a rose may be a rose, but memory isn't just memory. We've already discussed several diffent kinds of memory—for example, the difference between RAM and ROM. In very broad terms, engineers will talk about many different kinds of memory, each of which has an appropriate use.

- RAM: **Random Access Memory**. This is the most common type of memory that people think of when they hear about memory; binary values are stored as electrical signals. Each set of signals (usually sets are word- or byte-sized, but they can also be individual bits) can be addressed independently, in "random" order, hence the name. RAM is a kind of **volatile** memory in that the chips require electrical power in order to hold the signal; if the power goes out, all the information you have in RAM will disappear.

  There are two broad subtypes of RAM: **Dynamic RAM (DRAM)** and **Static RAM (SRAM)**. Most of the memory you buy or see is DRAM, which is cheaper and more compact. Each "bit" is simply stored as a charge on a single electrical capacitor (plus an associated transistor), a device that will hold energy for a short period of time. The problem with DRAM is that the memory trace decays inside the circuit even if the chip itself has power. SRAM will remember values as long as the computer has power without needing refreshes. In practical terms, this means that the computer must periodically generate refresh signals to recreate the DRAM memory patterns. ("Periodically," in this context, means a few thousand times a second. This is still a relatively long period of time for a 1-GHz processor.)

  By contrast, SRAM is built to be self-reinforcing, like the flip-flop circuits discussed in appendix A. Each memory bit will typically require about 6 to 10 transistors to create, which means that a byte of SRAM memory takes up to 10 times as much space on the chip and costs up to 10 times as much money. On the other hand, because SRAM requires no refresh cycles, it can be accessed more quickly. Whereas DRAM is usually used for main system memory (where the added cost of several hundred megabytes adds up), SRAM is usually used in small, speed-critical memory applications such as the computer's **cache memory**. (For this reason, the Atmel microcontroller uses exclusively SRAM for its writable memory; with less than 1,000 bytes, speed dominates over price.) Despite the fact that SRAM is self-refreshing, the transistors still need power in order to work, and SRAM will lose its signal if power is cut off for too long (milliseconds). Thus, SRAM is still considered to be volatile memory.

- ROM: **Read-Only Memory**. Whereas RAM can be both read from and written to, ROM chips cannot be written to. A better description is that writing to ROM chips, when possible at all, requires special operations and sometimes even special equipment. However, the advantage of ROM is that it's a form of **nonvolatile memory**, meaning that if power is removed from the chip, the data still remains. This makes it ideal for storing, for example, photographs taken by a digital camera.

  The simplest and oldest version of ROM is structured similarly to DRAM, except that instead of using a capacitor, each memory cell contains a **diode**, which is programmed by the chip manufacturer to pass current if and only if that memory cell is supposed to hold a 1. Since diodes do not need power and do not usually degrade, the pattern built into the chip will remain unchanged forever unless you jump on it or something. In addition the manufacturer must know exactly what memory values to use, and the consequences are

(continued)

serious if the manufacturer changes its decision or makes a mistake. (The infamous 1993 Pentium `fdiv` bug is an example of what can go wrong with a ROM.)

ROMs can be built extremely cheaply in quantity—for pennies per chip. But what happens if you need only 25 chips? It's probably not worthwhile to buy an entire chip factory. Instead, it is better to use **PROM (Programmable ROM)** chips. Like ROM chips, these are manufactured with a static electrical connection at every memory cell (instead of an active element like a capacitor or transistor). In a PROM, these connections are actually fuses that can be broken by the application of a high enough voltage. This process, for obvious reasons, is called "burning" a PROM. Once the PROM is burned, the electrical connections that remain (or are now broken) are still fixed and unchanging. But because it's impossible to unbreak a fuse, a PROM can only be burned once.

A final type of ROM avoids this issue. **EPROM (Erasable Programmable ROM)** chips use advanced quantum physics to create a semiconductor-based reusable fuse at each memory element. To create an electrical connection, the memory location is subjected to the same over-voltage used with the PROM. However, applying ultraviolet light for several minutes will cause the "fuse" to reset. This will erase the entire chip, allowing it to be reprogrammed and reused.

• **Hybrid memory.** In an effort to achieve the best of both worlds, manufacturers have started making so-called hybrid memory, which is supposed to be field-reprogrammable while still having the storage advantages of ROM. A variation on EPROM technology, such as **EEPROM (Electronically Erasable Programmable ROM)** chips, uses a localized electrical field to "erase" each memory cell instead of erasing the entire chip as a whole. Because this operation is performed electronically, it doesn't require the cabinet-sized ultraviolet light chamber and can be part of the distributed system.

On the other hand, writing to EEPROMs takes a long time because the cell must be exposed to the magnetic field to erase it, which takes several milliseconds. In theory, EEPROMs provide the same functionality as RAM, since each individual cell can be written, read, and rewritten, but the timing (and cost issues) make it impractical. Another major problem with EEPROMs is that they are typically capable of only a limited number of read/write cycles.

FLASH memory is one approach to speeding up the process of writing to EEPROMs. The basic idea is simple; instead of erasing each bit individually the electrical field (for erasing) is applied to large blocks on the chip. It takes more or less the same time to erase a block as it does to erase a single bit, but when data must be stored in mass quantities (say, on a pen drive like my beloved Jump Drive 2.0 Pro, manufactured by Lexar Media), the time needed to transfer a block of data to memory dominates over the time needed to erase the sector where it will be placed. Flash memory is widely used, not only in pen drives but also in digital camera memory, smart cards, memory cards for game consoles, and solid-state disks in PCIMCIA cards.

Another variation on hybrid memory is **NVRAM (Non-Volatile RAM)**, which is actually SRAM with an attached battery. In the event of power loss, the battery is capable of providing the power necessary to keep memory alive in an SRAM chip. Of course, the cost of the battery makes this kind of memory substantially more expensive than simple SRAM.

• **SAM (Sequential Access Memory):** No discussion of memory types would be complete without mentioning SAM. SAM is intuitively familiar to anyone who has tried to find a particular scene in a videotape. Unlike RAM, SAM can only be accessed in a particular (sequential) order, which can make it slow and awkward to use in small pieces of data. Most kinds of secondary storage—CD-ROMs, DVDs, hard drives, even magnetic tapes—are actually SAM devices, although they usually try to provide block-level random access.

EEPROM is electronically programmable, so the AVR CPU can write data to the EEPROM for persistent storage (although it takes a long time, on the order of 4 ms). Unlike the SRAM, though, there is a limited number of times that data can be rewritten (about 100,000 times, although technology is always improving). This is a physical problem related to the construction of the memory, but it should be borne in mind when writing programs for the AVR. Writing a piece of data to the EEPROM bank just once per second will still reach the 100,000 write limit in a little over a day. However, there's no limit to the number of times that the computer can safely read from the EEPROM. This makes the EEPROM bank ideal for storing field-modifiable data that needs to be kept but that doesn't change very often, such as setup/configuration information or infrequent data logging (say, once per hour, which would give you about a 10-year lifetime). On our standard example, the EEPROM bank is organized as a set of 128 bytes.

Each of these memory banks has its own address space, so the number 0 (0x00) could refer not only to the actual number 0, but to the lowest 2 bytes of the Flash memory, the lowest (single) byte of EEPROM, or the lowest byte of SRAM (also known as R0). As with all assembly language programs, the key to resolving this ambiguity is context; values stored in the PC refer to FLASH memory, while normal register values (when read as addresses) refer to locations in SRAM. EEPROM is accessed through special-purpose hardware that in practical terms can be treated as a peripherial.

9.2.3   Devices and Peripherials

The AVR implements a simple kind of memory-mapped I/O. It is not designed to be used in graphics-heavy environments, where one might be expected to display pictures consisting of millions of bytes 20 to 30 times per second. Instead, it is expected to drive a chip where the output goes through a few pins that are physically (and electrically) attached to the CPU circuitry. Specifically, these pins are addressable through specific defined locations in the I/O memory bank. Writing to I/O memory location 0x18 (SRAM memory location 0x38), for example, is defined as writing to the "Port B Data Register" (PORTB), which in turn is equivalent to setting an electrical signal at the eight output pins corresponding to Port B. The chip can generate enough power to turn on a simple light-emitting diode (LED), or throw an electrical switch to connect a stronger power source to a more power-hungry device. Similarly, reading the various bits from the register will cause the CPU to detect the voltage level currently present at the pins, perhaps to detect if a photocell (a so-called electric eye) is reacting to light or to determine the current temperature reading from an external sensor.

The AVR usually provides several bidirectional data ports that can be individually defined (on a per-pin basis) to be input or output devices. It also provides on-chip timer circuits that can be used to measure the passage of time and/or let the chip take action on a regular, recurring basis (such as changing a stop light every 30 seconds or taking an engine temperature reading every millisecond). Depending on the model, there may be other built-in peripherals such as a UART (Universal Asynchronous Receiver and Transmitter) for large-scale data transmission/reception, an analog comparator to compare two analog sensor readings, and so forth. Unlike with larger computers, many of the output devices (the pins) are shared by several different output devices; the pins used for the UART are the same physical connections used for data Port B. Without this sort of overlap, the chip would be physically much more difficult to use (having hundreds of pins needing individual connections), but the overlap itself means that there are several device sets that cannot be used together. If you are using Port B, you can't use the UART at the same time.

The I/O memory is also where information on the current state of the CPU itself is stored. For example, the AVR status register (SREG) is located at I/O location 0x3F (SRAM location 0x5F) and contains bits describing the current CPU status (such as whether or not the most recent computation resulted in a 0 and/or a negative number). The stack pointer is stored at location 0x3D (0x5D) and defines the location (in SRAM) of the active stack location. Because these registers are treated programmatically as memory locations, interacting with I/O peripherials is as simple as storing and reading memory locations.

9.3 Assembly Language

Like most chips, the registers on the AVR are not structured in any particular fashion. Assembly language instructions are thus written in a two-argument format, where the destination operand comes before the source operand. Thus

```
ADD       R0, R1           ; R0 = R0 + R1
```

will cause the value of R1 to be added to the value of R0, storing the result in R0 and setting the value of various SREG bits to reflect the outcome of the result. Confusingly, the numbers 0 and 1 will work just as well as the more understandable R0 and R1—the assembler will usually accept either. Although superficially this looks very much like an assembly language instruction for a Pentium or Power, it (of course) corresponds to a different machine language value specific to the Atmel AVR.

The AVR provides most of the normal set of arithmetic and logical operations that we have come to expect: ADD, SUB, MUL (unsigned multiply), MULS (signed multiply), INC, DEC, AND, OR, COM (bit complement, i.e., NOT), NEG (two's complement, i.e., negate), EOR (exclusive or), and TST (which tests a register value and sets the flags appropriately if the value is 0 or negative). Perhaps oddly in our view, the slow and expensive division operation is *not* available. Also not available is the modulus operator or any kind of floating point support.

To speed up the sorts of computations typically done by a microcontroller, there are a number of –I variants (SUBI, ORI, ANDI, etc.) that will take an immediate mode constant and perform that operation on the register. For example,

```
ADD       0, 1             ; R0 = R0 + R1
```

will add register 1 to register 0. The instruction

```
ADDI      0, 1             ; R0 = R0 + 1, or "increment R0"
```

will, by constrast, add the immediate value 1 to register 0.

There are also several instructions to perform operations on individual bits: for instance, SBR (set bit(s) in register) or CBI (clear bit in I/O register) will set/clear individual bits in a general-purpose or I/O register. For example,

```
SBR     R0, FF              ; R0 = R0 OR 0xFF
```

will set the lower 8 bits of register 0 to 1s.

The various control operations are also extensive. In addition to a wide range of branch/jump instructions (unconditionally: JMP; conditionally: BR??, where ?? refers to different flags and flags combinations in the SREG register; and jump to subroutine: CALL), there are a few new operations. The SB?? operation–the first ? is an R (general-purpose register) or an I (I/O register), the second is a C (clear bit) or S (set bit), hence SBIC = Skip if Bit in I/O register is Clear—performs a very limited branch that skips the single next instruction if the bit in the appropriate register is set/clear. The AVR also supports **indirect jumps** (unconditional: IJMP, to subroutine: ICALL) where the target location is taken from a register (pair), specifically the 16-bit value stored in R30:R31.

9.4 Memory Organization and Use

Normal data transfer instructions manipulate the SRAM memory bank by default. Since registers and I/O registers are for all practical purposes part of this same bank, there's no difference between writing to a register and writing to a simple SRAM byte. However, the arithmetic operations defined in the previous section work only with the general-purpose registers (R0..R31), so one must still be prepared to move data around within this bank. The normal instructions for this purpose are the LDS (Load Direct from SRAM) instruction, which takes a register as its first argument and a memory location as its second, or the corresponding SDS (Store Direct to SRAM) instruction, which reverses the arguments and the process. The AVR also provides three specific **indirect address registers**, X, Y, and Z, that can be used for indirect addressing. These are the last six general-purpose registers, taken in pairs (so the X register is really the R26:R27 pair), and can be used to hold (variable) addresses in memory. Using these registers and the LD (Load inDirect) instruction, the code

```
CLR     R26             ; Clear R26 (set it to 0)
LDI     R27, 0x5F       ; Load Immediate (constant value) 5F into R27
LD      R0, X           ; Move (X) [= value in location 5F] into R0
```

will copy memory location 0x005F into register 0. It first sets the two halves of the X register individually to 0x00 and 0x5F, then uses this as an index register (we have previously seen that 0x005F is actually the SREG register). An easier way of doing this would be to use the IN instruction, which reads the value from the specified I/O register:

```
IN      R0, 0x3F        ; Copy SREG  into R0
```

Note that although SREG is in memory location 0x5F, it is only in I/O port number 3F.

Access to FLASH memory (which can, of course only be read from, not written to) is obtained indirectly using the LPM (Load from Program Memory) instruction. The value stored in the Z register is used as a memory address inside the program (Flash) memory area, and the appropriate value is copied to the R0 register.

Accessing EEPROM is more difficult, largely for physics and electronics reasons. Although an EEPROM bank is in theory read/write, writing effects actual physical change to the memory bank. Therefore, it takes a long time to complete and can require substantial preparations (such as powering up "charge pumps" to provide the necessary energy for the changes) that need to take place before the write can be performed. On the AVR, the designers opted for a memory access scheme that closely resembles the one used to access a device.

The AVR defines three I/O registers (as part of the I/O register bank in SRAM): the EEAR (EEPROM Address Register), EEDR (EEPROM Data Register), and EECR (EEPROM Control Register). The EEAR contains a bit pattern corresponding to the address of interest (a value between 0 and .127 in our standard example, so the high bit should always be a 0). The EEDR contains either the data to be written or the data that has just been read, in either case using the data in the EEAR as the destination.

The EECR contains three control bits that individually **enable** read or write access to the EEPROM memory bank. In particular, bit 0 (the least significant bit) of the EECR is defined to be the **EERE** (EEPROM Read Enable) bit. To read from a given location in the EEPROM, the programmer should take these steps:

- Load the byte address of interest into the EEAR.
- Set the EERE set to 1, allowing the read to proceed.
- Read the data.
- After the read operation is completed, find relevant data in the EEDR.

The steps used to write are a little (not much!) more complex, because there are 2 enabling bits that need to be set. Bit 2 is defined to be the **EEMWE** (EEPROM Master Write Enable) bit; when it it set to 1, the CPU is enabled to write to the EEPROM. However, this doesn't actually do any writing; it simply performs the preparations for writing. The actual writing is performed by setting bit 1 (the **EEWE**/EEPROM Write Enable bit) to 1 *after the EEMWE has also been set to 1*. The EEMWE will automatically return to 0 after a short period of time (about four instructions). This two-phase commit process the computer from accidentally scribbling once the EEPROM (and damaging important data) in the event of an unexpected program bug.

In order to write to the EEPROM, the programmer should

- Load the byte address of interest into the EEAR.
- Load the new data into the EEDR.
- Set the EEMWE to 1, enabling writing to the EEPROM bank.
- (Within four clock cycles) Set the EEWE to 1, allowing the write to happen.
- Write the data.

The actual writing, however, can be extremely slow, taking as much as 4 ms. On a chip running at 10 MHz, this is enough time to perform 40,000 (!) other operations. For this reason, it's a good idea to make sure that the EEPROM isn't in the middle of writing (i.e., waiting for the EEWE bit to go to 0 after a potential current write completes) before trying any other EEPROM operations.

9.5 Issues of Interfacing

9.5.1 Interfacing with External Devices

The EEPROM interface described in the previous section is very similar to other peripherial interfaces. Each device is controlled (and interacted with) by a small set of defined registers in the I/O register bank. A few examples should suffice to give the flavor of interaction.

The AT90S2313 provides as one of its built-in devices a UART attached to a set of pins configured to drive a standard serial port. We will eliminate the physical details of the electrical connnections, which are interesting but would bring us more into the realm of electrical engineering than of computer architecture. The CPU interacts with the UART hardware through a set of four registers: the UART I/O Data Register (which stores the physical data to be transmitted or received), the UART Control Register (which controls the actual operation of UART, for example by enabling transmission or by setting operational parameters), the UART Baud Rate Register (which controls how rapidly/slowly data is transferred), and the UART Status Register (a read-only register that shows the current status of the UART). To send data across the UART, and thus across a serial line, the UART I/O Data Register must first be loaded with the data to be transmitted, and the Baud Rate Register must be loaded with a pattern representing the desired speed. To perform the data transfer, the Control Register must be set to "Transmitter Enable" (formally speaking, bit 3 of the UART Control Register must be set to 1). If an error occurs in transmission, appropriate bits will be set in the Status Register, where the computer can observe them and take appropriate corrective action.

SIDEBAR

Clocks, Clock Speed, and Timing

How do computers know what time it is? More importantly, how do they make sure that things that need to happen at the same time do so (like all bits in a register getting loaded at once)? The usual answer involves a controlling **clock** or **timing circuit**. This is just a simple circuit usually hooked up to a crystal oscillator like the one in a digital watch. This oscillator will vibrate zillions of times per second, and each vibration is captured as an electrical signal and sent to all the electronic components. This, technically, is where the "1.5 GHz" in a computer description comes from; the master clock circuit in such a computer is a signal with a 1.5-GHz frequency; in other words, vibrates 1,500,000,000 times per second. As will be seen in appendix A, this clock signal both allows needed computations to proceed and prevents spurious noise from introducing errors.

For actions that need to be performed repeatedly, such as refreshing the screen every 30th of a second, a slave circuit will simply count (in this case) 50,000,000 master clock cycles and then refresh the screen. Obviously, things that need to happen fast, such as the fetch-execute cycle, will be timed to be as short as possible, ideally occurring at a rate of one per

(continued)

clock cycle. The baud rate on the UART controller is controlled by a similar slave circuit. The "speed pattern" tells this circuit how many master clock ticks should occur before the UART must change signals.

This is also the reason that **overclocking** works. If you have a processor designed to run at 1.5 GHz, you can adjust the master clock circuit (perhaps even change crystals) to run at 2.0 Hz. The CPU doesn't know that its signal is coming in too fast and will try to respond at the higher rate. If it really is running at the rate of one fetch-execute per clock tick, it will try to fetch and execute faster. In a sense, it's like trying to play a record at a higher speed than normal (45 rpm instead of 33 rpm). (Ask your parents.) Sometimes this works and you just got an inexpensive 30% speed boost. On the other hand, the CPU may not be able to respond physically to the faster speed, and it might die horribly (for example, if the cooling is inadequate). Sometimes the CPU will overrun the rest of the components (by asking for data faster than the memory can provide it or the bus can move it).

Interacting with the data port(s) involves a similar process. Unlike the UART, the data ports are configured to allow up to eight independent electrical signals to be transferred simultaneously. Using this system, a single data port could simultaneously monitor three push buttons (as input devices) and a switch (as an input device), while controlling four output LEDs. Each data port is controlled by two registers, one (the Data Direction Register) defining for each bit whether it controls an input or output device and the other (the Data Register) holding the appropriate value. To turn on an LED connected (say) to pin 6, the programmer would first make sure that the sixth bit of the DDR was set to 1 (configuring the pin as an output device) and then set the value in the sixth bit of the data register to 1, bringing the pin voltage high (about 3–5 volts) and turning on the LED. Setting this bit to 0 would correspondingly turn off the LED by setting the pin voltage to (close to) 0 volts.

9.5.2   Interfacing with Timers

The AVR also includes several built-in timers to handle normal tasks such as measuring time or performing an operation at regular intervals. (Think about an elevator: the door opens, the elevator waits a fixed number of seconds, and then the door closes again. A door that stayed open only a microsecond would be unhelpful.) Conceptually, these timers are very simple: an internal register is set to an initial value. The timer then counts clock pulses (adding 1 to the internal register each time), either from the internal system clock or from an external source of timing pulses, until the internal register "rolls over" by counting from a set of all 1s to a set of all 0s. At this point, the timer goes off and the appropriate amount of time has passed.

An example would be appropriate here. I will assume that we have a source of clock pulses that comes once every 2 μs. Loading an 8-bit timing counter with the initial value of 6 will cause it to increment to 7, 8, 9,... every 2 μs. After 250 such increments (500 μs, or about 1/2000th of a second), the timer will "roll over" to 256, which will overflow the register to 0. At this point, the timer can somehow signal the CPU that an appropriate amount of time has passed so that the CPU can do whatever it was waiting for.

One common and important kind of timer is the **watchdog timer,** whose purpose is to prevent the system from locking up. For example, a badly written toaster program could have a bug that goes into an infinite loop right after the heating element is turned on. Since infinity is a very long time, the effect of such an infinite loop would be (at least) to burn your toast, and very likely your table, your kitchen, and possibly your apartment building. The **watchdog** works as a normal timer, except that the "signals" it sends the CPU are equivalent to pressing the reset button and thus restarting the system in a known (sane) state. It is the responsibility of the program to periodically reset the watchdog (sometimes called "kicking" it) to keep it from triggering.

Although the timer itself is simple, the CPU's actions can be less so. There are two ways in which the CPU can interact with the timer. The first, dumb, way, is for the CPU to put itself into a loop, **polling** the appropriate I/O register to see whether or not the timer has completed. If the timer has not completed, the CPU returns to the top of the loop. Unfortunately, this method of continuous polling (sometimes called **busy-waiting**) prevents the CPU from performing any other, more useful, processing. Busy-waiting can be thought of as the process of sitting by a telephone waiting for an important call instead of getting on with your life.

A more intelligent way of dealing with expected future events (which also applies to waiting by the phone) is to set up an **interrupt handler**. This is more or less how the AVR deals with expected but unpredictable events. The AVR knows a few general kinds of **interrupts** that are generated under hardware-defined circumstances, such as the timer overflowing, an electrical signal on an established pin, or even power-up. On the AVR in particular, the possible interrupts for a given chip are numbered from 0 to a small value (like 10). These numbers also correspond to locations in Flash ROM (program code) in the interrupt vector; when interrupt number 0 occurs, the CPU will jump to location 0x00 and execute whatever code is stored there. Interrupt number 1 will jump to location 0x01, and so forth. Usually, all that is stored in the interrupt location itself is a single JMP instruction to transfer control (still inside the interrupt handler) to a larger block of code that does the real work. (In particular, the watchdog timer is defined to generate the same interrupt that would be created by the reset button or a power-on event, thus providing some protection against infinite loops and other program bugs.)

9.6 Designing an AVR Program

As a final example, here is a design (but not completed code) showing how a microcontroller program might work in real life. The first observation is that microcontrollers are rather specialized computers, so there are many kinds of programs that it would be silly to write for a microcontroller. The physical structure of the AVR yields some obvious examples. It would be silly to try to write a program that involves many floating point calculations, for example, on a computer with no FPU or floating point instructions. However, the AVR is a very good chip for programs within its capacities.

For a semi-realistic example, we'll look at a type of software that could be run practically on a microcontroller—specifically, the design of a traffic light seen at any typical busy intersection. I will assume that there's a street running north/south that crosses another street running east/west, and the city traffic planners want to make sure that traffic on only one street can move at a time. (I also assume the usual pattern of red/yellow[amber]/green lights, meaning stop, caution, and go.)

In order for this to work, a set of four different patterns must be presented:

Pattern number	N/S light	E/W Light	Notes
0	Green	Red	Traffic flows N/S
1	Yellow	Red	Traffic slowing N/S
2	Red	Green	Traffic flows E/W
3	Red	Yellow	Traffic slowing E/W

Actually, this might not work. For safety's sake, we might want to set all the lights to red between the times when traffic goes from N/S to E/W and vice versa to allow the intersection to clear. It would also be nice to have an emergency setting of all red lights just in case. We can add these as three additional patterns:

Pattern number	N/S light	E/W Light	Notes
4	Red	Red	Traffic about to flow N/S
5	Red	Red	Traffic about to flow E/W
6	Red	Red	Emergency

This tabulation leads to two other observations. First, all the program needs to do is to transistion (with appropriate timing) between the patterns in the following order: 0, 1, 5, 2, 3, 4, 0,... Second, as with so many other microcontroller programs, there's no real stopping point for the program. For once, it's not only useful but probably essential that the program run in an infinite loop.

The easiest way to write such a program is to implement what's called a **state machine**. The "state" of such a program is simply a number representing the pattern the lights are currently displaying (e.g, if the state is 4, all lights should be red). Each state can be held for a certain length of time (as measured by the timer). When the timer interrupt occurs, the computer will change the state (and the lights) and reset the timer to measure the next amount of time.

We can also use other interrupts in this state table. For example, we can attach a special police-only switch to a pin corresponding to an external interrupt. The interrupt handler for this interrupt will be written such that the computer goes into a specific all-red emergency state. When that switch is closed (by the police pressing a button), the controller will immediately execute the interrupt. Similar use of external interrupts could cause the computer to detect when/if a passing pedestrian presses the "walk" button, causing the computer to transition to yet another state, where the appropriate walk light is turned on for the right amount of time. And, of course, we can use the watchdog timer to look for possible program bugs, kicking it as necessary (say, every time the lights change); in the unlikely event that the watchdog timer triggers, we could have the program go either to a specific preprogrammed normal state or to the emergency state on the grounds that something has gone wrong and the system needs to be checked.

9.7 Chapter Review

- A **microcontroller** is a small, single-chip, limited-capacity computer used for small-scale operations such as device control or monitoring.
- Microcontrollers are found in many kinds of gadgets and devices, most of which do not seem (offhand) to be computers at all, such as the braking system of a car.

- The Atmel AVR is a family of related microcontrollers with a specialized instruction set for these sorts of tasks. The architecture of the AVR is substantially different from that of a more typical full-service computer. For example, the AVR doesn't have support for floating point operations, and contains fewer than 10,000 bytes of memory, but does have extensive on-board peripherial device support.
- Like many microcontrollers, the Atmel AVR is an example of RISC processing. There is a relatively small number of machine instructions tuned for specific purposes.
- The AVR is an example of Harvard architecture, in which memory is divided into several (in this case, three) different banks, each with different functions and access methods. The registers (and I/O registers) of the AVR are located in one of the three memory banks, along with general-purpose RAM for variable storage. The AVR also has a bank of FLASH ROM for program storage and a bank of EEPROM for storage of static variables whose value must survive a power outage.
- Input and output in the Atmel AVR are accomplished through I/O registers in the memory bank. A typical device has a Control Register and a Data Register. Data to be read or written is placed in the Data Register, and then bits in the Control Register will be manipulated appropriately to cause the operation to happen. Different devices will have different registers and potentially different appropriate manipulations.
- Infrequent but expected events are handled efficiently using an **interrupt** and its corresponding **interrupt handler**. When an interrupt occurs, the normal fetch-execute cycle is modified to branch to a predefined location where appropriate (interrupt-specific) actions can be taken. Such interrupts are not restricted to the Atmel AVR but happen on most computers, including the Pentium and the Power architecture.
- The AVR is a good chip for only certain kinds of programs due to the limitations of its hardware and capacities. A typical microcontroller program is a **state machine** that runs forever (in an infinite loop), performing a well-defined set of actions (like changing traffic lights) in a fixed, predefined sequence.

9.8 Exercises

1. What are three typical characteristics of a microcontroller?
2. Why does the Atmel AVR use RISC principles in its design?
3. What components of a typical computer are not found on the Atmel AVR?
4. Is the Atmel an example of von Neumann architecture? Why or why not?
5. What's the difference between RAM and ROM?
6. Why does SRAM cost more per byte than DRAM?
7. What are the memory banks of the Atmel AVR, and what are their uses?
8. What is the function of a watchdog timer?
9. What is meant by "memory-mapped I/O"?
10. Describe the procedure that the Atmel uses to make an LED flash off and on repeatedly.
11. How would the traffic light example be modified if we wanted the lights in emergency mode to flash RED–OFF–RED–OFF...?

10

Advanced Programming Topics on the JVM

10.1 Complex and Derived Types

10.1.1   The Need for Derived Types

To this point, the discussion of computing has focused on operations on basic, elementary types such as integers and floating point numbers. Most problems, especially problems large or complex enough to need computers, focus instead on less basic types. For example, to answer the question "What's the cheapest way to fly from Baltimore to San Francisco?" you need to understand planes, routes, and money. The notion of money is intimately connected with floating point numbers, while the notion of routes is more closely connected with the idea of sequences of starting and stopping points.

From a software designer's point of view, it's much easier to understand a solution if it is presented in terms of these high-level types, while the computer can only operate on the basic types within its instruction set. The notion of derived types bridges this gap nicely. A **derived type** is a complex type built from (ultimately) basic types and on which high-order computations can be performed. The derived type "money" can be built in a straightforward fashion from a floating point number (or more accurately, if less straightforwardly, from a combination of integers for the various units, like dollars and cents or perhaps pounds, shillings, pence and farthings for a historical application). The derived type "geographical location" can be built in a straightforward fashion from two numbers representing latitude and longitude.

A very abstract concept such as "route" could be built from a "list" of "flights" between "geographic locations," each "flight" being associated with a cost, expressed in "money." In this example, "route" would be a derived type. The types "list," "flight," "money," and "geographic location" would also be derived types, ultimately stored and manipulated as an appropriate collection of primitive types. From the software designer's point of view, this is a powerful advantage—if such types can be implemented in the computer system itself and if the programmer can use computer implementations of the high-level operations. Using these derived types to describe abstract, derived types allows programmers and system designers to build complex systems more easily than they could build a single monolithic program.

Let's start by looking in detail at some examples of derived types.

10.1.2   An Example of a Derived Type: Arrays
The Theory

One of the simplest and most common kinds of derived types is the **array**. From a theoretical and platform-independent perspective, an **array** is a collection of elements of identical type indexed by an integer. You can use this definition to impress someone in a data structures class, if you have to. Meanwhile, let's unpack it a bit: An array is an example of what's sometimes called a "container type," meaning that its only purpose is to store other pieces of information for later use. In an array, all the pieces have to be of the same type, such as all integers or all characters—but, of course, they can have different values. Finally, the individual locations for data are addressed using a number—specifically, an integer that references that particular element. See, not so bad! (figure 10.1).

short figure [ ] = new short [5];

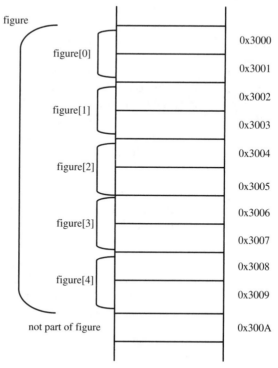

Figure 10.1   Diagram showing the memory layout for an array

If you have an array of 1,000 integers, how much space does that take up? Assuming a 4-byte integer, no bonus points are awarded for answering "at least 4,000 bytes." This is true no matter what machine one is using. However, a block of memory this big simply won't fit into a register. Fortunately, this isn't a problem, since computations have to be performed on individual data elements and not on the array as a whole. The programmer can thus use a trick to get at the data. She stores a number corresponding to the **base** of the array, a location from which all array accesses will be computed. In this case, it will be a block of memory at least 4,000 bytes long, typically the memory address of the initial element (element number 0) of the array. The programmer also stores an **offset**, an integer index of the element he or she wants to use. On the 8088 or Pentium, these numbers would be stored in two different registers, and a specific addressing mode would tell the computer to combine them appropriately to make an array access.

On the JVM, things are a little different, because "address modes" do not really exist. Instead, the two numbers are pushed on the stack and a special-purpose operation is performed to access the array appropriately. Actually, there are five special-purpose operations, depending upon what needs to be done. In approximately the order in which they are needed, these operations are:

- Creating a new array
- Loading a data item into an element of an array
- Retrieving a data item from an array element
- Determining the length of an array
- Destroying an array when it is no longer needed

More importantly, note that from the point of view of a high-level language programmer (or a computer science theorist), there's no real difference between these two approaches. That's because an array is fundamentally a derived type defined by its use. As long as there is some way of performing these actions—for example, loading a value into an array element at a particular index—the exact implementation doesn't matter from a theoretical point of view. This point will come up again in the discussion of classes proper.

Creation

Obviously, any array must be created before it can be used; the computer needs to reserve the appropriate (possibly very large) block of memory. In high-level languages such as C++ or Pascal, this is often done automatically when the array variable is declared. The statement

```
int sample[1000];
```

declares sample to be an array variable (holding elements of type "int") and at the same time reserves enough space for 1,000 integers, numbered from [0] to [999]. In Java, space for an array is reserved via explicit array creation, such as with

```
int[] sample = new int[1000];
```

There is a subtle difference here. In the first example, the creation of the array is implicit in the declaration, while in the second, the creation of the array (the allocation of the block of memory) is done via an explicit command ("new"). The JVM, of course, doesn't support variable declarations in the normal sense, but it does support array creation. This is accomplished through the use of the machine instruction newarray. In order to create an array, the programmer (and computer) needs to know both the size of the array to be created and the type of element it will contain.

The newarray instruction takes a single argument, the basic type of element for the array. The assembler is a little odd in this regard, as it expects the Java name of the type, not the type expression. For example, to create the sample array defined above, the type would be "int," not the type expression I. The length of the array to be created must be available on the stack as an integer. This length will be popped, space will be reserved for a new array of the appropriate length and type, and then an **address** corresponding to the new array will be pushed to the top of the stack. This address can be loaded and manipulated appropriately.

The JVM equivalent for defining the sample array above would look something like this:

```
ldc 1000             ; push 1000 as the new array length
newarray int         ; create an array of integers
astore   1           ; store the new array in #1\vspace*{-4pt}
```

Arrays are one place where the basic types of byte and char are actually used. In calculations on the stack, byte and char values are automatically promoted to integers, and in local variables they are still sized as 32-bit quantities. This is somewhat wasteful of space, but it wastes less space (at most 3 bytes per local variable, a tiny number) than it would to make the JVM capable of storing small quantities. With arrays, the wasted space could be much more significant as the arrays grow. In fact, the JVM even provides a basic type for **boolean** arrays, since a machine could choose to store up to eight boolean values in a single byte (32 in a single word) for a more than 95% improvement in space efficiency.

Technically speaking, the newarray instruction (opcode 0xBC) will only create one-dimensional arrays of primitive, basic types such as ints and floats. An array of derived types is more tricky to create because the type needs to be specified. Because derived objects can be defined more or less arbitrarily by the programmer, there is not and cannot be a standardized list of all the possible derived types. The JVM provides an anewarray instruction (opcode 0xBD) for one-dimensional arrays of a derived type. As before, the size must be popped off the stack, while the type is given as an argument. However, the argument is itself rather complex (as will be discussed below) and actually refers to a String constant in the constant pool that describes the element type. From the JVM's perspective, executing opcode 0xBD is much more complicated than executing opcode 0xBC, since it requires that the JVM look up the String in the constant pool, interpret it, check that it makes sense, and possibly load an entirely new class. From the programmer's perspective, there is very little difference between creating an array of a basic type and a derived type, and one possible enhancement to an assembler such as jasmin would be to allow the computer to determine (by examining the type of argument) whether opcode 0xBC or 0xBD is needed.

The most difficult part of creating an array of derived objects is specifying the type. For example, to create an array of String types (see below), the fully qualified type name "java/lang/String" must be used. The following example shows how to create an array of 1,000 Strings:

```
ldc 1000                    ; 1000 elements in the array
anewarray java/lang/String ; create an array of Strings
```

This particular instruction is very unusual and very specific to the JVM. Most computers do not provide this sort of support at the level of the instruction set for allocating blocks of memory, and even fewer support the idea of allocating typed blocks. However, the ability to support typed computations even when the types involved are user-defined is critical to the cross-platform security envisioned by the designers of the JVM.

In addition to creating simple, one-dimensional arrays, the JVM provides a shortcut instruction for the creation of multidimensional arrays. The multianewarray instruction (note the somewhat tricky spelling) pops a variable number of dimensions off the stack and creates an array of appropriate type. The first argument to multianewarray defines the type of the array (not, it should be noted, the type of the array element) in a shorthand notation of type expressions, while the second argument defines the number of dimensions and thus the number of stack elements that need to be popped. For example, the following code specifies that three numbers are to be popped off the stack, creating a three-dimensional array:

```
bipush 6              ; size of array in third dimension = 6
bipush 5              ; size of array in second dimension = 5
bipush 3              ; size of array in first dimension = 3
multianewarray [[[F 3 ; create a 3x5x6 array of floats
```

Note that the final array created has three dimensions and is of overall size 3x5x6. The first argument, "[[[F", defines the type of the final array as a three-dimensional array (three ['s) of floating point numbers.

The Type System Expanded

From previous work with System.out and printing various things, you should be somewhat familiar with the system for expressing types to the JVM. The top half of table 10.1 lists familiar basic types (which are used in the newarray instructions and their JVM expressions, as might be used in a call to invokevirtual or multianewarray). In addition to the basic computational types with which we are already familiar, the JVM recognizes as basic types the byte (B), the short (S), the char (C), and the boolean (Z), also listed in table 10.1.

Derived types, as might be expected, are derived from the expressions of underlying types. The type description of an array, for example, is an open square bracket ([) followed by the type of every element in the array. Note that no closing bracket is needed or, in fact, allowed. This has confused more than one programmer. The expression for an array of integers would thus be [I, while the expression for a two-dimensional array (a matrix) of floats would be [[F; this literally expresses an array ([) each of whose elements is an array of floats ([F).

Classes and class types are expressed using the fully qualified class name, bracketed in front by a capital L and in back by a semicolon (;). The system output System.out, for instance, is an

Type	JVM/Jasmin Expression
int	I
long	J
float	F
double	D
byte	B
short	S
char	C
boolean	Z
void (return type)	V
array of X	[X
class Y	LY;
function taking X and returning Y	(X) Y

Table 10.1   Type Description Expressions

object of class PrintStream, stored in the directory and package of java.io (or java/io). Thus, the proper class expression for System.out would be `Ljava/io/PrintStream;`, as has been used in many previous examples.

These type constructors can be combined as needed to express complex types. For example, the standard Java definition of the "main" routine takes as an argument an array of Strings. In Java, this is written with a line like this:

```
public static void main(String [] args)
```

String is typically a system-defined class in the java.lang package, so it would be expressed as `Ljava/lang/String;`, while the argument is an array of such Strings. The main method does not return anything to the calling environment and hence is declared with return type void. Thus, our by now familiar statement at the beginning of many methods:

```
.method public static main([Ljava/lang/String;)V
```

This declares that the main method accepts an array of Strings as its only argument and returns nothing (void). It is evident from this example that this type system is used not only in the description of array types, but also in the definitions of methods, as will be described later.

Storing

To store an item in an array, the JVM provides several similar instructions, depending upon the type of element. For simplicity, assume for the moment that it's an array of integers (`[I`). In order to store a value at a location in an array, the JVM needs to know three things: which array, which location, and which value. The programmer must push these three things (in that order) onto the stack and then execute the instruction `iastore`. This operation is somewhat unusual in that it doesn't push anything onto the stack afterward, so it has the net effect of decreasing the stack size by three.

```
      bipush 10       ; need 10 elements
      newarray I      ; create array of 10 integers
      astore_1        ; store array in location #1

      iconst_0        ; load a 0 for looping
      istore_2        ; and store in #2
Loop:
      aload_1         ; load the array
      iload_2         ; load the location
      iload_2         ; load the value (which is the same as the location)
      iastore         ; set array[location] = value
      iinc 2 1        ; add 1 to #2 (the location and value)
      iload_2         ; are we done yet (is location >= 10)?
      bipush 10       ; load 10 for comparison
      if_icmplt Loop    ; if not at 10 yet, jump to Loop and repeat
      ; and we're done!
```

Figure 10.2   Example of storing in an array

Figure 10.2 shows a simple example of how data can be stored in an array. This code fragment first creates an array of 10 integers and then stores the numbers 0–9 in the corresponding array elements (figure 10.3).

For other basic types, including the noncomputational types of chars and shorts, the JVM provides appropriate types using the standard method of initial letters to define variants. For

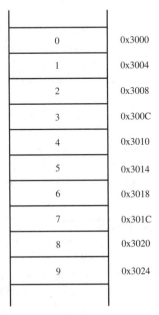

Figure 10.3   Memory layout for figure 10.2

Array Element Type	Store Operation	Load Operation
int	iastore	iaload
long	lastore	laload
double	dastore	daload
float	fastore	faload
char	castore	caload
short	sastore	saload
byte	bastore	baload
boolean	bastore	baload
array (address)	aastore	aaload
object (address)	aastore	aaload

Table 10.2 Array operations for loading and storing values

example, to store an element in an array of longs, use the lastore instruction. To store an element in an array of nonbasic types (address types, such as an array of arrays or an array of objects), the elements are stored as addresses (a), so the instruction is aastore (table 10.2). The only tricky aspect is in distinguishing between an array of booleans and an array of bytes, both of which begin with the letter b. Fortunately, the JVM itself can handle this ambiguity, as it uses the instruction bastore for both byte and boolean arrays and is capable of distinguishing between them on its own. (All right, this is a micro-lie. On most implementations of the JVM, especially the one from Sun Microsystems, the machine doesn't bother to distinguish and just uses bytes to store boolean array elements. This wastes about 7 bits per boolean element, which is still acceptably efficient.)

Storing in a multidimensional array must be performed as a sequence of stores. Because a multidimensional array is really stored (and treated) as an array of arrays, it is first necessary to load the relevant subarray and then to load or store in it. Figure 10.4 shows a code fragment for placing the number 100 in one slot (specifically location [1][2]) in a matrix of integers.

```
bipush 3                ; second dimension is 3
bipush 4                ; first dimension is 4
multianewarray [[I 2    ; create 4x3 array of integers
astore_1                ; store array in #1

aload_1                 ; load the array
iconst_1                ; we're interested in a[1][?]
aaload                  ; get a[1] (a row of 3 integers)
iconst_2                ; get location 2
bipush 100              ; load 100 to be placed in array a[1]
iastore                 ; store 100 in a[1][2]
```

Figure 10.4 Example of creating and storing in a multidimensional array

Loading

As with storing, so with loading. The JVM provides a set of instructions in the ?aload family that will extract an element from an array. To use these instructions, push the array and the desired location. The instruction will pop these arguments and then extract and push the value stored at that location, as in the following example.

```
aload_1    ; load the 1000 int array stored at #1
bipush 56  ; push the value (desired location) 56
iaload     ; extract and push the integer value array[56]
```

Getting the Length

Getting the length of an array is easy. The `arraylength` instruction pops the first entry off the stack (which must, of course, be an array) and pushes the length of the array. For example, the code below loads the previously created sample array, takes its length, and leaves the (int) value 1000 on the stack:

```
aload_1        ; load previously defined sample (1000 int array)
arraylength    ; pop sample, push sample's length
```

Destroying

In contrast to the previous operations, destroying an array when its contents are no longer needed is very simple. In fact, it's something that the programmer need not even think about. The JVM standard defines that the machine itself should periodically perform **garbage collection,** finding memory, class instances and variables that are no longer used by the program. Once such things are found, they are collected and made available for reuse.

The exact definition and operation of the garbage collection routine will vary from one JVM implementation to another. The general definition of "garbage" is that the memory location is no longer reachable from the program. For example, if local variable #1 holds (the only copy of the address of) an array, the array and every element in it are reachable and possibly available for computation. If the programmer were to write over local variable #1, then, although the array itself has not changed, it's no longer possible to access the information in it. At this point, the memory taken up by the array (which might be extensive) doesn't store anything useful and might as well be recycled for other useful purposes. The only problem is that there's no way to predict exactly when this recycling might happen, and it's technically legal for a JVM implementation not to perform garbage collection at all.

From the programmer's perspective, there is no need to explicitly destroy an array. Popping or overwriting all the references to the array, which will usually happen by itself in the normal course of running the program, will cause the array to become unreachable, garbage, and therefore recycled.

10.1.3   Records: Classes Without Methods

The Theory

The next simplest derived type is called, variously, a **structure** or a **record**. Again, like an array, this is a container type. Unlike an array, the data stored in a record is contained in named `fields`

Class Baseball Player

Name (String)	Babe Ruth
Year (I)	1923
Team (String)	
Games (I)	
At Bats (I)	
Runs (I)	
Hits (I)	
Batting Average (F)	0.393

Figure 10.5 A partially filled record for baseball card information

and may be of different types. The record provides a method of keeping related data together in a single logical location. If you like, you can think of a record as an electronic baseball trading card, which carries all the information relevant to a single player (batting average, home runs hit, times at bat, runs batted in, stolen bases, etc.) in one consistent, easy-to-transport format (figure 10.5). Each of these pieces of information would be associated with a particular field name (e.g. "RBI" for runs batted in) and possibly would have different types (batting average is defined as a float, while the number of home runs is an integer, and position—"shortstop"—might even be a String). A simpler example would be a fraction with just two integer fields (numerator and denominator).

Unlike an array, each record type must be defined separately at compile time by the programmer. The definition will mostly consist of a list of the necessary field names and their respective types. These will be stored in a suspiciously familiar-looking file, as shown in figure 10.6.

This example program shows a simple instance of a record type, specifically a fraction (or as a mathematician might put it, a rational number). Fractions are formally defined as the ratio between two integers, named the numerator (the number on the top) and the denominator (the number on the bottom), respectively. The two key lines in this file that define these fields are the ones beginning with the .field directive Specifically, the line

```
.field public numerator I
```

defines a field named numerator whose value is of type "I" (for integer, as discussed above). A field with a **long** value would use a 'J', while a field with a String (a derived type) would use the expression "Ljava/lang/String;" as we have seen before. The public keyword indicates that the numerator value is "public," meaning that it can be accessed, read, and modified by other functions and other objects in the system.

What about the rest of the file? Close inspection reveals that it's the same boilerplate we have been using since the first examples for the definitions of classes. The reason for this is very simple: a record in the JVM is implemented as a class, so there is a minimal class overhead

```
; structure definition for 'fraction' types

.class public fraction
.super java/lang/Object

.field public numerator I
.field public denominator I

; boilerplate -- needed because 'structures' are really 'classes'
.method public <init>()V
    aload_0
    invokespecial java/lang/Object/<init>()V
    return
.end method
```

Figure 10.6   A sample record defining "fraction" as a derived type

that also must be present to allow the rest of the system to interact with our newly defined record. So, without further ado, let's look specifically at classes as a derived type and see their advantages.

10.2   Classes and Inheritance

10.2.1   Defining Classes

A major advance in programming technology—or more accurately, in program design—was the development of **object-oriented** programming. Under this framework, large programs are designed using systems of smaller **interactive objects** that are individually responsible for their own data processing. A common metaphor is that of a restaurant. Diners can order any dish they like without having to worry about preparation details; that's the kitchen's responsibility. (And the cook doesn't worry about who ordered a particular dish; that's the server's responsibility.) This division of responsibility really pays off because a code fragment written for one purpose can often be coopted and reused for another purpose, and a large system can be built with relative ease as a collection of interacting objects. To continue a repeated example, the random number generator designed in section 3.4.1 can be used any time a random number is needed, whether for a Monte Carlo simulation, a Vegas-style casino game, or a first-person shoot-'em-up.

In order to structure these objects into a coherent framework, they are usually grouped into (and written as) **classes** of similarly propertied objects. One random number generator is much the same as any other, even if the detailed parameters or operations may differ. In particular, the things that an outside observer would want to do to or with a random number generator (seed it to a state to start generating or get a new random number from the generator) are the same. We can then define the idea of a "random number generator" operationally—in terms not of how it works, but of what we can do with it. Anything that calls itself a random number generator will have to perform those two operations.

This leads us to a familiar formal definition of a **class** as an abstract description of a derived type consisting of a set of named (instead of numbered) fields of potentially different types. (Sounds a lot like a record, doesn't it?) The difference is that a class also contains **methods**, functions that define legitimate ways to interact with the class. Finally, an **object** is an example or instantiation of a class, so where a class might be an abstract concept (like a "car"), an object would be a particular car, like the specific old VW Bug that I used to work on in high school.

As a quick review, a class (from the outside) is a way of grouping together similarly propertied objects that can all be interacted with in the same way. On a computer running Apple's OS X operating system, all windows have three buttons at the upper left corner: red, for deleting the window; yellow, for iconifying it; and green, for expanding it. Once the user understands how to work with any one window, she can work with all of them. This idea generalizes to the notion of classes, objects, and methods. In particular, each object (or instance of a class) shares the same methods or defined functions for interacting with that object. If you understand how to steer one example of a VW Bug, you know how to steer all of them, because the "method" of steering is identical.

This view continues to hold when programming on the JVM, because two objects are represented as independent instances of class files, where each class is largely independent and relies on the same methods for communicating at the JVM bytecode level. We have already seen examples of this in previous programs, mostly in interacting with the system output.

In detail:

- System.out (in jasmin, System/out) is a particular object.
- System/out instantiates the java/io/PrintStream class.
- All PrintStream objects have a println method.
- The println method causes a String to appear in the "usual" place, which can vary from object to object; for System/out it appears at the standard system output such as the screen.
- To make this happen, one uses the invokevirtual instruction, which triggers the appropriate method (println) on the appropriate object (System/out) [of the appropriate type (PrintStream)].

Each system is required (by the Java/JVM standards documents) to provide a PrintStream class and a System/out object as a member of that class. The exact details—for example, whether to print to a file on disk, a window on the screen, or a printer—are left to the individual classes. Furthermore, it's easy to set up another object (of class PrintStream) that prints its data in a different location. Then instead of invoking the println method of System/out, one invokes that same method of the new object and thereby prints to a file instead of to the screen.

Java does not enforce object-oriented programming, but the designed structure of the language makes it very easy and profitable to use it. In addition, the structure of the JVM does not enforce object-oriented programming, but it does encourage its use. In particular, the JVM specifically stores executable programs as **class files** and, as shown, makes it very easy to build a large-scale system using interoperating classes. We present some examples of such derived classes below.

10.2.2   A Sample Class: String

Classes, like arrays and fields, are derived types, but the various methods included as class definitions can make them much more difficult to understand. A typical, but still relatively understandable, example of a derived type is the standard Java String class, defined as part of the Java.lang (or Java/lang) package. The String class simply holds an immutable and un-changeable string such as "Hello, world!", perhaps to be printed; the class defines both the type of data used in a String (usually an array of characters) and a set of methods, func-tions, and operations which are defined as valid ways of interacting with the String class. We've been using String objects for some time without having a formal understanding of their properties.

Using a String

In addition to storing the actual string value, the String supports a wide collection of computational methods that will inspect the String to determine its properties. For example, the charAt() method takes an integer and returns the character at the location specified.

In Java (or an equivalent object-oriented high-level language), this function would be defined to fit a calling scheme something like

```
class java.lang.String {
    char charAt(int);
}
```

This scheme, used both for defining the function and for calling it, states that the method charAt() is part of the class String (itself part of the java/lang package), takes a single integer as a parameter and returns a character value. In jasmin, these same concepts would be expressed in a slightly different syntax, using the same syntax given in table 10.1.

```
java/lang/String/charAt(I)C
```

(Quick review: this means that the symbol "charAt" is a function taking type I and returning type C.) As we shall see, this kind of syntax is used both for defining the method itself and for invoking the method on any particular string.

The compareTo() method compares the current String with another and determines which one is alphabetically prior; if this (the current string) would come before the argument String in a dictionary, either by being shorter or by having a letter earlier in the usual sorting sequence, the integer returned will be negative. If this comes after the String argument, the return value will be positive, and if the Strings are exactly equal, a 0 is returned. In our jasmin notation, this method looks like this:

```
java/lang/String/compareTo(Ljava/lang/String;)I
```

Other methods specified (by the standard) as belonging to the String class include equals(), which returns a boolean value to indicate whether one string is identical to another;

equalsIgnoreCase(), which does the same calculation but ignoring case (so "Fred" and "fred" are not equal but would be equalIgnoreCase); indexOf(), which returns the location of the first occurrence of the character specified as an argument; length(), which returns the length of the String; and toUpperCase(), which returns a new String in which all characters have been converted to CAPITAL LETTERS. All in all, there are more than 50 separate methods, excluding the ones implicitly inherited from the Object class, that are defined by the standard as part of the JVM java.lang.String class.

10.2.3 Implementing a String

Under the hood, and at the bytecode level, how is a String actually implemented? The answer, annoying but brilliant, is that it doesn't matter! Any valid JVM class that implements the appropriate 50 methods, irrespective of the actual details, is a valid version of the class. As long as other classes use only the well-defined standard methods to interact with the String class, users will find that a well-behaved String class will serve their needs.

One (worthless) possibility for implementing a String, for example, would be as an ordered collection of individual character variables, each representing a separate character in the String. This has some obvious drawbacks from a programmer's point of view, as he would need to create many variables with names like seventyeighthcharacter. A better solution would be to use a simple derived type such as a character array (see above). Even here, there are a few choices. For instance, he could try to save space and use a byte array (if all of the Strings he the designer expects to deal with are ASCII strings, then there is no need to deal with UTF-16). He could also use an array of integer types to simplify any needed calculations. The String could be stored in this array in normal order, so that the first element of the array corresponds to the initial character of the string, or in reverse order (to simplify implementation of the endsWith() method).

Similarly, he may or may not want to create a special field holding the length of the string as an integer value. If he does so, this will make each individual String object a little larger and a little more complex, but it will also make it faster to use the length() method. Trade-offs like these can be important to the overall performance of the system, but they have no effect on whether or not the programmer's version of String is legitimate; and anyone else who uses his String class will find that, if all methods are there and correct, their program will still work. There doesn't need to be any specific relationship between the String class file and the class files that use String.

Constructing a String

String has a special method (usually called a **constructor** function that can be used to make a new String. This method takes no arguments and most of the time isn't very useful because the String created is of 0 length and has no characters. With the notation used so far in the book, this constructor function would be described as

java/lang/String/<init>()V

To make it easier and more useful, the String class also has many (about 11) other constructors that allow you to specify the contents of the String to be created. For example, a programmer can duplicate an existing String by creating a new String from it as follows:

```
java/lang/String/<init>(Ljava/lang/String;)V
```

He can also create a string from a StringBuffer (which makes an immutable string from a mutable one):

```
java/lang/String/<init>(Ljava/lang/StringBuffer;)V
```

or directly from an array of characters:

```
java/lang/String/<init>([C)V
```

any one of which would provide control over both the creation of the String as well as its contents.

10.3 Class Operations and Methods

10.3.1   Introduction to Class Operations

Classes are, in general, much more complex than arrays because they are required (or at least allowed) to provide many more operations and many more kinds of operations than arrays. Because of this complexity, it's not usually practical to create a new class on the fly (although one can always create a new object instantiating an existing class). Classes are, instead, defined via .class files as we have been doing; the basic class properties, such as fields and methods, are defined via jasmin directives at compile time. Once these fields and methods have been created, they can be used by anyone on the system (with appropriate access permission).

10.3.2   Field Operations

Creating Fields

Unlike arrays, fields within classes are named, not numbered. However, fields within different classes may be called the same thing, raising the possibility of ambiguity and confusion. For this reason, when fields are used, they should be fully described, including the name of the class that introduces the field.

To create a field, jasmin uses the directive .field, as illustrated below (and also in figure 10.6:

```
.field public AnExampleField I
```

This example creates a field in the current class named AnExampleField, which holds a variable of type int. Because this field is declared "public," it can be accessed and manipulated by methods that are not themselves part of the current class; presumably the programmer has some reason for this. A more realistic example (following the baseball metaphor above) can be seen in figure 10.7.

The .field directive allows several other access specifications and arguments. For example, a field can be declared "final," meaning that its value cannot be changed from the value set in

```
.field public Name Ljava/lang/String;
.field public Year I
.field public Team Ljava/lang/String;
.field public Games I
.field public AtBats I
.field public Runs I
.field public Hits I
.field public BattingAverage F
```

Figure 10.7   Fields for a hypothetical BaseballPlayer class (see figure 10.5)

the field definition, or it can be declared "static," meaning that the field is associated with a class rather than with individual objects within the class:

```
.field public static final double PI D = 3.1415926537898
```

This example defines "PI" as a static (class-oriented), final (unchangeable) double with the value of π. If for some reason the programmer wanted to restrict the use of PI to methods within the Example class, it could be declared "private" instead. Valid access specifications include private, public, protected, final, and static, all of which have their usual meaning in Java.

Using Fields
Since fields are automatically part of their objects/classes, they are automatically created as part of object creation (or, in the case of static fields, as part of class loading) and destroyed when the corresponding object/class is swept in garbage collection. The two operations of separate interest to the programmer are therefore storing data in a field and loading it from a field (placing it an the stack).

The procedure for storing in a field is similar to the procedure for storing in an array, with the significant difference that fields are named instead of numbered. As such, the putfield operation takes the name of the relevant field as an argument (because names, as such, cannot be placed on the stack). The programmer needs to push the address of the relevant object (whose field is to be set) and the new value (which must be of the correct type) and then execute the appropriate putfield instruction, as shown in figure 10.8. (The results of executing the code are show in figure 10.9.)

Static fields, being attached to a class instead of a particular object, have a similar structure but do not need to have an object on the stack. Instead, they are simply placed in the appropriate class field using the instruction putstatic. If the PI example above had not been defined as "final," then a programmer could adjust the internal value of PI using

```
ldc_2w 3.0        ; load 3.0 to become the new value of PI
putstatic Example/PI D ; set PI to be 3.0 for the Example class
                  ; of course, this wouldn't work, since PI
                  ; was defined as 'final' above
```

```
aload_1          ; #1 should hold the address (hence the 'a')
                 ; of an instance of the BaseballPlayer class
                 ; (an object of class Example)
                 ; and specifically, Babe Ruth
ldc "Babe Ruth"; push the name to be put into the Name field
putfield BaseballPlayer/Name Ljava/lang/String;
aload_1          ; reload our object
                 ; put 1923 into the field as an int
sipush 1923      ; push 1923 to be put into the Year field
putfield BaseballPlayer/Year I ; put 1923 into the field as an int
aload_1          ; reload our object
ldc 0.393        ; in 1923, Ruth's batting average was 0.393
putfield BaseballPlayer/BattingAverage F
                 ; put 0.393 into the field as a float
```

Figure 10.8 Storing information in object fields

Class Baseball Player

Name (String)	Babe Ruth
Year (I)	1923
Team (String)	
Games (I)	
At Bats (I)	
Runs (I)	
Hits (I)	
Batting Average (F)	0.393

Figure 10.9 Results of executing the code in figure 10.8

The JVM also provides instructions (getfield and getstatic for retrieving values from fields. The System class (defined in java.lang, and thus formally expressed as java/lang/System) contains a statically defined field called out that contains a PrintStream object. To get the value of this object, we use the by now familiar line

```
getstatic java/lang/System/out Ljava/io/PrintStream
```

Because java/lang/System is a class, nothing need be on the stack and nothing will be popped in the process of executing getstatic. When accessing a nonstatic field (using getfield), since the value must be selected from a particular object, the object must first be pushed onto the stack:

```
aload_1     ; load Example object from #1
getfield Example/AnExampleField I ; push AnExampleField as int
```

10.3.3 Methods

Method Introduction

In addition to fields, most classes also possess methods, ways of acting on the data stored in the class or its objects. Methods differ from fields in that they actually compute things and therefore contain bytecode. (As with fields, there are several different kinds of methods with different properties; the main method, for instance, must nearly always be defined as both public and static because of the way the JVM interpreter works. When the JVM attempts to execute a class file, it looks for a method defined as part of the class (and not as part of any particular object, since there are no objects of that class thus, static) to execute. Since there are no objects of that class, this method must be publicly accessible. For this reason, every program we have yet written includes the line

```
.method public static main([Ljava/lang/String;)V
```

as a definition of main as a public, static method.

Method Invocation Via invokevirtual

Methods are declared and defined in their corresponding class file. To use a method it must be **invoked** on an appropriate object or class. There are a few basic operations that correspond to method invocation, used in slightly different ways, depending upon the circumstances.

The most common and most straightforward way to invoke a method uses the invokevirtual operation (opcode 0xB6). We have been using this in several chapters, and there is nothing especially new or conceptually difficult about it. The operation pops an object (and the arguments to the method) from the stack, invokes the appropriate method on the object, and pushes the result, as in the following standard code:

```
getstatic java/lang/System/out Ljava/io/PrintStream
ldc "Hello, world!"
invokevirtual java/io/PrintStream/println(Ljava/lang/String;)V
```

This code pushes the object System.out (a PrintStream) and one argument. By inspection of the invokevirtual line, we can see that the stack must contain, at the top, a single argument of type java/lang/String and below it a PrintStream object A more complicated method might take several arguments, but they will all be specified in the invokevirtual line, so the computer knows exactly how many arguments to pop. Below all arguments is the object whose method is to be invoked (figure 10.10).

When such a method is invoked, control will be passed to the new method in similar fashion to a subroutine call. However, there are a few crucial differences. First, the arguments to the method are placed sequentially in local variables starting at #1. Local variable #0 gets a copy of the object itself whose method is being invoked (in Java terms, #0 gets a copy of this). The new method also gets a completely new set of local variables and a completely new (and empty) stack.

When computation is completed, the method must return, and return with the appropriate type expected by the method definition. From the calling environment's viewpoint, the method should push an element of the appropriate type at the top of the stack. From the method's viewpoint, it needs to know which element (and what type). There are several commands to return, starting

```
aload   1 ; load Object of class Class

bipush 3

bipush 5

ldc     5.0

invokevirtual Class/method (IIF)V
```

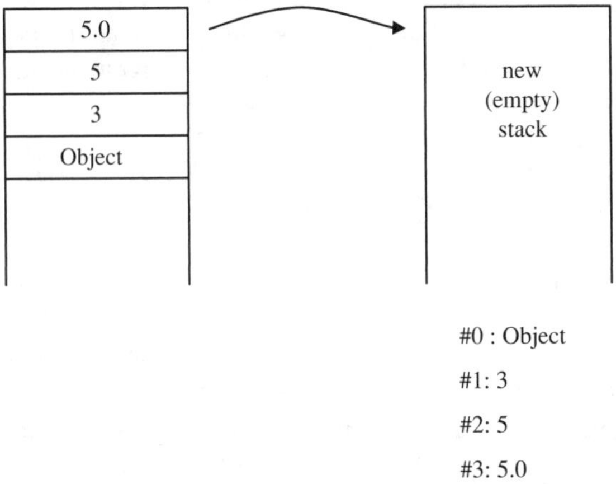

Figure 10.10   Method invocation using **invokevirtual**

with return, which returns nothing, i.e., is a void type, and the ?return family, which returns the appropriate element of the appropriate type at the top of the stack; members of this family include the usual suspects—ireturn, lreturn, freturn, dreturn—as well as areturn to return an address or object (figure 10.11). This family does not, however, include the ret instruction, which returns from a subroutine. It is also not legal to "fall off" the end of a method; unlike Java and most high-level languages, there is no implicit return at the end of a method.

This can be seen in the following very simple method, which simply returns 1 if and only if the argument is the integer 3:

```
.method public isThree(I)I
    .limit locals 2
    .limit stack  2
    iload_1                 ; argument, an int, is in #1
    bipush 3                ; load 3 for comparison
    if_icmpeq   Yes         ; if #1 == 3, then return 1
    bipush 0                ; not equal, so return 0
    ireturn
Yes:
    bipush 1                ; equal, so return 1
    ireturn
.end method
```

```
bipush  6

ldc     7.0

bipush  1

ireturn
```

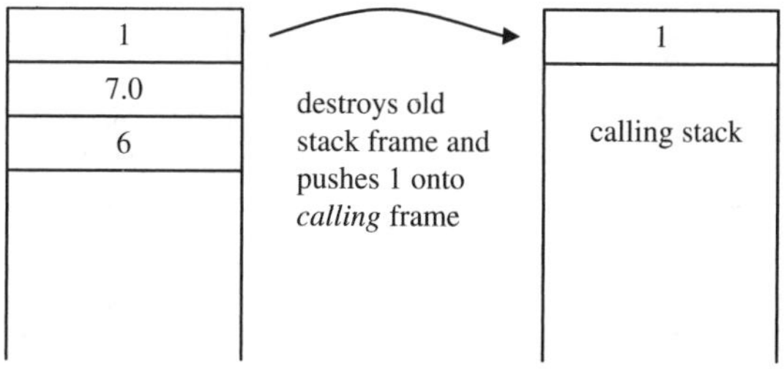

Figure 10.11   Method return using **ireturn**

There is a very important difference between subroutines (accessed via jsr/ret) and methods (accessed via invokevirtual/?return). When a subroutine is called, the calling environment and the called routine share local variables and the current stack state. With methods, each time you start a method, you get a brand new set of local variables (all uninitialized) and a brand new stack (empty). Because each new method invocation gets a new stack and a new set of local variables, methods support recursion (having a method reinvoke itself) in a way that subroutines do not. To invoke a method recursively, one can simply use the value stored in #0 as the target object and write the invokevirtual line normally. When the method executes, it will use its own version of the stack and local variables without affecting the main stream of computation. Upon return from the method, the calling environment can simply pick up where it left off, using the results of the method invocation.

Other invoke? Instructions

Since invokevirtual takes an object and its arguments to call a method, it (perhaps obviously) isn't suitable for use with a static method. Static methods don't have associated objects. The JVM provides a special invokestatic operation (as figure 10.12) for invoking static methods on classes. This operates just as invokevirtual would (and looks very similar), except that it does not attempt to pop an object from the stack; it only pops the arguments. It also does not bother to place the object (this) in #0 and instead fills up the local variables with the arguments starting from #0.

There are also a few special circumstances that call for special handling. Specifically, when one initializes a new object (using the

```
bipush  3
bipush  5
ldc     5.0
invokestatic Class/staticmethod(IIF)V
```

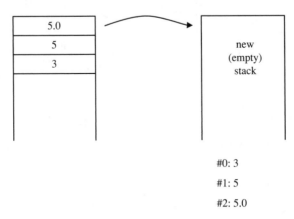

#0: 3

#1: 5

#2: 5.0

Figure 10.12 Static method invocation using **invokestatic**

method) or deals with a few tricky situations involving superclasses and private methods, there is a special operation, invokespecial, that must be used. From the programmer's viewpoint, there is no difference between invokevirtual and invokespecial, but our standard boilerplate code

```
.method public <init>()V
     aload_0
     invokespecial java/lang/Object/<init>()V
     return
.end method
```

illustrates the main use of invokespecial. In order to initialize an object (of any class), it is first necessary to confirm that it has all the properties of the superclasses (for example, if a Dog is a subclass of Animal, to initialize a Dog, one needs to make sure it's a valid Animal). This is accomplished by calling the initialization method on the current object (this, or local variable #0). But because it's an initialization method, the computer has to use invokespecial.

Declaring Classes
Classes are typically defined and declared in files with the .class extension. These files, though, contain necessary information about the classes themselves and their relationship with other classes that the JVM needs in order to operate properly.

For this reason, every class file created needs to have the two directives

```
.class Something
.super ParentOfSomething
```

to define the class itself and its place in the class hierarchy. Like fields and methods, the .class directive can also take various access specifications, such as public. The class name (Something in the above example) should be the fully qualified name, including the name of any packages; the class System, defined as part of the java.lang package, would contain the fully qualified class name of java/lang/System. Similarly, the superclass should include the fully qualified name of the immediate superclass and must be present; although most student-written classes are subclasses of java/lang/Object, this is not a default and must be specified explicitly.

There are a number of other directives that may or may not be present in a class file, mostly directives of use to source debuggers. For example the .source directive tells the JVM program the name of the file that was used to generate the class file; if something goes wrong with the program at run time, the JVM interpreter can use this information to print more useful error messages.

10.3.4   A Taxonomy of Classes

One important subtlety glossed over in the previous section is the existence of several different types of class files and methods. Although they are all very similar (the actual difference in storage usually involves just setting or clearing a few bits in the access flags in the class file), they represent profound differences in class semantics, especially as viewed from outside the class.

In the most common relationship between classes, objects, and methods, every object in a class has its own set of data but is operated on by a unified collection of methods. For example, consider the "class" of any specific model of car (let's take, as a specific, the 2007 Honda Accord). Obviously, these cars all operate (in theory) the same way, but they have individual properties such as color, amount of gas in the tank, and Vehicle Identification Number. These properties would be stored as fields in the individual Honda objects themselves. On the other hand, the headlights are controlled in exactly the same way on every car; the "method" of turning on the headlights is a property of the class, not of any individual car.

There are, however, certain properties of the class as a whole, such as the length of the car, the width of the wheelbase, and the size of the gas tank. These properties can even be read directly from the blueprints and do not need any cars to actually exist. We distinguish between **class variables**, which are properties of the class itself, and **instance variables**, which are properties of individual instances. In the JVM, fields that are class variables are declared as static and stored in the class itself, instead of in individual objects:

```
.field color Ljava/lang/String;
.field static carLength D
```

Similarly, fields can be declared as final to represent that the value, whether an instance variable or a class variable, cannot be changed:

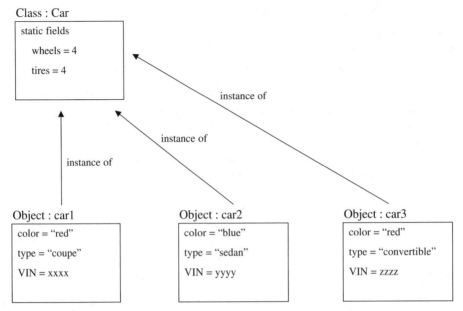

Figure 10.13 Class vs. static fields. All case have the same number of wheels, but each has its own color and vehicle identification number (VIN)

```
.field final vehicleIndentification Ljava/lang/String; = "whatever"
.field static final wheels I = 4
.field static final tires I = 4
```

In this example, the field vehicleIdentification is an instance variable that doesn't change (but may vary from car to car), while all cars in the class have the same fixed and immutable number of wheels (figure 10.13). The length of a car is a property of the class, while the color of a car is a property of the individual car object and can be changed (if one decides to repaint, for example).

A similar distinction between instance methods and class methods holds. Most of the programs written so far have involved a method defined as

```
.method public static main([Ljava/lang/String;)V
```

This main method is very important because, by default, whenever a Java program is run (or a class file is executed using java more exactly), the Java program will load the class file and look for a method named "main." If it finds one, it will then attempt to invoke that method with a single argument corresponding to the rest of the words typed on the command line. The static keyword indicates that the main method is associated with the class, not with any particular instance of the class. For this reason, it is not necessary to create any instances of the appropriate class in order to invoke the main method.

```
; program to illustrate use of 'fraction' structure type

.class public fractionfront
.super java/lang/Object

; boilerplate
.method public <init>()V
        aload_0
        invokespecial java/lang/Object/<init>()V
        return
.end method

.method public static main([Ljava/lang/String;)V

        new fraction
        invokespecial fraction/<init>()V

        return
.end method
```

Figure 10.14   Creating a "fraction" object

In addition, we have the necessary property "public," which indicates that this method (or field) can be accessed from outside the class. A public method (or class) is visible and executable to the entire system, including the JVM startup sequence, while a private method is executable only from objects/methods within the defining class. This is, of course, implicit in the structure of "main" itself, since it must be executable as the first method of the overall program. Other variations on the access flags can define a class, field, or method as "final," as before, or even as "abstract," which means that the class itself is just an abstraction from which no instances can be made and that we should use one of the subclasses of this class instead. Again, the details of these methods and properties are more relevant to an advanced Java programmer than to an understanding of how the JVM itself works.

10.4 Objects

10.4.1   Creating Objects as Instances of Classes

A class definition, by itself, is not usually very useful for performing computations. More useful are the instances of these "classes" as objects, actual examples of classes that can hold data, deal with method invocations, and in general, do useful stuff. For example, the "fraction" class defined above in the record section simply states that a fraction has two fields, a numerator and a denominator. An actual fraction would have a specific set of values in those fields that could be used in computation.

To create an instance of a class, it is first necessary to know the name of the class. The jasmin statement

```
new ExampleClassType
```

creates (allocates memory inside the computer for) a new instance of the `ExampleClassType` class and pushes an address onto the method stack pointing to the new object. Merely making space is not enough; it must also be initialized to a useful/meaningful state using one of the constructor methods defined for that type. To do this, it is necessary to use `invokespecial` with an appropriate method and set of arguments, as in figure 10.14.

Remember that the definition of the fraction class defined (using the standard boilerplate) a single constructor method `<init>`, which takes no arguments. Therefore, we construct our new fraction using the two lines

```
new fraction
invokespecial fraction/<init>()V
```

to create and initialize our fraction.

Actually, this is not very useful. The reason is that although we have just created and initialized it, the `invokespecial` instruction pops our only reference to the fraction away when it returns. As a result, our newly allocated block of memory has just been lost and is probably now being collected as garbage. In order to retain access to our new fraction object, we need to duplicate the address before calling `invokespecial` on it, as in figure 10.15 This figure also gives an example of how data can be moved to and from the fields of an object.

10.4.2 Destroying Objects

Object destruction, again, is handled by the garbage collection system and happens any time no pointers to an object remain in accessible locations (such as in a local variable or on the stack).

10.4.3 The Type Object

The fundamental type in any JVM system is named "Object" or, more completely, `java/lang/Object`. As the root of the entire inheritance hierarchy, everything on the system is an Object in some form. Therefore, the properties of Objects are basic properties shared by everything in the system, and the methods of Objects are methods that can be called on anything. These methods are not particularly exciting, because they are so basic; for example, all Objects support an `equals()` method, which returns "true" if two objects are the same and "false" if they are different.

As generic types Objects can be used as general places holders for data; a programmer could define (or, more likely, use) a standardized List type that holds a collection of Objects, and then use this type to store his grocery list, his class schedule, and the win/loss record of a favorite team without modification. Most of the standard data structures defined as part of the Java language are defined in this way so that the data they hold, being an Object, imposes no restrictions on how to use the structures.

10.5 Class Files and .class File Structure

10.5.1 Class Files

In a typical JVM system, each independent class is stored in a `class file` that maintains the necessary information for the use and execution of that particular class. Most of this information is fairly obvious—for example, the name of the class, its relationship to other classes in the

```
; second program to illustrate use of 'fraction' structure type

.class public fractionfront2
.super java/lang/Object

; boilerplate
.method public <init>()V
     aload_0
     invokespecial java/lang/Object/<init>()V
     return
.end method

.method public static main([Ljava/lang/String;)V
     .limit locals 2
     .limit stack 2

     ; create a new 'fraction' and store in local variable 1
     new fraction                        ; create a new 'fraction'
     dup                                 ; duplicate to call <init>
     invokespecial fraction/<init>()V    ; initialize
     astore_1                            ; store new fraction

     ; assign the numerator the value 2
     aload_1                             ; load the fraction
     iconst_2                            ; push numerator value
     putfield fraction/numerator I       ; place 2 in numerator (as int)
     ; n.b. restorage of the fraction not needed!

     ; assign the denominator the value 3
     aload_1                             ; load fraction (again)
     iconst_3                            ; push denominator
     putfield fraction/denominator I     ; place 3 in denominator (as int)


     ; print the numerator
     getstatic java/lang/System/out Ljava/io/PrintStream;
     aload_1                             ; load the fraction
     getfield fraction/numerator I       ; get and push the numerator
     invokevirtual java/io/PrintStream/print(I)V      ; ... and print

     ; print a slash
     getstatic java/lang/System/out Ljava/io/PrintStream;
     ldc "/"
     invokevirtual java/io/PrintStream/print(Ljava/lang/String;)V

     ; print(ln) the denominator
     getstatic java/lang/System/out Ljava/io/PrintStream;
     aload_1                             ; load the fraction
     getfield fraction/denominator I     ; get and push the denominator
     invokevirtual java/io/PrintStream/println(I)V       ; ... and print(ln)

     return
.end method
```

Figure 10.15   Creating and using a "fraction" object

Magic Number (4 bytes)	0xCAFEBABE
Minor Version Number (2 bytes)	
Major Version Number (2 bytes)	
Constant Pool Count (2 bytes)	
	1st Constant Pool entry (variable)
	2nd Constant Pool entry (variable)
	...
Access Flags (2 bytes)	
This Class (2 bytes)	refers to contant pool entry
Super Class (2 bytes)	refers to contant pool entry
Interfaces Count (2 bytes)	
	0th Interface (2 bytes) refers to constant pool entry
	1st Interface (2 bytes) refers to constant pool entry
	...
Fields Count (2 bytes)	
	0th Field (variable size)
	1st Field (variable size)
	...
Methods Count (2 bytes)	
	0th Method (variable size)
	1st Method (variable size)
	...
Attributes Count (2 bytes)	
	0th Attribute (variable size)
	1st Attribute (variable size)
	...

Figure 10.16   Overview of the class file format

inheritance hierarchy, and the methods defined by and characteristic of the class. The exact details of storage can be rather technical and can even vary from one JDK version to another, so if you have a specialist's need for the details of class file format (for example, if you are writing a compiler that outputs JVM machine instructions), you should probably consult a detailed technical reference like the JVM references specifications themselves.[1] For a nonspecialist, the following description (and appendix C in more detail) will give some of the flavor of a class file.

In broad terms, a class file is stored as a set of nested tables, as in figure 10.16. The top-level table contains basic information regarding the class, such as the version number of the JVM for which it is was compiled, the class name, and fundamental access properties. This table also contains a set of subtables, including a table of defined methods, fields, attributes, and direct interfaces that the class implements. Another subtable contains the **constant pool**, which stores the fundamental constant values and Strings used by the program. For example, if the value 3.1416 were needed by the class, instead of using the 4-byte floating point value itself every place it were needed, this value would be placed in a small table of constants and the table index would be used.

This has the effect of increasing the space efficiency of class files. Although there are overk 4 billion different floating point constants that a program might want to use, in practical terms few

---

[1] Tim Lindholm and Frank Yellin, *The Java Virtual Machine Specification*, 2nd ed. (Addison-Wesley, Boston, 1999).

programs will use more than 100 or so. A constant pool of only 200 entries can be addressed using a 1-byte index and thus save 3 bytes per constant access. Even a huge program that uses 60,000 constants can address any one of them with a 2-byte index. In addition to storing floating point constants, the constant pool will hold integers, longs, doubles, and even objects such as String constants (like the prompt "Please enter your password", which might be stored to be printed via a call to `println`). In fact, the `ldc` operation with which we are already familiar actually stands for "load from the constant pool" and can be used (as we have seen) for almost any type.

10.5.2 Starting up Classes

Before a class is available to be used by a running program it must be loaded from the disk, linked into an executable format, and finally initialized to a known state. This process is one of the fundamental services that a JVM program must provide in the form of the **primordial class loader**, an instantiation of the standard-defined type `java.lang.ClassLoader`. The JVM designer has a certain amount of leeway in determining what services the primordial class loader can provide above a certain minimum level.

For example, to **load** a class, the loader usually must be able to find the class on local storage (usually by adding the suffix `.class` to the name of the class), read the data stored there, and produce an instance of `java.lang.Class` to describe that class. In some circumstances (like a Web browser or a sophisticated JVM implementation), one may need to pull individual classes out of an archive or download appropriate applets across the network. The primordial loader must also understand enough of the class structure to pull out the superclasses as needed; if the class you have written extends Applet, then JVM needs to understand Applets and their properties to run your program correctly. It is the task of the linker (which is also usually grouped into the class loader) to connect (**link**) these different classes into a suitable runtime representation.

Another important task of the JVM class loader is to **verify** that the bytes in the bytecode are safe to execute. Trying to execute an integer multiplication when there are no integers on the stack would not be safe; nor would trying to create a new instance of a class that doesn't exist. The verifier is responsible for enforcing most of the security rules discussed throughout this book. Finally, the class is **initialized** by calling the appropriate routines to set static fields to appropriate values and otherwise make the class into a fit state for execution.

10.6 Class Hierarchy Directives

This section pertains mainly to advanced features of the Java class hierarchy, and it can be therefore skipped without loss of continuity.

In the real world, there can be problems with the strict type hierarchy that the JVM supports. Because each subclass can have only one superclass, each object (or class) will inherit at most one set of properties. Real life is rarely that neat or clean. For example, one fairly obvious hierarchy is the standard set of biological taxa. A dog is a mammal, which in turn is a vertebrate, which in turn is an animal, and so forth. This could be modeled easily in the JVM class hierarchy by making Dog a subclass of Mammal, and so forth. However, in practice, Dog also inherits many properties from the Pet category as well, a category that it shares with Cat and Hamster, but also with Guppy, Parakeet, and Iguana (and excludes Bear, Cheetah, and other non-Pet mammals).

So we can see that, whatever category Pet is, it crosses the lines of the standard biological taxonomy. And because there's no way to inherit from more than one class, there's no easy way within the class structure to create a class (or an Object) that is both a Mammal and a Pet.

Java and the JVM provide a process to cover these sorts of regularities via the mechanism of `interfaces`. An **interface** is a special sort of class-like Object (in fact, it's stored in a file of identical format; only a few access flags change) that defines a set of properties (fields) and functions (methods). Individual Objects are never instances of an interface; instead, they **implement** an interface by explicitly encoding these properties and functions within their classes. For example, it may be decided that among the defining properties of a Pet is the function of having a Name and an Owner (presumably these would be access methods returning a string value), and thus appropriate methods to determine what the name and owner actually are. Interfaces never actually define the code for a method, but they do define methods that a programmer is required to implement. Similarly, although interfaces can define fields, fields defined as part of an interface must be both **static** and **final**, reflecting the fact that an individual object is never an instance of an interface—and thus has no storage space available by virtue of the fields it implements.

At this point, a skilled programmer can define the Dog class such that it inherits from (extends) the Mammal class, and thus gets all the properties associated with Mammals. She can also define the class as "implementing" the Pet interface by making sure that, among the methods she writes in his Dog class are the appropriate methods required of every Pet.

The programmer would then define in her class file not only that the class Dog had Mammal as a superclass, but also that it implemented the Pet interface. This would involve a new directive as follows:

```
.class public Dog
.super Mammal
.implements Pet
```

The declaration and use of the Pet interface would be very similar to writing a normal class file, but with two major differences. First, instead of using the `.class` directive to define the name of the class, the programmer would use the `.interface` directive in the same way:

```
.interface public Pet
```

Second, the methods in the `Pet.j` files would have method declarations but no actual code associated with them (implying that they are `abstract`):

```
.method public abstract getName()Ljava/lang/String;
.end method
.method public abstract getOwner()Ljava/lang/String;
.end method
```

There are also a few minor differences in use between interface types and class types. First, interface types cannot be directly created as objects, although one can certainly create objects that implement interface types. In the example above, although creating a Dog is legal, creating a Pet is not:

```
new Dog          ; this is fine
new Pet          ; this would produce an error
```

However, interfaces are acceptable as argument types and return values of methods. The following code will accept any valid object whose class implements the Pet interface

```
invokespecial Dog/isFriendlyTo(LPet;)I
```

and will tell you, for example, whether or not any particular Dog is friendly to (for example) a particular Iguana. Finally, if you have an Object that implements a particular interface but you don't know what class it is (as in the isFriendlyTo example above), the JVM provides a basic instruction, invokeinterface, to allow interface methods to be invoked directly, without regard to the underlying class. The syntax of invokeinterface is similar to that of the other invoke? instructions but is slightly more complicated; it is also usually slower and less efficient than the other method invocation instructions. Unless you have a specific need for interfaces, they're best left to specialists.

10.7 An Annotated Example: Hello, World Revisited

At this point, we are in a position to give a detailed explanation of every line in the first jasmin example given, including the boilerplate:

```
.class public jasminExample
```

is a class directive that specifies the name of the current class

```
.super java/lang/Object
```

... and where it fits into the standard hierarchy (specifically, as a subclass of java/lang/Object)

```
.method public <init>()V
```

This is the method for constructing an element of type jasminExample. It takes no arguments, and returns nothing, with name <init>.

```
aload_0
invokespecial java/lang/Object/<init>()V
```

To initialize a jasminExample, we load the example itself and make sure it is successfully initialized as an Object first.

```
return
```

No other initialization steps are needed, so quit the method.

```
.end method
```

This directive ends the method definition.

```
.method public static main([Ljava/lang/String;)V
```

This is the main method, called by the Java program itself. It takes one argument, an array of Strings, and returns nothing. It is defined as both public and static, so it can be called from outside the class without the existence of any objects of that class.

```
.limit stack 2
```

We need two stack elements (one for System.out, one for the String).

```
getstatic java/lang/System/out Ljava/io/PrintStream;
```

Get the (static) field named "out" from the System class; it should be of type PrintStream, defined in the java.io package.

```
ldc "This is a sample program."
```

Push the string to be printed (more accurately, push the index of that string in the constant pool).

```
invokevirtual java/io/PrintStream/println(Ljava/lang/String;)V
```

Invoke the "println" method on System.out.

```
return
```

Quit the method.

```
.end method
```

This directive ends the method definition.

10.8   Input and Output: An Explanation

10.8.1   Problem Statement

The Java programming language defines much more than the syntax of the language itself. Key to the acceptance and widespread use of the language has been the existence of various packages to handle difficult aspects of programming, such as input and output. The java.io package, for example, is a set of packages specifically designed to handle system input and output at a sufficiently abstract level to be portable across platforms.

Using input and output peripherials is often one of the most difficult parts of any computer program, especially in assembly language programming. The reason, quite simply put, is the bewildering variety of devices and the ways they can work.

There is a big difference, at least in theory, between devices like disk drives, where the entire input is available at any one time, and devices like a network card, where the data is available only on a time-sensitive and limited basis. Not only are different kinds of devices available, but even within one broad category, there may be subtle but important differences, such as the placement of keys on a keyboard, the presence or absence of a second mouse button, and so forth. However, from the point of view of the programmer, these differences not only don't matter but would be actively confusing. An e-mail program, for instance, has the primary job of reading input (from the user), figuring out where and to whom the mail should go, and sending it on its way. The details of how the data arrives—does it come in bursts over an Ethernet connection? in single keystrokes from an attached keyboard? as a massive chunk of data arriving through a cut-and-paste operation? as a file on the hard disk?—don't (or shouldn't) matter to the e-mail program.

Unfortunately, at the level of basic machine instructions, these differences can be crucial; reading data from an Ethernet card is not the same as reading data from the disk or from the keyboard. The advantage of a class-based system such as the one supported by the JVM is that the classes themselves can be handled and unified, so that the programmer's task is made a little less confusing.

10.8.2 Two Systems Contrasted

General Peripherial Issues

To illustrate this confusion, consider the task of reading data and printing it somewhere (to the screen or the disk). For simplicity, assume that the input device (the spot where the data is coming) is either an attached keyboard or an attached disk. Without going into detail, a keyboard is just a complicated switch; when a key is pressed certain electrical connections are made that allow the computer to determine which key was pressed (and hence which character was intended) at that time. A disk is a gadget for information storage; logically, you can think of it as a huge array of "sectors," each of which holds a fixed number of bytes (often 512, but not always). In fact, it's a little more complicated, since the information is ordered as a set of multiple **platters** (each of which looks like a CD made out of magnetic tape), each platter having several numbered concentric **tracks**, each track being divided into several `sectors` like slices of pizza (figure 10.17). To read or write a sector of data, the computer needs to know the platter number, track number, and sector within the track—but most of the time (whew!) the hard drive controller will take care of this.

It's important to note a few crucial differences between these two gadgets. First, when you read from the keyboard, you will get at most one character of information, since you only learn the key that's being pressed at that instant. Reading from a disk, by contrast, gives you an entire sector of data at once. It's also possible to read ahead on a disk and see what the next sector contains; this is impossible on a keyboard.

Similar differences hold, depending upon the exact details of the screen to which we print. If a window manager is running on the computer, then (of course) we will print to an individual window and not to the screen, as we would in text mode. In text mode, for example, we always know that printing starts at the left-hand side of the physical screen, whereas we have no idea where the window is at any given time; it may even be moving while we're trying to print. And, of course, printing to the screen is entirely different from writing data to the disk, with all the structure defined above.

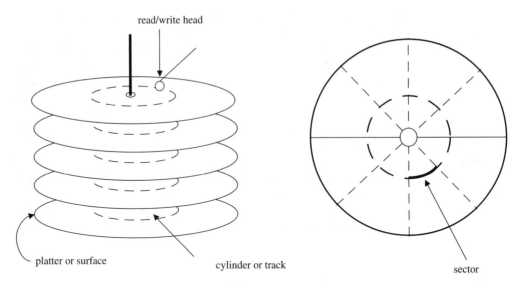

Figure 10.17 Structure of disks

As will be seen, the class structure of the JVM avoids much of this confusion by using a proper class structure, unlike another common system—the Intel Pentium, running Windows 98.

The Intel Pentium

Every device you attach to a Pentium comes with a set of **device drivers**. This is true, in fact, for every computer; the drivers define how to interact with the hardware. They are similar to classes and methods in this regard, except that they have no useful, unified interface. One of the simplest sets of device drivers on any Windows box is the BIOS (Basic Input-Output System) shipped as part of the operating system. (Actually, the BIOS predates the Pentium chip by nearly 20 years, but the functionalism, a holdout from the original IBM-PC, is still around.)

On the Intel Pentium, a single machine instruction (INT) is used to transfer control to the BIOS; when this is executed, the computer inspects the value stored in a particular location (the AX register) to determine what should be done. If the value stored is 0x7305, the computer will access the attached disk. To do this properly, it inspects a number of other values stored in other registers. Among these values is the number of the disk sector of interest, a memory location to place the new data, and whether the disk should be read from or written to. In either case, at least one sector of data will be transferred.

The same instruction that transfers control to the BIOS will also cause the computer to read a character if the value stored in the lower half of the AX register is a 0x01. Actually, the process is a little more complicated. If the value stored is 0x01, the computer will wait until a key is pressed and return that character (it will also print that character to the screen). If the value stored is 0x06, then the computer will check to see if a key is pressed this instant, and return it (without printing). If no key is being pressed, then nothing is returned (and a special flag is set to indicate that). Both of these functions read only one character at a time. To read several characters at once, if they are available in a typeahead buffer, use the stored value 0x0A, which does not return the characters, but instead stores them in main memory.

Output has similar issues of detail. To write to a disk, one uses the same BIOS operation used to read, while to write to the screen in text mode or a window system requires two different operations (which are different from the read operations/values).

All this occurs after the device drivers and hardware controllers have "simplified" the task of accessing the peripherials. The fundamental problem is that the various sorts of hardware are too different from each other. It would be possible for a programmer to write a special-purpose function whose sole job is, for instance, to handle input—*if* input is supposed to be read from the keyboard, use operation 0x01; if it is to be read from a disk, use operation 0x7305; and in either case, move the value read into a uniform place and in a uniform format. Such a program may or may not be difficult to write, but it requires attention to detail, hardware knowledge, and time that not every programmer wants to spend.

This mess is part of why Windows, the operating system, exists. Part of the functionality of Windows is to provide this broad-brush interface for the programmer. Microsoft programmers have taken the time to write these detailed, case-laden functions.

The JVM

By contrast, in a properly designed and constructed class-based system, this unification is delivered by the class structure itself. In Java (and by extension in the JVM), most input and output is handled by the class system. This allows the classes to take care of information hiding and only present the important shared properties via methods.

To briefly review: the java.io.* package, as defined for Java 1.4, provides a variety of classes, each with different properties for reading and writing. The most useful class for input, and the one most often used, is `BufferedReader`. This is a fairly powerful high-level class that allows reading from many sorts of generalized "stream" objects (figure 10.18). Version 1.5 of Java includes additional classes, such as a `Scanner`, that are handled in a similar manner.

Unfortunately, the keyboard lacks many properties that are typical of these BufferedReader objects, but the class system provides a way to construct a BufferedReader object from other sorts of objects. The standard Java libraries do provide an object, a field in the System class, called `System.in` that usually attaches to the keyboard. This field is defined, however, to hold one of the lowest, most primitive types of input objects—a java.io.InputStream. (Key differences between an InputStream and a BufferedReader include the absence of buffering and the inability to read any type other than a byte array.)

The java.io.* package also provides a special type for reading from the disk, either as a FileInputStream or as a FileReader, both of which can be used to construct a BufferedReader. Once this is done, access to a file is identical to access to the keyboard, since both use the some methods as the BufferedReader class.

In the following section, we will construct a program (using the more widely available Java 1.4 semantics) to read a line from the keyboard and to copy that line to the standard output.

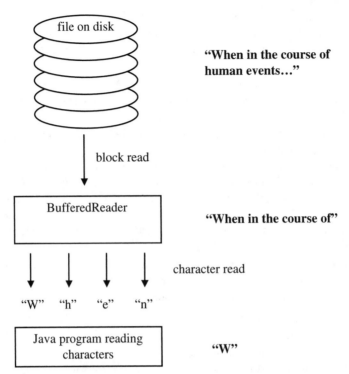

Figure 10.18   Reading a file from the disk using BufferedReader

Although the process is still complex, the complexity lies in the construction of the BufferedReader, not in the actual data reading. For a simple one-time cost of Object construction, any data can be read through a BufferedReader, while the corresponding program on the Intel would need special cases and magic numbers for every I/O operation.

10.8.3   Example: Reading from the Keyboard in the JVM
An example of the code used to perform this task in Java is presented in figure 10.19. Note that two conversions are needed, first to construct an InputStreamReader from the InputStream and second to construct a BufferedReader from the InputStreamReader. In fact, there is even a bit of complexity hidden in the Java code, since the actual constructor function for the BufferedReader is defined as

```
public BufferedReader(Reader in)
```

meaning that one can construct a BufferedReader out of any sort of Reader, of which InputStream-Reader is merely one subclass.

Object construction is handled as before in two steps. First, the new Object itself must be created (via the new instruction), and then an appropriate initialization method must be invoked (via invokespecial). This program will require two new Objects to be created, an InputStreamReader

```
    import java.io.*;

    class jvmReaderExample {
        public static void main(String[] args) throws IOException {

            InputStreamReader i = new InputStreamReader(System.in);
            BufferedReader b = new BufferedReader(i);

            String s = b.readLine();
            System.out.println(s);
        }
    }
```

Figure 10.19   Sample Java program to read and echo a line from the keyboard

and a BufferedReader. Once these have been created, the BufferedReader class defines a standard method (called "readLine") that will read a line of text from the keyboard and return it as a String (Ljava/lang/String;). Using this method, we can get a string and then print as usual through System.out's println method.

10.8.4   Solution

```
.class public jvmReader
.super java/lang/Object

; boilerplate needed for object creation
.method public <init>()V
   aload_0
   invokespecial java/lang/Object/<init>()V
   return
.end method

.method public static main([Ljava/lang/String;)V

.limit stack 4

; create a new object of type InputStreamReader
new java/io/InputStreamReader

; initialize constructor from System.in (InputStream)
dup
getstatic java/lang/System/in Ljava/io/InputStream;
invokespecial java/io/InputStreamReader/<init>(Ljava/io/InputStream;)V
; equivalent to new InputStreamReader(InputStream)
```

```
; now create a new BufferedReader
new java/io/BufferedReader
; duplicate it and put it underneath InputStreamReader
dup_x1

; duplicate again and put it underneath InputStreamReader
dup_x1
; stack now holds BR, BR, ISR, BR

; eliminate unneeded BufferedReader
pop

; call constructor of BufferedReader using InputStreamReader
invokespecial java/io/BufferedReader/<init>(Ljava/io/Reader;)V


    ; initialized BufferedStreamReader now at top of stack

    ; invoke readline method to get a string (and leave at top of stack)
    invokevirtual java/io/BufferedReader/readLine()Ljava/lang/String;

    ; get System.out
    getstatic java/lang/System/out Ljava/io/PrintStream;
    swap
    invokevirtual java/io/PrintStream/println(Ljava/lang/String;)V

    return
.end method
```

10.9 Example: Factorials Via Recursion

10.9.1   Problem Statement

As a final example, we present code to do recursion (where one function or method invokes itself) on the JVM using the class system. The factorial function is a widely used mathematical operation in combinatorics and probability. For example, if someone wants to know how many different ways there are to shuffle a (52-card) deck of cards, the answer is 52!, or $52 \cdot 51 \cdot \ldots \cdot 1$. One nice property of factorials is that they have an easy recursive definition in that

$N! = N \cdot (N-1)!$ for $N >= 1$, and $0! = 1$

Using this identity, we can construct a recursive method that accepts an integer (as a value of N) and returns $N!$.

10.9.2   Design

The pseudocode for solving such a problem is straightforward and is presented as an example in most first-year programming texts.

```
To calculate N!
      if (N <= 0) then
            return 1
      else begin
            recursively calculate (N-1)!
            multiply by N to get N * (N-1)!
            return N * (N-1)!
      end
end calculation
```

(Strict mathematicians will note that this pseudocode also defines the factorial of a negative integer as 1 as well.)

In addition, a (public, static) main routine will be needed to set the initial value of N and to print the final results. Because the main method is static, if the factorial method is not static, we would need to create an Object instance of the appropriate class; if we defined the factorial method as static, it can be invoked directly.

10.9.3   Solution

A worked-out solution to calculate 5! is presented here. Similar code can be used to solve almost any recursively defined problem.

```
.class public factorialCalculator
.super java/lang/Object

; boilerplate needed for object creation
.method public <init>()V
   aload_0

   invokespecial java/lang/Object/<init>()V
   return
.end method

.method public static main([Ljava/lang/String;)V
   ; we need two stack elements, one for System.out, one for the string
   .limit stack 2

   bipush 5           ;   push 5 to calculate 5!
   invokestatic factorialCalculator/fact(I)I
   ; 5! is now on stack to be calculated

   ; get and push System.out
   getstatic java/lang/System/out Ljava/io/PrintStream;

   ; put System.out and 5! in right order
   swap

   ; invoke the PrintStream/println method
   invokevirtual java/io/PrintStream/println(I)V

   return
.end method
```

```
.method static fact(I)I
   .limit stack 2
   iload_0        ; check if argument <= 0
   ifle  Exit     ; if so, return 1 immediately

   iload_0        ; push N

   iinc 0 -1      ; compute (N-1)
   iload_0        ; load (N-1)
   ; calculate (N-1)!
   invokestatic factorialCalculator/fact(I)I
   ; N and (N-1)! are both on the stack
   imul           ; multiply to get final answer
   ireturn        ; and return it
Exit:
   iconst_1       ; 0! is defined as 1
   ireturn
.end method
```

10.10 Chapter Review

- The JVM, because of its strong association with the object-oriented programming language Java, provides direct support for object-oriented programming and user-defined class types. Both array and Object references are supported by the basic type **address**.
- An array is a collection of identical types indexed by an integer(s). There are individual machine-level instructions to create, read from, or write to single-dimensional and multidimensional arrays, as well as to get the length of an array.
- When arrays (or any data) are no longer useful or accessible, the JVM will automatically reclaim the used memory via **garbage collection** and make it available for reuse.
- The JVM also supports **records** as collections of named **fields** and **classes** as records with defined access methods. It also supports **interfaces** as collections of abstract methods. The class file is the basic unit of program storage for the JVM and incorporates all three of these types.
- Fields are accessed via `getfield` and `putfield` instructions; `static` (class) fields use `getstatic` and `putstatic`.
- Classes are accessed via one of four `invoke?` instructions, depending on the class and the method involved.
- Objects are created as instances of classes by the `new` instruction. Every class must include appropriate constructor functions (typically named <init>) to initialize a new instance to a sane value.
- Access to the outside world via I/O primitives is accomplished on the JVM by a standardized set of classes and methods. For example, `System.in` is a static field of type InputStream whose properties and access methods are defined by the standards documents. Reading from

the keyboard can be accomplished by invoking the proper methods and creating the proper classes using System.in as a base.

- Recursion can also be supported using the class system by creating new sets of local variables at each new method invocation. This differs from the previous jsr/ret techniques, as well as from the techniques employed on systems like the Pentium or PowerPC, where new local variables are created on stack frames.

10.11 Exercises

1. How does the implementation of user-defined types on the JVM differ from implementations on other machines like the 8088 or PowerPC?
2. How would space for a local array be created on a PowerPC? How would the space be reclaimed? How do these answers differ on a JVM?
3. An array element is usually accessed via index mode on a typical computer like the Pentium. What does the JVM use instead?
4. How are standard methods like String.toUpperCase() incorporated into the JVM?
5. What is the difference between a field and a local variable?
6. What is the difference between invokevirtual and invokestatic?
7. Why do static methods take one fewer than nonstatic arguments?
8. What is the corresponding type string for the following methods?
   a. float toFloat(int)
   b. void printString(String)
   c. float average(int, int, int, int)
   d. float average(int [])
   e. double [][] convert(long [][])
   f. boolean isTrue(boolean)
9. What is special about the <init> method?
10. What is the fourth byte in every class file (see appendix D)?
11. Approximately how many different String values could a single method use?

10.12 Programming Exercises

1. Write a jasmin program using the Java 1.5 **Scanner** class to read a line from the keyboard and echo it.
2. Write a jasmin program using the Java AWT (or a similar graphics package) to display a copy of the Jamaican flag on the screen.
3. Write a jasmin program to determine the current date and time.
4. Write a Time class to support arithmetic operations on times. For example, 1:35 + 2:15 is 3:50, but 1:45 + 2:25 is 4:10.
5. Write a Complex class to support addition, subtraction, and multiplication of complex numbers, such as $3 + 4i$.
6. The **Fibonacci sequence** can be recursively defined as follows: the first and second elements of the sequence have the value 1. The third element is the sum of the first and second, elements, or 2. In general, the Nth Fibonacci number is the sum of the $N - 1$st and $N - 2$nd numbers.

Write a program to read a value N from the keyboard and to (recursively) determine the Nth Fibonacci number. Why is this an inefficient way to solve this problem?

7. Write a program (in any language approved by the instructor) to read a class file from the disk and print the number of elements in the constant pool.

8. Write a program (in any language approved by the instructor) to read a class file from the disk and print the names of the methods defined in it.

Digital Logic

A.1 Gates

Without the transistor, the modern computer would not be possible. As suggested by Moore's Law (transistor density doubles every eighteen months), the ability to fabricate and arrange transistors is the fundamental way that data is controlled, moved, and processed within the chips at the heart of a computer.

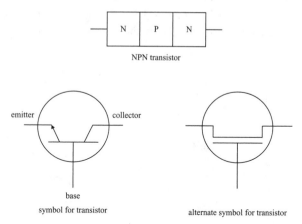

Figure A.1 Sample transistors and symbols

   A transistor can be regarded as a kind of electronically controlled switch. A typical transistor and its electronic diagram are shown in figure A.1. Under normal circumstances, electricity flows from the emitter to the collector like water through a pipe or cars through a tunnel. However, this is possible only as long as appropriate application of an electrical signal to the base permits the flow of electricity to pass. Without this control signal, it's as though someone had turned off a faucet (or set up a traffic light). When this happens, electricity can't get through. By combining these switches in combination, engineers can create dependency structures; electricity will flow only if all transistors are energized, for example.

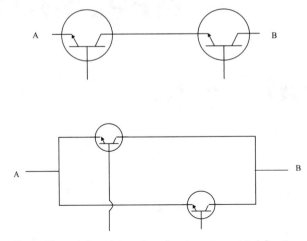

Figure A.2   Transistors in series (top) and parallel (bottom)

Figure A.2 shows two examples of dependency structure. In the **series** circuit, both transistors share a common path, and electricity must be able to flow through both circuits at the same time if it is to flow from point A to point B. In the **parallel** circuit, each transistor has its own current path, and any transistor can allow current to flow across the circuit.

The electrical circuit shown in figure A.3 is an example of two transistors connected in series. In order for electricity to flow from the power source (V_{cc}) to the output, both

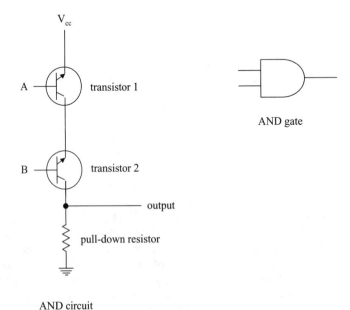

Figure A.3   Simplified AND gate and symbol

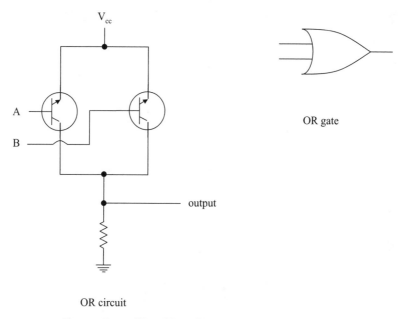

OR gate

OR circuit

Figure A.4 Simplified OR gate and symbol

transistors need to be signaled to allow current to pass. If either transistor is an open switch, then electricity can't flow. This implies that electricity can flow (there is power at the output) only if transistor 1 is closed **AND** transistor 2 is closed. Similarly, in figure A.4, two transistors in parallel, will allow current to flow if either the first transistor **OR** the second transistor is closed (or both).

The basic building blocks of a computer consist of simple circuits, called **gates**, that implement these simple, logical signals. These gates typically contain between one and six transistors each and implement basic logical or arithmetic operations. Remember that the basic values used in logic are True and False. If "current is flowing" represents True, then the circuit in figure A.3 is an implementation of the logical function AND in a simple (and somewhat idealized—don't try to build this at home out of Radio Shack components!) gate. Other functions available include OR (figure A.4), NOT, NAND, and NOR. The symbols used for drawing various gates are given in figure A.5. Note that each gate (except NOT) has two inputs and a single output. Also noted that the NOT gate symbol has a circle (representing signal inversion) at the output line. The symbol for a NAND (Not-AND) gate is the same as the symbol for an AND gate, but with the little inversion circle at the output. Similarly, a NOR (Not-OR) gate is just an OR gate with the inversion circle.

A.2 Combinational Circuits

Complicated networks of gates can implement any desired logical response. For example, the XOR (eXclusive OR) function is True if and only if exactly one, but not both, of the inputs is

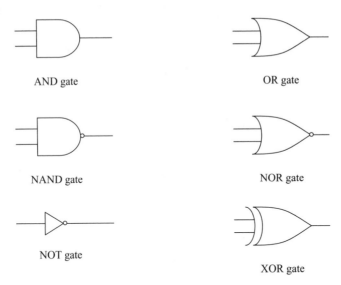

Figure A.5   Gate types and symbols

True. In logical notation, this can be written

As: A XOR B = (A OR B) AND (NOT (A AND B))
As a truth table, this can be written as in table A.1
And finally, as a circuit, as figure A.6

   The basic concept of combinatorial circuits is that the output is always a function of the current input signal(s) without regard to signal history. Such circuits can be very useful for implementing simple decisions or arithmetic operations. Although a full description of how to design such circuits is beyond the scope of this appendix, figure A.7 shows how a set of gates could implement simple binary addition (as part of the ALU of a computer).

   Specifically, this circuit will accept two single-bit signals (A and B) and output both their sum and whether or not there is a carry. (This circuit is sometimes called a "half adder.") Examination of the binary addition table shows that the sum of two bits is simply their XOR, while a carry is generated if and only if both bits are 1s, or in other words, their AND. Similar analysis can yield a more complicated design capable of incorporating a carry bit from a previous addition stage (a "full adder"; see figure A.8) or adding several bits at one time (as in a register). Figure A.9 shows how a 4-bit addition can be performed by four

A	B	Result
True	True	False
True	False	True
False	True	True
False	False	False

Table A.1   Truth table defining eXclusive OR

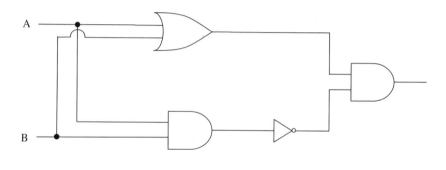

A XOR B

Figure A.6   Implementation of XOR in gates

replications of the full adder circuit; 32 replications, of course, could add together two registers on the Pentium. One can also build a circuit to perform binary multiplication and other operations. Multiply these simple gates by several billion, and you approach the power and complexity of a Pentium.

A.3 Sequential Circuits

In contrast to a combinatorial circuit, a sequential circuit retains some notion of memory and of the history of the circuit. The output of a sequential circuit depends not only on the present input, but also on the past inputs. Another way of expressing this is to say that such a circuit has an internal state. By using the internal state, one can store information for later use, essentially creating the sort of memory necessary for a register.

One of the simplest sequential circuits is the **S–R flip-flop**, illustrated in figure A.10. To understand this circuit, let's first pretend that S and R are both 0 (False), Q is 0, and $\bar{Q}$ is 1 (True). Since $\bar{Q}$ is True, R NOR $\bar{Q}$ is 1. Similarly, S NOR Q is 1. We thus see that this configuration is internally consistent and will remain stable as long as the individual components

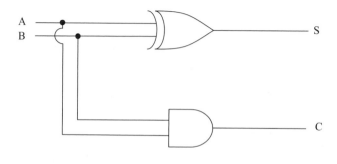

A + B

Figure A.7   Single-bit half adder

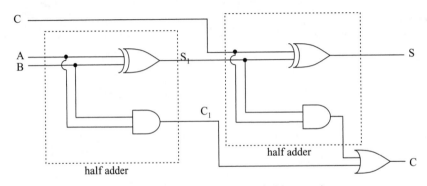

Figure A.8   Single-bit full adder (with carry)

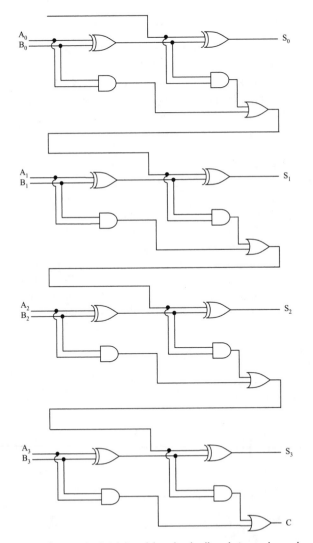

Figure A.9   Cascaded 4-bit adder, including internal carries

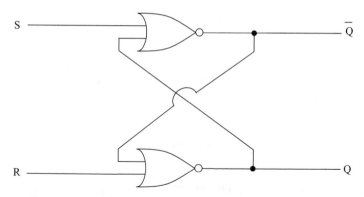

Figure A.10   S–R flip-flop, a circuit with memory

work (which usually means as long as they have power). A similar analysis will show that if S and R are both 0, while Q is 1, the result will be a self-consistent, stable state.

This simple flip-flop can be used as a 1-bit memory; the value of Q is the value stored in the memory. The signals S and R can be used to set or reset (set to 1 or 0) the flip-flop, respectively. Observe that if S becomes 1, this will force the output of the upper NOR gate to be 0. With R 0 and $\bar{Q}$ 0, the output of the lower NOR gate is 1, so the value stored is now 1. A similar process, if R is set to 1, forces Q to 1 and Q to 0.

Unfortunately, if S and R are both 1, then bad things happen. According to the notation, Q and $\bar{Q}$ should always be opposites of each other, but if both inputs are 1, both outputs will be 0 (you can confirm this for yourself). In a purely mathematical sense, we can regard this as the logical equivalent of dividing by 0—something to be avoided instead of analyzed. Similarly, even a brief power spike on one input wire can cause the flip-flop to unexpectedly change state—something to be avoided if possible.

However, since this is to be avoided, other sorts of sequential circuits are more commonly used in computers. Most common circuits combine control signals with timing signals (usually called a **clock signal**) to synchronize the control signals and keep short-term fluctuations from influencing the circuit's memory. Notice that in figure A.11, the clock signal acts to enable the flip-flop to change state. If the clock signal is low, then changes on S or R cannot affect the memory state of the circuit.

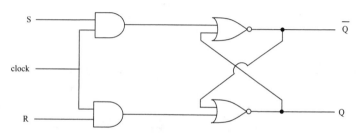

Figure A.11   A clocked S–R flip-flop

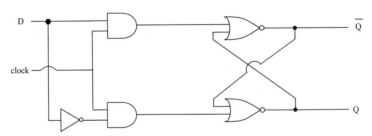

Figure A.12   A D flip-flop

We can extend this clocked flip-flop further to something perhaps more useful as well as safer. The circuit diagram in figure A.12 illustrates a D flip-flop. As you can see, this circuit has only one input beyond the clock. The D input is tied to the S input of the flip-flop, while $\bar{D}$, the complement of D, is tied to the R input. This keeps both S and R from being 1 at the same time. When a clock pulse occurs, the value of D will be stored in the flip-flop (if the value of D is 1, then Q becomes 1; if the value of D is 0, Q becomes 0). Until a clock pulse occurs, changes in D will have no effect on the value of the flip-flop. This makes a D flip-flop very valuable for copying and storing data—for example, in reading from an I/O device to a register for later use.

Another variation on the SR flip-flop yields the T flip-flop (figure A.13). Like the D flip flop, this is a single-input extension of the clocked S–R flip-flop, but the additional feedback wires control how the input/clock pulse is gated through; in this circuit, the flip-flop will change state ("toggle") each time the input is triggered. For example, if Q is 1 (and $\bar{Q}$ is 0, by extension), then the next pulse will trigger the bottom input wire (essentially the R input in the previous circuits) and reset the flip-flop so that Q is 0.

A.4 Computer Operations

Using these building blocks, it's possible to build the higher-level structures associated with computer architectures. In particular, a collection of simple 1-bit flip-flops (such as the S–R flip-flop) can implement a simple register and hold data until it is needed. To add, for example,

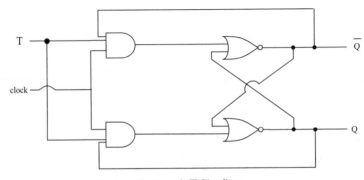

Figure A.13   A T flip-flop

two 1-bit registers, the Q output of each register can be electrically connected to one input of a simple addition circuit. The Q output of the other register would be connected to the other adder input. The resulting output bit would be the addition of these 2 register bits, which could be captured and stored (via a D flip-flop) in yet another register. The T flip-flop could be used in conjunction with adder circuits to build a simple pulse counter. Of course, these descriptions oversimplify dreadfully, but they give something of the feel for the task presented to the computer designer.

APPENDIX B

JVM Instruction Set

Sample mnemonic in context (Numeric opcode value in hex)—
description

Summary: This opcode doesn't exist but illustrates the entry format. To the right are the required initial and final stack states as needed/created by the operation in question. Note that long and double types take two stack slots, as shown.

Initial: long
long
Final: float

aaload (0x32)—Load value from array of addresses

Summary: Pops an integer and an array of addresses (object references) from the stack, then retrieves a value from that location in the one-dimensional array of addresses. The value retrieved is pushed on the top of the stack.

Initial: int(index)
address(array ref)
Final: address (object)

aastore (0x53)—Store value in array of addresses

Summary: Stores an address (array reference) in an array of such addresses. The top argument popped is the index defining the array location to be used. The second argument popped is the address value to be stored, and the third and final argument is the array itself.

Initial: int(index)
address (object)
address(array ref)
Final: —

aconst_null (0x1)—Push array constant *null*

Summary: Pushes the machine-defined constant value *null* as an address onto the operand stack.

Initial: —
Final: address(null)

aload <varnum> (0x19) [byte/short]—Load the address from local variable

Summary: Loads the address (object reference) from local variable #<varnum> and pushes the value. The value of <varnum> is a byte in the range 0..255 unless the wide operand prefix is used, in which case it is a short in the range 0..65536. Note that subroutine return locations cannot be loaded from stored locations via aload or any other opcode.

Initial: —
Final: address

250

aload_0 (0x2a)—Load address from local variable #0
Summary: Loads address (object reference) from local variable #0 and
pushes the value loaded onto the stack. This is functionally equivalent
to `aload 0` but takes fewer bytes and is faster.

Initial: —
Final: address

aload_1 (0x2b)—Load address from local variable #1
Summary: Loads address (object reference) from local variable #1 and
pushes the value loaded onto the stack. This is functionally equivalent
to `aload 1` but takes fewer bytes and is faster.

Initial: —
Final: address

aload_2 (0x2c)—Load address from local variable #2
Summary: Loads address (object reference) from local variable #2 and
pushes the value loaded onto the stack. This is functionally equivalent
to `aload 2` but takes fewer bytes and is faster.

Initial: —
Final: address

aload_3 (0x2d)—Load address from local variable #3
Summary: Loads address (object reference) from local variable #3 and
pushes the value loaded onto the stack. This is functionally equivalent
to `aload 3` but takes fewer bytes and is faster.

Initial: —
Final: address

anewarray <type> (0xbd) [int]—Create unidimensional array of
objects
Summary: Allocates space for an <one>-dimensional array of type
<type> and pushes a reference to the new array. The type is stored
in bytecode as a 4-byte index into the constant pool. The size of the
new array is popped as an integer from the top of the stack.

Initial: int(size)
Final: address(array)

anewarray_quick (0xde)—Quick version of `anewarray` opcode
Summary: Optimized version of `anewarray` opcode used internally in
Sun's Just In Time (**JIT**) compiler. This opcode should never appear
in a `.class` file that isn't currently loaded and being executed.

Initial: see original
opcode
Final: see original
opcode

areturn (0xb0)—Return from method with address result
Summary: Pops an address (object reference) from the current method
stack. This object is pushed onto the method stack of the calling environment. The current method is terminated, and control is transferred
to the calling environment.

Initial: address
Final: (n/a)

arraylength (0xbe)—Take length of an array
Summary: Pops an array (address) off the stack and pushes the length
associated with that array (as an integer). For multidimensinal arrays,
the length of the first dimension is returned.

Initial: address(array)
ref
Final: int

astore <varnum> (0x3a) [byte/short]—Store address in local
variable
Summary: Pops an address (object reference or subroutine return location) from the top of the stack and stores that address in local variable
#<varnum>. The value of <varnum> is a byte in the range 0..255
unless the `wide` operand prefix is used, in which case it is a short in
the range 0..65536.

Initial: address
Final: —

astore_0 (0x4b)—Store address in local variable #0

Summary: Pops an address (object reference) from the top of the stack
   and stores that address value in local variable #0. This is functionally
   equivalent to `astore 0` but takes fewer bytes and is faster.

Initial: address
Final: —

astore_1 (0x4c)—Store address in local variable #1

Summary: Pops an address (object reference) from the top of the stack
   and stores that address value in local variable #1. This is functionally
   equivalent to `astore 1` but takes fewer bytes and is faster.

Initial: address
Final: —

astore_2 (0x4d)—Store address in local variable #2

Summary: Pops an address (object reference) from the top of the stack
   and stores that address value in local variable #2. This is functionally
   equivalent to `astore 2` but takes fewer bytes and is faster.

Initial: address
Final: —

astore_3 (0x4e)—Store address in local variable #3

Summary: Pops an address (object reference) from the top of the stack
   and stores that address value in local variable #3. This is functionally
   equivalent to `astore 3` but takes fewer bytes and is faster.

Initial: address
Final: —

athrow (0xbf)—Throw an exception/error

Summary: Pops an address (object reference) and "throws" that object
   as an exception to a predefined handler. The object must be of type
   Throwable. If no handler is defined, the current method is terminated and the exception is rethrown in the calling environment. This
   process is repeated until either a handler is found or there are no more
   calling environments, at which point the process/thread terminates.
   If a handler is found, the object is pushed onto the handler's stack
   and control is transferred to the handler.

Initial:
address(Throwable)
Final: (n/a)

baload (0x33)—Load value from array of bytes

Summary: Pops an integer and an array from the stack, then retrieves
   a value from that location in the one-dimensional array of bytes. The
   value retrieved is converted to an integer and pushed on the top of
   the stack.

   The `baload` operand is also used to load values from a `boolean`
array using similar semantics.

Initial: int(index)
address(array ref)
Final: int

bastore (0x54)—Store value in array of bytes

Summary: Stores an 8-bit byte in a byte array. The top argument
   popped is the index defining the array location to be used. The second argument popped is the byte value to be stored, and the third and
   final argument is the array itself. The second argument is truncated
   from an int to a byte and stored in the array.

   The `bastore` operand is also used to store values in a `boolean`
array using similar semantics.

Initial: int(index)
int(byte or boolean)
address(array ref)
Final:—

bipush <constant> (0x10 [byte])—Push [integer] byte
Summary: The byte value given as an argument (−128..127) is sign-
extended to an integer and pushed on the stack.

Initial: —
Final: int

breakpoint (0xca)—Breakpoint (reserved opcode)
Summary: This opcode is reserved for internal use by a JVM implementation, typically for debugging support. It is illegal for such
an opcode to appear in a a class file, and such a class file will fail
verification.

Initial: (n/a)
Final: (n/a)

caload (0x34)—Load value from array of bytes
Summary: Pops an integer and an array from the stack, then retrieves
a value from that location in the one-dimensional array of characters.
The value retrieved is converted to an integer and pushed on the top
of the stack.

Initial: int(index)
address(array ref)
Final: int

castore (0x55)—Store value in array of characters
Summary: Stores a 16-bit UTF-16 character in an array of characters.
The top argument popped is the index defining the array location
to be used. The second argument popped is the character value to
be stored, and the third and final argument is the array itself. The
second argument is truncated from an int to a character and stored in
the array.

Initial: int(index)
int(character)
address(array ref)
Final: —

checkcast <type> (0xc0 [constant pool index])—Confirm type compatibility
Summary: Examines (but does not pop) the top element of the stack
to confirm that it is an address (object or arrray reference) that can
be cast to the type given as an argument—in other words, that the
object is either **null**, an instance of <type> (see `instanceof`), or
of a superclass of <type>. In bytecode, the type is represented as a
2-byte index into the **constant pool** (see Glossary). If the types are
not compatible, a ClassCastException will be thrown (see `athrow`).

Initial: address
Final: address

checkcast_quick (0xe0)—Quick version of `checkcast` opcode
Summary: Optimized version of `checkcast` opcode used internally in
Sun's Just In Time (**JIT**) compiler. This opcode should never appear
in a `.class` file that isn't currently loaded and being executed.

Initial: see original
opcode
Final: see original
opcode

d2f (0x90)—Convert double to float
Summary: Pops a two-word double off the stack, converts it to a single-
word floating point number, and pushes the result.

Initial: double
double
Final: float

d2i (0x8e)—Convert double to integer
Summary: Pops a two-word double off the stack, converts it to a single-
word intger, and pushes the result.

Initial: double
double
Final: int

d2l (0x8f)—Convert double to long

Summary: Pops a two-word double off the stack, converts it to a two-word long, and pushes the result.

Initial: double
double
Final: long
long

dadd (0x63)—Double precision addition

Summary: Pops two doubles and pushes their sum.

Initial: double-1
double-1
double-2
double-2
Final: double
double

daload (0x31)—Load value from array of bytes

Summary: Pops an integer and an array from the stack, then retrieves a value from that location in the one-dimensional array of doubles. The value retrieved is pushed on the top of the stack.

Initial: int(index)
address(array ref)
Final: double
double

dastore (0x52)—Store value in array of doubles

Summary: Stores a two-word double in an array of such a double. The top argument popped is the index defining the array location to be used. The second/third arguments popped are the double value to be stored, and the final argument is the array itself.

Initial: int(index)
double
double
address(array ref)
Final: —

dcmpg (0x98)—compare doubles, returning 1 on NaN

Summary: Pops two two-word doubles off the operand stack and pushes a −1, 0, or +1 (as an integer) as a result. If the next-to-top number is greater than the top number, the value pushed is +1. If the two numbers are equal, the value pushed is 0; otherwise, the value is −1. If either or both words popped equal IEEE NaN (*Not a Number*) when interpreted as a double, the result pushed is 1.

Initial: double-1
double-1
double-2
double-2
Final: int

dcmpl (0x97)—compare doubles, returning −11 on NaN

Summary: Pops two two-word doubles off the operand stack and pushes a −1, 0, or +1 (as an integer) as a result. If the next-to-top number is greater than the top number, the value pushed is +1. If the two numbers are equal, the value pushed is 0; otherwise, the value is −1. If either or both words popped equal IEEE NaN (Not a Number) when interpreted as a double, the result pushed is −1.

Initial: double-1
double-1
double-2
double-2
Final: int

dconst_0 (0xe)—Push double constant 0.0

Summary: Pushes the constant value 0.0 as a 64-bit IEEE double-precision floating point value onto the operand stack.

Initial: —
Final: double(0.0)
double(0.0)

dconst_1 (0xf)—Push double constant 1.0

Summary: Pushes the constant value 1.0 as a 64-bit IEEE double-precision floating point value onto the operand stack.

Initial: —
Final: double(1.0)
double(1.0)

ddiv (0x6f)—Double precision division

Summary: Pops two two-word double precision floating point numbers, then pushes the result of the next-to-top number divided by the top number.

Initial: double-1
double-1
double-2
double-2
Final: double
double

dload <**varnum**> **(0x18 [byte/short])**—Load double from local variable

Summary: Loads a two-word double precision floating point number from local variables #<varnum> and #<varnum> +1 and pushes the value. The value of <varnum> is a byte in the range 0..255 unless the wide operand prefix is used, in which case it is a short in the range 0..65536.

Initial: —
Final: double
double

dload_0 (0x26)—Load double from local variable #0/#1

Summary: Loads a double precision floating point number from local variables #0 and #1, and pushes the value loaded onto the stack. This is functionally equivalent to dload 0 but takes fewer bytes and is faster.

Initial: —
Final: double
double

dload_1 (0x27)—Load double from local variable #1/#2

Summary: Loads a double precision floating point number from local variables #1 and #2 and pushes the value loaded onto the stack. This is functionally equivalent to dload 1 but takes fewer bytes and is faster.

Initial: —
Final: double
double

dload_2 (0x28)—Load double from local variable #2/#3

Summary: Loads a double precision floating point number from local variables #2 and #3 and pushes the value loaded onto the stack. This is functionally equivalent to dload 2 but takes fewer bytes and is faster.

Initial: —
Final: double
double

dload_3 (0x29)—Load double from local variable #3/#4

Summary: Loads a double precision floating point number from local variables #3 and #4 and pushes the value loaded onto the stack. This is functionally equivalent to dload 3 but takes fewer bytes and is faster.

Initial: —
Final: double
double

dmul (0x6b)—Double precision multiplication

Summary: Pops two doubles and pushes their product.

Initial: double-1
double-1
double-2
double-2
Final: double
double

dneg (0x77)—Double precision negation

Summary: Pops a two-word double precision floating point number from the stack, reverses its sign (multiplies by −1), then pushes the result.

Initial: double
double
Final: double
double

drem (0x73)—Double precision remainder

Summary: Pops two two-word double precision floating point numbers, then pushes the remainder resulting when the next-to-top number is divided by the top number.

Initial: double-1
double-1
double-2
double-2
Final: double
double

dreturn (0xaf)—Return from method with double result

Summary: Pops a 2-byte double precision floating point number from the current method stack. This number is pushed onto the method stack of the calling environment. The current method is terminated, and control is transferred to the calling environment.

Initial: double
double
Final: (n/a)

dstore <varnum> 0x39 [byte/short])—Store double in local variable

Summary: Pops a double from the top of the stack and stores that double value in local variables #<varnum> and #<varnum> +1. The value of <varnum> is a byte in the range 0..255 unless the wide operand prefix is used, in which case it is a short in the range 0..65536.

Initial: double
double
Final: —

dstore_0 (0x47)—Store double in local variable #0/#1

Summary: Pops an integer from the top of the stack and stores that integer value in local variables #0 and #1. This is functionally equivalent to dstore 0 but takes fewer bytes and is faster.

Initial: double
double
Final: —

dstore_1 (0x48)—Store double in local variable #1/#2

Summary: Pops a double from the top of the stack and stores that double value in local variables #1 and #2. This is functionally equivalent to dstore 1 but takes fewer bytes and is faster.

Initial: double
double
Final: —

dstore_2 (0x49)—Store double in local variable #2/#3

Summary: Pops a double from the top of the stack and stores that double value in local variables #2 and #3. This is functionally equivalent to dstore 2 but takes fewer bytes and is faster.

Initial: double
double
Final: —

dstore_3 (0x4a)—Store double in local variable #3/#4

Summary: Pops a double from the top of the stack and stores that double value in local variables #3 and #4. This is functionally equivalent to dstore 3 but takes fewer bytes and is faster.

Initial: double
double
Final: —

dsub (0x67)—Double precision subtraction

Summary: Pops two two-word double precision floating point numbers, then pushes the result of the next-to-top number minus the top number.

Initial: double-1
double-1
double-2
double-2
Final: double
double

dup (0x59)—Duplicate top stack word

Summary: Duplicates the top word of the stack and pushes a copy.

Initial: word-1
Final: word-1
word-1

dup2 (0x5c)—Duplicate top two stack words

Summary: Duplicates the top two words of the stack and pushes copies at the top of the stack. Items duplicated can be two separate one-word entries (such as ints, floats, or addresses) or a single two-word entry (such as a long or a double).

Initial: word-1
word-2
Final: word-1
word-2
word-1
word-2

dup2_x1 (0x5d)—Duplicate top two words of stack and insert under third word

Summary: Duplicates the top two words of the stack and inserts the duplicate below the third word as new fourth and fifth words. Items duplicated can be two separate one-word entries (such as ints, floats, or addresses) or a single two-word entry (such as a long or a double).

Initial: word-1
word-2
word-3
Final: word-1
word-2
word-3
word-1
word-2

dup2_x2 (0x5e)—Duplicate top two words of stack and insert under fourth word

Summary: Duplicates the top two words of the stack and inserts the duplicate below the fourth word as new fifth and sixth words. Items duplicated can be two separate one-word entries (such as ints, floats, or addresses) or a single two-word entry (such as a long or a double).

Initial: word-1
word-2
word-3
word-4
Final: word-1
word-2
word-3
word-4
word-1
word-2

dup_x1 (0x5a)—Duplicate top word of stack and insert under second word

Summary: Duplicates the top word of the stack and inserts the duplicate below the second word as a new third word.

Initial: word-1
word-2
Final: word-1
word-2
word-1

dup_x2 (0x5b)—Duplicate top word of stack and insert under third word

Summary: Duplicates the top word of the stack and inserts the duplicate below the third word as a new fourth word.

Initial: word-1
word-2
word-3
Final: word-1
word-2
word-3
word-1

f2d (0x8d)—Convert float to double

Summary: Pops a single-word floating point number off the stack, converts it to a two-word double, and pushes the result.

Initial: float
Final: double
double

f2i (0x8b)—Convert float to int

Summary: Pops a single-word floating point number off the stack, converts it to a single-word integer, and pushes the result.

Initial: float
Final: int

f2l (0x8c)—Convert float to long

Summary: Pops a single-word floating point number off the stack, converts it to a two-word long integer, and pushes the result.

Initial: float
Final: long
long

fadd (0x62)—Floating point addition

Summary: Pops two floats and pushes their sum.

Initial: float
float
Final: float

faload (0x30)—Load value from array of bytes

Summary: Pops an integer and an array from the stack, then retrieves a value from that location in the one-dimensional array of floats. The value retrieved is pushed on the top of the stack.

Initial: int(index)
address(array ref)
Final: float

fastore (0x51)—Store value in array of addresses

Summary: Stores a single-word floating point number in an array of such floats. The top argument popped is the index defining the array location to be used. The second argument popped is the float value to be stored, and the third and final argument is the array itself.

Initial: int(index)
float
address(array ref)
Final: —

fcmpg (0x96)—compare floats, returning −1 on NaN

Summary: Pops two single-word floating point numbers off the operand stack and pushes a −1, 0, or +1 (as an integer) as a result. If the next-to-top number is greater than the top number, the value pushed is +1. If the two numbers are equal, the value pushed is 0; otherwise, the value is −1. If either or both words popped equal IEEE NaN (Not a Number) when interpreted as a floating point number, the result pushed is −1.

Initial: float
float
Final: int

fcmpl (0x95)—compare floats, returning −1 on NaN

Summary: Pops two single-word floating point numbers off the operand stack and pushes a −1, 0, or +1 (as an integer) as a result. If the next-to-top number is greater than the top number, the value pushed is +1. If the two numbers are equal, the value pushed is 0; otherwise, the value is −1. If either or both words popped equal IEEE NaN (Not a Number) when interpreted as a floating point number, the result pushed is −1.

Initial: float
float
Final: int

fconst_0 (0xb)—Push floating point constant 0.0

Summary: Pushes the constant value 0.0 as an IEEE 32-bit floating point value onto the operand stack.

Initial: —
Final: float(0.0)

fconst_1 (0xc)—Push floating point constant 1.0

Summary: Pushes the constant value 1.0 as an IEEE 32-bit floating point value onto the operand stack.

Initial: —
Final: float(1.0)

fconst_2 (0xd)—Push floating point constant 2.0
Summary: Pushes the constant value 1.0 as an IEEE 32-bit floating point value onto the operand stack.

Initial: —
Final: float(1.0)

fdiv (0x6e)—Floating point division
Summary: Pops two single-word floating point numbers, then pushes the result of the next-to-top number divided by the top number.

Initial: float
float
Final: float

fload <varnum> **(0x17 [byte/short])**—Load int from local variable
Summary: Loads a single-word floating point number from local variable #<varnum> and pushes the value. The value of <varnum> is a byte in the range 0..255 unless the wide operand prefix is used, in which case it is a short in the range 0..65536.

Initial: —
Final: float

fmul (0x6a)—Floating point multiplication
Summary: Pops two floats and pushes their product.

Initial: float
float
Final: float

fload_0 (0x22)—Load float from local variable #0
Summary: Loads a single-word floating point number from local variable #0 and pushes the value loaded onto the stack. This is functionally equivalent to fload 0 but takes fewer bytes and is faster.

Initial: —
Final: float

fload_1 (0x23)—Load float from local variable #1
Summary: Loads a single-word floating point number from local variable #1 and pushes the value loaded onto the stack. This is functionally equivalent to fload 1 but takes fewer bytes and is faster.

Initial: —
Final: float

fload_2 (0x24)—Load float from local variable #2
Summary: Loads a single-word floating point number from local variable #2 and pushes the value loaded onto the stack. This is functionally equivalent to fload 2 but takes fewer bytes and is faster.

Initial: —
Final: float

fload_3 (0x25)—Load float from local variable #3
Summary: Loads a single-word floating point number from local variable #3 and pushes the value loaded onto the stack. This is functionally equivalent to fload 3 but takes fewer bytes and is faster.

Initial: —
Final: float

fneg (0x76)—Floating point negation
Summary: Pops a floating point number from the stack, reverses its sign (multiplies by −1), then pushes the result.

Initial: float
Final: float

frem (0x72)—Floating point remainder
Summary: Pops two single-word floating point numbers, then pushes the remainder resulting when the next-to-top number is divided by the top number.

Initial: float
float
Final: float

freturn (0xae)—Return from method with float result
Summary: Pops a single-word floating point number from the current method stack. This number is pushed onto the method stack of the

Initial: float
Final: (n/a)

calling environment. The current method is terminated, and control is transferred to the calling environment.

fstore <varnum> (0x38 [byte/short])—Store float in local variable
Summary: Pops a float from the top of the stack and stores that float value in local variable #<varnum>. The value of <varnum> is a byte in the range 0..255 unless the wide operand prefix is used, in which case it is a short in the range 0..65536.

Initial: float
Final: —

fstore_0 (0x43)—Store float in local variable #0
Summary: Pops a float from the top of the stack and stores that float value in local variable #0. This is functionally equivalent to fstore 0 but takes fewer bytes and is faster.

Initial: float
Final: —

fstore_1 (0x44)—Store float in local variable #1
Summary: Pops a float from the top of the stack and stores that float value in local variable #0. This is functionally equivalent to fstore 1 but takes fewer bytes and is faster.

Initial: float
Final: —

fstore_2 (0x45)—Store float in local variable #2
Summary: Pops a float from the top of the stack and stores that float value in local variable #0. This is functionally equivalent to fstore 2 but takes fewer bytes and is faster.

Initial: float
Final: —

fstore_3 (0x46)—Store float in local variable #3
Summary: Pops a float from the top of the stack and stores that float value in local variable #0. This is functionally equivalent to fstore 3 but takes fewer bytes and is faster.

Initial: float
Final: —

fsub (0x66)—Floating point subtraction
Summary: Pops two single-word floating point numbers, then pushes the result of the next-to-top number minus the top number.

Initial: float
float
Final: float

getfield <fieldname> <type> (0xb4 [short][short])—Get object field
Summary: Pops an address (object reference) from the stack and retrieves and pushes the value of the identified field. The getfield opcode takes two parameters, the field identifier and the field type. These are stored in the bytecode as 2-byte indices in the **constant pool** (see Glossary). Unlike in Java, the field name must always be fully qualified, including the name of the relevant class and any relevant packages.

Initial: address(object)
Final: value

getfield2_quick (0xd0)—Quick version of getfield for two-word fields
Summary: Optimized version of getfield opcode used internally in Sun's Just In Time (**JIT**) compiler. This opcode should never appear in a .class file that isn't currently loaded and being executed.

Initial: see original opcode
Final: see original opcode

getfield_quick (0xce)—Quick version of `getfield` opcode

Summary: Optimized version of `getfield` opcode used internally in Sun's Just In Time (**JIT**) compiler. This opcode should never appear in a `.class` file that isn't currently loaded and being executed.

Initial: see original opcode
Final: see original opcode

getfield_quick_w (0xe3)—Quick, wide version of `getfield` opcode

Summary: Optimized version of `getfield` opcodes used internally in Sun's Just In Time (**JIT**) compiler. This opcode should never appear in a `.class` file that isn't currently loaded and being executed.

Initial: see original opcode
Final: see original opcode

getstatic <**fieldname**> <**type**> **(0xb2 [short][short])**—Get class field

Summary: Retrieves and pushes the value of the identified class field. The `getfield` opcode takes two parameters, the field identifier and the field type. These are stored in the bytecode as 2-byte indices in the **constant pool** (see Glossary). Unlike in Java, the field name must always be fully qualified, including the name of the relevant class and any relevant packages.

Initial: —
Final: value

getstatic_quick (0xd2)—Quick version of `getstatic` opcode

Summary: Optimized version of `getstatic` opcode used internally in Sun's Just In Time (**JIT**) compiler. This opcode should never appear in a `.class` file that isn't currently loaded and being executed.

Initial: initstack
Final: finalstack

getstatic2_quick (0xd4)—Quick version of `getstatic` opcode for 2-byte fields

Summary: Optimized version of `getstatic` opcode used internally in Sun's Just In Time (**JIT**) compiler. This opcode should never appear in a `.class` file that isn't currently loaded and being executed.

Initial: see original opcode
Final: see original opcode

goto <**label**> **(0xa7 [short])**—Go to label unconditionally

Summary: Transfers control unconditionally to the location marked by <label>. In bytecode, this opcode is followed by a 2-byte offset to be added to the current value in the PC. If the label is further away than can be represented in a 2-byte offset, use `goto_w` instead; the **jasmin** assembler is capable of determining which opcode to use based on its analysis of the distances.

Initial: —
Final: —

goto_w <**label**> **(0xc8 [int])**—Go to label unconditionally using wide offset

Summary: Transfers control unconditionally to the location marked by <label>. In bytecode, this opcode is followed by a 4-byte offset to be added to the current value in the PC. Using this opcode makes it possible to branch to locations more than 32,767 bytes away from the current locations. The **jasmin** assembler will automatically determine whether `goto` or `goto_w` should be used based on its analysis of the distances.

Initial: —
Final: —

i2b (0x91)—Convert integer to byte

Summary: Pops a single-word integer off the stack, converts it by

Initial: int
Final: int

truncation to a single byte (value 0..255), zero extends the result to 32 bits, and pushes the result (as an integer).

i2c (0x92)—Convert integer to character

Summary: Pops a single-word integer off the stack, converts it by truncation to a 2-byte UTF-16 character, zero extends the result to 32 bits, and pushes the result (as an integer).

Initial: int
Final: int

i2d (0x87)—Convert integer to double

Summary: Pops a single-word integer off the stack, converts it to a two-word double, and pushes the result.

Initial: int
Final: double
double

i2f (0x86)—Convert integer to float

Summary: Pops a single-word integer off the stack, converts it to a single-word floating point number, and pushes the result.

Initial: int
Final: float

i2l (0x85)—Convert integer to long

Summary: Pops a single-word integer off the stack, sign extends it to a two-word long integer, and pushes the result.

Initial: int
Final: long
long

i2s (0x93)—Convert integer to short

Summary: Pops a single-word integer off the stack, converts it by truncation to a signed short integer (value −32768..32767), sign extends the result to 32 bits, and pushes the result (as an integer). Note that the truncation can cause a change in sign as the integer's original sign bit is lost.

Initial: int
Final: int

iadd (0x60)—Integer addition

Summary: Pops two integers and pushes their sum.

Initial: int
int
Final: int

iaload (0x2e)—Load value from array of bytes

Summary: Pops an integer and an array from the stack, then retrieves a value from that location in the one-dimensional array of integers. The value retrieved is pushed on the top of the stack.

Initial: int(index)
address(array ref)
Final: int

iand (0x7e)—Integer logical AND

Summary: Pops two integers from the stack, calculates their bitwise AND, and pushes the 32-bit result as an integer.

Initial: int
int
Final: int

iastore (0x4f)—Store value in array of integers

Summary: Stores a single-word integer in an array of such ints. The top argument popped is the index defining the array location to be used. The second argument popped is the integer value to be stored, and the third and final argument is the array itself.

Initial: int(index)
int(value
address(array ref)
Final: —

iconst_0 (0x03)—Push integer constant 0

Summary: Pushes the constant value 0 (0x0) as a 32-bit integer onto the operand stack.

Initial: —
Final: int(0)

iconst_1 (0x4)—Push integer constant 1

Summary: Pushes the constant value 1 (0x1) as a 32-bit integer onto the operand stack.

Initial: —
Final: int(1)

iconst_2 (0x5)—Push integer constant 2
Summary: Pushes the constant value 2 (0x2) as a 32-bit integer onto
the operand stack.

Initial: —
Final: int(2)

iconst_3 (0x6)—Push integer constant 3
Summary: Pushes the constant value 3 (0x3) as a 32-bit integer onto
the operand stack.

Initial: —
Final: int(3)

iconst_4 (0x7)—Push integer constant 4
Summary: Pushes the constant value 4 (0x4) as a 32-bit integer onto
the operand stack.

Initial: —
Final: int(4)

iconst_5 (0x8)—Push integer constant 5
Summary: Pushes the constant value 5 (0x5) as a 32-bit integer onto
the operand stack.

Initial: —
Final: int(5)

iconst_m1 (0x2)—Push integer constant −1
Summary: Pushes the constant value −1 (0xFFFF) as a 32-bit integer
onto the operand stack.

Initial: —
Final: int(−1)

idiv (0x6c)—Integer division
Summary: Pops two integers, then pushes the integer part of the result
of the next-to-top number divided by the top number.

Initial: int
int
Final: int

if_acmpeq <label> (0xa5 [short])—Compare addresses and branch if
equal
Summary: Pops two addresses (object references) from the stack. If the
next-to-top element is equal to the top element, control is transferred
to <label>. Internally, the opcode is followed by a 2-byte quantity
which is treated as an offset and added to the current value of the PC
if the branch is to be taken.

Initial: address
address
Final: —

if_acmpne <label> (0xa6 [short])—Compare addresses and branch if
not equal
Summary: Pops two addresses (object references) from the stack. If
the next-to-top element is not equal to the top element, control is
transferred to <label>. Internally, the opcode is followed by a 2-
byte quantity which is treated as an offset and added to the current
value of the PC if the branch is to be taken.

Initial: address
address
Final: —

if_icmpeq <label> (0x9f [short])—Compare integers and branch if
equal
Summary: Pops two integers from the stack. If the next-to-top element
is equal to the top element, control is transferred to <label>. Internally, the opcode is followed by a 2-byte quantity which is treated as
an offset and added to the current value of the PC if the branch is to
be taken.

Initial: int
int
Final: —

if_icmpge <label> (0xa2 [short])—Compare integers and branch if
greater than or equal
Summary: Pops two integers from the stack. If the next-to-top element

Initial: int
Final: int

is greater than or equal to the top element, control is transferred to <label>. Internally, the opcode is followed by a 2-byte quantity which is treated as an offset and added to the current value of the PC if the branch is to be taken.

if_icmpgt <label> (0xa3 [short])—Compare integers and branch if greater than

Summary: Pops two integers from the stack. If the next-to-top element is greater than the top element, control is transferred to <label>. Internally, the opcode is followed by a 2-byte quantity which is treated as an offset and added to the current value of the PC if the branch is to be taken.

Initial: int
int
Final: —

if_icmple <label> (0xa4 [short])—Compare integers and branch if less than or equal

Summary: Pops two integers from the stack. If the next-to-top element is less than or equal to the top element, control is transferred to <label>. Internally, the opcode is followed by a 2-byte quantity which is treated as an offset and added to the current value of the PC if the branch is to be taken.

Initial: int
int
Final: —

if_icmplt <label> (0xa1 [short])—Compare integers and branch if less than

Summary: Pops two integers from the stack. If the next-to-top element is less than the top element, control is transferred to <label>. Internally, the opcode is followed by a 2-byte quantity which is treated as an offset and added to the current value of the PC if the branch is to be taken.

Initial: int
int
Final: —

if_icmpne <label> (0xa0 [short])—Compare integers and branch if not equal

Summary: Pops two integers from the stack. If the next-to-top element is not equal to the top element, control is transferred to <label>. Internally, the opcode is followed by a 2-byte quantity which is treated as an offset and added to the current value of the PC if the branch is to be taken.

Initial: int
int
Final: —

ifeq <label> (0x99 [short])—Branch if equal

Summary: Pops an integer off the top of the operand stack. If the value of the integer popped is equal to 0, control is transferred to <label>. Internally, the opcode is followed by a 2-byte quantity which is treated as an offset and added to the current value of the PC if the branch is to be taken.

Initial: int
int
Final: —

ifge <label> (0x9c [short])—Branch if greater than or equal

Summary: Pops an integer off the top of the operand stack. If the value of the integer popped is greater than or equal to 0, control is transferred to <label>. Internally, the opcode is followed by a 2-byte

Initial: int
Final: —

quantity which is treated as an offset and added to the current value of the PC if the branch is to be taken.

ifgt <label> (0x9d [short])—Branch if greater than

Summary: Pops an integer off the top of the operand stack. If the value of the integer popped is greater than 0, control is transferred to <label>. Internally, the opcode is followed by a 2-byte quantity which is treated as an offset and added to the current value of the PC if the branch is to be taken.

Initial: int
Final: —

ifle <label> (0x9e [short])—Branch if less than or equal

Summary: Pops an integer off the top of the operand stack. If the value of the integer popped less than or equal to 0, control is transferred to <label>. Internally, the opcode is followed by a 2-byte quantity which is treated as an offset and added to the current value of the PC if the branch is to be taken.

Initial: int
Final: —

iflt <label> (0x9b [short])—Branch if less than

Summary: Pops an integer off the top of the operand stack. If the value of the integer popped is less than 0, control is transferred to <label>. Internally, the opcode is followed by a 2-byte quantity which is treated as an offset and added to the current value of the PC if the branch is to be taken.

Initial: int
Final: —

ifne <label> (0x9a [short])—Branch if not equal

Summary: Pops an integer off the top of the operand stack. If the value of the integer popped is not equal to 0, control is transferred to <label>. Internally, the opcode is followed by a 2-byte quantity which is treated as an offset and added to the current value of the PC if the branch is to be taken.

Initial: int
Final: —

ifnonnull <label> (0xc7 [short])—Branch if not null

Summary: Pops an address (object reference) off the top of the operand stack. If the value of the address popped is not null, control is transferred to <label>. Internally, the opcode is followed by a 2-byte quantity which is treated as an offset and added to the current value of the PC if the branch is to be taken.

Initial: int
Final: —

ifnull <label> (0xc6 [short])—Branch if null

Summary: Pops an address (object reference) off the top of the operand stack. If the value of the address popped is null, control is transferred to <label>. Internally, the opcode is followed by a 2-byte quantity which is treated as an offset and added to the current value of the PC if the branch is to be taken.

Initial: address
Final: —

iinc <varnum> <increment> (0x84 [byte/short] [byte/short])—Increment integer in local variable

Summary: Increments a local variable containing an increment. The first argument defines the variable number to be adjusted, while the

Initial: —
Final: —

second is a signed constant amount of adjustment. Normally, the variable can be from 0 to 255, while the increment can be any number from −128 to 127. If the wide prefix is specified, the variable can be from 0 to 65536 and the increment can range from −32768 to 32767. The stack is not changed.

iload <varnum> (0x15 [byte/short])—Load int from local variable

Summary: Loads an integer from local variable #<varnum> and pushes the value. The value of <varnum> is a byte in the range 0..255 unless the wide operand prefix is used, in which case it is a short in the range 0..65536.

Initial: —
Final: int

iload_0 (0x1a)—Load int from local variable #0

Summary: Loads a single-word integer from local variable #0 and pushes the value loaded onto the stack. This is functionally equivalent to iload 0 but takes fewer bytes and is faster.

Initial: —
Final: int

iload_1 (0x1b)—Load int from local variable #1

Summary: Loads a single-word integer from local variable #1 and pushes the value loaded onto the stack. This is functionally equivalent to iload 1 but takes fewer bytes and is faster.

Initial: —
Final: int

iload_2 (0x1c)—Load int from local variable #2

Summary: Loads a single-word integer from local variable #2 and pushes the value loaded onto the stack. This is functionally equivalent to iload 2 but takes fewer bytes and is faster.

Initial: —
Final: int

iload_3 (0x1d)—Load int from local variable #3

Summary: Loads a single-word integer from local variable #3 and pushes the value loaded onto the stack. This is functionally equivalent to iload 3 but takes fewer bytes and is faster.

Initial: —
Final: int

impdep1 (0xfe)—Reserved opcode

Summary: This opcode is reserved for internal use by a JVM implementation. It is illegal for such an opcode to appear in class file, and such a class file will fail verification.

Initial: (n/a)
Final: (n/a)

impdep2 (0xff)—Reserved opcode

Summary: This opcode is reserved for internal use by a JVM implementation. It is illegal for such an opcode to appear in a class file, and such a class file will fail verification.

Initial: (n/a)
Final: (n/a)

imul (0x68)—Integer multiplication

Summary: Pops two integers and pushes their product.

Initial: int
int
Final: int

ineg (0x74)—Integer negation

Summary: Pops an integer from the stack, reverses its sign (multiplies by −1), then pushes the result.

Initial: int
Final: int

instanceof <type> (0xc1 [short])—Test if object/array is of specified type

Summary: Pops an address (object or array reference) from the stack and determines if that object/array is compatible with that type—either an instance of that type, an implementation of that interface, or an instance of a relevant supertype. If it is compatible, the integer value 1 is pushed; otherwise, 0 is pushed.

Initial: address
Final: int

instanceof_quick (0xe1)—Quick version of `instanceof` opcode

Summary: Optimized version of `instanceof` opcode used internally in Sun's Just In Time (**JIT**) compiler. This opcode should never appear in a `.class` file that isn't currently loaded and being executed.

Initial: see original opcode
Final: see original opcode

invokeinterface <method> <Nargs> (0xb9 [short][byte][byte])—Invoke interface method

Summary: Invokes a method defined within an interface (as opposed to a class). Arguments to `invokeinterface` include the fully qualified name of the method to be invoked (including the interface name, parameter types, and return type) and the number of arguments. These arguments are popped from the stack along with an address (object reference) of an object implementing that interface. A new stack frame is created for the called environment, and the object and arguments are pushed onto this environment's stack. Control then passes to the new method/environment. Upon return, the return value (given by `?return`) is pushed onto the calling environment's stack.

Initial: argN
...
arg2
arg1
address(object)
Final: (result)

In bytecode, the method name is stored as a 2-byte index in the **constant pool** (see Glossary). The next byte stores the number of argument *words*, up to 255 passed to the method. The next byte must store the value 0 and can be used internally by the JVM to store hash values to speed up method lookup.

invokeinterface_quick (0xda)—Quick version of `invokeinterface` opcode

Summary: Optimized version of `invokeinterface` opcode used internally in Sun's Just In Time (**JIT**) compiler. This opcode should never appear in a `.class` file that isn't currently loaded and being executed.

Initial: see original opcode
Final: see original opcode

invokenonvirtual_quick (0xd7)—Quick version of `invokespecial` opcode

Summary: Optimized version of `invokespecial` opcode used internally in Sun's Just In Time (**JIT**) compiler. This opcode should never appear in a `.class` file that isn't currently loaded and being executed.

Initial: see original opcode
Final: see original opcode

invokespecial **<method>** **(0xb7 [short])**—Invoke instance method

Summary: Invokes an instance method on an object in certain special cases. Specifically, use invokespecial to invoke.

- the instance initialization method <init>,
- a private method of **this**, or
- a method in a superclass of **this**.

This opcode is otherwise similar to invokevirtual (q.v.). Arguments to invokespecial include the fully qualified name of the method to be invoked (including the class name, parameter types, and return type) and the number of arguments. These arguments are popped from the stack along with an address (object reference) of an instance of the relevant class. A new stack frame is created for the called environment, and the object and arguments are pushed onto this environment's stack. Control then passes to the new method/environment. Upon return, the return value (given by ?return) is pushed onto the calling environment's stack. In bytecode, the method name is stored as a two-byte index into the **constant pool** (See Glossary).

Initial: argN
. . .
arg2
arg1
address(object)
Final: (result)

invokestatic **<method>** **(0xb8 [short])**—Invoke static method

Summary: Invokes a static method on a class. Arguments to invokestatic include the fully qualified name of the method to be invoked (including the class name, parameter types, and return type) and the number of arguments. These arguments are popped from the stack. A new stack frame is created for the called environment, and arguments are pushed onto this environment's stack. Control then passes to the new method/environment. Upon return, the return value (given by ?return) is pushed onto the calling environment's stack.

In bytecode, the method name is stored as a 2-byte index into the **constant pool** (see Glossary).

Initial: argN
. . .
arg2
arg1
Final: (result)

invokestatic_quick **(0xd9)**—Quick version of invokestatic opcode

Summary: Optimized version of invokestatic opcode used internally in Sun's Just In Time (**JIT**) compiler. This opcode should never appear in a .class file that isn't currently loaded and being executed.

Initial: see original opcode
Final: see original opcode

invokesuper_quick **(0xd8)**—Quick version of invokespecial opcode

Summary: Optimized version of invokespecial opcode used internally in Sun's Just In Time (**JIT**) compiler. This opcode should never appear in a .class file that isn't currently loaded and being executed.

Initial: see original opcode
Final: see original opcode

invokevirtual <method> (0xb6 [short])—Invoke instance method

Summary: Invokes an instance method on an object. Arguments to invokevirtual include the fully-qualified name of the method to be invoked (including the class name, parameter types, and return type) and the number of arguments. These arguments are popped from the stack along with an address (object reference) of an instance of the relevant class. A new stack frame is created for the called environment, and the object and arguments are pushed onto this environment's stack. Control then passes to the new method/environment. Upon return, the return value (given by ?return) is pushed onto the calling environment's stack. In bytecode, the method name is stored as a 2-byte index into the **constant pool** (see Glossary).

Initial: argN
...
arg2
arg1
address(object)
Final: (result)

invokevirtual_quick (0xd6)—Quick version of invokevirtual opcode

Summary: Optimized version of invokevirtual opcode used internally in Sun's Just In Time (**JIT**) compiler. This opcode should never appear in a .class file that isn't currently loaded and being executed.

Initial: see original opcode
Final: see original opcode

invokevirtual_quick_w (0xe2)—Quick version of invokevirtual opcode (wide index)

Summary: Optimized version of invokevirtual opcode used internally in Sun's Just In Time (**JIT**) compiler. This opcode should never appear in a .class file that isn't currently loaded and being executed.

Initial: see original opcode
Final: see original opcode

invokevirtualobject_quick (0xdb)—Quick version of invokevirtual for methods on Object

Summary: Optimized version of invokevirtual opcode used internally in Sun's Just In Time (**JIT**) compiler. This opcode should never appear in a .class file that isn't currently loaded and being executed.

Initial: see original opcode
Final: see original opcode

ior (0x80)—integer logical OR

Summary: Pops two integers from the stack, calculates their bitwise inclusive AOR, and pushes the 32-bit result as an integer.

Initial: int
int
Final: int

irem (0x70)—Integer remainder

Summary: Pops two single-word integers, then pushes the remainder resulting when the next-to-top number is divided by the top number. This operation is rather like the C or Java % operation.

Initial: int
int
Final: int

ireturn (0xac)—Return from method with integer result

Summary: Pops an integer from the current method stack. This integer is pushed onto the method stack of the calling environment. The current method is terminated, and control is transferred to the calling environment.

Initial: int
Final: (n/a)

ishl (0x78)—Shift integer to the left

Summary: Pops an integer and another integer from the stack. The
value of the next-to-top integer is shifted to the left by the number of
bits indicated by the lower 6 bits of the top integer; then the resulting
long is pushed. Newly emptied places are filled with 0 bits. This is
equivalent to multiplying the value by a power of 2 but may be faster.

Initial: int(shift)
int(value)
Final: int

ishr (0x7a)—Shift integer to the right

Summary: Pops an integer and another integer from the stack. The
value of the next-to-top integer is shifted to the right by the number
of bits indicated by the lower 6 bits of the top integer; then the
resulting value is pushed. Note: this is an arithmetic shift, meaning
that the sign bit is copied to fill the newly emptied places.

Initial: int(shift)
int(value)
Final: int

istore <varnum> (0x36 [byte/short])—Store integer in local variable

Summary: Pops an integer from the top of the stack and stores that
integer value in local variable #<varnum>. The value of <varnum>
is a byte in the range 0..255 unless the wide operand prefix is used,
in which case it is a short in the range 0..65536.

Initial: int
Final: —

istore_0 (0x3b)—Store integer in local variable #0

Summary: Pops an integer from the top of the stack and stores that
integer value in local variable #0. This is functionally equivalent to
istore 0 but takes fewer bytes and is faster.

Initial: int
Final: —

istore_1 (0x3c)—Store integer in local variable #1

Summary: Pops an integer from the top of the stack and stores that
integer value in local variable #1. This is functionally equivalent to
istore 1 but takes fewer bytes and is faster.

Initial: int
Final: —

istore_2 (0x3d)—Store integer in local variable #2

Summary: Pops an integer from the top of the stack and stores that
integer value in local variable #3. This is functionally equivalent to
istore 2 but takes fewer bytes and is faster.

Initial: int
Final: —

istore_3 (0x3e)—Store integer in local variable #3

Summary: Pops an integer from the top of the stack and stores that
integer value in local variable #3. This is functionally equivalent to
istore 3 but takes fewer bytes and is faster.

Initial: int
Final: —

isub (0x64)—Integer subtraction

Summary: Pops two single-word integers, then pushes the result of
the next-to-top number minus the top number.

Initial: int
int
Final: int

iushr (0x7c)—Shift unsigned int to the right

Summary: Pops an integer and another integer from the stack. The
value of the next-to-top integer is shifted to the right by the number
of bits indicated by the lower 6 bits of the top; then the resulting
value is pushed. Note: this is a logical shift, meaning that the sign bit
is ignored and the bit value 0 is used to fill the newly emptied places.

Initial: int(shift)
int(value)
Final: int

ixor (0x82)—integer logical XOR
Summary: Pops two integers from the stack, calculates their bitwise XOR (exclusive OR), and pushes the 32-bit result as an integer.

Initial: int
int
Final: int

jsr_w <label> (0xc9 [int])—Jump to subroutine using wide offset
Summary: Pushes the location of the next instruction (PC + 5, representing the length of the jsr_w insruction itself), then executes an unconditional branch to <label>.

Initial: —
Final: address(locn)

jsr <label> (0xa8 [short])—Jump to subroutine
Summary: Pushes the location of the next instruction (PC + 3, representing the length of the jsr insruction itself), then executes an unconditional branch to <label>.

Initial: —
Final: address(locn

l2d (0x8a)—Convert long to double
Summary: Pops a doubleword long integer point number off the stack, converts it to a two-word double, and pushes the result.

Initial: long
long
Final: double
double

l2f (0x89)—Convert long to float
Summary: Pops a doubleword long integer point number off the stack, converts it to a single-word floating point number, and pushes the result.

Initial: long
long
Final: float

l2i (0x88)—Convert long to int
Summary: Pops a doubleword long integer point number off the stack, converts it to a single-word integer, and pushes the result. Note that this may cause a change in sign as the long's original sign bit is lost.

Initial: long
long
Final: int

ladd (0x61)—Long addition
Summary: Pops two longs and pushes their sum.

Initial: long-1
long-1
long-2
long-2
Final: long
long

laload (0x2f)—Load value from array of bytes
Summary: Pops an integer and an array from the stack, then retrieves a value from that location in the one-dimensional array of longs. The value retrieved is pushed onto the top of the stack.

Initial: int(index)
address(array ref)
Final: long
long

land (0x7f)—Long logical AND
Summary: Pops two longs from the stack, calculates their bitwise AND, and pushes the 64-bit result as a long.

Initial: long-1
long-1
long-2
long-2
Final: long
long

lastore (0x50)—Store value in array of longs

Summary: Stores a two-word long integer in an array of such longs. The top argument popped is the index defining the array location to be used. The second/third arguments popped are the long value to be stored, and the final argument is the array itself.

Initial: int(index)
long
long
address(array ref)
Final: —

lcmp (0x94)—Compare longs

Summary: Pops two two-word integers off the operand stack and compares them. If the next-to-top value is greater than the top value, the integer 1 is pushed. If the two values are equal, the integer 0 is pushed; otherwise, the integer −1 is pushed.

Initial: long-1
long-1
long-2
long-2
Final: int

lconst_0 (0x9)—Push integer constant zero

Summary: Pushes the constant value 0 (0x0) as a 64-bit long integer onto the operand stack.

Initial: —
Final: long(0)
long(0)

lconst_1 (0xa)—Push integer constant 1

Summary: Pushes the constant value 1 (0x1) as a 64-bit long integer onto the operand stack.

Initial: —
Final: long(1)
long(1)

ldc <constant> (0x12 [short])—Load one-word constant

Summary: Loads and pushes a single-word entry from the **constant pool** (See Glossary). <constant> can be an int, a float, or a literal string, which is stored as an entry numbered from 0 to 255 in the constant pool.

Initial: —
Final: word

ldc2_w <constant> (0x14 [int])—Load two-word constant

Summary: Loads and pushes a doubleword entry from the **constant pool** (see Glossary). <constant> can be a double or long, which is stored as an entry numbered from 0 to 65536 in the constant pool.

Initial: —
Final: word

ldc_quick (0xcb)—Quick version of ldc opcode

Summary: Optimized version of ldc opcode used internally in Sun's Just In Time (**JIT**) compiler. This opcode should never appear in a .class file that isn't currently loaded and being executed.

Initial: see original opcode
Final: see original opcode

ldc_w <constant> (0x13 [int])—Load one-word constant with wide access

Summary: Loads and pushes a single-word entry from the **constant pool** (see Glossary). <constant> can be an int, a float, or a literal string, which is stored as an entry numbered from 0 to 65536 in the constant pool.

Initial: —
Final: word

ldc_w_quick (0xcd)—Quick, wide version of ldc opcode

Summary: Optimized version of ldc opcodes used internally in Sun's Just In Time (**JIT**) compiler. This opcode should never appear in a .class file that isn't currently loaded and being executed.

Initial: see original opcode
Final: see original opcode

ldiv (0x6d)—Long integer division
Summary: Pops two two-word long integers, then pushes the integer part of the result of the next-to-top number divided by the top number.

Initial: long-1
long-1
long-2
long-2
Final: long
long

lload <varnum> (0x16 [byte/short])—Load long from local variable
Summary: Loads a two-word long integer from local variables #<varnum> and #<varnum>+1 and pushes the value. The value of <varnum> is a byte in the range 0..255 unless the wide operand prefix is used, in which case it is a short in the range 0..65536.

Initial: —
Final: long
long

lload_0 (0x1e)—Load long from local variable #0/#1
Summary: Loads a 2-byte long integer from local variables #0 and #1 and pushes the value loaded onto the stack. This is functionally equivalent to lload 0 but takes fewer bytes and is faster.

Initial: —
Final: long
long

lload_1 (0x1f)—Load long from local variable #1/#2
Summary: Loads a 2-byte long integer from local variables #1 and #2 and pushes the value loaded onto the stack. This is functionally equivalent to lload 1 but takes fewer bytes and is faster.

Initial: —
Final: long
long

lload_2 (0x20)—Load long from local variable #2/#3
Summary: Loads a 2-byte long integer from local variables #2 and #3 and pushes the value loaded onto the stack. This is functionally equivalent to lload 2 but takes fewer bytes and is faster.

Initial: —
Final: long
long

lload_3 (0x21)—Load long from local variable #3/#4
Summary: Loads a 2-byte long integer from local variables #3 and #4 and pushes the value loaded onto the stack. This is functionally equivalent to lload 3 but takes fewer bytes and is faster.

Initial: —
Final: long
long

lmul (0x69)—Long integer multiplication
Summary: Pops two longs and pushes their product.

Initial: long-1
long-1
long-2
long-2
Final: long
long

lneg (0x75)—Long integer negation
Summary: Pops a two-word long integer from the stack, reverses its sign (multiplies by −1), then pushes the result.

Initial: long
long
Final: long
long

lookupswitch <args> (0xab [args])—Multiway branch
Summary: Performs a multiway branch, like the Java/C++ switch statement. The integer at the top of the stack is popped and

Initial: int
Final: —

```
lookupswitch
    1 : One
    2 : Two
    3 : Three
    5 : Five
default:Elsewhere
```

Figure B.1   Example of `lookupswitch`

opcode (0xab) and padding
default offset
number of entries (N)
value 1
offset 1
value 2
offset 2
. . .
value N
offset N

Table B.1   Bytecode layout for `lookupswitch`

compared to a set of value:label pairs. If the integer is equal to value, control is passed to the correponding label. If no value matches the integer, control passes instead to a defined default label. Labels are implemented as relative offsets and added to the current contents of the PC to get the location of the next instruction to execute.

See figure B.1 for example of this statement in use.

The `lookupswitch` instruction has a variable number of arguments, so its bytecode storage is rather tricky. After the opcode (0xab) itself, 0 to 3 bytes of padding follow, so that the the 4-byte `default offset` begins at a byte that is a mutiple of 4. The next 4 bytes define the number of value:label pairs. Each pair is stored in succession, in order of increasing value, as a 4-byte integer and a corresponding 4-byte offset. Table B.1 illustrates this.

lor (0x81)—Long logical OR

Summary: Pops two longs from the stack, calculates their bitwise inclusive OR, and pushes the 64-bit result as a long.

Initial: long-1
long-1
long-2
long-2
Final: long
long

lrem (0x71)—Long integer remainder

Summary: Pops two two-word integers, then pushes the remainder resulting when the next-to-top number is divided by the top number. This operation is rather like the C or Java % operation.

Initial: long-1
long-1
long-2
long-2
Final: long
long

lreturn (0xad)—Return from method with address result

Summary: Pops a 2-byte long integer from the current method stack. This long is pushed onto the method stack of the calling environment. The current method is terminated, and control is transferred to the calling environment.

Initial: long
long
Final: (n/a)

lshl (0x79)—Shift long to the left

Summary: Pops an integer and a 64-bit long integer from the stack. The value of the long is shifted to the left by the number of bits indicated by the lower 6 bits of the integer; then the resulting long is pushed. Newly emptied places are filled with 0 bits. This is equivalent to multiplying the value by a power of 2 but may be faster.

Initial: int(shift)
long
long
Final: long
long

lshr (0x7b)—Shift long to the right

Summary: Pops an integer and a 64-bit long integer from the stack. The value of the long is shifted to the right by the number of bits indicated by the lower 6 bits of the integer; then the resulting long is pushed. Note: this is an arithmetic shift, meaning that the sign bit is copied to fill the newly emptied places.

Initial: int(shift)
long
long
Final: long
long

lstore <varnum> (0x37 [byte/short])—Store long in local variable

Summary: Pops a long from the top of the stack and stores that long value in local variables #<varnum> and #<varnum> +1. The value of <varnum> is a byte in the range 0..255 unless the wide operand prefix is used, in which case it is a short in the range 0..65536.

Initial: long
long
Final: —

lstore_0 (0x3f)—Store long in local variable #0/#1

Summary: Pops a long from the top of the stack and stores that long value in local variables #0 and #1. This is functionally equivalent to lstore 0 but takes fewer bytes and is faster.

Initial: long
long
Final: —

lstore_1 (0x40)—Store long in local variable #1/#2

Summary: Pops a long from the top of the stack and stores that long value in local variables #1 and #2. This is functionally equivalent to lstore 1 but takes fewer bytes and is faster.

Initial: long
long
Final: —

lstore_2 (0x41)—Store long in local variable #2/#3

Summary: Pops a long from the top of the stack and stores that long value in local variables #2 and #3. This is functionally equivalent to lstore 2 but takes fewer bytes and is faster.

Initial: long
long
Final: —

lstore_3 (0x42)—Store long in local variable #3/#4

Summary: Pops a long from the top of the stack and stores that long value in local variables #3 and #4. This is functionally equivalent to lstore 3 but takes fewer bytes and is faster.

Initial: long
long
Final: —

lsub (0x65)—Long integer subtraction

Summary: Pops two two-word long integers, then pushes the result of the next-to-top number minus the top number.

Initial: long-1
long-1
long-2
long-2
Final: long
long

lushr (0x7d)—Shift unsigned long to the right

Summary: Pops an integer and a 64-bit long integer from the stack. The value of the long is shifted to the right by the number of bits indicated by the lower 6 bits of the integer; then the resulting long is pushed. Note: this is a logical shift, meaning that the sign bit is ignored and the bit value 0 is used to fill the newly emptied places.

Initial: int(shift)
long
long
Final: long
long

lxor (0x83)—Long logical XOR

Summary: Pops two longs from the stack, calculates their bitwise XOR (exclusive OR), and pushes the 64-bit result as a long.

Initial: long-1
long-1
long-2
long-2
Final: long
long

monitorenter (0xc2)—Obtain lock on object

Summary: The JVM **monitor** system enables synchronization and coordinated access to objects among multiple threads. The monitorenter statement pops an address (object reference) and requests an exclusive lock on that object from the JVM. If no other thread has locked that object, the lock is granted and execution continues. If the object is already locked, the thread blocks and ceases to execute until the other thread releases the lock via monitorexit.

Initial: address
Final: —

monitorexit (0xc3)—Release lock on object

Summary: Pops an address (object reference) and releases a previously obtained (via monitorenter) lock on that object, enabling other threads to get locks in their turn.

Initial: address
Final: —

multianewarray <type> <N> (0xc5 [short] [byte])—Create multi-dimensional array

Summary: Allocates space for an <N>-dimensional array of type <type> and pushes a reference to the new array. The type is stored in bytecode as a 2-byte index in the **constant pool** (see Glossary), while the number of dimensions <N> is stored as a byte value from 0 to 255. Executing this opcode pops <N> integer elements off the stack, representing the size of the array in each of the dimensions. The array is actually built as an array of (sub) arrays.

Initial: dimension N
dimension N-1
.

.
dimension 1
Final: address

multianewarray_quick (0xdf)—Quick version of `multianewarray` opcode

Summary: Optimized version of `multianewarray` opcode used internally in Sun's Just In Time (**JIT**) compiler. This opcode should never appear in a `.class` file that isn't currently loaded and being executed.

Initial: see original opcode
Final: see original opcode

new <class> **(0xbb [short])**—Create new object

Summary: Creates a new object of the class specified. The type is stored internally as a 2-byte index in the **constant pool** (see Glossary).

Initial: —
Final: address(object)

new_quick (0xdd)—Quick version of `new` opcode

Summary: Optimized version of `new` opcode used internally in Sun's Just In Time (**JIT**) compiler. This opcode should never appear in a `.class` file that isn't currently loaded and being executed.

Initial: see original opcode
Final: see original opcode

newarray <typename> **(0xbc [type-byte])**—Create unidimensional array of objects

Summary: Allocates space for an <1>-dimensional array of type <typename> and pushes a reference to the new array. The new array is popped as an integer from the top of the stack, while the type of the array is determined by examining the byte following this opcode according to the following table:

Initial: int(size)
Final: address(array)

boolean	4	byte	8
char	5	short	9
float	6	int	10
double	7	long	11

nop (0x0)—No operation

Summary: Does nothing. An operation that does nothing is sometimes useful for timing or debugging or as a placeholder for future code.

Initial: —
Final: —

pop (0x57)—Pop single word from stack

Summary: Pops and discards the top word (an integer, float, or address). Note that there is no matching `push` instruction, as pushing is a typed operation; use, for instance, `sipush` or `ldc`.

Initial: word
Final: —

pop2 (0x58)—Pop two words from stack

Summary: Pops and discards the top two words (either two singleword quantities like integers, floats, or addresses, or a single two-word quantity such as a long or a double). Note that there is no matching `push` instruction, as pushing is a typed operation; use, for instance, `ldc2_w`.

Initial: word
word
Final: —

putfield <fieldname> <type> **(0xb5 [short][short])**—Put object field

Summary: Pops an address (object reference) and a value from the stack and stores that value in the identified field of the object. The

Initial: value
address(object)
Final: —

putfield opcode takes two parameters, the field identifier and the field type. These are stored in the bytecode as 2-byte indices in the **constant pool** (see Glossary). Unlike in Java, the field name must always be fully qualified, including the name of the relevant class and any relevant packages.

putfield2_quick (0xd1)—Quick version of putfield opcode for 2-byte fields

Summary: Optimized version of putfield opcode used internally in Sun's Just In Time (**JIT**) compiler. This opcode should never appear in a .class file that isn't currently loaded and being executed.

Initial: see original opcode
Final: see original opcode

putfield_quick (0xcf)—Quick version of putfield opcode

Summary: Optimized version of putfield opcode used internally in Sun's Just In Time (**JIT**) compiler. This opcode should never appear in a .class file that isn't currently loaded and being executed.

Initial: see original opcode
Final: see original opcode

putfield_quick_w (0xe4)—Quick, wide version of putfield opcode

Summary: Optimized version of putfield opcodes used internally in Sun's Just In Time (**JIT**) compiler. This opcode should never appear in a .class file that isn't currently loaded and being executed.

Initial: see original opcode
Final: see original opcode

putstatic <fieldname> <type> (0xb3 [short][short])—Put class field

Summary: Pops a value from the stack and stores that value in the identified field of the specified class. The putstatic opcode takes two parameters, the field identifier and the field type. These are stored in the bytecode as 2-byte indices in the **constant pool** (see Glossary). Unlike in Java, the field name must always be fully qualified, including the name of the relevant class and any relevant packages.

Initial: value
Final: —

putstatic2_quick (0xd5)—Alternate quick version of putstatic opcode

Summary: Optimized version of putstatic opcode used internally in Sun's Just In Time (**JIT**) compiler. This opcode should never appear in a .class file that isn't currently loaded and being executed.

Initial: see original opcode
Final: see original opcode

putstatic_quick (0xd3)—Quick version of putstatic opcode

Summary: Optimized version of putstatic opcode used internally in Sun's Just In Time (**JIT**) compiler. This opcode should never appear in a .class file that isn't currently loaded and being executed.

Initial: see original opcode
Final: see original opcode

ret <varnum> (0xa9 [byte/short])—Return from subroutine

Summary: Returns to the address stored in <varnum> after a jump to a subroutine via jsr or jsr_w. The variable number is stored as a byte

Initial: —
Final: —

in the range 0..255 unless the wide prefix is used, which causes the variable to be stored as a 2-byte quantity (range 0..65536) instead.

return (0xb1)—Return from method without result

Summary: Terminates the current method and transfers control back to the calling environment.

Initial: —
Final: (n/a)

saload (0x35—Load value from array of bytes

Summary: Pops an integer and an array from the stack, then retrieves a value from that location in the one-dimensional array of a 16-bit short. The value retrieved is sign-extended to an integer and pushed on the top of the stack.

Initial: int(index)
address(array ref)
Final: int

sastore (0x56)—Store value in array of characters

Summary: Stores a 16-bit short integer in an array of shorts. The top argument popped is the index defining the array location to be used. The second argument popped is the short value to be stored, and the third and final argument is the array itself. The second argument is truncated from an int to a short and stored in the array.

Initial: int(index)
int(short)
address(array ref)
Final: —

sipush <constant> (0x11 [short])—Push [integer] short

Summary: The short value given as an argument (−32768..32767) is sign-extended to an integer and pushed on the stack.

Initial: —
Final: int

swap (0x5f)—Swap top two stack elements

Summary: Swaps the top two singleword elements on the stack. There is, unfortunately, no swap2 instruction.

Initial: word-1
word-2
Final: word-2
word-1

tableswitch <args> (0xaa [args])—Computed branch

Summary: Performs a multiway branch, like the Java/C++ switch statement. The integer at the top of the stack is popped and compared to a set of value:label pairs. If the integer is equal to the value, control is passed to the correponding label. If no value matches the integer, control passes instead to a defined default label. Labels are implemented as relative offsets and added to the current contents of the PC to get the location of the next instruction to execute. This instruction can be executed more efficiently than the similar lookupswitch statement (q.v.), but the values need to be consecutive and sequential.

Initial: int
Final: —

The arguments to tableswitch include the lowest and highest values represented by values in the table. If the integer popped from the stack is less than the lowest value or greater than the highest value, control is transferred to the default label. Otherwise, control is transferred directly (without a need for comparisons) to the (integer-low)-th label in the table.

See figure B.2 for an example of this operation in use.

The tableswitch instruction has a variable number of arguments, and thus its bytecode storage is rather tricky. After the opcode (0xaa) itself, 0 to 3 bytes of padding follow, so that the the four-byte

```
tableswitch 1 3
    One
    Two
    Three
    default:Elsewhere
```

Figure B.2   Example of `tableswitch`

| opcode (0xaa) and padding |
| default offset |
| low value |
| high value |
| offset 1 |
| offset 2 |
| ... |
| offset N |

Table B.2   Bytecode layout for `tableswitch`

`default offset` begins at a byte that is a mutiple of 4. The next 8 bytes define the lowest table entry and highest table values. Each offset is then stored in numerical order as a 4-byte offset. Table B.2 illustrates this.

wide (0xc4)—Specify "wide" interpretation of next opcode

Summary: This is not an opcode, but rather an opcode prefix. It indicates that the arguments of the next operation are potentially larger than usual—for example, using a local variable greater than 255 in `iload`. The `jasmin` assembler will generate this prefix as needed automatically.

Initial: —
Final: —

Opcode Summary by Number

C.1 Standard Opcodes

0	0x0	nop	101	0x65	lsub
1	0x1	aconst_null	102	0x66	fsub
2	0x2	iconst_m1	103	0x67	dsub
3	0x3	iconst_0	104	0x68	imul
4	0x4	iconst_1	105	0x69	lmul
5	0x5	iconst_2	106	0x6a	fmul
6	0x6	iconst_3	107	0x6b	dmul
7	0x7	iconst_4	108	0x6c	idiv
8	0x8	iconst_5	109	0x6d	ldiv
9	0x9	lconst_0	110	0x6e	fdiv
10	0xa	lconst_1	111	0x6f	ddiv
11	0xb	fconst_0	112	0x70	irem
12	0xc	fconst_1	113	0x71	lrem
13	0xd	fconst_2	114	0x72	frem
14	0xe	dconst_0	115	0x73	drem
15	0xf	dconst_1	116	0x74	ineg
16	0x10	bipush	117	0x75	lneg
17	0x11	sipush	118	0x76	fneg
18	0x12	ldc	119	0x77	dneg
19	0x13	ldc_w	120	0x78	ishl
20	0x14	ldc2_w	121	0x79	lshl
21	0x15	iload	122	0x7a	ishr
22	0x16	lload	123	0x7b	lshr
23	0x17	fload	124	0x7c	iushr
24	0x18	dload	125	0x7d	lushr

(*continued*)

25	0x19	aload	126	0x7e	iand
26	0x1a	iload_0	127	0x7f	land
27	0x1b	iload_1	128	0x80	ior
28	0x1c	iload_2	129	0x81	lor
29	0x1d	iload_3	130	0x82	ixor
30	0x1e	lload_0	131	0x83	lxor
31	0x1f	lload_1	132	0x84	iinc
32	0x20	lload_2	133	0x85	i2l
33	0x21	lload_3	134	0x86	i2f
34	0x22	fload_0	135	0x87	i2d
35	0x23	fload_1	136	0x88	l2i
36	0x24	fload_2	137	0x89	l2f
37	0x25	fload_3	138	0x8a	l2d
38	0x26	dload_0	139	0x8b	f2i
39	0x27	dload_1	140	0x8c	f2l
40	0x28	dload_2	141	0x8d	f2d
41	0x29	dload_3	142	0x8e	d2i
42	0x2a	aload_0	143	0x8f	d2l
43	0x2b	aload_1	144	0x90	d2f
44	0x2c	aload_2	145	0x91	i2b
45	0x2d	aload_3	146	0x92	i2c
46	0x2e	iaload	147	0x93	i2s
47	0x2f	laload	148	0x94	lcmp
48	0x30	faload	149	0x95	fcmpl
49	0x31	daload	150	0x96	fcmpg
50	0x32	aaload	151	0x97	dcmpl
51	0x33	baload	152	0x98	dcmpg
52	0x34	caload	153	0x99	ifeq
53	0x35	saload	154	0x9a	ifne
54	0x36	istore	155	0x9b	iflt
55	0x37	lstore	156	0x9c	ifge
56	0x38	fstore	157	0x9d	ifgt
57	0x39	dstore	158	0x9e	ifle
58	0x3a	astore	159	0x9f	if_icmpeq
59	0x3b	istore_0	160	0xa0	if_icmpne
60	0x3c	istore_1	161	0xa1	if_icmplt
61	0x3d	istore_2	162	0xa2	if_icmpge
62	0x3e	istore_3	163	0xa3	if_icmpgt
63	0x3f	lstore_0	164	0xa4	if_icmple
64	0x40	lstore_1	165	0xa5	if_acmpeq
65	0x41	lstore_2	166	0xa6	if_acmpne
66	0x42	lstore_3	167	0xa7	goto
67	0x43	fstore_0	168	0xa8	jsr
68	0x44	fstore_1	169	0xa9	ret

(continued)

69	0x45	fstore_2	170	0xaa	tableswitch
70	0x46	fstore_3	171	0xab	lookupswitch
71	0x47	dstore_0	172	0xac	ireturn
72	0x48	dstore_1	173	0xad	lreturn
73	0x49	dstore_2	174	0xae	freturn
74	0x4a	dstore_3	175	0xaf	dreturn
75	0x4b	astore_0	176	0xb0	areturn
76	0x4c	astore_1	177	0xb1	return
77	0x4d	astore_2	178	0xb2	getstatic
78	0x4e	astore_3	179	0xb3	putstatic
79	0x4f	iastore	180	0xb4	getfield
80	0x50	lastore	181	0xb5	putfield
81	0x51	fastore	182	0xb6	invokevirtual
82	0x52	dastore	183	0xb7	invokespecial
83	0x53	aastore	184	0xb8	invokestatic
84	0x54	bastore	185	0xb9	invokeinterface
85	0x55	castore	186	0xba	*xxxunusedxxx*
86	0x56	sastore	187	0xbb	new
87	0x57	pop	188	0xbc	newarray
88	0x58	pop2	189	0xbd	anewarray
89	0x59	dup	190	0xbe	arraylength
90	0x5a	dup_x1	191	0xbf	athrow
91	0x5b	dup_x2	192	0xc0	checkcast
92	0x5c	dup2	193	0xc1	instanceof
93	0x5d	dup2_x1	194	0xc2	monitorenter
94	0x5e	dup2_x2	195	0xc3	monitorexit
95	0x5f	swap	196	0xc4	wide
96	0x60	iadd	197	0xc5	multianewarray
97	0x61	ladd	198	0xc6	ifnull
98	0x62	fadd	199	0xc7	ifnonnull
99	0x63	dadd	200	0xc8	goto_w
100	0x64	isub	201	0xc9	jsr_w

C.2 Reserved Opcodes

The JVM standard also reserves the following opcodes:

202	0xca	breakpoint
254	0xfe	impdep1
255	0xff	impdep2

Opcode 202 (breakpoint) is used by debuggers, while opcodes 254 and 255 are reserved for internal use by the JVM itself. They should never appear in a stored class file; in fact, a class file with these opcodes should fail verification.

C.3 "Quick" Pseudo-Opcodes

In 1995, researchers at Sun Microsystems proposed the use of internal "quick" opcodes as a method of increasing the speed and efficiency of the Java compiler. Normally, when an entry in the constant pool is referenced, the entry must be resolved to confirm its availability and type compatibility. If a single statement must be executed several times, this reresolution can slow the computer down. As part of its **Just-In-Time** (JIT) compiler, Sun has proposed a set of opcodes that assume that the entry has already been resolved. When a normal opcode is executed (successfully), it can be replaced internally with a "quick" pseudo-opcode to skip the resolution step and speed up subsequent executions.

These pseudo-opcodes should never appear in a class file in long-term storage. Instead, the JVM itself may rewrite the opcodes on an executing class. If done properly, this change is completely invisible to a Java programmer or even a writer of compilers. The set of optimization pseudo-opcodes proposed includes the following:

```
203   0xcb   ldc_quick
205   0xcd   ldc_w_quick
206   0xce   getfield_quick
207   0xcf   putfield_quick
208   0xd0   getfield2_quick
209   0xd1   putfield2_quick
210   0xd2   getstatic_quick
211   0xd3   putstatic_quick
212   0xd4   getstatic2_quick
213   0xd5   putstatic2_quick
214   0xd6   invokevirtual_quick
215   0xd7   invokenonvirtual_quick
216   0xd8   invokesuper_quick
217   0xd9   invokestatic_quick
218   0xda   invokeinterface_quick
219   0xdb   invokevirtualobject_quick
221   0xdd   new_quick
222   0xde   anewarray_quick
223   0xdf   multianewarray_quick
224   0xe0   checkcast_quick
225   0xe1   instanceof_quick
226   0xe2   invokevirtual_quick_w
227   0xe3   getfield_quick_w
228   0xe4   putfield_quick_w
```

There is, of course, nothing to prevent a different implementor from using a different optimization method or set of quick opcodes.

C.4 Unused Opcodes

Opcode 186 is unused for historical reasons, as its previous use is no longer valid in the current version of the JVM. Opcodes 204, 220, and 229–253 are unassigned in the current JVM specifications but might acquire assignments (and uses) in later versions.

APPENDIX **D**

Class File Format

D.1 Overview and Fundamentals

As alluded to briefly in chapter 10, class files for the JVM are stored as a set of nested tables. This is actually a slight misnomer, as the same format is used whenever classes are stored or transmitted, so a class received over the network comes across in exactly the same format—as a "file." Each "file" contains the information needed for exactly one class, including the bytecode for all of the methods, fields and data internal to the class, and properties for interacting with the rest of the class system including name and inheritance details.

All data in class files is stored as 8-bit bytes or as multiple byte groups of 16, 32, or 64 bits. These are referred to in standards documents as u1, u2, u4, and u8, respectively, but it's probably easier to think of them just as bytes, shorts, ints, and longs. To prevent any confusion between machines with different storage conventions (such as the 8088 with its byte swapping), the bytes are defined as coming in "network order" (also called "big-endian" or "most significant byte [MSB]" order), where the most significant byte comes first. For example, the first 4 bytes of any JVM class file must be the so-called magic number 0xCAFEBABE (an int, obviously). This would be stored as a sequence of 4 bytes in the order 0xCA, 0xFE, 0xBA, 0xBE.

The top-level table of a class file contains some housekeeping information (of fixed size) and five variable-sized lower-level tables. There is no padding or alignment between the various components, which makes it somewhat difficult to pull a specific part (such as the name of a method) out of a class file.

The detailed top-level format of a class file (table D.1) is as follows:

The "magic number" has already been described; it serves no real purpose except to make it easy to identify class files quickly on a system. The major and minor version numbers help track compatibility. For example, a very old class file (or a class file compiled with a very old version of Java) might use opcodes that no longer exist or that have changed semantics. The current version of Java (as of early 2006) uses minor version 0 and major version 46 (0x2e), corresponding to the new Java 5.0 release.

The fields for this class and the superclass refer to entries in the constant table (see the next section for details) and define the name of the current class, as well as the immediate

285

Size	Identifier	Notes
int	magic number	Defined value of 0xCAFEBABE
short	minor version	Defines which version (major and minor revisions)
short	major version	of JVM class file is compatible with
short	constant pool count	Maximum entry number in following table
variable	constant pool	Pool of constants used by class
short	access flags	Valid access types (public, static, interface, etc.)
short	this class	Identifier of this class type
short	superclass	Identifier of this class's superclass type
short	interfaces count	Number of entries in following table
variable	interfaces	Interfaces implemented by this class
short	fields count	Number of entries in following table
variable	fields	Fields declared as part of this class
short	methods count	Number of entries in following table
variable	methods	Methods defined as part of this class
short	attributes count	Number of entries in following table
variable	attributes	Other attributes of this class

Table D.1   Detailed diagram of class-file format

superclass. Finally, the access flags field defines the access-related properties of the current class—for example, if this class is defined as **abstract**, which prevents other classes from using it as an argument to the new instruction. These properties are stored as individual flags in a single two-word bit vector as follows:

Meaning	Bit value	Interpretation
public	0x0001	Class is accessible to others
final	0x0010	Class cannot be subclassed
super	0x0020	New invocation semantics
interface	0x0200	File is actually an interface
abstract	0x0400	Class can't be instantiated

So, an access flags field of 0x0601 would define a "public" "abstract" "interface."

D.2   Subtable Structures

D.2.1   Constant Pool

The constant pool is structured as a sequence of individual entries representing constants used by the program. For example, a constant representing the integer value 1010 would be stored in 5 successive bytes. The last 4 bytes would be the binary representation of 1010 (as an integer), while the first byte is a tag value defining this entry as an integer (and thus as having 5 bytes).

Depending upon the tag types, the size and internal format of entries vary as in the following table.

Type	Value
UTF8 string	1
Integer	3
Float	4
Long	5
Double	6
Class	7
String	8
Field reference	9
Method reference	10
Interface method reference	11
Name and type	12

The structure of integers, longs, floats, and doubles is self-explanatory. For example, a constant pool entry for an integer consists of 5 bytes, an initial byte with the value 3 (defining the entry as an integer) and 4 bytes for the integer value itself. UTF8 strings are stored as an unsigned length value (2 bytes in length, allowing string of up to 65,536 characters) and a variable-length array of bytes containing the character values in the string. All literal strings in Java class files— string constants, class names, methods and field names, etc.—are stored internally as UTF8 string constants.

The internal fields in other types refer to the (2-byte) indices of other entries in the constant pool. For example, a field reference contains 5 bytes. The first byte would be the tag value defining a field (value 9). The second and third bytes holds the index of another entry in the constant pool defining the class to which the field belongs. The fourth and fifth bytes hold the index of a "name and type" entry defining the name and field. This name and type entry has an appropriate tag (value 12) and then the indices of two UTF8 strings defining the name/ type.

There are two important caveats regarding the constant pool. For historical reasons, constant pool entry number 0 is never used, and the initial element takes index 1. For this reason, unlike most other array-type elements in Java (and other class file entries), if there are k constant pool entries, the highest entry is k, not $k - 1$. Also, for historical reasons, constant pool entries of type long or double are treated as two entries; if constant pool entry 6 is a long, then the next pool entry would have index 8. Index 7, in this case, would be unused and illegal.

D.2.2   Field Table
Each field of the class is defined internally as a table entry with the following fields:

Size	Identifier	Notes
short	access flags	Access properties of this field
short	name	Index of name in constant pool
short	descriptor	Index of type string
short	attributes count	Number of field attributes
variable	attributes	Array of field attributes

The name and type fields are simply indices into the constant pool for the name and type descriptor strings, respectively, of the field. The access flags field is a bit vector of flags, as before (interpretation given by the following table), defining valid access attributes for the field. Finally, the attributes table defines field attributes just as the class attributes table does for the class as a whole.

Meaning	Bit value	Interpretation
public	0x0001	Field is accessible to others
private	0x0002	Field is usable only by defining class
protected	0x0004	Field is accessible to class and subclasses
static	0x0008	Class, not instance, field
final	0x0010	Field cannot be changed
volatile	0x0040	Field cannot be cached
transient	0x0080	Field cannot be written/read by object manager

D.2.3 Methods Table

Each method defined in a class is described internally as a table entry with a format almost identified to that of the field entry described above. The only difference is the specific values used to represent different access flags, as given in the following table.

Meaning	Bit value	Interpretation
public	0x0001	Field is accessible to others
private	0x0002	Field is usable only by defining class
protected	0x0004	Field is accessible to class and subclasses
static	0x0008	Class, not instance, field
final	0x0010	Field cannot be changed
synchronized	0x0020	Invocation is locked
native	0x0100	Implemented in hardware-native language
abstract	0x0400	No implementation defined
strict	0x0800	Strict floating point semantics

D.2.4   Attributes

Almost all parts of the class file, including the top-level table itself, contain a possible **attributes** subtable. This subtable contains "attributes" created by the compiler to describe or support computations. Each compiler is permitted to define specific attributes, and JVM implementations are required to ignore attributes that they don't recognize, so this appendix cannot provide a complete list of possible attributes. On the other hand, certain attributes must be present, and the JVM may not run correctly if it requires a certain attribute that is absent.

Each attribute is stored as a table with the following format:

Size	Identifier	Notes
short	attribute name	Name of attribute
int	attribute length	Length of attribute in bytes
variable	info	Contents of attribute

Probably the most obvious (and important) attribute is the **Code** attribute, which, as as an attribute for a method, contains the bytecode for that particular method. The **Exceptions** attribute defines the types of exceptions that a particular method may throw. In support of debuggers, the **Sourcefile** attribute stores the name of the source file from which this class file was created, and the **LineNumberTable** stores which byte(s) in bytecode correspond to which individual lines in the source code. The **LocalVariableTable** attribute similarly define which variable (in the source file) corresponds to which local variable in the JVM. Compiling (or assembling) with the -g flag (on a *NIX system) will usually cause these attributes to be placed in the class file. Without this flag, they are often omitted to save space and time.

The ASCII Table

E.1 The Table

Hex	Char	Hex	Char	Hex	Char	Hex	Char	Hex	Char	Hex	Char	Hex	Char	Hex	Char
00	nul	01	soh	02	stx	03	etx	04	eot	05	enq	06	ack	07	bel
08	bs	09	ht	0a	lf	0b	vt	0c	ff	0d	cr	0e	so	0f	si
10	dle	11	dc1	12	dc2	13	dc3	14	dc4	15	nak	16	syn	17	etb
18	can	19	em	1a	sub	1b	esc	1c	fs	1d	gs	1e	rs	1f	us
20		21	!	22	"	23	#	24	£	25	%	26	&	27	'
28	(	29	)	2a	*	2b	+	2c	,	2d	-	2e	.	2f	/
30	0	31	1	32	2	33	3	34	4	35	5	36	6	37	7
38	8	39	9	3a	:	3b	;	3c	<	3d	=	3e	>	3f	?
40	@	41	A	42	B	43	C	44	D	45	E	46	F	47	G
48	H	49	I	4a	J	4b	K	4c	L	4d	M	4e	N	4f	O
50	P	51	Q	52	R	53	S	54	T	55	U	56	V	57	W
58	X	59	Y	5a	Z	5b	[	5c		5d	]	5e	^	5f	_
60	`	61	a	62	b	63	c	64	d	65	e	66	f	67	g
68	h	69	i	6a	j	6b	k	6c	l	6d	m	6e	n	6f	o
70	p	71	q	72	r	73	s	74	t	75	u	76	v	77	w
78	x	79	y	7a	z	7b	{	7c	}	7d	}	7e	~	7f	del

Note that ASCII 0x20 (32 decimal) is a space (" ") character.

E.2 History and Overview

ASCII, the **American Standard Code for Information Interchange**, has for decades (it was formalized in 1963, internationalized in 1968) been the most common standard for encoding character data in binary format. Other once common formats, such as EBCDIC and Baudot, are largely of historical interest only. The original ASCII character set defined a 7-bit standard for encoding 128 different "characters," including a complete set of both upper- and lowercase letters (for American English), digits, and many symbols and punctuation marks. In addition, the first 32 entries in the ASCII table define mostly unprintable **control characters** such as a backspace (entry 0x08), [horizontal] tab (entry 0x09), vertical tab (0x10), or even an audible "bell" (now usually a beep, entry 0x07). Unfortunately, ASCII does not well support non-English languages or even many commonly useful symbols such as $\rightarrow$, $\leq$, or the British pound sign (£).

Since almost all computers store 8-bit bytes, byte values 0x80...0xFF, which do not have a standard character interpretation, are often used for machine-dependent proprietary extensions to the ASCII table. For example, the letter ö is used in German but not English. Microsoft has defined an extended ASCII table (among several different sets in use by various Windows-based programs) that uses entry 0x94 to represent this value as part of a fairly complete set of German-specific characters; this same table defines entry 0xE2 as an uppercase Γ, but oddly enough does not define an entry for lowercase γ. I suppose that the German-speaking market was more important to the designers of this character set than the Greek-speaking one. Apple, by contrast, does not define a meaning for the extended characters (at least for its "terminal" environment under OS X).

The core of the problem is that a single byte, with only 256 different storage patterns, can't store enough different characters. Java's solution is to use a larger character set (Unicode) and store them as 2-byte quantities instead.

Glossary

80x86 family A family of chips manufactured by Intel, beginning with the Intel 4004 and extending through the 8008, 8088, 80086, 80286, 80386, 80486, and the various Pentiums. These chips form the basis of the IBM-PC and its successors and are the most common chip architecture in use today.

absolute address The 20-bit address obtained by combining the segment:offset memory address in an 8086-based computer.

abstract A class that contains no direct instances, only subclasses. Alternatively, an unimplemented method that must be implemented in subclasses.

accumulator A designated single register for high-speed arithmetic, particularly addition and multiplication. On **80x86** computers, the [E]AX register.

actual parameter The actual value used in place of the **formal parameter** in a call to a function or method.

address A location in memory; alternatively, a number used to refer to a location in memory.

addressing mode The way to interpret a bit pattern to define the actual operand for a statement. For example, the bit pattern 0x0001 could refer to the actual constant 1, the first register, the contents of memory location 1, and so forth. See individual modes: **immediate mode**, **register mode**, **direct mode**, **indirect mode**, **index mode**.

algorithm A step-by-step, unambiguous procedure for achieving a desired goal or performing a computation.

ALU A component of a typical machine architecture where the arithmetic and logical operations are performed. Part of the **CPU**.

American Standard Code for Information Interchange See **ASCII**.

AND A **boolean** function that returns True if and only if all arguments are True; otherwise, it returns False. An **AND gate** is a hardware circuit that implements an AND function on the input electrical signals.

applet A small, portable program (application), typically delivered as part of a Web page.

Arithmetic and Logical Unit See **ALU**.

arithmetic shift A **shift operation** where the leftmost (rightmost) bit is duplicated to fill the emptied bit locations.

array A derived type; a collection of subelements of identical type indexed by an integer.

ASCII A standard way of representing character data in binary format. The ASCII set defines a 7-bit pattern for letters, digits, and some commonly used punctuation marks.

assembler A program to convert a source file written in **assembly language** to an executable file.

assembly language   A low-level language where each human-readable statement corresponds to exactly one machine instruction. Different computer types have different assembly languages.

attributes   A data structure in the **JVM** class file format used to store miscellaneous information.

backward compatibility   The ability of a computer or system to duplicate the operations of previous versions. For example, the Pentium is **backward compatible** with the 8088 and so will still run programs written for the original IBM-PC.

base   1. The numeric value represented by a digit place in the numbering system. For example, binary is base 2, while decimal is base 10 and hexadecimal is base 16.
    2. The electrical connection in a transistor that controls the flow of current from the emitter to the collecter.

BAT   A method of translating logical addresses inside a memory manager to a fixed block of physical memory.

BCD   A method used by the math processor in the 80x86 family where each decimal digit of a number is written as a corresponding 4-bit binary pattern. The number 4096, for example, would be written in BCD as 0100 0000 1001 0110.

big-endian   A storage format where the most significant bit is stored as the first and highest-numbered bit in a word. In big-endian format, the number 32770 would be stored as binary 10000010.

binary   1. A number system where all digits are 1 or 0 and successive digits are larger by a factor of 2. The number 31 in binary would be written as 11111.
    2. A mathematical operator such as addition that takes exactly two operands.

Binary Coded Decimal   See **BCD**.

bit   A binary digit, the basic unit of information inside a computer. A bit can take two basic values, O or 1.

bitwise   Of a Boolean operation when an operation is applied individually to each respective bit in a multi-bit structure like a byte or an integer.

block address translation   See **BAT**.

boolean logic   A logic system, named after George Boole, where operations are defined and performed as functions on binary quantities.

branch   A machine instruction that changes the value of the program counter (PC) and thus causes the computer to begin executing at a different memory location. An equivalent term is **goto**.

branch prediction   An optimization technique to speed up a computer by predicting whether or not a conditional branch will be taken.

bus   A component of a typical machine architecture that acts as a connection between the **CPU**, the memory, and/or peripherals.

busy-waiting   Waiting for an expected event by checking to see if the event has happened inside a loop. Compare **interrupt**.

byte   A collection of 8 bits. Used as a unit of memory, of representation size, or of register capacity.

bytecode   The **machine language** of the **JVM**.

cache memory   A bank of high-speed memory to store frequently accessed items to improve overall memory performance.

Central Processing Unit   See **CPU**.

CF   The Carry Flag, set when the most recent operation generated a carry out of the register, as when two numbers are added for which the sum is too large.

CISC   A computer design philosophy using many complicated special-purpose instructions. Compare **RISC**.

class   A collection of fields and methods defining a type of object in an object-oriented programming environment.

class files   The format used by the JVM to store classes (including records and interfaces) in long-term storage or to deliver them over a network.

class method   A method defined by an object-oriented system as a property of a class, rather than of any particular instance of that class.

class variable   A variable defined by an object-oriented system as a property of a class, rather than of any particular instance of that class.

clock signal   An electrical signal used by the computer to synchronize events and to measure the passage of time.

CLR   The virtual machine underlying Microsoft's .NET framework.

code   Executable machine instructions, as opposed to data.

collector   Part of a standard transistor to which current from the emitter flows unless shut off by a current at the base.

comment   A statement in a programming language that is ignored by the computer but that may contain information readable by and useful to humans. In jasmin, comments begin with a semicolon (;) and extend to the end of the line.

Common Language Runtime   See **CLR**.

compiler   A program to convert a source file written in a **high-level language** to an executable file.

complete/writeback   A typical phase in a pipelined architecture, where the results of an operation are stored in the target locations.

Complex Instruction Set Computing   See **CISC**.

conditional branch   A branch (like ifle) that may or may not be taken, depending upon the current machine state.

constant pool   The set of constants used by a particular JVM class, as stored in the **class file**.

control characters   The ASCII characters with values below 0x20, which represent nonprinting characters such as a carriage return or a ringing bell.

Control Unit   The part of the **CPU** that moves data in and out of the CPU and determines which instruction to execute.

CPU   The heart of the computer, where calculations take place and the program is actually executed. Usually consists of the **Control Unit** and the **ALU**.

data memory   Memory used to store program data (such as variables) instead of program code.

decimal   Base 10. The usual way of writing numbers.

derived type   A representation for data built up by combining basic types. For example, a fraction type could be derived from two integers, the numerator and the denominator.

destination   Where data goes. For example, in the instruction `istore_3`, the destination is local variable #3.

destination index   A register in the 80x86 family that controls the destination of string primitive operations.

destination operand   An operand defining the `destination` of an instruction; in the Pentium instruction set, the destination operand is typically the first, as in `MOV AX, BX`.

device   Another name for a **peripheral**.

device driver   A program (or part of the **operating system** that controls a device).

diode   An electrical component that lets electricity pass in only one direction; part of the makeup of a transistor.

Direct Memory Access   The capacity of a computer to let data move between main memory and a peripheral like a graphics card without having to go through the **CPU**.

direct mode   An addressing mode where a bit pattern is interpreted as a location in memory holding the desired operand. In direct mode, the bit pattern 0x0001 would be interpreted as memory location 1.

directive   A statement in assembly language [in `jasmin`, beginning with a period (.)] that does not translate into a machine instruction but instead gives instructions to the assembler itself. The .limit directive is one example.

dispatch   A typical state in a **pipelined** architecture where the computer analyzes the instruction to determine what kind it is, gets the source arguments from the appropriate locations, and prepares the instruction for actual execution.

dopants   Impurities deliberately added to semiconductors like silicon to affect their electrical properties. Introducing these impurities allows the construction of diodes and transistors that are the key components of electronic equipments like computers.

DRAM   A kind of **RAM** that requires continuous refreshing to hold data. Slower but cheaper than **SRAM**. As with all RAM, if the power goes out, the memory loses its data.

dst   An abbreviation for **destination**.

Dynamic RAM   See **DRAM**.

EEPROM   A kind of **hybrid** memory combining the field programmability of **RAM** with the data persistence of **ROM**.

Electronically Erasable Programmable ROM   See **EEPROM**.

embedded system   A computer system where the computer is an integral part of a larger environment, not an independently usable tool. An example is the computer that runs a DVD player.

emitter   Part of a standard **transistor** through which current flows to the **collector** unless shut off at the **base**.

EPROM   A type of **PROM** that can be erased, typically by several seconds of exposure to high-powered ultraviolet light. These memories are reprogrammable, but typically not in the field.

Erasable Programmable ROM   See **EPROM**.

execute   1. To run a program or machine instruction.
           2. A typical state in a **pipelined** architecture where the computer runs a previously fetched (and dispatched) instruction.

exponent   A field in an IEEE **floating point** representation controlling the power of 2 by which the **mantissa** is multiplied.

extended AX register   The 32-bit **accumulator** on an 80386 or later chip in the **80x86 family**, including the Pentium.

fetch   1. To load a machine instruction in preparate for performing it.
           2. A typical state in a **pipelined** architecture where the computer loads an instruction from main memory.

fetch-execute cycle   The process by which a computer **fetches** an instruction to be performed, **executes** that instruction, and then cyclically fetches the next instruction in sequence until the program ends.

Fibonacci sequence   The sequence 1, 1, 2, 3,..., where every term is the sum of its two immediate predecessors.

fields   Named data storage locations in a record or class.

flags   Binary variables used to store data. See also **flags register.**

flags register   A special register in the **CPU** that holds a set of binary **flags** regarding the current state of computation. For example, if machine overflow occurs on an arithmetic calculation, a **flag** (typically called the "overflow flag" or **OF**) will be **set** to 1. A later **conditional branch** can examine this flag.

Flash   A kind of **hybrid memory** combining the field programmability of **RAM** with the data persistence of **ROM**. Commonly used in pen drives and digital cameras.

floating point   1. Any noninteger value stored by a computer.
           2. A specific format for storing noninteger values in a binary form of scientific notation. Values are stored as the product of a **mantissa** times 2 raised to the power of a biased **exponent**.

Floating Point Unit   See **FPU**.

FPU   Special-purpose hardware attached to the CPU to handle floating point (as opposed to integer) calculations. Now somewhat rare, as most CPUs can handle floating point operations on board.

formal parameter   The variables used in the definition of a function or method that serve as place holders for later **actual parameters**.

garbage collection   The process of reclaiming memory locations that are no longer in use. Automatic on the JVM.

gates   Electrical circuits that implement **boolean** functions.

goto   See **branch**.

Harvard architecture   A kind of non–von Neumann architecture where code storage (for programs) is separated from data storage (for variables).

hexadecimal   Base 16. A number system where all digits are 0–9 or the letters A–F and successive digits are larger by a factor of 16. The number 33 in hexadecimal would be written as 0x31.

high   1. The upper part of a register or data value; in particular, the most significant byte of a general-purpose regiser on the 8088.
2. See **high-level.**

high-level   A language like Java, C++, or Pascal where a single statement may correspond to several **machine language** instructions.

hybrid memory   A kind of memory designed to combine the field rewritability of **RAM** with the data persistence of **ROM**. For examples, see **EEPROM** or **Flash**.

immediate mode   An addressing mode where a bit pattern is interpreted as a constant operand. In direct mode, the bit pattern 0x0001 would be the constant 1.

implement   Of an interface, to follow the interface without being an instance of it.

index mode   An addressing mode where a bit pattern is interpreted as an offset from a memory address stored in a register.

indirect address register   A register, like the Pentium's BX or the Atmel's Y register, tuned to be used in indirect or index mode.

indirect mode   An addressing mode where a bit pattern is interpreted as a memory location holding a pointer to the actual operand. In indirect mode, the bit pattern 0x0001 would be interpreted as the value stored at the location referred to by the pattern in memory location 1.

infix   A method of writing expressions where a binary operation comes between its arguments, as in $3 + 4$. Compare **postfix** or **prefix**.

initialize   To set to a particular initial value prior to use or to call a function that performs this task.

instance method   A method defined by an object-oriented system as a property of an object rather than its controlling class.

instance variable   A variable defined by an object-oriented system as a property of an object rather than its controlling class.

instruction   In general, a command to a computer. In machine code, an individual bit pattern representing a single operation. In assembly language, a type of statement that translates directly into a machine instruction.

instruction pointer   See **IP**.

instruction queue   An ordered set of instructions either waiting to be loaded or already loaded and waiting to be executed.

instruction register (IR)   The register inside the **CPU** that holds the **current instruction** for dispatch and execution.

instruction set   The set of operations that a specific CPU can carry out.

integrated circuit   A circuit fabricated as a single sillicon chip instead of as many individual components.

interface   An abstract class that defines behavior shared by different objects but outside of the normal inheritance structure.

interrupt   1. A small piece of code set up in advance to be executed when a particular event occurs.
2. The notification to the CPU that such an event has happened and that this piece of code should be executed.

interrupt handler   A system for dealing with expected events without the overhead of **busy-waiting**.

invoke   To execute a method.

I/O controller   A component of a typical machine architecture that controls a particular **peripherial** for input and output. The I/O controller usually accepts and interprets signals from the **bus** and takes care of the details of operating a particular component like a hard drive.

I/O registers   Registers used to send signals to an I/O controller, especially on the Atmel AVR.

IP   The `instruction pointer`, a standard CPU register that holds the memory location of the current instruction being executed.

jasmin   An **assembler** written by Meyer and Downing for the **JVM** and the primary teaching language of this book.

Java Virtual Machine   See **JVM**.

JIT compilation   A technique for speeding up execution of **JVM** programs by converting each statement to an equivalent **native machine language** instruction.

Just In Time   See **JIT compilation**.

JVM   A virtual machine used as the basis for the Java programming language and the primary teaching machine of this book.

label   In assembly langauge, a human-readable marker for a particular line of code so that that line can be the target of a **branch** instruction.

latency   The amount of time it takes to accomplish something. On a computer with an instruction latency of 1 μs, executing an instruction will take at least that much time.

linear congruential generator   A common pseudorandom number generator where successive values of equations of the form $newvalue = (a \cdot oldvalue + c)\%m$ are returned from the generator.

link   The process of converting a set of bytecode (or machine instructions) stored on disk into an executable format.

little-endian   A storage format where the least significant bit is stored as the first and highest-numbered bit in a word. In little-endian format, the number 32770 would be stored as binary 01000001.

llasm   The assembler used with Microsoft's .NET Framework.

load   The process of transferring a set of bytecode (or machine instructions) from disk to memory.

logical address   The bit pattern stored in a **register** and used to access memory prior to interpretation by any **memory management** or **virtual memory** routines.

logical memory   The address space defined by the set of logical addresses, as distinguished from the physical memory where the **memory manager** stores data.

logical shift   A **shift operation** where the newly emptied bit location(s) are filled with the value 0. Compare **arithmetic shift**.

long   In Java or **jasmin**, a data storage format for 64-bit (two-word)integer types.

low-level   A language like **jasmin** or other assembly languages where a single statement corresponds to a single **machine language** instruction.

machine code   See **machine language**.

machine cycle   A basic time unit of a computer, typically defined as the time needed to execute a single instruction or, alternatively, as one unit of the system clock.

machine language   The binary encoding of the basic instructions of a computer program. This is not typically written by humans, but by other programs such as **compilers** or **assemblers**.

machine state register   A register describing the overall state of the computer as a set of flags.

mantissa   The fractional part of a **floating point** number, to be multiplied by a scale factor consisting of 2 raised to the power of a specific **exponent**.

math coprococessor   An auxiliary chip, usually used for **floating-point** calculations, while the **ALU** handles integer calculations.

memory manager   A system for controlling a program's access to physical memory. It typically improves performance, increases security, and enhances the amount of memory that a program can use.

memory-mapped I/O   A method of performing I/O where specific memory locations are automatically read by the I/O controller instead of using the bus.

microcontroller   A small computer, usually part of an **embedded system** instead of a standalone, independently programmable computer.

microprogramming   Implementing a computer's (complex) instruction set as a sequence of smaller, RISC-like instructions.

Microsoft Intermediate Language   See **MSIL**.

MIMD   The ability of a computer to carry out two different instructions on two different pieces of data at the same time.

MMX instructions   Instructions implementing SIMD parallelism on later models of the **80x86 family** of chips.

mnemonic A human-readable statement written as part of an assembly language program that corresponds to a specific operation or opcode.

mode See **addressing mode**.

modulus The formal mathematical definition of "remainder."

monitor A subsystem of the **JVM** used to ensure that only one method/thread has access to a piece of data at one time.

Monte Carlo simulation A technique for exploring a large space of possible answers by repeated use of random numbers.

most significant The digit or byte corresponding to the highest power of the base. For example, in the number 361,402, the number 3 is the most significant digit. See also **big-endian**, **little-endian**.

motherboard The board of a computer to which the **CPU** and the most crucial other components are attached.

MSIL The language, corresponding to JVM bytecode, underlying Microsoft's .NET Framework.

MSR See machine state **register**.

nonvolatile memory Memory where the stored data is still present even after power is lost to the system.

Non-Volatile RAM See **NVRAM**.

normalized form The standard format of a typical floating point number according to the IEEE 754 standard. This includes a sign bit, an 8-bit biased exponent, and a 23-bit mantissa with an implicit leading 1.

n-type A semiconductor that has been doped with an electron-donating substance, making these electrons available for passing current.

null A designated address referring to nothing in particular.

NVRAM **Hybrid** memory combining the field programmability of **RAM** with the data persistence of **ROM**.

nybble A collection of 4 bits referring to a single hexadecimal digit. Used as a unit of memory, of representation size, or of register capacity. Rare.

object-oriented programming A style of programming, popularized by languages like Smalltalk, C++, and Java, where programs are composed of interactive collections of classes and objects, and communication is performed by invoking methods on specific objects.

octal Base 8. Rarely used today.

OF The Overflow Flag, set when the most recent operation on signed numbers generated an answer too large for the register.

offset The distance in memory between two locations. Usually used with regard to either a base register (as in the 8088 memory segmentation) or the amount by which a **branch** instruction changes the **PC**.

opcode The byte(s) corresponding to a particular operation in machine code. Compare **mnemonic**.

operands   The arguments given with a particular operation; for example, the ADD instruction usually takes two operands. On the JVM, however, the iadd instruction takes no operands, because both arguments are already available on the stack.

operating system   A program-control program used to control the availability of the machine to user-level programs and to launch and recover from them at the appropriate time. Common examples of operating systems include Windows, Linux, MacOS, and OS X.

operator   The symbol or code indicating which particular mathematical or logical function should be performed. For example, the operator + usually indicates addition.

OR   A **boolean** function that returns True if and only if all arguments are True; otherwise, it returns False. An **OR gate** is a hardware circuit that implements an OR function on the input electrical signals.

overclocking   Attempting to run a computer chip with a **clock** running faster than the chip's rated capacity.

overflow   Broadly, when an arithmetic operation results in a value too large to be stored in the destination. For example, multiplying two 8-bit numbers is likely to produce up to a 16-bit result, which would overflow an 8-bit destination register.

page   A block of memory used in the memory management system.

page table   A table used by the **memory manager** to determine which logical addresses correspond to which physical addresses.

paging   Dividing memory into "pages." Alternatively, the ability of a computer to move pages from main memory to long-term storage and back in an effort to expand the memory available to a program and to improve performance.

parallel   In an electrial circuit, two components are in parallel if there is a separate path for current that passes through each component individually. Cf. **series**.

parallelism   In a computer, the ability to perform multiple operations at the same time. See also **MIMD** and **SIMD**.

PC   A register holding the memory location of the instruction currently being executed; changing the value of this register will result in loading the next instruction from a different location. This is how a **branch** instruction works.

peripheral   A component of a computer used to read, write, display, or store data or, more generally, to interact with the outside world.

pipelining   Breaking a process (typically a machine instruction execution) into several phases like an assembly line. For example, a computer might be executing one instruction while fetching the next one. A typical pipelined architecture can execute several different instructions at once.

platter   An individual storage surface in a hard drive.

polling   Testing to see whether or not an event has happened. See **busy-waiting**.

port-mapped I/O   A method of performing I/O where communication with the I/O controller happens through specific ports attached to the main bus.

postfix   A method of writing expressions where a binary operation comes between its arguments, as in 34+. Compare **infix** or **prefix**.

prefetch   Fetching an instruction before the previous instruction has been executed; a crude form of **pipelining**.

prefix   A method of writing expressions where a binary operation comes between its arguments, as in +34. Compare **infix** or **postfix**.

primordial class loader   The main class loader responsible for loading and linking all classes in the JVM.

program counter   See **PC**.

programmable ROM   Field-programmable but not erasable **ROM**. Unlike conventional **ROM** chips, these chips can be programmed in small quantities without needing to set up an entire fabrication line.

programming models (modes)   A defined view of the architecture and capacity of a computer that may be limited for security reasons.

PROM   See **programmable ROM**.

protected mode   A programming model where the capacity of the programs is typically limited by memory management and security issues; useful for user-level programs on a multiprocessing system.

pseudorandom   An algorithmically generated approximation of randomness.

p-type   A type of semiconductor that has been doped with an electron-capturing (or "hole-donating") substance, making these electrons unavailable for passing current.

radix point   A generalization of the idea of "decimal point" to bases other than base 10.

RAM   Memory that can be both read from and written to in arbitrary locations. RAM is typically **volatile** in that if power is lost, the data stored in memory will also be lost.

Random Access Memory   See **RAM**.

Read-Only Memory   See **ROM**.

real mode   A **programming model** where the program has access to the entire capability of the machine, bypassing security and memory management. Useful primarily for **operating systems** and other **supervisor**-level programs.

record   A collection of named fields but without methods.

reduced instruction set computing   See **RISC**.

register   A memory location within the CPU used to store the data or instructions currently being operated upon.

register mode   An addressing mode where a bit pattern is interpreted as a specific register. In register mode, the bit pattern 0x0001 would be interpreted as the first register.

return   The process (and typically the instruction used) to transfer control back to the calling environment at the termination of a subroutine.

RISC   A computer design philosophy using a few short general-purpose instructions. Compare **CISC**.

ROM   Memory that can be read from but not written to ROM is typically **nonvolatile** in that if power is lost, the data stored in memory will persist.

roundoff error   Error that happens when a **floating point** representation is unable to represent the exact value, usually because the defined mantissa is too short. The desired value will be "rounded off" to the closest available representable quantity.

SAM   Memory that cannot be accessed in arbitrary order but that must be accessed in a predefined sequence, like a tape recording.

seed   A value used to begin a sequence of generation of **pseudorandom numbers**.

segment   Broadly speaking, a contiguous section of memory. More specifically, a section of memory referenced by one of the **segment registers** of the **80x86 family**.

segment:offset   An alternative way of representing up to 20-bit **logical addresses** within the 16-bit **registers** of an Intel 8088 (or later models).

segment register   A register in the **80x86 family** used to define blocks of memory for purposes such as code, stack, and data storage and to extend the available address space.

semiconductor   An electrical material, midway between a conductor and an insulator, that can be used to produce diodes, transistors, and integrated circuits.

Sequential access memory   See **SAM**.

series   In an electrial circuit, two components are in series if there is only a single path for current that passes through both components. Cf. **parallel**.

SF   The Sign Flag, set when the most recent operation generated a negative result.

shift   An operation where bits are moved to adjacent locations (left or right) within a register.

sign bit   In a **signed** numeric representation, a bit used to indicate whether the value is negative or nonnegative. Typically, a sign bit value of 1 is used to represent a negative number. This is true for both integer and floating point representations.

signed   A quantity that can be both positive and negative, as opposed to **unsigned** quantities, which can only be positive.

SIMD   The ability of a computer to carry out the same instructions on two different pieces of data at the same time—for example, to zero out several elements in memory simultaneously.

Single Instruction Multiple Data   See **SIMD**.

source   Where data comes from. For example, in the instruction `iload_3`, the source is local variable #3.

source index   A register in the 80x86 family that controls the source of string primitive operations.

source operand   An operand defining the `source` of an instruction; in the Pentium instruction set, the source operand is typically the source, as in `MOV AX, BX`.

src   An abbreviation for **source**.

S–R flip-flop   A circuit used to store a single bit value as voltage across a self-reinforcing set of transistors.

stack   A data structure where elements can be inserted (pushed) and removed only (popped) at one end. Stacks are useful in machine architectures as ways of creating and destroying new locations for short-term storage.

stack frame A stack-based internal data structure used to store the local environment of a currently executing program or **subroutine**.

state machine A computer program where the the computer simply changes from one named "state" to another upon receipt of a specific input or event.

static See **class method**.

static RAM See **SRAM**.

string primitive An operation on the 80x86 family that moves, copies, or otherwise manipulates byte arrays such as strings.

structure See **record**.

subroutine An encapsulated block of code, to be called (possibly) from several different locations over the course of a program, after which control is passed back to the point from which it was called.

superscalar A method of achieving MIMD parallelism by duplicating pipelines or pipeline stages to enhance performance.

supervisor A privileged **programming model** where the computers have the capacity to control the system in a way normally prohibited by the security architecture, usually used by the operating systems. See also **real mode**.

this In Java, the current object whose instance method is being invoked. In jasmin, an object reference to **this** is always passed as local variable #0.

throughput The number of operations that can be accomplished per time unit. This may be different from the **latency** on a multiprocessor that may (for example) be able to complete several operations with identical latency at the same time, achieving effectively several times the expected throughput.

Throwable In the JVM, an Object that can be thrown by the athrow instruction; an exception or error.

timer A circuit that counts pulses of a **clock** in order to determine the amount of lapsed time.

time-sharing A form of multiprocessing where the CPU runs one program at a time in small blocks of time, giving the illusion of running multiple programs at once.

two's complement notation A method of storing **signed** integers such that addition is an identical operation with both positive and negative numbers. In two's complement notation, the representation of -1 is a vector of bits whose values are all 1.

typed In a computation, representation, or operation, where the type of data processed affects the legitimacy or validity of the results. For example, istore_0 is a typed operation, as it will only store integers. The **dup** operation, by contrast, is untyped, as it will duplicate any stack element.

U One of the two five-stage pipelines on the Intel Pentium.

unary A mathematical operator such as negation or cosine that takes exactly one operand.

unconditional Always, as in an an unconditional **branch** that is always taken.

Unicode   A set of character representations designed to include a greater variety of letters than ASCII. See **UTF-16**.

unsigned   A quantity that can be only positive or negative, as opposed to **signed** quantities, which can be both positive and negative; typically, unsigned quantities cannot express as large a range of positive values.

update mode   An addressing mode where the value of a register is updated after access—for example, by incrementing to the next array location.

user mode   A programming model where the capacities of the program are limited by the security architecture and operating system to prevent two programs from interacting harmfully.

UTF-16   An alternate character encoding to **ASCII** where each character is stored as a 16-bit quantity. This allows up to 65,536 different characters in the character set, enough to include a large number of non-English or non-Latin characters.

V   One of the two five-stage pipelines on the Intel Pentium.

verifier   The phase of loading where the class file is **verified**, or the program that performs such verification.

verify   On the JVM, the process of validating that a method or class can be successfully run without causing security problems. For example, attempting to store a value as an integer that had previously loaded as a floating point number will cause an error, but this error can be caught when the class file is **verified**.

virtual address   An abstract address in virtual memory that may or may not be physically present in memory (and may otherwise reside in long-term storage). Cf. **logical address**.

virtual address space   See **virtual address**.

virtual memory   The capacity of a computer to interpret logical addresses and to convert them to physical addresses. Also, the ability of a computer to access logical addresses that are not physically present in main memory by storing parts of the logical address space on disk and loading them into memory as necessary.

virtual segment identifier   See **VSID**.

VSID   A bit pattern used to expand a logical address into a much larger address space for use by the memory manager.

watchdog timer   A **timer** that, when triggered, resets the computer or checks to confirm that the machine has not gone into an infinite loop or an otherwise unresponsive state.

word   The basic unit of data processing in a machine, formally the size of the general-purpose **registers**. As of this writing (2006), 32-bit words are typical of most commerically available computers.

ZF   The Carry Flag, set when the result of the most recent operation is a 0.

Index